FEMINIST PERSPECTIVES ON THE FOUNDATIONAL SUBJECTS OF LAW

Cavendish
Publishing
Limited

FEMINIST PERSPECTIVES ON THE FOUNDATIONAL SUBJECTS OF LAW

EDITOR
Anne Bottomley
Kent Law School
University of Kent at Canterbury

Cavendish
Publishing
Limited

First published in Great Britain 1996 by Cavendish Publishing Limited, The Glass House, Wharton Street, London WC1X 9PX.

Telephone: 0171-278 8000 Facsimile: 0171-278 8080

British Library Cataloguing in Publication Data

A catalogue record for this book is available from the British Library

ISBN 1 85941 194 0

Printed and bound in Great Britain by
Biddles Ltd, Guildford and King's Lynn

PREFACE

This collection is composed of a series of papers inspired by a commitment to feminist scholarship, written and presented within a framework of the 'foundational' courses found in every English (and Welsh) law degree. In taking this approach it is the first collection, to the best of our knowledge, of its kind. Until now published work has tended to focus on those aspects of law, and legal education, where feminist approaches have most obviously had an impact. In this set of papers the starting-point is quite different: it is to explore issues of gender in relation to the focus given to us (in legal education) by the demands of the professional bodies in their requirement that certain areas of substantive law are taught as part of a law degree. We have therefore necessarily taken as axiomatic an approach to law which focuses on the languages, ideas and concepts of the so-called 'foundation'. Of course such a presentation of the cultural complex called 'law' is highly contentious; even the professional bodies in holding to the idea of 'foundational' courses are constantly renegotiating what should fall under this definition. Are we talking about a simple set of classifications organised around key conceptual ideas or, rather, a looser set of organising principles around which we can situate clusters of ideas and practices? These questions are crucial; they are fundamental to our understanding of law and therefore of the possibilities of our use of law. Although our framework means that they are not directly addressed, these issues permeate many of the papers.

Even in choosing how to name the sections under which the papers are organised certain choices have had to be made which reflect some of the uncertainties behind the seeming intransigence of the 'fundamentals' approach and the different patterns of reception of them into the academic agenda. 'Contracts' and 'torts' remain as two separate areas, despite the propensity on many degrees to fuse them into 'obligations'; equally 'land' and 'equity and trusts' remain as two separate identities rather than appearing as 'property'. Conversely 'constitutional' and 'administrative' law appear here as 'public law'. Law of the European Union, or European Community law, is given a separate heading rather than being subsumed into a 'public law' section, reflecting not only its growth in importance but its newly acquired status in relation to the 'foundational' subjects.

Because of the organising focus it might be thought that the collection will only be of interest to students of English law; and indeed in terms of reading the collection from beginning to end this might be true. However, the issues explored, the themes and materials used, make the study much broader. Indeed two papers come from overseas (and two were written in Scotland!) and any student of a common law jurisdiction will find much to engage them here.

It is hoped that the collection will present, and help develop, feminist work in a number of ways. Firstly, it can simply be used in each seemingly discrete subject area. In each of the 'foundational' subjects it presents ideas and issues, introduces methodologies, which we hope will be utilised within those areas to bring new perspectives to them. We do not attempt to present, or even allude to, all that has been written in the name of feminist work in any one of these areas but these papers can be used as an introduction to thinking more critically about material all students will encounter on their degree. Secondly, bringing together feminist work on the different subject areas in this way allows for an overview of issues: ideas developed in one area may well have an impact on the way in which we can think about other areas. In this sense readers are encouraged not merely to read in those areas which are of immediate interest to them, but to explore the papers as a group for what they have to say, more generally, about the styles and possibilities of feminist work *per se.*

Within the collection are many different 'feminisms': the authors do not hold in common an agreed formula for what feminism is about other than a shared commitment to the exploration of gender relations. You will find many different perspectives here and, again, the collection can be used to explore these differences.

Finally, the astute reader will begin to recognise the limitations of working within the confines of the 'foundations' and want to ask questions of the relationship, or lack of relationship, between the different subject areas and the emerging areas of legal work which do not so simply fit within this formula. The collection will have really worked if it leaves you with more questions than you, the reader, began with!

The idea for the collection was originally conceived during a seminar at Birkbeck College, London and the first outline was planned in the following hours at a local bar. Gestation has been long and sometimes uncomfortable. Many lent their support, advice etc (often more crucially than they realised) and so many thanks to Belinda Meteyard, Joanne Scott, Jo Shaw, Lesley Bender, Nicola Lacey, Peter Fitzpatrick, Jane Hinde, Marie-Claire Bellou, Lesley Turano, Andrew Dart, Mary Jane Mossman, Michaela Twyford and others.

Many thanks also to the authors of these papers, many of whom were working on very tight schedules, and all of whom agreed to donate the proceeds due to them from the sale of this book to the journal *Feminist Legal Studies.* Finally many thanks to Jo Reddy for her tolerance and her insistence – and her insight in knowing which to exercise at which time.

In recent years we have mourned the deaths of four pioneers in feminist legal scholarship: Vicki Fisher (United Kingdom), Lois Brunnot (The Netherlands), Mary Joe Frug (United States) and Tove Stang Dahl (Norway). This collection is dedicated to them in celebration of their lives, their work and the inspiration they gave, and continue to give, to others.

Anne Bottomley
New Year's Day 1996

CONTRIBUTORS

Anne Bottomley teaches land law and equity and trusts at the University of Kent, Canterbury. She has published papers in the areas of family law, feminist jurisprudence and property law. She is a member of the editorial board of *Feminist Legal Studies* and has been an active member of Critical Legal Conference (UK). She is currently working on a book entitled *In Search of Dike: the Quest for a Feminist Jurisprudence*.

Beverley Brown teaches at the University of Edinburgh. She has published widely, particularly in the areas of criminology and legal theory.

Joanne Conaghan is a senior lecturer in law at the University of Kent. Her areas of research include labour law, tort law and feminist legal theory and she has published widely in all three fields. She is also the co–author (with Wade Mansell) of *The Wrongs of Tort* (1993) Pluto Press, and co–editor (with Anne Bottomley) of *Feminist Theory and Legal Strategy* (1993) Blackwell Publishers.

Sheila Duncan teaches law and social theory at the University of Warwick. Her research focuses on feminist and post-modernist theory applied to the text and politics of criminal law. She was a practising defence solicitor. She now also writes scripts for the television series *The Bill*.

Leo Flynn lectures at the School of Law in King's College, London. A graduate of the National University of Ireland and the University of Cambridge, he has also lectured at the Universities of Leeds and Lund, Sweden. He teaches EC law and jurisprudence, and has written widely in those areas. Apart from the theory and practice of equality law, his other major research interest is that of state intervention in the market in the EU.

Peter Goodrich teaches contracts at Birkbeck College, University of London. His most recent books are *Oedipus Lex: Psychoanalysis, History, Law* (1995) and *Law in the Courts of Love: Literature and Other Minor Jurisprudences* (1996). He is currently working on a history of the law and procedures of women's courts.

Kate Green is a principal lecturer at the University of East London. Her main teaching and research interests lie in land law, women and law and legal theory. Currently, her work focuses on the contributions which feminist legal theorists can make to an understanding of property law.

Hilary Lim teaches at the University of East London. Her main teaching and research interests lie in equity and trusts and legal theory. She is co-author (with Kate Green) of *Cases and Materials in Land Law* (1995, 2nd edn) Pitmans.

Robin Mackenzie has taught law in England, Scotland and New Zealand. She currently convenes banking and finance law, family law and feminist perspectives in law at the University of Kent, and has published articles on feminist legal thought, compensation for gender-specific injury, transsexuals' legal sexual status and risk management aspects of equity.

Gillian More has held positions as a lecturer in law at the Europa Institute and the Universities of Edinburgh and Keele. She is currently studying for the English Bar, based at Middle Temple. Her particular interest is in EC employment law.

Sheila Noonan is Professor of Law at Queen's University, Ontario, Canada. She has published a number of papers on aspects of criminal law and legal theory.

Katherine O'Donovan is Professor of Law at the University of London, Queen Mary College. She is author of *Sexual Divisions in Law* (1985), *Equality and Sex Discrimination Law* (1988, co-author) and *Family Law Matters* (1993). Her current research interests are in human rights and family rights, particularly the rights of the child.

Stephanie Palmer is a lecturer in law at the University of Cambridge and a Fellow of Girton College. She is Australian and did her graduate degree at Harvard Law School.

Patricia Peppin teaches at Queen's University, Ontario, Canada. She has published a number of papers on issues of torts law, health law and feminist work.

CONTENTS

FEMINIST PERSPECTIVES ON THE FOUNDATIONAL SUBJECTS OF LAW

LAW OF THE EUROPEAN COMMUNITY

EXPLORING FOUNDATIONAL SUBJECTS

A 'foundation' suggests a beginning: that which makes possible what follows and upon which what follows can be securely based. It is therefore a crucial, determining, beginning. It involves selection, choice, and therefore necessarily excludes as much as it includes, refuses as much as makes possible. 'Foundational subjects' suggest fully constituted subjects; clearly recognisable, describable, integrated and defined. Constituted as complete. Not only visible but knowable. Knowable as what they are and what they are not.

It is a crucial part of the claim to law-in-modernity that law is so founded and is of itself foundational of civic order. Enmeshed in the claims and aspirations of enlightenment philosophies of order and rationality, the narratives spun of law-in-modernity assert the existence of a threshold over which the prefigurative elements of 'law' were drawn and pulled, woven into a web of discourse about the rule of law and a set of practices of law, rational, regulated and integrated, which could be known by the whole as well as the parts. Each section defined and classified and then placed into relation; each section underpinned by key foundational concepts; for instance, the legal subject.

The construction of these narratives, their partiality and their violence towards the excluded, has been of interest to post-modernists and feminists alike. In these papers Goodrich recovers other histories of contracts, Brown explores shifts in the political theories informing contracts, and Duncan interrogates criminal law as predicated on the legal subject as being not-woman. The use of the figure of woman, of narratives of the feminine, as constitutive of law-in-modernity by exclusion, by difference and by denial, is a major theme of feminist work. Exposing and countering this foundational element has led some feminists to argue that there is no possible space in law for W/women;[1] for others a form of transcendent inversion, the transgressive claim to a parallel law of/for W/women, is a way to break from a seemingly defeatist collapse in the face of the power of law.[2] Both approaches reject the claims of law-in-modernity; both aspire to transformative change but they divide on the possibilities of the use, rather than simply the critique, of law.[3]

Within this volume the approaches taken are often more tentative and exploratory; eschewing grand themes and solutions and rather testing out possibilities. Some papers are overtly strategic: thinking through legal strategies which might help some women now, but setting this against the impact they

---

1   See eg Carol Smart, *Feminism and The Power of Law* (1989) Routledge.

2   Most notably Luce Irigaray, see eg *Je, Tu, Nous* (1993) Routledge.

3   The counterposing of Smart and Irigaray here may seem a little disingenuous if not set within the context that while the first works primarily as a sociologist and focuses very much on law as practice, the latter as a cultural theorist is much more interested in law as a set of ideas, a way of imagining ourselves and our relation to others. However, there are points of intersection in their work: for Smart, her engagements with theory and, for Irigaray, her call for law reform.

might have on other groups or on the overall dynamic of ideas, images and subjects constituted through law. For Noonan it is an examination of criminal defences, for Conaghan whether a feminist ethical base can be argued in torts law. In More and Flynn, the possible uses of European Union law; in O'Donovan and Palmer, strategies based on rights language and constitutionalist issues are the focus. The possible 'spaces' to be found in law continually raise issues of judgment; pragmatic in seeking to measure effect, ethical in seeking to test against some measure of what feminism is about.

Running through many of the papers (eg Conaghan and Palmer) is the problem of 'knowledge of women'; if feminism is predicated on a claim to speak not only 'for' but 'of' women, then what actually is 'woman'? Does she hold some essential, foundational identity which allows us to recognise, describe and know (sic) her, separate and apart from her construction through male discourse? Can this hold together claims of/for all women as a group, a category, which differentiates them not only from men but holds them as one despite all their cultural diversity? These questions go beyond simply a recognition of 'need' to questions of distinctive forms of knowledge, ethical claims and dreams and desires.

Some papers in this collection exhibit a willingness and a wish to explore different narrative forms as not only a mode of revealing partiality in law but also of exploring the very possibilities of feminism in finding voices as women. The use of story telling, of imaginative literature, of drawing on fairy-tales (Green, Lim, Mackenzie) and of biography utilises creative forms of thought and speech which seem particularly conducive to women and allow explorations, feminist perspectives being developed and explored at the very same time as law stories are explored.

In this sense feminism is being tested and tried as much as law; a series of possibilities for being or becoming woman. Not a given, not a theory, not even a perspective in the sense that there is one coherent gaze watching; but rather a series of incidents, situations and possibilities. All that is certain is the need for change which will transform relations between men and women to the advantage of both.

This sense of not being able to make any great claims or construct any grand narratives, but rather of needing to explore, test, and continually re-question, set against a horizon of dreams and aspirations for a better world, gives rise to a rejection of foundational ideas as knowledge and a rejection of an assertion that we can ourselves construct ourselves as foundational subjects. It gives rise to the recognition of the contingency of attempting to form, of asserting or claiming, subject status. We may recognise the strategic need to make such a claim, we may use the assertion to explore the issues involved; but we do not have to 'believe' in it as absolute. It is simply a matter of what it makes possible and, at the same time, a crucial awareness of the process of construction:

> To deconstruct these terms means ... to continue to use them, to repeat them, to treat them subversively, and to displace them from the contexts in which they have been deployed as instruments of oppressive power.[4]

Recovering histories, genealogies, of law allows us to not only examine foundational claims, but also the processes which made possible those assertions. Thus Butler argues:

> ... the subject is constituted through an exclusion and differentiation, perhaps a repression, that is subsequently concealed, covered over, by the effect of autonomy. In this sense, autonomy is the logical consequence of a disavowed dependency ...[5]

The act of recovery becomes then a revelation of the partiality and fragility of the claim to autonomy, to the foundational subject. The continued contortions required to assert and reassert law-as-modernity in its construction of the legal subject in criminal law are examined by Duncan. It is as if the tension between the discourses of law and the practices of law (between the assumed premises and the actual experiences) is dealt with by an attempt re-negotiate 'the margins' in a move which allows 'the centre' to be reconfirmed (Noonan). The more 'fragile' the assumptions the more powerful the assertions; the greater the need to try and present the continuing presence and value of the foundational. The greater the fear of the 'irrational', the greater the attempts at repression. But the attempts to exclude, to repress or simply to deny can never finally succeed. The legal subject, the practices of law and the discourse of the rule of law are not reducible to a simply rational base. We can examine, and expose, these attempts and these failures and, in doing so, reveal not only power but also the fragility of that power.

Thus interrogating 'the law' in its fullest sense reveals the many contingent factors which lie behind the presentation of 'the law' as some kind of unitary, univocal, model operating one-directionally. Not only does an examination of the practices of law reveal unevenness and inconsistency but an examination of the way in which narratives of, and about, law are constructed reveals crucial choices being made which may reveal or hide this unevenness (Green, Lim, Mackenzie, Bottomley). This form of interrogation is not carried out simply to criticise law, in the sense of exposing the operative myths, but to consider the ways in which not simply the practices but the presentation of the practices, may be made more enabling within feminist terms. How cases are reported, used in texts, indeed how the practices of law are constructed into topics for legal education become issues of engagement – of questioning the possibilities of bringing not simply feminist perspectives on to the agenda but feminist aspirations for change.

'Foundational subjects' was taken as the title for this collection as echoing the most recent way of 'naming' the aspects of legal education which the legal

---

4   Judith Butler, 'Contingent Foundations' in Benhabib etc (eds), *Feminist Contentions* (1995) Routledge at p 51. See also Rosi Braidotti, *Nomadic Subjects* (1994) Columbia.

5   At p 45.

profession requires students to undertake on exempting degrees.[6] Replacing the terminology of the 'core' subjects, topics which students must now study are grouped, or clustered, under seven 'foundational' headings. The product of much negotiation between interested parties, what is interesting is that behind the seeming certainty of the presentation of these 'foundational' elements lies a great deal of contention about the groupings, the nomenclature and the actual topics selected for study. Lim supports the decision, hard-won, to keep equity and trusts as a separate heading, rather than its being subsumed under a new property grouping. What is revealed is not only the contingency of choice but also that in this act of mapping, the introduction of feminist perspectives may be more enabled by some foci rather than others. It is moot to argue that some areas of law seem more conducive to feminist thinking than others (Brown, Conaghan, Peppin, Lim) but what is clearly the case is that feminists, and others, need to recognise the contingent aspects of constructing foci, and even more so categories, within law. The need to think laterally, in terms of relations, through and over categories, has often been important in feminist analysis: in Peppin's paper the Canadian experience of the use of constitutional principles in relation to tortious actions raises possibilities for the interaction of private/public law which have only recently entered the agenda for English lawyers (O'Donovan and Palmer). Further Peppin's paper may well reflect the strength of 'naming' an area for women, in this case 'health law', as a site around which actions can be consolidated for the client, drawing on distinctive areas of law and litigation. Thus the act of naming, of organising, of providing foci, has very real consequences. These acts of mapping do not have to be presented as impermeable, impenetrable and absolute; we can take comfort from difficulties the professional bodies faced when presenting their 'foundational subjects' and recognise that the clusters of practices and ideas brought into relation under the status of 'foundational subjects' are not, in fact, anywhere near as 'foundational' as they sound! We may query whether they do offer, here and now, the best 'foundation' for an education in (or rather through) law rather than a training for legal practice; but we can at least recognise that they are simply heuristic devices.[7] In this sense the new 'foundational' approach, ironically, poses exactly the same questions as the feminist approaching the mass and mess of law: how do I begin to make sense of this and use it as best I can for the purposes I have?

6　The seven 'foundations of legal knowledge' are: obligations I, obligations II, foundations of criminal law, foundations of equity and the law of trusts, the foundations of the law of the European Union, foundations of property law and foundations of public law, *Preliminary Notice to Law Schools Registering Qualifying (Law) Degrees* (July 1993) Law Society and CLE. Because law schools tend to add the term 'subjects', I have played on the concept of 'foundational subjects' to open up the questions of 'subject status' and 'subjectivity'.

7　A number of commentators have pointed out that the 'foundations' approach now taken by the professional bodies is actually a loosening up of the educational agenda and offers more freedom and choice to the academic curricula than the more prescriptive attitude taken previously, see, eg, G Hottor, 'Trusts Law: A Song Without End?' (1992) *Modern Law Review* 123, and P Scott, review of William Twining, 'Blackstone's Tower: The English Law School' (1995) *Journal of Law and Society* 429.

CHAPTER ONE

CONTRACTING OUT/CONTRACTING IN: SOME FEMINIST CONSIDERATIONS

BEVERLEY BROWN

Feminist legal theory has approached the law of contracts from two directions: exclusion and inclusion. The exclusionary is the more familiar mode, portraying women and the family as historically multiply disbarred from all that the world of contracts empowers and is prepared to remedy. Approached from this angle, the question of inclusion can be addressed only as a possible prescription for the future: should the family become more like the market (or *vice versa*)? Olsen and O'Donovan ask this question.[1] Inclusionist analyses, by contrast, tend to argue I say 'tend' as this is a far less established approach that there is a feminine, 'familial', presence *already installed*, comfortably or uncomfortably, within the gates of contract law, even as its commercial norm. Why focus on the foothills when the fortress is already invaded? This is the polarity around which this essay is arranged.

The purpose is to indicate some of the pitfalls of reading off contract doctrine from political models of liberalism. The interrogation of gender and contract, beginning from the simple rhetoric of exclusion, is becomes an account of different contract 'logics' accumulated within the law. Law thus appears to be both bad and good at the basic art of housewifery. Unwilling to waste anything, nothing can be quite thrown out; the drawers are full of a jumble of 'rainy day' subcategories; occasionally a spring cleaning rationalisation will come along.

Whether reading for exclusion or inclusion, feminism has approached the law of contracts in terms of a great polarity between the market and the family. Contract and the market are read as coextensive. The market sphere is also male in its monopoly and masculine in its manners. Perhaps nothing could better embody – or, more precisely, disembody – men's abstracted relations with each other than the model of the discrete transaction, usually taken to supply the focal meaning of the law of contract:

> ... no duties exist between the parties prior to the contract formation and in which the duties of the parties are determined at the transaction stage. Prior to the transaction, Smith has no duty to Brown; at the time they enter into their agreement in a single joint exercise of their free choice; they determine their respective duties to each other for the duration of the agreement; completion of the promised performance terminates the party's obligations.[2]

---

1 K O'Donovan, *Sexual Divisions in Law* (1985) Weidenfeld and Nicolson at pp 191-94; F Olsen,'The Family and the Market: A Study of Ideology and Legal Reform' (1983) *Harvard Law Review* 96.

2 J Swan and B J Retier, *Contracts* (1982) Butterworths at pp 43-46.

'One-shot', 'arm's length', founded in the hostile egoism of possessive individualism, even the names in the example, those mere ciphers 'Smith' and 'Brown', evoke the ethos of strangers.

By contrast, the family is the domain of non-contract, female in its distinctive occupancy and feminine in its personal rather than impersonal mode, affective rather than instrumental – and, for that reason, also associated with forms of power, archaic or/and brutal, incompatible with contractual presumptions of equality. As Unger, though not exactly a feminist, puts it, the family appears as both 'too good' and 'too bad' to be included in the realm of contract.[3]

This, at least, is held to be law's picture, and also the picture that law has done its best to make (or keep) true. Law's motive here may be attributed to crude sexist bias, whether conscious or unconscious, a deliberate failure to apply the principle of equal freedom, that politically made contract which is not just a commercial technique but a political revolution. All is signally disclosed in the way the potential linguistic openness of the 'Rights of Man' in 18th century social contract theory turned out to conceal a literalist closure. Or, law may be moved by a more sophisticated perception of the market as propped on the family for its economic survival as a system and, a 'haven in a heartless world' for the emotional survival of its male agents, everything neatly coalescing in the family's role in reproducing the next generation of market-competent male and masculine actors, and their feminine carers and caterers. In its exclusionist mode, this dominant picture has largely been used to show how women and the family, and women in the name of the family, have been disbarred from entry into the enjoyments of contract regimes.

Two aspects of this rendition are particularly notable; indeed, they are closely configured. The first is the very short circuit between the legal, the political and the economic. This shows up in the frequent invocation of the term 'public' as meaning the sphere of commercial life *and* the sphere of participation in government, especially in the form of political representation. Similarly, in 'history of ideas' accounts of the genesis of social contract theory, commentary has it that, in reformulating the presumptions of political power against traditionalist claims to legitimacy, the contract metaphor flowed naturally from the merchant class, for whom 'contract honeycombed their lives'.[4] Contract and the market become coextensive because they are seen as sharing the same ideas of individual liberty and consent found in classic liberal political theory, even sometimes down to its modern democratic inscriptions.[5] Thus, with contract already instituted as a central metaphor of political rights and relations, 19th

---

3   R Unger, *The Critical Legal Studies Movement* (1983) Harvard University Press at pp 63–65.
4   R S Peters, *Hobbes* (1967) Penguin.
5   Q Skinner, 'Meaning and Understanding in the History of Ideas' (1969) *History and Theory*, vol 8 at pp 13-14.

century denunciations of the exclusion of married women from commercial contracts and 20th century battles over entry into the labour market take on all the symbolics of citizenship, all at par with suffrage. Feminist analysis of contract law, in line with a wider tendency, is thus already preoccupied by a certain politicisation of the market.

The second notable feature is the way 'the family' is inscribed in history, the family's non-contract status registered as 'pre-contract', somehow a remnant of earlier social modes stranded in the present. As 'too good' for contracts, the family (and hence women) stands for some enchanted lost community of love and gifts and altruism; as 'too bad', the family represents those forms of traditional status and authority given up in a world of meritocracy, along with recourse to brutal forms of bodily power now officially renounced as uncivilised. (This 'fossil' picture of the family contrasts with the way the family has been dealt with, in other areas of law, as being in the forefront of social developments, as in Mary Ann Glendon's *The New Family and the New Property*.[6])

In both these aspects, there is a certain concurrence between the conventional and the feminist versions. In both stories, freedom of contract is located as a conjoint economic and political 'moment' (occurring over a very long stretch of time). The doctrine of freedom of contract tells the historical story of a double disembedding of persons from the pre-existing web of community relations and traditional authority. As freedom *to* contract, it means freedom to choose one's contract partner, no longer tied through obligations of birth and status, liberated from or bereft of the social linkages that constituted the personal/public world of superiors and inferiors. Legally untied, such connections appear in retrospect as sources of undue influence, whether of sentiment or coercion (mixed legally as unconscionability and duress), that compromise the voluntary nature of the transaction. This half of freedom of contract can, in turn, be seen by reference to the law of marriage where 'party freedom' to choose the partner is an immense revolution in the system of alliance marriage which, tied to property, arguably had as much meaning at the level of peasant smallholdings as of grand dynasties.

Yet, at the same time, the choice of partners is only the first half of full freedom of contract. For the second half, freedom *of* contract allows what marriage does not, the parties' ability to define the terms of their agreement: to create the obligations, and only those obligations, one desires. Marriage, by contrast, is a fixed-term contract, an all or nothing package. Hence, as Pateman notes in *The Sexual Contract*, many 'feminist writers have stressed the deficiencies of a contract in which the parties cannot set the terms themselves',[7] and hence at least one possible reason why lawyers hesitate to see marriage as a true contract.

This story can even be tied together with the law on marital rape. Both in Scotland and England, Hale is cited as the authority for non-recognition of the

---

6   M A Glendon, *The New Family and the New Property* (1981) Butterworths.

7   C Pateman, *The Sexual Contract* (1988) Polity/Blackwell at p 155.

crime of rape within marriage, the doctrine on rape often subsumed to the general civil status of wives under '*coverture*':

> But the husband cannot be guilty of a rape committed by himself upon his lawful wife, for by their mutual matrimonial consent and contract, the wife hath given up herself in this kind unto her husband, which she cannot retract.[8]

Historically this type of 'contract' is not even specific to marriage. It has at least a general resemblance to contracts of oath and fealty in which the prime focus was on the person to whom one was swearing loyalty. Social contract theory, with its distinction between a pact of submission and a pact of union, also offers some parallels. In the Hobbesian model, submission to the sovereign is total and irrevocable. Consent is given at the moment of choosing one's sovereign-partner – for Hobbes, no natural lawyer, the social bond has no external foundation in natural or divine, but is artificial, and voluntary – based on the act of will in which, submitting by that contract, the subject's right to further non-consent is given up. If this version of the sovereignty of marriage represents the law as it was before the recent changes, then the current law on marital rape is more like Locke's version: consent now revocable, the presumption of consent has not disappeared but rather become factual, requiring non-consent to be positively evidenced.[9]

Hence a Whiggish tale in which it merely remains to institute the second half of full freedom of contract:

> The solution to the problem of the marriage contract is presented as completion of the reforms that have eroded *coverture*; wives can even take their place as 'individuals' and contract appears once again as the enemy of the old world of status or patriarchy.[10]

What is interesting in Pateman's argument is not her criticisms of late 20th century contracting-in prescription. (She is hardly unique in that.) Rather, it is her argument that, far from being stranded in the past or the pre-modern, it is the modern family and, by implication, modern forms of contract, that are at stake. Her main argument is that the era of social contract theory instituted a new form of domination between men and women and one very much in the form of a contract. Marriage (and the wider social and political order), she argues, came to be based on a hidden contract, an exchange based on the woman's sexual services. Further, in this regard, marriage had at its core the same sort of exchange as non-marital cohabitation, the two in turn bearing a generic relation to prostitution; precisely, in legal terms, one of the ways in which

---

8   M Hale, *Historia Placitorum Coronae* (1736) vol 1 at p 629. See also *Stallard v HMA* (1987) 9 SCCR 248 and *R v R* [1991] 1 All ER 747, the Scottish and English cases that inaugurate the recognition of material rape as a competent charge.

9   For Locke, the sovereign could justifiably presume the subjects were tacitly consenting unless they actively rebelled or otherwise showed non-consent. This comparison between social contract theory and the law of rape is adapted from J Vega, 'Coercion and Consent:. Classic Liberal Concepts in Texts on Sexual Violence' (February 1988) vol 16 no 1, (although she uses 'tacit' rather confusingly also to mean 'irrevocable').

10 Pateman *op cit* n 7 at p 156.

cohabitation may be construed as a contract for immoral purposes (the other being that it is immoral as an arrangement, 'unlawful sex' meaning simply sex outside marriage). No wonder, she says, lawyers are so reticent about precisely why the marriage contract is unlike other contracts.

But is it? For, in speaking of sexual exchange, Pateman has begun to use the language of the successor theory of contract, *bargain theory*. The older, will theory, is indeed much closer to political theories of the social contract.[11] Its key concerns are intentions and meetings of minds, whether a contract was truly willed. Where the will theory begins from the subjects who make the contract, and searches for their mutual agreements, the bargain theory begins from the putative contract asks.

WILL THEORY AND BARGAIN THEORY

The will theory begins from the parties' status as entirely free agents, capable of forming their relationship and their obligations *ex nihilo*. Narratively, the will theory begins from the parties' inner intentions and moves, as it were, outward to find a public manifestation of their meeting of minds. Hence, historically, the evidential role of consideration, sometimes punningly used to distinguish rash from considered promises, as signifying that a legally binding agreement is intended. Consideration as form has therefore been compared to a seal, or any ritual, that would mark out a change in the parties' legal relations. As a mark it says nothing more than that a change is willed; it does not speak to the content.

In general, the bargain theory institutes a quite different approach from the will theory. It involves no preliminary narrative, and tends to discount the discourse of private intentions. Indeed the whole formalism of marking out contracts becomes redundant. It begins, simply and crudely, with the substantive requirement that for a contract to exist, there must be an exchange. The role of consideration and intentions is reversed. Now it is intentions, somewhat peripheral, that become evidence of a true exchange, while consideration is no longer evidential but material, forming the substance of the contract. But what is crucial is that the rational agent replaces the free agent. General objective criteria of human conduct make contract regimes legible. This is installed in the notion of exchange itself: no rational person would do something for nothing, or, in market-theory terms, groups behave on the premise that all the members act rationally (which is not incompatible with the knowledge that not all of them do).

Taken to its logical extreme, the bargain theory would make individual intentions entirely redundant (and hence too the need to express them minutely and distinctly): there would be simply no need to find out about individual

---

11   But see J Gordley, *The Philosophical Origins of Modern Contract Doctrine* (1981) Clarendon.

intentions of parties: they have either behaved within the parameters of what can be recognised as rational or they have not. Where bargain theory imputes intentions, this is not a *faute de mieux* substitute for lack of access to the real subjective thing; on the contrary, imputed rationality is *better* than the real thing.

The will theory is often criticised for its metaphysics, assuming a contract already exists in that mythical moment of the meeting of minds (*when* precisely?) to be merely recorded externally. The written document itself becomes but evidence of intentions. Yet this is too literal; as Fuller[12] combined with Ricoeur[13] might argue, this metaphysical approach simply misunderstands the character of legibility installed in a contract, the implications of its necessarily public 'readability' by a third party. This is most obvious when put in terms of enforcement: if the purpose of contracts is to guarantee security of transaction, the ability to assume promises are backed up by legal requirement, then the agreement must be intelligible to law. But it also applies even between the parties themselves, as they may themselves at a later date come back (as it were, as third parties to their previous selves) to read the document to discover their commitments. Thus, as with Parliamentary intentions, reading statutes is not a recovery of empirically existing past thought (even when *Hansard* may be used as evidence). Rather, to impute an intention; an author is to read a document assuming, for example, that it makes sense, has some overall unity or consistency.

There is a second crucial element in both the will theory and the bargain theory which may be put as the degree of risk which the parties are presumed to have to bear for themselves. The logic of the will theory, mimicking political theory of freedom of the individual, would in principle allow potentially *any* agreement to count as a contract, however risky, however ruinous. The only concern, this being based in the theory of freedom, would be undue influence, the forces of duress or sentiment. Unger describes this as the gambler's view, with contracts as bets on the future, and gambling debts fully enforceable. It assumes not only freedom but equality. Hence the early 19th century refusal to accept excuses such as impossibility, recognised in tort, as a release from contractual liability on the grounds that such excuses were rightly restricted to the realm of imposed obligations. By contrast, in the realm of contracts, voluntarily created obligations, parties should be held totally responsible for dealing with the consequences if things went wrong.

Famously, checks on this pure risk have been provided by the state, in regulating the limits of freedom in terms of fairness. Less familiar is the way that the bargain theory also performs this task, but in a different way, an internal mutation within private contracts. To refuse to count a contract as a contract on the grounds that no rational person would have made such a bargain is a way of

---

12   L Fuller, 'Consideration and Form' (1941) *Columbia Law Review* vol 41.

13   P Ricoeur, 'The Model of the Text: Meaningful Action Considered as a Text' in P Rabinow and W M Sullivan (eds), *Interpretive Social Science: A Reader* (1979) University of California Press.

checking 'deep play'. At the same time, emphasis shifts to knowledge-conditions.

The problematic area of cohabitation contracts displays some of these co-existing elements in contract law rather well. First, consider the idea of a discrete transaction as common to both will theory and bargain theory. It is based on the idea that the relationship has been entirely created by the contract, and that once all the terms are fulfilled, the contract is complete, and the relationship thus ceases to exist. Performance exhausts the contract. What then should one make of those cohabitation contracts seeking solely to set up post-termination arrangements (for instance, limiting property rights)? How is classic contract law to conceptualise this: a contract whose terms come into force only after the relation has ended? The co-extensiveness of contract and relationship is violated. (There is of course a different area of law regulating such post-termination situations, the law of marriage, divorce and custody.)

Second, there is the notorious 'double bind' in which the courts interpret a cohabitation contract as an exchange of sexual services for money (and hence not a contract because immoral) or, conversely, see the relationship as based on the gift of love (and hence not a contract because a gift). Again, one can see a source, besides prejudice, for this approach. For bargain theory asks: where is the exchange? (Hence if, as in *Marvin v Marvin*, the possibility of finding an acceptable exchange in domestic services with a computable market value.)[14]

Finally, there is the complaint that the courts refuse to read even express contracts as expressions of the parties' intentions, insisting that they simply could not have intended legal consequences to follow. Here the query merely concerns whether this is best expressed, as it often is, in terms of imposing public standards of interpretation: for that, as we have seen, is a necessary condition of their being contracts at all. But it bodes ill for those instances of implied contract that retrospectively tell the story beginning, 'I thought it was love but ...'.

INCLUSIONIST VISIONS

In Chapter 7 of *Postmodern Legal Feminism*,[15] Mary Joe Frug stages a feminist examination of the Posner-Macneil debate about the law of contracts. It is, as it were, a rehearsal of a debate that has not yet occurred, in which principles associated with the feminine or the family may already be found within contract law – although in a marginalised form still in comparison with classical models. This section offers a brief analysis of this vision, and its pitfalls, as well as filling in the basic debate.

---

14   18 Cal 3d 660, 557 p 2d 106, 134 Cal Rptr 815 (1976) as discussed in C Dalton, 'Deconstructing Contract Doctrine' in K T Bartlett and R Kennedy (eds), *Feminist Legal Theory: Reading in Law and Gender* (1991) Westview Press.

15   (1992) Routledge.

The Posner-Macneil debate is about how to construe the law of contracts. Each side takes one of the existing contract types and gives it paradigm status as standing for contract law as whole. For Posner it is the discrete transaction as inflected through neoclassical economics whereas for Macneil the relational contract is the true norm especially as supplemented by anthropological and sociological understandings of reciprocity and solidarity. They are fighting about the nature of exchange.

Both of these approaches are in conflict with standard legal doctrine, whether deep legal dogmatics or the 'textbook' version. Characterising the official position as mixed and muddled, both Posner and Macneil seek the alternative authority of current practice. Yet Macneil goes even further than Posner, seeking a mandate not only in the courts, but in the world of settled business practice. For him, the courts represent the pathology of contract law, not its norms; what happens when things go wrong, not when they go right.

This is a debate that lends itself easily to masculine/feminine casting, the whole made the more piquant because these are actually competing characterisations of commercial life. Posnerian masculinity has all the high-octane values on its side: performance, control, security of transaction, high presentation demands (ie make terms explicit), standardisation, all built on the 'stranger' mode of the one-off, arm's length, atomistic, discrete transaction. Macneil's feminisation is equally easily wrought for here is a vocabulary of the courts' hidden but real commitment to preserving ongoing relationships, recognising the importance of trust, which includes respecting not only unarticulated but inarticulate understandings, for 'ordinary people' are important here, and overall a plea for diversity and multiple standards of interpretation and enforcement as part of the general emphasis on a wider context-sensitive regime. Similarly, too, the emphasis on negotiation rather than either/ors and hierarchies. Here, too, is an awareness of the risks inherent in relationships, and concern for their possible need of mending. Hence risk planning characterises discrete transactions while performance planning is the mark of the discrete transaction. Cohabitation contracts may not be so unusual after all.

Recognising these debates on the gender axis is at the same time to recognise the various mappings claimed in the name of gender: individualism/community and the feminist 'appropriation', as Joan Williams[16] calls it, of the critique of possessive individualism; the contestation of rationalist ethics and epistemologies, for Joan Williams another feminist appropriation of the terms of already existing critique; so too feminist claims to the world of negotiated justice and the reorienting of law as not the centre but the edge of systems of social ordering; as it were approaching law from the good woman's, rather than the bad man's, though equally external, point of view. Hence the temptation to read the debate

---

16 J Williams, 'Deconstructing Gender' in P Smith (ed), *Feminist Jurisprudence* (1993) Oxford University Press.

in terms of the well-worn master opposition: individualism/community with its mix and match of subheadings (atomism/relations, general rules/particularism and context-sensitivity, self-interest/altruism). In other words, to begin once again with the reading of classic contract doctrine as merely the application of classical liberal theory to be opposed to the sentimental virtues. Gilligan[17] offers a responsive chord the relational world.

It is certainly true that Posner approaches law from the perspectives of maximising choice and minimising state intervention. Indeed, so enamoured is Posner of market principles that he has, notoriously, sought to extend them to personal life. Sexual events and 'contracts' are thus to be seen as market transactions, adapting to the available conditions and constraints, but essentially still a matter of individuals rationally pursuing their own self-regarding preferences. The criminal law of rape, for example, has been analysed in Posnerian terms by reference to marriage as a justifiable monopoly on the free circulation of sexual partners. And, while there have been many feminist howls of outrage about the terms of his prescriptions, it can also been noted that descriptively, there are obvious continuities with feminist accounts of rape law as the protection of male property, and marriage as the exchange of women between men.

By contrast, if Posner wants to make the family more like the market, it seems that Macneil proceeds in the opposite direction in emphasising the 'relational' subtext of contract law as an everyday practice and, with it, a rather less formalistic attitude to precision than is suggested in the classical, or even neoclassical, concern for highly specified-in-advance contract forms. Business relations between, say, suppliers and producers, operate in terms of commercial understandings of a 'more or less at that price', 'on or around that date' variety that, in turn, both facilitate and rely on the existence of ongoing relationships of trust and informal understandings between familiar business 'pairings'. Any new relationships are, similarly, initiated on the basis that they will soon become such ongoing situations. In attacking the discrete transaction and developing the idea of 'relational' principles, Macneil draws upon that old legal realist favourite, the doctrine of reliance, also discussed by Unger as a an instance of the counter-principle of community: 'the freedom to choose a contract partner will not be allowed to work in ways that subvert the communal aspects of social life'.[18] The courts know the importance of keeping relations afloat over time and will often elevate relational principles over the competing principle of imposing strict contractual liability.

What a present, it seems, for feminism: an account of contract law's 'familial' understandings that at the same time can summon the weight of legal realism and critical legal studies, to put 'the feminine' on the side of nascent counter-

---

17   C Gilligan, *In A Different Voice* (1982) Harvard University Press.

18   Unger *op cit* n 3 at p 61.

principles against the dominance of the discrete transaction, and the ideology of freedom and classic individualism.

Yet certain aspects of Posner, for example, become very puzzling. Why does he espouse standard form contracts (citing Lellellyn and the Uniform Commercial Code)? For pure freedom of contract is best embodied in the individually-tailored set of terms. He seems to be making the market transaction more like marriage as freedom-to, not freedom-of, contract. The answer is not only that he is clearly a bargain theorist, but that he would like to purge contract theory of the confusions of the will theory, to seek absolute presentation, maximum security of transaction, to gain maximum control over future outcomes. The aim of contracts is complete and certain planning. In sociological terms, this is a Weberian account of the role that contracts play for capitalist entrepreneurship, the ability to pursue profit systematically by controlling the future, instrumental rationality's preference for formal rationality.

The rationalism of neoclassical economics focuses centrally on problems of *knowledge*. For Posner, the market place is crucially an information system, price is solely an allocative device that provides information to the market about the current balance/degree of equilibrium of supply and demand. Similarly, one of his justifications for the existence of law is that it reduces 'the complexity and hence cost of transactions by supplying a set of normal terms that, in the absence of the law of contracts, the parties have to negotiate expressly.' This is not to defend Posner but merely to require intelligibility conditions.

Yet – at least polemically – one could go further when examining the Posnerian solution[19] offered to the problem of contracts having become impossible to fulfil for reasons either not known ('subjectively') or unknowable ('objectively'). He sweeps aside this distinction as meaningless. There is no 'objective' transpersonal standpoint of foreseeability. (Strange, how reminiscent this is of certain themes in feminist critiques of inequality.) Claims to objectivity are in practice always based on a particular point of view. The important thing is that there is a correlation between power and the amount of knowledge one can command: more can be seen from a hilltop than a valley. This argument, in turn, meets up with an approach most highly developed outside of contract law, primarily in the world of tort liability: risk allocation. The basic logic of this, at least in tort, does seem to be inspired by a sense that, in this world of non-voluntarily chosen obligations to others, it is more appropriate to share losses between parties rather than allocating them in either/or fashion to one or the other. Hence, in those situations the risk ought to be borne by the more powerful party. (Again, of course, this has the economy of not needing to investigate subjectivities: it is a type of strict liability strategy.)

Conversely, one should equally be wary of talk of community. Pluralistic and fragmented solutions have not been their typical form. The language of

---

19 R Posner and A Rosenfield, 'Impossibility and Related Doctrines in Contract Law: An Economic Analysis' (1977) *Journal of Legal Studies* vol 6.

unspoken agreements, as much as it may, speaks the language of caring, and is also the mode of gentleman's agreements and the 'insiders' knowledge' school of business talk, favoured by airport books that offer to tell you 'everything they didn't teach you at Harvard Law School': making deals, the art of bluffing, avoiding going to court, and how to keep your useful contacts while ditching 'losers'. All those unspoken rules of reciprocity, the informal appreciations of how things are done, the community relations that determine a person's social credit, have, far from being culturally alien to masculinity, been its greatest standby. In the world of economics and the theory of the firm it was precisely in such quasi-market calculations that insiders could be trained and promoted.

Indeed, when one examines Macneil's work at greater length, it transpires that it is very much predicated on the, probably correct, perception that many corporate relationships, especially in labour law, operate as, in effect, private jurisdictions (or fiefdoms), small polities that must work out their own principles of private vertical command and internal rules of justice. Thus the correlate of the law-independency of his thesis is that law is replaced not only by custom but by corporate regimes of governance. 'Informality works best in settled contexts such as business.'

Hence the need for caution.

CHAPTER TWO

GENDER AND CONTRACTS

PETER GOODRICH*

An unusual contract, reported in a mid 15th century treatise on judgments of love, gave rise to a curious litigation.[1] The action was brought by a male petitioner against a woman defendant for breach of an amorous contract or *alliance d'amours*. The parties had entered into a formal agreement, publicly sworn and sealed with tears and kisses, declaring their mutual love and promising, amongst other things, that they would never have any other lovers. The petitioner pleaded that the woman defendant had broken that promise. His argument was a complicated and tenuous one. The greatest good of love, he claimed, was that of keeping the heart and affections of one's lover. Every time a lover becomes distracted (*est vaquant*) or involves herself with pleasing others, it is to be taken as a sign that her heart is not entirely loyal and should not be wholly trusted. Despite her promise, the petitioner claimed, his lover had almost immediately begun to entertain other suitors and had accepted small gifts, amorous speeches and in some cases bouquets of flowers from other men. His argument was that the attention she had shown to other men through accepting visits and gifts was in breach of her promise of fidelity which in his view required that she accept gifts and attention only from him.

In what could well appear to be a reversal of traditional gender roles, the defendant opposed the plea, claiming that her promise should be understood in less absolute terms and interpreted more hedonistically.[2] Her argument was that no one should be given such great authority, power or domination over another's pleasures and desires as the petitioner had claimed. Her promise of love could not be interpreted in any specific or predetermined way nor could their contract be taken to preclude her talking to other men or accepting gifts or laughter. In short, the contract could only be maintained if love was understood as requiring neither possession nor exclusion but rather a 'space in between the lovers'[3] within which inherently public or social sphere they could genuinely

---

*   My thanks to Richard Collier, Hugh Collins, Niki Lacey, Anton Schütz and Linda Mills for discussion and comments that led me to change much of this essay.

1   Martial d'Auvergne, *Les arrêts d'amour* (1460/1951 edn) Picard at pp 38–42.

2   It should be noted here that the specific construction of gender identities can neither be assumed as given nor interpreted exclusively in terms of the contingent characteristics of gender identities at a given time and in a particular institution or place. On the 'social temporality' of gender identity, see Judith Butler, *Gender Trouble. Feminism and the Subversion of Identity* (1990) Routledge. For an eloquent analysis of the contingency of gender identities in law, see Jeanne Schroeder, 'Feminism Historicized: Medieval Misogynist Stereotypes in Contemporary Feminist Jurisprudence' (1990) 75 *Iowa Law Review* 1135.

3   Auvergne, *Arrêts d'amour* at p 40. For contemporary feminist discussion of the 'space in between' or *entre deux*, see particularly Luce Irigaray, *Thinking the Difference* (1994) Athlone Press. For commentary, see Alain Pottage, 'Recreating Difference' (1993) 5 *Law and Critique* 131.

appreciate, honour and love each other. The petitioner had thus failed to understand her promise because he did not appreciate either the nature of love or the relational and temporal qualities of a contract. The court held that the petitioner's plea was contrary to the code of love and that he had acted in such a manner as to drive love away. There was no breach of promise because nothing in the contract could in law be interpreted as preventing the defendant from pursuing her pleasures, accepting compliments and gifts and enjoying the company of others. Judgment was thus for the defendant together with an award of full costs.

The case is interesting because it is argued upon the basis of two very different conceptions of relationship and so also of contracts and their interpretation. For the petitioner, the contract is in essence proprietary and restrictive: its terms should give him control over the behaviour of another and should be interpreted strictly: in the modern idiom, objectively. The contractual rights which he wishes to assert are formal and invariant, and their assertion should pay no attention to subsequent changes in mood, emotion or amorous circumstance. The contract is thus to be understood as instituting absolute and unchanging terms. Although the subject matter of the agreement is the relation between lovers, the terms are to be understood impersonally and interpreted formally. Law in this construction of contract should impose upon and define life. For the defendant the contract is to be interpreted quite differently. The agreement is expressive of love and is to be interpreted symbolically or aesthetically. The contract symbolises certain feelings or emotions and is attached to a relationship at a particular time and place. To give a true interpretation of the contract would be to follow and interpret the subsequent relationship between the two lovers and most importantly to recognise the space of relationship, the temporality, intensity and duration of the desires that constitute the relationship and that precede and post-exist any legal qualification or definition. The contract itself is thus viewed as a space of communication and of desire; its interpretation is a matter of insight and adaptation to both circumstance and change. The point to be stressed is that both interpretations construct an image of gender identities – of the role that each gender performs within a relationship – and so also of the affective or emotional structure of contracts and their interpretation. One, it could be argued, is predicated upon distance and the addiction to a phantasm of certainty. It attempts both to control – to own or exploit – its subjects and to deny the effects of time upon the content of relationships. The other is more fluid and flexible. It conceives of the contract as an aspect of relationship and recognises that both time and feelings change.

Despite its aura of historical distance and procedural curiosity the contract of love can usefully introduce several features of the gender of contracts. The agreement between lovers belongs to an alternative history of contracts, one that has yet to be written. It belongs to a repressed history of emotions and fidelities, of conscience and of spiritual promises, of subjective and aesthetic interpretations of terms. To draw upon that other history is to allude initially to the diversity of contexts, forms and uses of contracts and to suggest that both in terms of doctrine and of substance a concern with the gender of contracts can lead to a radical rethinking of contemporary law. The principal argument of the present essay will take the form of tracing in outline the history and significance of gender in contracts, and most notably in the original and exemplary form of contract, that of the marriage. It will be argued, that it is the marriage contract, the contract of one gender with the other, that forms the dominant western model of legal prescription of gender identity. Using the marriage contract as an illustration of the contractual construction of gender identities, it will be argued subsequently that while it may frequently be denied, the substantive rules and doctrinal interpretations of contracts manifest a very strict set of images of gender and of the relationships within and between the genders. A contract is a social form of human relationship and as such it necessarily has a gender dimension whether the relationship in question is between man and man, man and woman, woman and woman, or some other corporate fiction of personality of which men and women are the bearers. It will be argued finally, that this gendered and intrinsically relational dimension of contracts cannot be denied simply by asserting that contracts are to be construed objectively or, in the language of case law, that one should search for 'a stiff contractual arrangement'.[4] To the extent that the objectivity of contracts appears to remove agreements from the domain of relationships and so of corporeality or gender it simply imposes a specific and, I will argue, specifically homosocial construction of gender identity upon the relationships so analysed and adjudicated. Such is not to argue that masculine or feminine gender identities are necessarily uniform or constant over time. It is rather to observe that to the degree that contemporary contract doctrine privileges formality and distance over relationship or intimacy it necessarily constructs a gendered identity and performs a particular role in the context of the current hierarchy and opposition of the sexes.

MARRIAGE AND CONTRACTS

The history of the exclusion of women from legal institutions gains an exemplary expression in the common law of contracts. Such exclusion is both paradoxical and ironic. It is paradoxical because one of the earliest and most consistent uses of the term contract within the legal tradition refers to the contract of marriage.[5] It is ironic because the hierarchical and gendered

---

4   *Jones v Padavatton* [1969] 1 WLR 328 (*per* Dankwerts LJ).

5   Bracton, *De legibus et consuetudinibus Angliae* (1968 edn) Harvard University Press at p 97 refers to marriage as a public contract (*publice contractum*). On the history of the marriage contract, I will refer primarily to Henry Swinburne, *A Treatise of Spousals, or Matrimonial Contracts* (1686/1711 edn) D Brown.

character of the marriage contract gave rise to many of the equitable principles and substantive rules relating to the formation and the policing of contracts to which, it will be argued, contemporary common law seeks to return. The irony is thus that so long as the common law continues to ignore the gender relationships expressed in or constituted by contracts it will persist in its 'august tradition' of 'sublime irrelevance'[6] to the practical world of agreements and the continuing relations which they engender.

The hidden gender of contracts can be approached from a number of historical and political perspectives. In using the contract of marriage as the emblem of what is at stake in the history and regulation of contracts I am only marginally concerned to correct the imbalance in existing narratives of the exclusively commercial provenance and character of contract doctrine. My initial concern is somewhat different. It is that of recalling the questions of gender that attach to the history of contracts. I will argue that contracts are relationships and should be understood as relationships, as forms of communication, of emotional exchange and development over time. The intensity, development and duration of a relationship are crucial features of the marriage contract, as also are the dimensions of power and gender hierarchy. That doctrinal writers and judges alike have tended historically to ignore the emotive and relational dimensions of contracts and the various unconscious and affective connotations of agreement is not simply a failure of will, understanding or procedure.

It is both historically implausible and interpretatively incompetent to attempt to understand any contractual agreement in terms which do not address the substantive quality of the relationships at stake in both promise and exchange. In historical terms, the western legal tradition has always viewed marriage as the perfect species of union and the most binding form of relationship and that model of union is found throughout the development of religious and legal institutions, in the law of both church and state.[7] In hermeneutic terms the purely formal analysis of contracts as momentary and objective forms of exchange or as dealings at a distance or at 'arm's length',[8] does not merely deprive legal culture of relevance, it disempowers those subjects who might otherwise benefit from contractual rights or equitable protections. Dealings at 'arm's length' do not indicate the absence of a relationship but rather a communicative and emotive distance, the pretence of objectivity or externality which legal doctrine has aspired to in the hope of being mistaken for a science. In psychoanalytic terms such distance or separation is best interpreted as a denial

6   Hugh Collins, *The Law of Contract* (1993, 2nd edn) Butterworths at p xi.

7   The metaphor of contract gains its most forceful classical expression in Cicero, who describes society as a marriage (*conjugere*), the most perfect form of union. The marriage contract as a model of contracting forms a consistent element in the later traditions of canon law. An action for breach of faith (*pro laesione fidei*) was the spiritual law's equivalent of an action for breach of a secular contract.

8   For recent judicial discussion of this term, in the context of economic duress, see *CTN Cash and Carry Ltd v Gallaher Ltd* [1994] 4 All ER 714.

of relation and of emotion rather than its absence. It can be understood as repression or more simply as fear of contact or engagement because such proximity is threatening to the authority of law and the status of its professional bearers. Whatever the case, be it fear, jealousy, greed or an essentially homosocial lack of care that promotes this distance, it cannot be denied that the interactions, communications and institutions of such exchange actively express, and in a broader sense constitute, a series of gender identities. The distance of exchange, in short, expresses a specific kind of relationship and a peculiar structure of emotion, one which, I will suggest, excludes certain types of relationship or gender identity while privileging others.

To argue that the marriage contract has been of considerable, though unacknowledged, significance to the development of contract doctrine, to argue that 'all contracts resemble a marriage'[9] has further implications which will be pursued in the following analysis. First, it places the question of the gender of contracts within a context of promise and of faith or, more broadly, within a symbolic framework. Promising was historically conceived as a form of communication with God as well as with a mundane person and the law. A promise would be pleaded and enforced in spiritual courts or courts of conscience as well as within the secular jurisdiction and positive law.[10] The hierarchy of the church and the repressions, both physical and emotional, of religious institutions were intrinisic to the interpretation and development of contracts and particularly to the conception of the absolute character of the written obligation or deed. Second, the religious context of the marriage contract is also significant in explaining the specific historical character of the exclusion of women from contracts. The church, like the law, was a masculine profession and its history and practice was predominantly one of relationships between men. Modern society, the 'civil and ecclesiastical polity' elaborated in early doctrine, was conceived as being based upon agreement or contract and that contract was an agreement between men. The homosocial and frequently homoerotic character of religious and political relationships meant that the feminine remained external to the institution of faith and practice of law throughout a hierarchically conceived polity or social body. What was true at the level of the social contract was also true of the specific legal conceptions of good faith or contractual intent: the exchanges, unions or contracts made in the market and the household were made between men, their subjectivity was the prevalent objectivity and the gender of their documentation, language and

---

9   Collins, *Law of Contract*, at p 287: 'In other words, contractual rights and duties remain personal to those who create them; all contracts resemble a marriage in so far as no third party can claim the right to share the intimate relations established between the spouses'. See further on this H Collins, 'The Decline of Privacy in Private Law' (1987) 14 *Journal of Law and Society* 91. For a discussion of broader trends, see Milton Reagan, *Family Law and the Pursuit of Intimacy* (1993) New York University Press.

10   The action for breach of promise, or in strict terms *pro laesione fidei* for breach of faith, would be sued in the spiritual courts before the ecclesiastical judges and the remedies would be corporal penance or performance of the promise. For the history of spiritual contracts, see Richard Cosin, *An Apologie for Sundrie Proceedings by Jurisdiction Ecclesiastical* (1591) J Norton.

interpretation was exclusive of the frequently feminine objects which contracts exchanged.[11] Finally, it will be argued that there is another history of contracts to which the relational conception of marriage provides a certain access. It is that of the plural history of differing forms, institutions and procedures of liaison, alliance and relationship. To understand the intimacy of contracting is to address the plurality of relationships expressed in agreements, be they those of commercial networks, of love or of other species of sexual exchange.

THE HOMOSOCIALITY OF CONTRACTS

The question of gender has not and does not figure very greatly in writings on contracts. Neither doctrine nor case law make more than passing reference to gender in contractual relationship and even progressive or critical contract theory has largely ignored the dimension of gender. While the doctrine of contract has been a privileged object or focus of critical theories of law, the concerns of feminist legal theory have remained by and large within the confines of feminist writings on law. While some critical accounts of the history of modern contracts recognise the fact that family law has been excluded artificially from contract theory,[12] the analysis of doctrine is concerned most usually with principle and counter-principle played out in the domains of the market economy and commercial exchange. The immediate reason for this absence from critical theory is probably the Marxist origin of such doctrine. While Marxist theory paid considerable attention to contract as a social and economic form, it reduced the substance of contract to the analysis of commodity production and the relations between classes. It then criticised the commodity market for reducing human relations to the callous cash nexus. Contracts expressed real relations between subjects but the nature of these relations was unconscious because it was determined not by the (imaginary) ideas which subjects had about their relations but by the reality of the economy and the relations of production.[13]

---

11   Specifically on this theme, see C Pateman, *The Sexual Contract* (1988) Polity Press; on the heterosexual character of the social contract see Monique Wittig, *The Straight Mind* (1992) Beacon Press; on the homosexual character of amorous exchange, see Jean-Charles Huchet, *L'Amour discourtois* (1987) Privat.

12   Roberto Unger, *The Critical Legal Studies Movement* (1986) Harvard University Press at p 58: 'First, there are the exclusions: whole areas of law, such as family law, labor law, antitrust, corporate law, and even international law, which were once regarded as branches of a unified contract theory but gradually came to be seen as requiring categories unassimilable to that theory'.

13   The most sophisticated analysis of the Marxist theory of contracts is still Eugeny Pashukanis, *Law and Marxism: A General Theory* (1978) Ink Links, ch 4. At p 68: 'Law in its general definitions, law as a form, does not exist in the heads and theories of learned jurists. It has a parallel, real history which unfolds not as a set of ideas, but as a specific set of relations which men enter into not by conscious choice, but because the relations of production compel them to do so'. For a general discussion of this issue, see P Goodrich *et al*, 'Introduction' in Douzinas *et al* (eds), *Politics, Postmodernity and Critical Legal Studies* (1994) Routledge.

Contract is assumed to belong to the market, and commercial exchange is assumed to take place at arm's length or at a distance. It is further assumed that such impersonal dealings exist, by virtue of their distance, beyond the terrain of the body and so outside of the confines of sex, of gender or even of desire. The conflicts which critical lawyers analyse are thus formulated in terms of logical oppositions between categories, as, for example, between liberalism and socialism, autonomy and solidarity, self-interest and altruism, volition and reliance or even freedom and paternalism, but these are not viewed as terms with either a gender content or any necessary link to the relations between the sexes. Where contract law is analysed as an ideology and its imagery is examined in terms of subjective aspirations the focus is similarly almost exclusively conceived in terms of the generic possibilities of empowerment in the relation between individuals and large-scale enterprises.[14] Most recently, a European collection of *Perspectives of Critical Contract Law* ranges in scope across a vast territory of European legal systems and addresses issues in consumer protection, insurance law and a variety of other specialised domains of contracting.[15] Some contributions allude very vaguely to questions of gender, as, for example, in a reference to 'Piercing the Contractual Veil',[16] but the panoply of critical perspectives does not include any analysis of contracts from the perspective of gender or of feminism. The only explicit reference to women and contracts is in the form of a rhetorical question which receives neither discussion nor answer.[17]

The absence of any specific representation of women either in contract doctrine or in its jurisprudence can be explained both at the level of history and at that of the form of law. From an historical perspective women have been directly excluded from the principal domains of commercial contract by virtue of their status. From Bracton onwards, women were defined at common law as being of an inferior status to men.[18] This legal inferiority was significant in numerous domains of politics and law but it meant in general that women could neither succeed to public office nor hold political positions nor practise within the professions.[19] Women were in this sense excluded from the social contract.

---

14 Jay Feinman and Peter Gabel, 'Contract Law as Ideology' in David Kairys (ed), *The Politics of Law* (1990) Pantheon Books.

15 Thomas Wilhelmsson, *Perspectives of Critical Contract Law* (1993) Dartmouth Publishing.

16 *Ibid* Gunther Teubner, 'Piercing the Contractual Veil? The Social Responsibility of Contractual Networks'. A veiled woman was a married one in legal terminology. See further: Anon, *The Lawes Resolutions of Women's Rights* (1632) J More at p 125: 'A woman as soon as she is married is called covert, in Latin *nupta*, that is veiled, as it were clouded and over-shadowed ... she has lost her streame, she is continually *sub potestate viri*'.

17 Thomas Wilhelmsson, in his synoptic overview of critical contract law, 'Questions for a Critical Contract Law' makes only one allusion to women and law, and this in the form of a question and accompanying reference to a feminist work on Nordic tort law: 'What can the rapidly growing women's law contribute ...?' Wilhelmsson (1993) *supra* n 15 at p 29.

18 Bracton *supra* n 5 at p 31: 'Women differ in many respects, for their position is inferior to that of men'.

19 This restricted status is first spelled out in detail as a topic in its own right in John Fortescue, *De natura legis naturae* (1462, 1869 edn) Private Distribution.

The social union or compact was made between men and expressive of the masculine order of both succession and of law. With a few exceptions, unable to inherit office or dignity and incapable of political action or power in their own right, women's role within the social drama of contracts or public life was either hidden (*covert*), indirect or the exception rather than the rule.[20] The specific destiny of women, according to the doctrines of both medieval and modern common law, was that of marriage or, in the words of one early treatise on the subject: 'All women are understood either married or to be married and their desires are subject to their husband.'[21] The principal effect of such a destiny was to expunge both the political and the contractual power of the feminine within the manifest transactions of the public sphere: 'The original contract is a sexual-social pact, but the story of the sexual contract has been repressed.'[22] It is the history of that repression and of the specific forms of the marginalisation or denial of gender which critical analysis still needs to address.

The legal effect of marriage or *coverture* was to place the wife not simply within the power or under the control of the husband but it was also to annex the woman to the husband such that husband and wife were in law one person. The wife's state of non-being, signalled by her loss of name and her adoption of her husband's dignity or status, led one early treatise to comment that 'a married woman perhaps may doubt whether she be either no one or no more than half a person ... they be by intent and wise fiction of law, one person, yet in nature and in some other cases by the law of God and man, they remain diverse'.[23] The contract of marriage was the civil death of the woman and while married she could make no contract in her own right. A *feme covert* or wife could neither complain of rape nor enter a contract of sale nor make a will without the consent of her husband. In its starkest description, women were the property of their husbands and where unmarried they were subject to their father or guardian. The life of a woman was depicted in law in terms of the statuses of maiden, wife and widow, each defined by reference to ownership by or guardianship of men, a status referred to by Glanvill as being always in some form, *in custodia dominorum*.[24] The principle which determined the varying statuses of the feminine was that of the law of the father or *patria potestas*, a power purportedly derived from God, nature or time immemorial and which gave the

---

20 Thus in one of the earliest constitutional treatises, Sir Thomas Smith, *De Republica Anglorum* (1565/1583 edn) H Middleton at pp 19-20, arguing that women monarchs were the exception which proved the rule of royal succession through male heirs: where women succeeded to the Crown 'such authority is annexed to blood and progeny ... for there the blood is respected, not the age nor the sex'.

21 Anon, *The Lawes Resolutions of Women's Rights* (1632) J More at p 9. For discussion, see Ian Maclean, *The Renaissance Notion of Woman* (1980) Cambridge University Press; Peter Goodrich, *Oedipus Lex* (1995) University of California Press.

22 Pateman, *Sexual Contract* at p 1.

23 Anon *supra* n 21 at p 4.

24 *Tractatus de legibus et consuetudinibus regni Angliae* (1187), translated as *The Treatise on the Laws and Customs of the Realm of England commonly called Glanvill* (1965) T Nelson at p 85.

father an absolute dominion, power or *potestas*, over his wife, servants and children: from Glanvill through to the modern law, 'legally a woman is completely in the power of her husband'.[25] Within this historical context, the marriage contract must be understood as a complicated form of property transaction between men. Its effect was that it transferred a woman into another family, or, in the language of law, *in alienam familiam*.[26] The contract defined the status of a woman and the legitimacy of her children; it transferred a woman from one position of subjection to another, and equally importantly passed other property (dowry or *maritagium*) between the families. While the consent of the woman, her acceptance of the offer of marriage, was necessary to the transaction, that consent was closer in form to an election between alternatives, to a response to a proposition or question, than it could properly be regarded as a free promise or freely engendered exchange: it was, one might say, the exemplary form of what American law calls a 'contract of adhesion' and English law a 'standard form contract'. Further still, the structure of exchanges in the network of relationships surrounding the marriage contract indicate clearly that the consent of the woman was of less significance than the consent of the parents or the guardian, that the relationship between the partners was of much less importance than that between the families whose blood and property was to be transferred.[27]

The marriage contract reflected far more than the will of the woman who consented to an offer. Its effects ranged across a series of domains of property and office to which she was disentitled. The contract, in short, was made between men and its significance was contained in a series of continuing relationships implied by, but in no sense co-extensive with, the contract itself. The subordinate position of the female party was compounded upon completion (and consummation) of the marriage. Husband and wife were in law one person and that person was the husband: 'A *feme covert* in our Books is often compared to an infant, both being persons disabled in the Law, but they differ much; an infant is capable of doing any act for his own advantage, so is not a *feme covert*. A lease made by an infant without rent is not void, but voidable; but is void in the case of a *feme covert*. If a *feme covert* enter into bond, *non est factum* may be pleaded to it ... An infant may bind himself for conveniences, as necessaries ... and the law gives him authority so to bind himself; but a *feme covert* cannot do so without the consent, actual or implied of the Husband ...'[28] Translated into a more contemporary terminology the legal position of the woman was that of non-existence. Her marriage was her civil death (*civiliter mortua*) and after marriage

---

25 Glanvill *supra* n 24 at p 59. The general best description of the common law position of the father comes from Sir Thomas Smith, *De Republica Anglorum. The maner of Government or policie of the Realme of England* (1584) Middleton at pp 12–14.

26 Anon *supra* n 21 at pp 9–10.

27 Thus Swinburne, *Treatise of Spousals* at pp 4–6.

28 Anon, *Baron and Feme: A Treatise of the Common Law Concerning Husbands and Wives* (1700) J Walthoe at p 4.

she lacked the capacity to enter contracts because she no longer had the will or volition necessary to intend and so to consent. Two features of this incapacity deserve specific recollection in relation to subsequent and contemporary legal developments.

First, the woman's lack of legal personality for purposes of contract, amongst other things, defines the woman as a species of non-being. The common law develops a paternalistic limitation upon the public sphere of contracts, a limitation which defines and protects the feminine in terms of a series of inabilities. For legal purposes the wife historically had independent capacity and a power to act only in relation to dower, to the period of time between her husband's death and her own demise. Within that space, defined as no longer subject to the power of another, but finally *sui iuris* or at her own law, she has a momentary after-life or temporary freedom and will. Outside of her survival of the husband the wife lacks contractual capacity because her will is not her own but that of her masculine partner. She cannot intend, consent or agree except in the name, person or identity of her husband. So too if husband and wife purport to enter into an agreement, to enfeoff each other or convey land to each other it is void upon the assumption that the consent of the wife is not genuine but obtained by the husband by coercion, by duress, constraint or 'some other sinister means'.[29]

If the argument that the marriage contract is emblematic of the legal conception of contract is to some degree accurate it does much to explain the continuing and contemporary exclusion of women from the domain of contracts. While I will return to the contemporary dimensions of this exclusion and specifically to the much commented on unenforceability of domestic agreements, it is worth observing here that the feminine is legally conceived not simply as private but further as powerless. As early as 1700 a feminist defence of women's civil identity makes the essential point that *potestas* means absolute or sovereign power and such power is incompatible with obligations: 'For covenants between husband and wife, like laws in an arbitrary government, are of little force, the will of the sovereign is all in all. Thus it is in matter of fact ... men happily sign articles but then retract them ... because being absolute master, she and all her grants he makes her, are in his power, and there have been but too many instances of Husbands that have persuaded or forced wives out of what has been settled on them.'[30] The image of women within the common law thus developed predominantly in the negative terms of an absence and appeared in the contract case law primarily in the form of a series of disabilities or as defenceless and powerless victims of obligations which they had either failed to understand or had been forced to consent to: 'A quick review of almost any

---

29 Henry Swinburne, *A Brief Treatise of Testaments and Last Wills, very profitable to be understood by all the subjects of this Realme of England* (1590) Society of Stationers at p 82.

30 Mary Astell, *Some Reflections upon Marriage Occasioned by the Duke and Dutchess of Mazarine's Case* (1700) J Nutt at pp 38–39.

contracts text will show that most successful defences feature women, particularly if they are old and widowed; illiterates; blacks and other minorities; the abjectly poor; and the old and infirm.'[31]

The second observation to be made is that such incapacity or legal disability, the treatment of the married woman as less than an infant, is not only a form of absence or invisibility. It is also a repression of the varied forms and identities of the feminine. Where women do appear in the public sphere of contracts they do so historically in the identity, the guise or *persona*, of men. The sphere of contracts, like the language and the interpretation of contracts, is defined by a history of masculine markets and exchanges between men. In the words of an early text subtitled the *Woman's Lawyer* it is remarked acutely that, 'women have nothing to do in constituting lawes, or consenting to them, in interpreting of lawes, or in hearing them interpreted at lectures, leets or charges, and yet they stand strictly tied to men's establishment of them'.[32] Such a general accusation is no less true of the specific domain of contracts. In its early commercial definition, a written bond is defined as 'a contract whereby a man confesses himself by his writing orderly made, sealed and delivered, to owe any thing unto him with whom he so contracts'. Slightly later, discussing proof of written contracts, the same author remarked that, 'deeds in old times were wont to be delivered in the presence of men of greatest credit and worship that could be gotten'.[33] If such is the common law paradigm of contract it is easy to remark that the feminine gender of exclusion or of absence is matched only by the masculine gender of display and publicity, in contemporary terms manifestation or objectivity, in the domain of commercial exchange.

The broad principle of construction and interpretation of contracts within modern common law is that of objectivity: words and behaviour are to be construed according to the judicial designation of the meaning a reasonable man, or occasionally an officious bystander, at the time of exchange, would have placed upon those words or that behaviour.[34] While it is not possible to generalise adequately across the range of the contemporary law of contracts, the objective meaning of contractual words or behaviour has generally reflected both the perceptions and the practices of a masculine public sphere. The broad heremeneutic principle elaborated by feminist jurisprudence, namely that objectivity in the construction and interpretation of contracts is expressive of a strongly homosocial view of communication, is borne out by the very language

---

31 Patricia Williams, *The Alchemy of Race and Rights. Diary of a Law Professor* (1991) Harvard University Press at pp 156-57.

32 Anon at p 2.

33 William West, *The First Part of Symbolaeography* (1603) T Wright at fol A 8 a and at fol B 8 b.

34 The principle is most recently discussed by the House of Lords in *The Hannah Blumenthal* [1983] 1 AC 834. The principle of objectivity is if anything stricter in the US. See, for example, *Kabil Developments Corpn v Mignot* (1977) 279 Or 151, 566 P 2d 505. The general issue of objectivity in contracts is well discussed in Clare Dalton, 'An Essay in the Deconstruction of Contract Doctrine' (1985) 94 *Yale Law Journal* 997.

in which construction and interpretation occur. At its most extreme, the language of contract formation is straightforwardly belligerent.

In *Butler Machine Tool v Ex-Cell-O Corpn*[35] the question of which documents and so which terms constituted the contact is discussed in terms of a 'battle of forms' and the difficulty of determining which form or which part of which form is a term of the contract: 'In some cases the battle is won by the man who fires the last shot. He is the man who put forward the latest terms and conditions: and, if they are not objected to by the other party, he may be taken to have agreed to them ... That may however go too far. In some cases ... the battle is won by the man who gets the blow in first ... There are yet other cases where the battle depends on the shots fired on both sides.'[36] The other judges in the case use equally bellicose descriptions of standard form commercial communication. For Lord Justice Lawton, the issue is that of how 'the battle should be conducted? The view taken by the judge was that the battle should extend over a wide area and the court should do its best to look into the minds of the parties and make certain assumptions. In my judgment, the battle has to be conducted in accordance with set rules ...'.[37] Within this agonistic context counsel were commended for having 'struggled manfully'[38] with the agreement.

The one dimensional depiction of the negotiation of agreement in such conflictive or military terms is not limited to standard form contracts. The House of Lords, in a recent case concerned with the enforceability of an 'agreement to negotiate', refused to recognise such an agreement because 'the concept of a duty to carry on negotiations in good faith is inherently repugnant to the adversarial position of the parties when involved in negotiations. Each party to the negotiations is entitled to pursue his (or her) own interest, so long as he avoids making misrepresentations'.[39] The examples could be multiplied but the point would not be greatly altered. The objective theory of contracts is constructed within a language of antagonism and uses figures of communicative reasonableness ranging from war to silence, from officiousness to abandonment, from threat to the impersonality of arm's length dealings, as suits the purposes of the judge. What is true across the range of a case law which prides itself upon its particularistic focus on 'concrete cases' and piecemeal solutions is that its concept of objectivity expresses a particular and partial conception of manifest relationship in a particular context and over a limited period of time. While such a concept of objective interpretation of relationships might seem adequately to reflect the world of financial relations and the interactions of commercial institutions, the homosociality of that world and the gendered quality of its institutional relations needs further exposure. It is important to repeat that

---

35 *Butler Machine Tool Co Ltd v Ex-Cell-O Corpn (England) Ltd* [1979] 1 All ER 965.

36 *Ibid (per* Denning LJ).

37 *Ibid (per* Lawton LJ).

38 *Ibid (per* Bridge LJ).

39 *Walford and Others v Miles and Another* [1992] 2 WLR 174 *(per* Lord Ackner).

objectivity, and the distance or separation upon which it is based, does not exclude emotion or relation, it represses and so internalises or more simply hides them. Such repression does not and cannot obliterate the relational, it simply institutes gender identities in an unconscious or habitual form. Objectivity, in short, expresses a particular type of emotion, broadly speaking fear of contingency or contact, and a specific structure of relation, that of power or exploitation. In both contexts the doctrine and imagery of objectivity constructs gender identities in the form of denial. The manner in which such identities are performed in legal texts must in consequence be read symptomatically: in psychoanalytic terms the denial of history and of relationship, of the body or of emotions, is the strongest of signs of trauma and so of the need to re-examine such features of identity.

To analyse the masculine gender of contracts doctrine and substantive decisions is to transgress the legally constituted boundaries of public and private spheres. Most particularly, it denies that questions of gender can be relegated to the non-legal domains of domesticity, femininity or subjectivity. The construction and maintenance of identities, whether professional, legal, judicial or commercial is always a subjective performance and entails a crossing of the boundaries between the differing realms and presentations of personality. While the construction of male professional identity may involve an endeavour to deny or negate the private, emotional, sexual, or subjective states of personal being, such denial, like identity itself, is necessarily fantasmatic. Various masculinities pervade the domains of the institution as specific forms of affectivity, identity, relationship and interaction. It is not simply that 'the suppressed subjective constantly erupts to threaten the priority accorded the objective ...',[40] that the personal and biographical are never far from the surface, but also that the construction of objectivity as an abstraction, as non-corporeal and gender blind is a specific exercise of power. It institutes a professional order or complex based upon the suppression of desire and the denial of the personal and proximate. Freud speaks directly of the pathology of homosocial professional relations, of aggressive rivalry and the ambitious jealousy of colleagues, 'who resemble each other too closely. Thus it was necessary to stress the difference, displace the accent, inflect the resemblance from one of rivalry to one of gender'.[41] The invisibility of gender within the masculine or homosocial domains of the institution is itself a very specific and powerful form of sexuality: 'So long as the individual is functioning normally and it is consequently impossible to see into the depths of his mental life, we may doubt whether his emotional relations to his neighbours in society have anything to do with sexuality, either actually or in their genesis. But delusions never fail to uncover these relations and to trace back the social feelings to their roots in a directly sensual erotic wish.'[42] That the field

40 Clare Dalton *supra* n 14 at p 1039.

41 Mikkel Borch-Jacobsen, *The Freudian Subject* (1989) Macmillan at pp 76-77. See further Richard Collier, *Masculinity, Law and the Family* (1994) Routledge at pp 271-76.

42 Freud, *Letters*, cited in Borch-Jacobsen, *Freudian Subject* at p 79.

of social and more specifically professional relations is desexualised does not mean that it is asexual but rather that the homosexuality of professional relations is repressed. The rivalry, competitiveness, emulation, admiration, fear and aspiration which characterise professional interactions are only thinly disguised or sublimated forms of libidinal or erotic relation, replete with its fears and jealousies and with love and hate. Returning to the substance of contracts, certain features of homosociality can be briefly outlined.

First, as already alluded to, the language and interpretative rules of contract doctrine are impersonal and broadly purport to be objective. Such objectivity endeavours to establish a norm of rationality which escapes the domains of affection and subjectivity.[43] It does so, I have argued, precisely by evacuating the reality of contracts, namely the reality, the intensity, duration and development of the relationships which contracts express. Even where the courts endeavour to give effect to equitable sentiments of fairness or to rectify inequalities or injustices within existing relationships, their tendency is to manipulate formal categories of contract in such a way as to achieve the intended result without directly addressing the emotive basis or affective cause of judgment. I will address the issue briefly from two perspectives, the first elliptical, the second substantive.

In a case already referred to concerning a plea of economic duress, the Court of Appeal addressed the grounds upon which a plea of economic duress might succeed in a commercial setting. Counsel for the plaintiffs was a 'Miss Heilbron QC' who, in Lord Justice Steyn's words, 'submitted that the deputy judge erred in rejecting the plea of duress'.[44] After briefly summarising the grounds of her submission, Steyn LJ proceeds to dismiss the now demoted Miss Heilbron's arguments in the following condescending and somewhat extraordinary manner: 'Miss Heilbron cited a number of authorities which illustrate the developments in this branch of the law. While I found the exercise of interest, I was reminded of the famous aphorism of Oliver Wendell Holmes that general propositions do not solve concrete cases. It may only be a half-truth but in my view the true part applies to this case. It is necessary to focus on the distinctive features of this case, and then to ask whether it amounts to a case of duress.'[45] Beyond being patronising and superior in tone, the comment is elliptical to say the least. The reference to Oliver Wendell Holmes' 'famous aphorism' offers some species of extraordinarily vague or simply abstract justification for the refusal to address the grounds upon which the courts will strike agreements down for inequality of bargaining power, for policy reasons or simply so as to do justice to meritorious claimants. Miss Heilbron QC had referred to cases which would appear to have set out rules allowing in principle for a plea of economic

---

43   This argument is put forcefully in Mary Joe Frug, *Postmodern Legal Feminism* (1992) Routledge at pp 115-18.

44   *CTN Cash and Carry Ltd v Gallaher Ltd* [1994] 4 All ER at p 717.

45   *Ibid.*

duress in the context of 'arm's length commercial dealings'. In one case the defendants were a small company 'whose directors were personally committed to its success',[46] in another case the plea of economic duress was made against a union which organised industrial action on a ship owned by the plaintiffs.[47] In ignoring Hilary Heilbron's presentation of concrete cases Steyn LJ not only allows himself the greatest degree possible of subjective discretion but also hides the basis for its exercise, namely the different nature of the commercial relationships involved in the cases cited and their correspondingly different access to the affections, conscious or unconscious, of the judge.

The example of Lord Justice Steyn's somewhat problematic relationship to a woman Queen's Counsel is elliptical in the sense that the appeal to superior authorities or the dressing up of judgments in the apparent technicalities of doctrine are not specific to contract doctrine. The feature of Steyn LJ's judgment which deserves substantive comment is that what differentiated *CTN Cash and Carry* from the earlier cases was that the dispute arose within the context of an established and continuing long-term contractual relationship which was not affected by the specific duress alleged. The issue which Steyn LJ did not wish to address was not only that of a female barrister's arguments as to relevant law but also the correlation between the doctrine of economic duress and a network of relationships over time which exceeded the bounds of any single contract. The second substantive feature of the objectivity of contract relates directly to this point. The courts, in seeking to give the appearance of interpreting contracts in an objective and professionally valid manner, rely heavily upon the fiction that what is at issue is the meaning of words and behaviour at the specific and momentary point of entry into the contract.

In a much-taught decision of the Missouri Court of Appeals the appellant was a travelling salesman employed by the respondents, a wholesale dry goods company. The appellant, Embry, was employed under a one year written contract which expired on 15 December 1903. The evidence proved that several times prior to the termination of his written contract, Embry had endeavoured to get an understanding with the president of the company, Thos H McKittrick, for another year, but had been 'put off from time to time'.[48] On 23 December, Embry called on McKittrick, in the latter's office, and said to him that as his employment had lapsed and as there were only a few days between then and 1 January in which to seek employment with other firms, if McKittrick wished to retain his services longer, he must have a contract for another year, or he would quit there and then. He also observed that he had already been put off twice before and wanted an understanding or contract at once 'so that he could go ahead without worry'. McKittrick, after a brief discussion, said: 'Go ahead, you're all right. Get your men out, and don't let that worry you.' The action was

46   *Atlas Express Ltd v Kafko Ltd* [1989] QB 833.

47   *Universe Tankships of Monrovia v International Transport Workers Federation* [1982] 2 All ER 67.

48   *Embry v Hargadine-McKittrick Dry Goods Co* (1904) 127 Mo App 383, 105 SW 777 (*per* Goode J).

brought by Embry the following March when he was fired. The Missouri Court of Appeals dealt with the matter as a question of the objective meaning of the words used at the time they were exchanged: 'The law imputes to a person an intention corresponding to the reasonable meaning of his words and acts. It judges his intention by his outward expressions and excludes all questions in regard to his unexpressed intention. If his words or acts, judged by a reasonable standard, manifest an intention to agree in regard to the matter in question, that agreement is established.'

In neither of the cases discussed would I argue that the decisions were either wrong in law or incoherent in fact. In *Embry v Hargadine-McKittrick* the problem is the same as in *CTN Cash and Carry*, namely that what is in issue is not determinable by reference to the interpretation of the words used at the time of purported agreement. The decision in *Embry* shares the inability of the English courts to directly address the substantive ground of decision, namely the equality or here inequality of the relationship between the parties and their behaviour both before and after the specifically cited exchange of words and behaviour. The culture of law and specifically the profession of judge does not allow direct analysis either of the non-communication evidenced by the reported facts or of the evasion of conversation contained in the actual exchange. The words used by McKittrick specifically avoid offering a contract and precisely fail to address directly the contractual concern expressed by *Embry*. The prior and continuing relationship between the parties, the rather sorry history of non-communication and the explicitly hierarchical and patriarchal nature both of the prior non-exchanges and the specific interaction, are far more important determinants of the meaning or significance of the words used than any standard or norm of objectivity against which the jury was supposed to measure them. *Embry v Hargadine-McKittrick* is interesting in sum not simply because of its representation of the failings of homosocial communication in commerce as well as in law. It illustrates with all the unconscious force of masculine communication both the complexity and the indirection of the rituals of two separate professional interactions. Here, within the peculiar and peculiarly recognisable structure of the public sphere, face to face interaction is conducted at 'arm's length', the proximity of oral exchange is conducted at a distance: the words of a man appear to avoid the question; McKittrick evades the question and in doing so clearly avoids saying yes, and by implication says no, while the court, equally indirectly or 'objectively', interprets his no to mean yes. Objectivity in such circumstances implies power rather than logic, authority rather than interpretation.

FEMINISM AND CONTRACTS

The most obvious feature of modern contract doctrine, and specifically of the theory of an objectively ascertainable moment of agreement or *consensus ad idem* is its irrelevance to the practice of agreement in commercial and other domains.

A series of studies over the past half century have amply indicated that the formalistic and objectivistic doctrines and rules of contracts have never been of great significance to commercial practice. The claim that the black letter rules or formal principles of freedom of contract provide a context of certainty for business transactions has never been supported by any extensive empirical evidence and is particularly inaccurate in relation to contemporary business practice.[49] In part the reason for the irrelevance of contract doctrine mirrors the general distance between law and society.[50] In specific terms commercial and other relationships are far more likely to be governed by their own codes of practice and of dispute resolution than they are to depend upon the lengthy, expensive, unpredictable and obscure procedures and remedies of the law of contract. In commercial situations numerous studies have shown that recourse to contract law and remedies is the exception rather than the rule and, in the words of one recent study, 'the conclusion which should be drawn ... is that classical contract law should be completely rejected as an explanation of long–term contracting'.[51]

The reasons which make contract doctrine so frequently irrelevant to the practice of commercial and other relationships can in feminist terms be grouped broadly around the failures of an historically and contemporarily masculine profession to address the issues of communication and interrelationship from which both contact and contract grow. The adversarial form and inflexible rules of dispute settlement within contract law ensure that wherever possible, and particularly where some vestige of relationship remains or can be salvaged, common law will not be the forum of settlement. Ambiguity, flexibility, mediation, negotiation and variation are much closer to the needs of relationship than are supposedly invariant, or simply opaque, and on occasion unintelligible, rules of the objective formation and interpretation of contracts. The rules and categories of contract formation do, of course, express, engender and organise relationships but they do so in the indirect and repressed style of homosocial objectivity or in the complex and distanced form of sublimated desires. The gendered character of the categories and constructions of contract doctrine

---

49 On the historical evidence, see Robert Ferguson, 'Commercial Expectations and the Guarantee of the Law: Sales Transactions in Mid-Nineteenth Century England' in Gerry Rubin and David Sugarman (eds), *Law, Economy and Society* (1984) Professional Books. On the more contemporary debate, see Stewart Macaulay, 'Non-Contractual Relations in Business: A Preliminary Study' (1963) XXVIII *American Sociological Review* 55; Macaulay, 'An Empirical View of Contract' (1985) *Wisconsin Law Rev* 465; Hugh Beale and Tony Dugdale, 'Contracts between Businessmen: Planning and the Use of Contractual Remedies' (1975) 2 *British Journal of Law and Society* 45; David Campbell and Donald Harris, 'Flexibility in Long-Term Contractual Relationships: The Role of Co-operation' (1993) 20 *Journal of Law and Society* 166.

50 On the interaction of differing systems of norms, see Marc Galanter, 'Justice in Many Rooms' in Mauro Capelletti (ed), *Access to Justice and the Welfare State* (1981); Roberto Unger, *Law in Modern Society* (1976) Free Press. See also Carol Smart, *Feminism and the Power of Law* (1989) Routledge.

51 Campbell and Harris *supra* n 49 at p 173. For a recent account of the marginal relevance of contracts within the National Health Service, see Pauline Allen, 'Contracts in the National Health Service Internal Market' (1995) 58 *Modern Law Review* 321.

should not be deemed lost or non-existent simply because it is ignored or denied.

The legal concept of contract was born as a form of relationship. A contract creates a union, society, partnership or engagement and in doing so it borrows in reality from a model which is still much closer to the contract of spousals or of marriage than it is to the aggressive and jealous 19th century legal fantasies of commercial certainty and absolute rules.[52] To a limited but growing degree, I will argue, contemporary common law is moving in the direction of recognising that the 'survival' of contracts lies in returning to the model of contract as an interaction and communication between subjects which develops, intensifies or wanes over time. Whether consciously or unconsciously, this entails a return to the plural histories of alternative models of contract and can learn much from the duration and symbolic effectiveness of the marriage contract. The rules developed around spousals constantly return in the form of equitable variations or reforms of the later and largely unsuccessful commercial model of impersonal or purely instrumental exchange. The marriage contract reminds law of the feminine, it recollects that interpretation is always an exercise of subjectivity, and that in strict historical terms the rules of communication and formation of a contract were developed around a man proposing marriage to a woman.[53]

The common law periodically recognises changes in the ethical and political basis of social relations. At its best it endeavours to respond to such change by interpreting or reinterpreting both instruments and rules in a novel or dynamic fashion. Such periods of hermeneutic activism force the law to draw extensively from quasi-legal and extra-legal sources and feminism has undoubtedly been one such institutionally separate, cross-disciplinary source of legal change.[54] In its crudest form, the common law simply asserts the need to reform the law in recognition of social change. At the level of interpretation, comments such as, 'I do not forget that this is 1961 and what might have been said of the position, independence, and the like, of women in 1848 would have to be seriously

---

52 Frug, *Postmodern Legal Feminism* at p 116, discussing what in English would be termed rules of frustration of contract (or *contractus interruptum*) remarks that: 'Like a phallus, this conceptual proposal is singular, daunting, rigid and cocksure'. For a striking critique of Frug's position, see Beverley Brown's characteristically crystalline analysis in 'Risking the Feminine: Mary Joe Frug on Law' (1994) 23 *Economy and Society* 355, particularly at p 366.

53 My favourite example of this is that of the postal rule. As I have argued at length elsewhere, the postal rule's enigmatic protection of the offeree is a product of the fact that what was originally at issue was a woman who responded to a proposal of marriage by post. The reason that the offeror bears the burden of risk is simply that the offeror was a man and was therefore much better able to take that risk than the woman offeree. See Peter Goodrich, *Oedipus Lex: Psychoanalysis, History, Law* (1995) University of California Press at pp 198-210.

54 Which, sadly, is not to suggest that feminism has yet changed law to nearly the degree to which law has subverted feminism. See Martha Fineman and Nancy Thomasden (eds) at *the Boundaries of Law: Feminism and Legal Theory* (1991) Routledge at p xii: 'I, for one, am a legal scholar who has lost faith. Feminism, it seems, has not and, perhaps, cannot transform the law. Rather, the law, when it becomes the battleground, threatens to transform feminism.' For a slightly more optimistic view, see Helena Kennedy, *Eve was Framed: Women and British Justice* (1992) Vintage.

qualified today', are not uncommon.[55] They do not, of course, provide any very direct indication of how the hermeneutic power to reinterpret or to update the law will be used but they do at least indicate some minimal concern with the historicity of law and the need, in potential at least, to rethink what it means to say in a contractual context that, 'the courts do not normally infer or apply the strictest legal canons to what passes between husband and wife in the ordinary course of marriage'.[56]

Occasionally the question of law reform or judicial legislation is directly addressed, as in a recent example drawn, appropriately enough, from the sphere of domestic contracts and specifically concerned with the terms of the marriage contract. Discussing, in 1991, towards the end of the 20th century, arguably rather late in the day, whether or not the marriage contract gives the husband absolute power over the wife for sexual purposes, Lord Keith states that, '[t]he common law is, however, capable of evolving in the light of changing social, economic and cultural developments. Hale's proposition [on the marriage contract] reflected the state of affairs in these respects at the time it was enunciated. Since then the status of women, and particularly of married women, has changed out of all recognition in various ways which are very familiar and upon which it is unnecessary to go into detail ... marriage is in modern times regarded as a partnership of equals, and no longer one in which the wife must be the subservient chattel of the husband'.[57] If a wife may now be deemed capable of forming an intention of consenting to or rejecting an offer of sexual contact it would be logical to suppose that she can in civil law agree or disagree to other offers. This, curiously, remains an open question in English law, the general presumption being still that domestic agreements are not intended to be binding and so cannot be enforced at law. Nor, with a few exceptions, can a contract be implied in relation to domestic labour, child care, emotional support or self-sacrifice such as giving up of a job: in the view of the judiciary these are all motivated by 'natural love and affection' and not by venal concern.[58] I would suggest, however, that the traditional contract doctrine cannot survive long in conjunction with the broadening scope of the judiciary's willingness to recognise the equality of married women in criminal law and equity. The question I will now address is that of the extent to which this changing perception of gender, though only, it must be admitted, of the feminine gender, has or is likely to enter the common law of contracts. Rather than working directly with the classical

---

55   *Zamet and Others v Hyman and Another* [1961] 3 All ER 933 at 937-38.

56   *Ibid* at p 937.

57   *R v R (rape: marital exemption)* [1991] 4 All ER 481 at 483-84.

58   Thus, most famously, *Balfour v Balfour* [1919] 2 KB 571; *Jones v Padavatton* [1969] 2 All ER 616. For the religious variation on this theme, see *Davies v Presbyterian Church of Wales* [1986] 1 All ER 705. For discussion of the gender implications of equitable remedies in these circumstances, see Leo Flynn and Anna Lawson, 'Gender, Sexuality and the Doctrine of Detrimental Reliance' (1995) 3 *Feminist Legal Studies* 105.

(and discredited) categories, I will address the questions of gender relationship and contract synoptically and in terms of affective exchange and emotional duress.

Affective exchange

The question of the proper objects of contractual relationship have traditionally been addressed at common law in terms of the requirement of consideration: to be enforceable at law an agreement must have as its object an exchange or bargain or in civil law a cause that justifies such enforcement. The agreement is otherwise *nudum pactum*, a naked pact, and cannot give rise to an action. Although, historically, 'the [common law judges] had no clear idea of what consideration meant'[59] the modern view has been that sufficient consideration simply means evidence of a bargain in which something of economic value or some 'material benefit'[60] passes between the parties. Since the late 18th century a mere promise, moral obligation, spiritual advantage and in most circumstances simple affection have been insufficient to constitute consideration. The economic model of consideration, however, has not worked well and contemporary case law has arguably reverted to an alternative conception of spiritual cause or affective exchange based upon the marriage contract and cognisant of the issues of hierarchy, duration and gender implied in the interpretation of any legally enforceable exchange.

The doctrine of consideration has its historical roots less in commercial practice than in spiritual conceptions of promising and in allied notions of the cause or motivation for agreements, including spousals and marriage contracts.[61]

---

59 James Gordley, *The Philosophical Origins of Modern Contract Doctrine* (1991) Oxford University Press at p 137.

60 *Webb v McGowin* (1935) 27 Ala App 82, 1168 So 196. In *Webb* the material benefit concerned was the life of one J Greeley McGowin. The appellant, while employed in a saw mill, was engaged in clearing the upper floor of the mill by dropping pine blocks to the ground below. The blocks weighed in the region of 75 pounds. 'As the appellant was in the act of dropping [a] block to the ground below ... he saw McGowin on the ground below and directly under where the block would have fallen.' Had he turned it loose it would have seriously harmed or killed McGowin, so the appellant held on to the block and fell with it, thereby diverting its direction. The appellant 'was badly crippled for life'. McGowin promised subsequently to pay the appellant a maintenance allowance for the rest of his life. The court held that such a promise was enforceable: 'It is well settled that a moral obligation is a sufficient consideration to support a subsequent promise to pay where the promisor has received a material benefit.' Interestingly and indicatively where similar facts occurred in a domestic setting there was no contract. In *Harrington v Taylor* (1945) 225 NC 690, 36 SE 2d 227 the defendant had assaulted his wife. She took refuge in the plaintiff's house. The next day the defendant gained access to the house and resumed the attack. The wife took an axe, knocked down the defendant and was about to split open his head when the plaintiff intervened, catching the axe on her hand. The hand was badly mutilated and the defendant promised to pay damages. The promise was held to be unenforceable: common gratitude or 'a humanitarian act of this kind, voluntarily performed, is not such consideration as would entitle her to recover at law'.

61 From a rather different perspective, the details of the historical development are well spelled out in A W B Simpson, *A History of the Common Law of Contract. The Rise of the Action of Assumpsit* (1987) Clarendon Press at pp 156–60, 270, 390–93, 475–85.

The early modern law recognised that 'advantage' could comprise any of a number of material and immaterial benefits. In general principle a promise would be enforced where it either created a 'charge' or advanced the purposes of the promisor.[62] Recognised benefits from promising included promotion of charitable purposes; the marriage of a child or relative;[63] the 'natural obligation' of father to son in another case was 'apparent consideration of affection ... for there is such nearness of relation between the father and the child, and 'tis a kind of debt to the child to be provided for ...;'[64] and elsewhere again performance of a *'voluntarie Courtesie'*[65] or simple 'amicable consideration'[66] were recognised when such were performed at the request of the promisor. Consideration, in short, was not predicated merely upon economic benefit or material bargain but upon a much broader conception of cause and moral obligation. The notion of cause or motive for promising had also the additional advantages of flexibility and of engagement with the relational context of interaction and exchange. The later common law reflects that early history in a number of residual categories of consideration and contemporary law arguably seeks to return to the broader principle of cause or of moral obligation that such residues recollect.

The principal direct form of survival of the early conception of cause can be found in the willingness of the courts from time to time to recognise moral obligation as a ground for enforcement of promises. Where, for example, a married woman borrowed money without the consent of her husband and subsequently promised to settle the bond then in strict law her promise was without foundation or consideration. Lord Mansfield, in a celebrated judgment, enforced the bare promise on the strength of the equity grounding it: 'Where a person is bound morally and conscientiously to pay a debt, though not legally bound, a subsequent promise will give a right of action ... the new promise creates a new ligamen.'[67] While the concept of moral obligation has not had any extensive life within common law, it clearly grounds a number of other developments. In general terms a number of affective relations gain contractual expression and enforcement on grounds that come very close to recognising simple obligations enforceable for ethical reasons. Justice, equity or fairness have thus allowed recovery where strict law or the economic model of instantaneous relationship could not do so.

A few examples from the case law can clearly evidence a continuing though unacknowledged role for moral obligation or simple cause or charge. In *Shadwell*

---

62 Christopher St Germain, *Doctor and Student* (1530) at p 134: '... if he to whom the promise is made have a charge by means of the promise, which he has also performed, then in that case he shall have an action for the thing promised, although he that made the promise have no worldly profit by it.'

63 *Lever v Heys* (1598) Moo KB 550, Cro Eliz 619, 650.

64 *Dutton v Poole* (1677) 3 KEB 786, 814, 830, 836, 1 Vent 318.

65 *Lampleigh v Braithwait* (1616) Hob 105, 80 ER 255.

66 *Hunt v Bate* (1568) Dyer 272a.

67 *Lee v Muggeridge and Another* (1813) 128 ER 599.

v Shadwell a nephew successfully sued his uncle for an allowance promised in consideration of his marriage. According to Erle CJ, 'the importance of enforcing promises which have been made to induce parties to marry has been often recognised'. Reviewing the facts, Erle CJ had no trouble in observing that the uncle had benefited from the marriage because it was 'an object of interest with a near relative and in that sense a benefit'. In reaching this conclusion the Lord Chief Justice observed: 'I am at liberty to consider the relation in which the parties stood, and the interest in the status of the nephew which the uncle declares.'[68] Subsequent case law can provide numerous examples of morally and relationally motivated decisions. In *Allegheny College v National Chautauqua County Bank*, Cardozo CJ memorably remarked of a charitable bequest that it was enforceable in that, '[t]he longing for posthumous remembrance is an emotion not so weak as to justify us in saying that its gratification is a negligible good'.[69] In other cases, a promise to pay money posthumously to a nephew who attended her funeral was posthumously enforced; a promise given by a nephew to an uncle to 'refrain from drinking, using tobacco, swearing and playing cards or billiards for money' was enforceable; in a further case a grandfather promised his granddaughter $2,000 if she quit work on the ground that 'none of my grandchildren work and you don't have to', and the promise was enforced.[70]

The reason for enforcement of promises of the kind delineated is often formulated in terms of reliance detriment but the principle I wish to focus upon is somewhat broader and less mundane. Contemporary English case law has increasingly recognised the need and assumed the power to transgress the boundaries of public and private and to intervene within both spheres through recognising consideration in contexts where a relationship or affective bond requires – on grounds of justice, common sense, commercial reality or simple policy – some species of legal protection. Within modern common law the recognition of affective bonds and moral obligations can be found across a spectrum of legal categories ranging from promissory estoppel to the concept of network contracts which, in what, borrowing again from the law of marriage and the conception of privity of blood, might be termed privity of endeavour, joins a party to a contract she has not signed.[71] The example I will use, however, is that of nominal or invented consideration. Again developed unconsciously out of a concern with gender issues it has gradually become accepted by the courts that performance of existing legal or contractual duties can constitute

---

68   *Shadwell v Shadwell* (1860) 142 ER 62.

69   *Allegheny College v National Chautauqua County Bank* (1927) 246 NY 369, NE 173.

70   Respectively *Earle v Angell* (1892) 157 Mass 294, 32 NE 164; *Hamer v Sidway* (1891) 124 NY 538, 27 NE 256; *Ricketts v Scothorn* (1898) 57 Neb 51, 77 NW 365.

71   On privity of endeavour, see *Norwich City Council v Harvey and Others* [1989] 1 WLR 828; see further the reasoning in *London Drugs Ltd v Kuehne and Nagel International Ltd* (1992) 3 SCR 299; 97 DLR 261. The theory of network contracts and their avoidance of the privity rule is spelled out in John Adams and Roger Brownsword, 'Privity and the Concept of a Network Contract' (1990) 10 *Legal Studies* 12; John Adams and Roger Brownsword, 'Privity of Contract – That Pestilential Nuisance' (1993) 56 *Modern Law Review* 722.

consideration. In a spirit of broadly paternalistic control the courts have recognised consideration in the form of a promise made by an ex-spouse to 'conduct herself with sobriety, and in a respectable, orderly, and virtuous manner'.[72] A later English decision found consideration where the mother of an illegitimate child had promised to keep the child 'well looked after and happy'.[73] In a further case the Court of Appeal found consideration where a wife who had deserted her husband had promised to 'lead a chaste life' and maintain herself.[74]

Whatever the justificatory language used to legitimate decisions which protect women or wives, the gender content of such considerations is not altogether surprising. That such decisions and more profoundly the history of the gender of contracts should constantly be a fissure within the commercial realm of contracts is less well-recognised. It is, as one judge recently observed, altogether more 'radical' a thing when such subjective, emotive or simply different criteria emerge in the public domain of commerce.[75] In *Williams v Roffey* a subcontractor who had encountered financial difficulties during performance of the contract had agreed, for an additional sum, to do what he was already obliged to do under the original contract. In giving judgment in relation to such an agreement, based as it was upon a promise to perform an existing duty and nothing more, Glidewell LJ in the Court of Appeal took the view that, '[i]n the late 20th century I do not believe that the rigid approach to the concept of consideration ... is either necessary or desirable'.[76] Adopting the 'modern' and labile approach to consideration, one judge was happy to find consideration even though 'one party did not suffer a detriment'.[77] The leading judgment specified a rather inelegant criterion, namely that provided the promisor 'obtains in practice a benefit, or obviates a disbenefit'[78] then there is in theory no reason why this should not be deemed consideration. The justification for such a decision does not, however, lie in the theory of consideration nor in the technical details of the variation agreement. As all the judges recognised, the decision was based on pragmatic or practical concerns. What weighed with the court was the pre-existing relationship between the parties and the fairness or good faith of the variation. All of the judges were particularly swayed by the evidence of the plaintiff's surveyor, Mr Cottrell, who had testified that the original contract price agreed between the defendant and the plaintiff was less than he himself regarded as a reasonable price, and that, 'there was a desire on Mr Cottrell's part to retain the services of the plaintiff so

---

72   *Dunton v Dunton* (1892) 18 VLR 114.

73   *Ward v Byham* [1956] 2 All ER 318.

74   *Williams v Williams* [1957] 1 WLR 148.

75   *Anangel Atlas Compania Naviera SA v Ishikawajima Harima Heavy Industries Co Ltd (No 2)* [1990] 2 Lloyd's Rep 526.

76   *Williams v Roffey Bros and Nicholls (Contractors) Ltd* [1990] 1 All ER 512 at 522.

77   *Ibid* at 527 (*per* Purchas LJ).

78   *Ibid* at 522 (*per* Glidewell LJ).

that work could be completed without the need to employ another subcontractor'.[79] Similarly Glidewell LJ was minded to comment with approval on Mr Cottrell's view that, 'a main contractor who agrees too low a price with a subcontractor is acting contrary to his own interests. He will never get the job done without paying more money ...'.[80] All the judges thus concurred that the main contractor gained a benefit from the new contract even though such benefits were clearly already owing to them under the original contract.

The pragmatic approach adopted in *Williams v Roffey* was developed by reasoning which moved directly from cases concerning domestic promises to the negotiated variation of a building contract. The court moved from contact to contract, from proximity to that which occurs 'where businessmen are negotiating at arm's length'.[81] The significance of the decision, in short, lies in the willingness of the court to bend the rules by virtue of attending to the pre-existing and continuing relation between the parties. What the court in effect decided was that the variation of contract was in the circumstances, and in light of disparities of power or inequalities between the parties at the time of the original agreement, fair. The unitary concept of contract doctrine and the habits of reasoning of the English judiciary may have made the expression of such a decision somewhat less than direct but the willingness of the court to attend to the specific differences of different situations, to listen to the parties and to recognise the complexities, the intensity and most particularly the duration of their relationship, was in many senses commendable.

Emotional duress

My final example can be relatively brief as it draws together many of the themes already elaborated. It is evident from the reasoning of *Williams v Roffey* and explicitly stated in *R v R* that the private sphere can no longer sensibly be regarded as in any way external to law. I have argued further that the norms developed in relation to spousals and marriage contracts have had a considerable influence upon the common law's ability to reinterpret formal categories or invent new forms for policing bargains or intervening in contractual relations where justice, conscience, fairness, common sense or practical reality so dictate. Such interventions or reinterpretations and inventions do not come explicitly dressed in the language of spousals nor do they directly address questions of gender but such are nevertheless both historically and linguistically implicit in the desire of equity to strike down unfair bargains. The relevance of such a history is all the more immediate by virtue of its largely unconscious role within the common lawyer's discussions of fairness. In the words of one judge: 'English law has characteristically, committed itself to no ... overriding principle [of

---

79 *Ibid* at 524 (*per* Russell LJ).
80 *Ibid* at 518 (*per* Glidewell LJ).
81 *Pao On v Lau Yiu* [1980] AC 614 at 643 (*per* Lord Scarman).

fairness], but has developed piecemeal solutions in response to demonstrated problems of unfairness ... equity has intervened to strike down unconscionable bargains. Parliament has stepped in to regulate the imposition of exemption clauses ... The common law has also made its contribution, by holding that certain classes of contract require utmost good faith ...'[82] I will look at only one dimension of that piecemeal or hotchpotch approach, namely the use of the concept of undue influence and, tentatively, emotional duress.

Glanvill and Bracton as well as the early modern treatise writers all commented upon the danger of duress in relation to any agreement, gift or conveyance, between husband and wife. They recognised that inequalities of power, the threat of violence by husbands and of sexual bargains or the consideration of lust (*propter libidinem*) manipulated by wives meant that such agreements were presumed at law involuntary. Bracton, to take the earliest example, comments that 'if gifts could be made because of love (*ob amorem*) between husband and wife, one of them might be destroyed by want and poverty, which cannot be tolerated'.[83] A somewhat later discussion of the same problem in relation to agreements made between husband and wife with regard to property which belonged to the wife prior to marriage recognises that the husband is likely to coerce the wife: 'What cannot men get wives to do if they list, she shall be barred and forever excluded of a great many acres of ground, for a few kisses and a gay gowne ... for till it be done and dispatch, the poore woman can have no quiet, her husband keeps such a jawling.'[84] Later case law borrowed directly from such a concept of inequality of power and recognised frequently that, 'no one can say what may be the extent of the influence of a man over a woman, whose consent to marriage he has obtained'.[85] Attempts to develop a general principle of contractual fairness or of inequality of bargaining power have been precluded, however, by the insistence of the courts that whatever developments occur should remain within the existing and specific categories of undue influence and duress.[86]

Recent developments have been marginally influenced by European law and by the possibility of reinterpreting the existing equitable category of undue influence into something approaching the concepts of fairness and good faith specifically required by current directives.[87] The principle of undue influence, as developed in modern law, is an equitable jurisdiction whereby courts have protected weaker parties from abuse: 'The equitable doctrine of undue influence has grown out of and been developed by the necessity of grappling with

---

82 *Interfoto Picture Library Ltd v Stiletto Visual Programmes Ltd* [1988] 1 All ER 348 (*per* Bingham LJ).

83 Bracton *supra* n 5 at p 99.

84 Anon *supra* n 21 at pp 179–180.

85 *Page v Horne* (1848) 11 Beav 227 at p 235.

86 See *National Westminster Bank plc v Morgan* [1985] AC 686.

87 Particularly 1993 Directive on Unfair Terms in Consumer Contracts, 93/13/EEC, 5 April 1993, OJ L 95/29, 21/4/93, Article 3(1). For comment, see Hugh Collins, 'Good Faith in European Contract Law' (1994) 14 *Oxford Journal of Legal Studies* 229.

insidious forms of spiritual tyranny and with the infinite varieties of fraud.' To this it is added that, 'no court has ever attempted to define undue influence ... [because] the influence of one mind over another is very subtle ... dangerous and powerful'.[88] The example I will use is again one which crosses the boundaries of public and private. It involves undue influence exercised by a husband over a wife so as to secure her signature on a charge over the matrimonial home. The relevant facts were simply that the husband misrepresented the nature of the charge over the matrimonial home while the Bank which benefited from the charge failed to provide independent advice for the wife and so were held to have had constructive notice of the misrepresentation.[89]

It was held by the House of Lords as settled law that the relationship of husband and wife no longer automatically gives rise to a presumption of undue influence. Equity, however, 'will have more jealousy' over dispositions by a wife to a husband and will offer a 'special tenderness of treatment ... to wives'. The source of this tender treatment or jealous protection has two causes. The first is stated as being the frequency with which wives are able to prove that they placed trust and confidence in their husband in relation to financial affairs and so raise a presumption of undue influence. The second is that, 'sexual and emotional ties between the parties provide a ready weapon for undue influence: a wife's true wishes can easily be overborne because of her fear of destroying or damaging the wider relationship'.[90] The protection of the wife was based on a broader principle than simple marriage. The court held that the same principles were applicable to any situation in which there was an emotional relationship between cohabitees. 'The tenderness shown by the law to married women is not based on the marriage ceremony but reflects the underlying risk of one cohabitee exploiting the emotional involvement and trust of the other. Now that unmarried cohabitation, whether heterosexual or homosexual, is widespread in our society, the law should recognise this'.[91]

The recognition of abuse of affections or emotional duress as effective defences is significant primarily for its willingness to acknowledge the affectivity of relationships as a proper object of legal attention within the law of contracts.[92] More than that, the decision is remarkable for recognising, if only most fleetingly, that the questions raised by affection and relationship are also questions of gender and not only of a heterosexually designated femininity. It is unlikely that the decision in *Barclays Bank v O'Brien* will be interpreted by the courts as directly relevant to questions of fairness outside of the category of undue influence but in its small way the decision does exemplify a flexibility and

---

88   *Allcard v Skinner* (1887) 36 Ch D 145 (*per* Lindley LJ).

89   *Barclays Bank plc v O'Brien and Another* [1993] 4 All ER 417.

90   *Ibid* at p 424 (*per* Lord Browne-Wilkinson).

91   *Ibid* at p 431.

92   It should be noted that subsequent litigation has only succeeded once to date, see *TSB Bank v Camfield* [1995] 1 All ER 951.

fluidity that can take account of the affective reality of relationships unimpeded by any artificial separation or isolation of the private sphere. The decision in a sense is even more radical than that. It reinvokes a history of marriage and contract so as to imply that questions of fairness, of strength and weakness, balances of power or imbalances of obligations, questions of equality and inequality, domination and influence are questions of gender and even more specifically of the relationships both within and between genders.

Ironically, the recognition of emotional abuse or of constructive notice of undue influence is an indirect form of acknowledging the capacity of a woman and specifically of a wife or cohabitee to form a contractual intention in domestic settings. The traditional rule that the wife had no independent will and hence no capacity to enter a contract or indeed any other legal relation without the consent of her husband or baron was reformulated in the early 20th century in the form of the presumption that there was no 'intention to create legal relations'. The effect of this presumption was that of assuming that in domestic contexts the wife's domestic labour or indeed help with business ventures was in principle donated out of affection and for free. In the spiritual terms from which, I have argued, the model of contract developed, one could regard domestic labour as the woman's vocation or calling and submission as her fate. Recognition of emotional duress allows the courts an indirect way of rewriting that presumption and recent case law suggests that such a reformulation is beginning to occur. In *Midland Bank plc v Cooke*[93] the line of equitable authorities that runs from *Tanner v Tanner*[94] and allowed the courts to offer partial and temporary relief outside of contract was used to imply a contract in circumstances where husband and wife had explicitly stated that they reached no agreement. Adopting the view that, '[e]quity has traditionally been a system which matches established principle to the demands of social change', the Court of Appeal came to the radically constructivist conclusion that, 'positive evidence that the parties neither discussed nor intended any agreement ... does not preclude the court, on general equitable principles, from inferring one'.[95] Using the evidence of undue influence or what I have termed emotional duress as a positive indication of intention to create legal relations, the court was happy to find a legally enforceable agreement. The gendered character of the relation between the parties, the specific character or qualities of inequality that it implied, were used by the court to find – to construct – an intimate contract.

The significance of the category of emotional duress, of the possibility of feminine intention or *anima contrahendi*, can be interpreted finally from the perspective of gender itself. If gender is a performance – 'an identity tenuously

---

93   *Midland Bank plc v Cooke and Another* [1995] 3 All ER 562.

94   *Tanner v Tanner* [1975] 3 All ER 776.

95   *Midland Bank v Cooke* at 575 (Waite LJ).

constituted in time, instituted in an exterior space through a stylised repetition of acts ...'.[96] Then the repetitive life of the law of contracts might be said to perform a series of gender identities. Such performances or precedents constitute what Judith Butler terms 'the social temporality' of gender identities.[97] It has been my contention that the dominant doctrinal model of contracts within modernity has been narrowly obsessed with commodity markets and fantasies of legal certainty engendering commercial security. The gender characteristics of such a market are aligned to representations of an acquisitive and antagonistic individuality and corresponding legal personality. Typifications of the contracting subject have in general been variously officious and calculating, rationalistic and aloof, competitive, cold and disjunctive.

Where contemporary law has endeavoured to subvert or redefine the purposes and social meanings of contracts, it has of necessity had either to subvert the precedent forms of gender identities or to invent different representations of contracting subjects. Contemporary recognition of the relational nature of contracts and specifically, in the examples analysed, of the affectivity of exchange and the possibility of the abuse of such affectivity opens up a further dimension to the relationships engaged in contracts. More than that it relates the volitional dimension of contract to the terrain of desire, and to its use and abuse. The dark figures of that desire and of its exclusion from the proper domain of the law of contract have been those of woman and of femininity. They have existed on the boundaries of law, and like desire itself they have formed the limit of legal reason and the mirror image of its truth. One might say that whereas historically the courts have recognised affectivity only as an excluding characteristic of the private sphere and of the feminine, recent case law can be creatively interpreted as taking some tentative steps towards recognising the gender of contracts in the public sphere. Law, in this sense, to adapt a phrase of Aristotle's, has become a wisdom not without desire. To analyse the gender of contracts is thus to cross the boundary that historically both marks and separates femininity from contract and desire from law.

AFTERWORD

I have suffered throughout this essay under the constraint of the history and metaphor of the marriage contract. Its history is significant not least because the law of such contracts crossed the boundaries of both spiritual and secular, interior and exterior law. It is thus amongst other things a mechanism for focusing upon the plurality of jurisdictions and of procedures and rules of law. To take the plurality of laws seriously,[98] however, involves tracing the much

---

96   Judith Butler, 'Gender Trouble, Feminist Theory and Psychoanalytic Discourse' in I Nicholson (ed), *Feminism/Post-Modernism* (1990) Routledge at p 140.

97   *Ibid* at p 141.

98   Nikolas Rose, 'Beyond the Public/Private Division: Law, Power and the Family' (1987) 14 *Journal of Law and Society* 61 at p 68.

more numerous sites and agencies of contract and of gender both within the contemporary state and across the social temporality of law. The marriage contract is a mechanism for thinking through both the plurality of laws and the contingency of identities. It is hard, however, not to be struck by how little the legal conceptions of gender identity in contracts have changed. It is hard not to feel that men make bad lawyers and poor judges because the gender identity and professional persona necessary for such homosocial callings is both experientially restricted and emotionally shallow. To focus upon that professional persona and upon the masculine gender identities of law's procedures and reasons is bound to be a somewhat melancholic undertaking. To understand the construction of identity, however, is the initial step toward the possibility of changing it. In that sense it would be unfortunate to end on a negative or antagonistic note. The invocation of other identities, and alternative jurisdictions or procedures and rules of law, allows for a different and fonder conclusion.

In his reports of cases of love heard before the High Court of Love in Paris, in the mid 15th century, Martial d'Auvergne notes several disputes relating to amorous contracts, alliances or unions of love. One such case concerned an action for rescission of a usurious amorous contract.[99] The petitioner was a man who had fallen in love with a woman. He had promised her his undying love and desperate to please her took it upon himself to offer her goods and gifts of all kinds. In the heat of such passion he 'promised and obligated' himself to come with musicians and instruments and play outside her house from midnight to dawn on every public holiday of the year. He further promised to love her and to bring her each month a dress of her choosing and a hat and a dress each first of May. He fulfilled his promises for a very long time and now complained that he had grown tired of his obligations. The burden of the contract was, he argued, too great and could not be maintained. His specific complaint was that for all that he had done to improve the life of the defendant, for all the goods and pleasures he had given her, he had in return received but one single kiss 'and this on the cheek and not even on the mouth'.[100] This he argued was such insufficient recompense for his amorous labours as to be usurious and he therefore pleaded that the contract be rescinded and annulled, and further demanded costs.

The woman defendant responded with the argument that she had gained little from the lover and that he had pursued her for his own pleasure rather than hers. She had not initiated the agreement but had eventually consented to the ardour and pleading of the complainant. It was he who had wanted the contract and she had no doubt that it was of great value to him and it was for this reason that he had pursued it so insistently in the first place. She received his gifts so as to give him pleasure and she wore his dresses and hats so as to honour his desire and to show her love. She argued finally that 'all the money in the world, all the

---

99 Martial d'Auvergne *supra* n 1.

100 *Ibid* at p 43.

dresses and gifts could not compare to half a kiss; and half a kiss, given with good heart was worth far more than he had given',[101] for within the code of love a kiss was a singular and spiritual thing and could not be either bought or sold. The court found for the defendant woman in all respects and awarded her both judgment and costs.

The plaintiff's attempt to reduce love to property, or to quantify the economy of desire and the forms of amorous exchange received an appropriately swift dismissal from the High Court of love. The decision attended, I would like to suggest, to the different character of amorous contracts and provided a judgment which was sensitive not simply to the meanness (the inappropriateness) of the plaintiff's arguments but also recognised the spiritual force and the virtue of desire. The jurisdiction of love was predicated upon an intrinsically poetic concern to give juristic definition and effective protection to the phantasmatic character and imaginary boundaries of gender identities and their interaction. Just as amorous liaisons, marriages and other forms of sexual exchange have been conceived historically as agreements or species of contract, so the law of contract could greatly benefit from recognising the varying intensities of emotion and of desire that motivate and accompany contractual exchange. Here is not the place to embark upon an analysis of the jurisdiction of love; it is enough to observe that the courts of love provide one further way of thinking through the power and the potential of gender as it emerges as an issue in the courts of law.

---

101 *Ibid* at p 44.

CHAPTER THREE

TORT LAW AND THE FEMINIST CRITIQUE OF REASON

JOANNE CONAGHAN

INTRODUCTION

In recent years, feminist legal theory has sought to address the law of tort and the values and assumptions which shape and inform it. This engagement has taken a number of different forms. One approach has been to focus on the formal exposition of tort law as a set of legal rules which embody and protect individual rights. Feminist (and critical legal) scholars have argued that such traditional presentations are misleading in presenting as coherent a body of knowledge which is better characterised as conflicting (or, at the very least, confused), and loaded, in the sense of privileging (often covertly) principles and values, such as individual responsibility or freedom of contract, over other desirable goals such as the promotion of social responsibility[1] or the empowerment of vulnerable groups.[2]

In addition, feminist writers have argued that the way in which tort cases (and legal disputes in general) are resolved reflects a mode of analysis which is distinctly 'male'. Thus, the tendency of judges to abstract a dispute from its particular context, to reformulate it in terms of a conflict of rights and seek a universal guiding principle by which the conflict can be resolved, is said to contrast with more 'feminine' approaches to dispute resolution which emphasise the relevance of context and the importance of preserving and developing particular relationships. In short, while tort law, as traditionally presented, presupposes the essential separateness of individuals from each other, feminist perspectives recognise, from the very outset, our necessary interconnectedness.[3]

---

1   J Conaghan and W Mansell, *The Wrongs of Tort* (1993) Pluto.

2   L Bender, 'Changing the Values in Tort Law' (1990) 25 *Tulsa LJ* 759, hereinafter cited as Bender, 'Values'; 'Feminist (Re)Torts: Thoughts on the Liability Crisis, Mass Torts, Power and Responsibilities' (1990) *Duke LJ* 848, hereinafter cited as Bender, '(Re)Torts'.

3   The characterisation of legal modes of analysis as predominantly 'male' derives particularly from the controversial work of Carol Gilligan, *In a Different Voice: Psychological Theory and Women's Development* (1982) Harvard University Press. Her work has focused significant feminist attention on gendered aspects of legal method, analysis and education and has resulted (*inter alia*) in efforts to identify and articulate distinctively female styles of analysis, decision-making and judgment. The literature is extensive but see, in particular, M J Frug, 'Re-Reading Contracts: A Feminist Analysis of a Contracts Casebook' (1985) 34 *American University L R* 1065; K C Worden, 'Overshooting the Target: A Feminist Deconstruction of Legal Education' (1985) 34 *American University LR* 1141; C Menkel-Meadow, 'Portia in a Different Voice: Speculation on a Woman's Lawyering Process' (1985) 1 *Berkeley Women's LJ* 38; also the following collections/symposiums: 'Women in Legal Education – Pedagogy, Law, Theory and Practice' in (1988) 38 *Journal of Legal Education* nos 1 & 2; 'Women in Legal Education' 77 *Iowa LR* (1991) pp 1-179; 'Legal Education, Feminist Values and Gender Bias' (1993) 45 *Stanford LR* pp 1525-80.

Just as feminist scholars have questioned the form which tort law takes, so also have they closely scrutinised its content. Many of the doctrines of which tort law is comprised – the test of reasonableness which governs the standard of care,[4] the traditional distinction between acts and omissions entailing the assertion that there is 'no duty to rescue',[5] the burden of proof both on negligence and causation,[6] the assessment of damages[7] and the availability of remedies generally[8] have all been the subject of critical feminist appraisal. Moreover, the deployment of the concept of 'gendered harm' has also proved fruitful in revealing the interest bias which traditional tort law reflects.[9] Thus, it has been asserted that tort law, while quick to defend and protect interests traditionally valued by men (such as a good reputation), is slow to respond to the concerns which typically involve women, for example, freedom from sexual harassment[10] or sexual abuse.[11] By emphasising the way in which tort law recognises and remedies some harms while at the same time overlooking or marginalising others, feminist theory challenges traditional assumptions about what constitutes 'harm' in tort and, at the same time, highlights its gendered content.

The overall thrust of the feminist critique of tort law is concerned with the justice of the system. Put bluntly, feminists challenge the assumption that tort law is fair. The allocation of rights and responsibilities may reflect, for the most part, a 'common sense' view of how people should behave towards one another and the degree of responsibility they should have for their acts, but that common sense reflects male rather than female perceptions about the scope and nature of human relationships. If women were to set about articulating principles to

---

4   L Bender, 'A Lawyer's Primer on Feminist Theory and Tort' (1988) 38 *J Legal Education* 3; L Finley, 'A Break in the Silence: Including Women's Issues in a Torts Course' (1989) 1 *Yale J Law and Feminism* 41; R Martyn, 'A Feminist View of the Reasonable Man: An Alternative Approach to Liability in Negligence for Personal Injury' (1994) 25 *Anglo-American LR* 334.

5   Bender *supra* n 4 at pp 33-36; L McClain, 'Atomistic Man Revisited: Liberalism, Connection and Feminist Jurisprudence' (1992) 65 *Southern California LR* 1171; R Lee, 'A Look at God, Feminism and Tort Law' (1992) 75 *Marquand LR* 369.

6   Bender *supra* n 2.

7   Finley, *supra* n 4; R Graycar, 'Women's Work: Who Cares?' (1992) 14 *Sydney LR* 86; 'Love's Labour's Cost: The High Court Decision in *Van Gervan v Fenton*' (1993) 1 *Torts LJ*.

8   Bender *supra* n 2.

9   The concept of 'gendered harm' builds on the perception that men and women are likely to suffer or experience injury in different ways: R West, 'The Difference in Women's Hedonic lives: A Phenomenological Critique of Feminist Legal Theory' in M Fineman and N Thomsaden, *At the Boundaries of Law: Feminism and Legal Theory* (1991) Routledge 115; R Graycar and J Morgan, *The Hidden Gender of Law* (1989) Federation Press. So, for example, women are more likely to be raped, or sexually harassed than men. Likewise, some suffering is exclusive to women, for example the pain of childbirth. The concept derives from the notion of 'social injury', that is the idea that the distribution of injury and suffering is shaped by social as well as individual factors: A Howe 'The Problem of Privatised Injuries: Feminist Strategies in Litigation' in Fineman and Thomsaden *supra* at p 148.

10   J Conaghan, 'Gendered Harms and the Law of Tort' (1996) 16 *Oxford J Legal Studies* (forthcoming).

11   J McConnell, 'Incest as Conundrum: Judicial Discourse on Private Wrong and Public Harm' (1992) 1 *Texas J Women and Law* 143.

inform and govern human behaviour, then, feminists claim, the system emerging would probably look very different: it would be based on a set of ethical principles placing greater emphasis on our dependence on, and involvement with, others rather than giving prominence to our separate and individual status.[12] Moreover, it would address those harms which pervade the biographies of women rather than ignore or diminish them.

Such a critique of tort law is also significant in focusing attention on aspects of tort doctrine with which we feel morally uncomfortable: Why is there no duty to rescue a child drowning in two feet of water when it is freely acknowledged that such a failure to act fully offends the bounds of human decency?[13] Why should we accept that it is 'reasonable' to let an accident happen when it is more expensive to avoid it when such a calculated approach to human suffering so affronts us? Why should people who act irresponsibly and without regard to others so often be able to pay their way out of a situation which in no real sense recompenses the victim for the loss she has sustained?[14] And, finally, why is the pervasive harm of sexual harassment not formally recognised by tort law? Surely, if this was a problem commonly suffered by men there would be a host of legal remedies to accommodate it?[15]

In challenging the common sense perceptions which pervade and at the same time disturb us, feminism can be very liberating. However, as a mode of analysis, feminism is not without its problems. One particular problem lies in the consequences which flow from a (not exclusively) feminist distrust of traditional philosophical claims to 'rationality' and/or 'objectivity'.[16] This is well-illustrated in the context of tort law. What feminist legal scholars have purported to do here is to question the alleged objectivity of tort standards by revealing their

---

12   Debate as to the existence and content of a distinctly feminine/feminist ethics forms a current preoccupation of feminist philosophical discourse. See, in particular, Gilligan *supra* n 3; N Noddings, *Caring: A Feminist Approach to Ethics and Moral Education* (1984) University of California Press; J Grimshaw, *Feminist Philosophers: Women's Perspectives on Philosophical Traditions* (1986) Harvester Wheatsheaf; S Ruddick, *Maternal Thinking* (1989) The Women's Press.

13   Bender *supra* n 4 at pp 33–36; Lee, McClain *supra* n 5.

14   Bender *supra* n 2.

15   Conaghan *supra* n 10.

16   The feminist critique of reason/objectivity can be located within a larger post-modern attack on Enlightenment thinking and in particular on the concept of universal reason (for a useful introduction to the issues, see A Thomson, 'Critical Legal Education in Britain' (1987) 14 *J Law and Society* 183 at pp 189–191). In a feminist context, universal reason has been identified as 'male' reason (G Lloyd, *The Man of Reason: 'Male' and 'Female' in Western Philosophy* (1984) University of Minnesota Press) and this in turn has resulted in close scrutiny and frequent rejection by (many) feminists of the idea of pure objective knowledge, for example L Stanley and S Wise, *Breaking Out: Feminist Consciousness and Feminist Research* (1983) Routledge; C MacKinnon, *Feminism Unmodified* (1986) Harvard University Press; and see generally, S Hekman, *Gender and Knowledge: Elements of a Post-Modern Feminism* (1990) Polity Press at pp 30–47. It has also generated attempts to articulate a 'feminist knowledge' in an effort to subvert the dominance of masculine epistemology: S Gunew, *Feminist Knowledge: Critiques and Construct* (1990) Routledge. However, the feminist critique of reason is the subject of acute controversy even within feminist circles: see L Anthony and C Witt, *Essays on Reason and Objectivity* (1994) Westview Press and Martha Nussbaum's review in 'Feminists and Philosophy' (20 October 1994) *New York Review of Books* 59.

partial and gendered content. The justice of the tort system, as expressed most typically by the 'reasonable man' standard, is, it is contended, 'male' justice and has no higher claim to universality or truth. Moreover the application of such a skewed and partial standard, *inter alia*, to women results in injustice because women are measured according to a standard which was devised without them in mind.[17] One solution is to articulate a concept of justice which does take account of women's perceptions and experiences. But the question then raised becomes: is a feminist conception of justice in tort law any more just given that it too may reflect a partial and gendered viewpoint? Indeed it is a viewpoint which can be just as oppressive and exclusionary as traditional male standards in that, while purporting to represent the experiences of 'women' as a group, it, more often than not, expresses the values and outlooks of some women, typically middle-class, white, educated, able-bodied women. Applied to working-class, non-white or disabled women, the articulation of a feminist conception of justice in tort law may work the same kind of injustice as feminists attribute to allegedly male standards.

Thus, while the question of what standards to adopt can no longer be resolved by appeals to higher, abstract, universal principles (because none, it is alleged, exist), nor can it easily accommodate the post-modernist insistence on a multiplicity of perspectives, none of which appears to have any greater or less weight than any other. How can law devise just standards to govern human behaviour in the absence of a concept of justice which is good for all? Indeed even the project of feminism becomes suspect, based as it is on the assumption that women as a group possess a commonality of interests. After all, if the differences between women are greater than their convergences, feminism may cease to have any meaningful content.[18]

Can these dilemmas be resolved? The object of this essay is to explore the issues raised in the context of a specific debate which is currently occupying feminist scholars in tort: the critique of the 'reasonable man' standard which traditionally governs the standard of care in negligence. By tracing and unpacking the progress of this debate, I hope to reveal the presence of the same

---

17 See, for example Bender *supra* n 4 at pp 20-25; Martyn *supra* n 4.

18 This concern reflects a growing preoccupation within and beyond feminist theory with the pitfalls of 'essentialism'. Thus, it has been argued that by portraying woman's oppression as a generalised and unitary experience, some feminist writers have relied on and reinforced a particular conception of the 'essential woman', thereby denying the diversity of experiences which characterise women's lives: E Spelman, *The Inessential Woman: Problems of Exclusion in Feminist Thought* (1988) Beacon Press. This critique is most effectively expressed in the context of the experiences of women of colour: bell hooks, *Ain't I a Woman? Black Women and Feminism* (1981) South End Press; A Harris, 'Race and Essentialism in Feminist Legal Theory' (1989) 42 *Stanford LR* 588. But it has left feminism with a genuine crisis of identity in the wake of the apparent collapse of the category 'woman': J Butler, 'Gender Trouble, Feminist Theory and Psychoanalytical Discourse' in L Nicholson (ed), *Feminism/Post-Modernism* (1990) Routledge; J Kristeva, 'Woman Can Never be Defined' in E Marks and I de Courtrivon (eds), *New French Feminisms* (1984) Schocken. Post-modernist feminists are now faced with the challenge of giving feminism a meaning and purpose which does not rely on notions of essentialism; see, for example E Jackson, 'Contradictions and Coherence in Feminist Responses to Law' (1993) 20 *J Law and Society* 398.

tensions which inform and shape the discussion of broader philosophical issues in feminist theory such as the feminist critique of reason and objectivity and the pursuit of an alternative feminist ethics. In this way I hope to shed some useful light on both the feminist critique of tort law and the broader issues concerning feminist theory in general.

THE FEMINIST CRITIQUE OF THE REASONABLE MAN

It is commonly asserted that the standard of care in negligence is determined by recourse to the ubiquitous 'reasonable man'. He is said to originate in the early 19th century decision of *Vaughan v Menlove*[19] which established that for purposes of determining negligence, the question was not whether or not a defendant had acted '*bona fide* and honestly to the best of his own judgment' but rather whether or not his conduct was that of 'a man of ordinary prudence'.[20] Thus the emphasis of the court was on an objective standard to which all must conform rather than a subjective one which took account of individual human frailty.

Such a view has been confirmed by subsequent cases which have emphasised the abstract and 'impersonal'[21] nature of the standard being applied although it is also true that the reasonable man is not devoid of all characteristics which make him human: age,[22] special skills[23] and, in some instances, disability[24] may all find their way into the fiction which the courts invoke. However, by and large, neither the personal characteristics nor the particular weaknesses of the defendant are considered when evaluating his behaviour and he may be liable even in circumstances where, in no moral sense, can he be said to be at fault.[25]

However, despite his prestigious pedigree and briskly confident persona, the reasonable man is not without his critics. Even at his birth there was considerable disagreement as to his merits: defence counsel in *Vaughan* contended he established a standard 'too uncertain to act upon'.[26] Moreover, in subsequent years judges and commentators have continued to acknowledge the uncertainty entailed in articulating a standard which, while purporting to be universal, nevertheless may produce considerable variety. As L MacMillan has forthrightly observed:

---

19 (1837) 3 Bing NC 468, reproduced in W Prosser, J Wade and V Schwarz, *Torts: Cases and Materials* (1988, 8th edn) Foundation Press at p 149.

20 *Per* Tindal CJ, *supra* n 19 at 150.

21 *Glasgow Corpn v Muir* [1943] 2 All ER 44 *per* L MacMillan at 48.

22 *McHale v Watson* [1966] 115 CLR 199.

23 *Philips v William Whitely Ltd* [1938] 1 All ER 566.

24 *Roberts v Ramsbottom* [1980] 1 All ER 7.

25 *Nettleship v Weston* [1971] 3 All ER 581.

26 *Supra* n 20.

> It is still left to the judge to decide what in the circumstances of the particular case the reasonable man would have had in contemplation ... Here there is room for a diversity of view.[27]

This has led some judges and commentators to conclude that the reasonable man is no more than a convenient legal fiction disguising the application of subjective judicial preferences and value judgments.[28] He is merely one of a range of legal devices which operate to 'obscure the policy content of judicial decision-making'.[29]

Thus, the reasonable man's claims to universality have long been questioned and recent feminist scrutiny has further compromised his reputation for impartiality. In particular, it is frequently asserted that his gender-specificity is not just a linguistic convention, whereby both sexes are denoted by reference to the masculine: the reasonable man is, in fact, male. It follows that the standard he expresses has a significant gender content.[30]

Such a claim can be evidenced in a variety of ways. That judges and textbook writers invariably have a man, rather than a woman, in mind when they apply the test of reasonableness is well illustrated by the images they invoke. Tort law is populated with references to 'the man on the Clapham omnibus' (or, in Australia, the 'Bondi tram'), 'the man who takes the magazine at home and in the evening pushes the lawn mower in his shirt sleeves'.[31] The image of a man occupying the busy public realm by day and the leisure of domestic life in the evening may reflect the aspirations of the suburban middle-class male but it certainly does not capture the experience of women juggling duties between home and work.

The maleness of the reasonable man standard is further suggested by the absence of women, by and large, from his birth and subsequent upbringing. The reasonable man possesses an exclusively male parentage and even today, some 150 years after his birth, his continued sustenance remains in the hands of a predominantly male judiciary.[32] In so far as the application of the reasonableness standard expresses, at least in part, the subjective preferences of particular judges, those preferences will inevitably be coloured by perceptions which derive from their sex (as well as class, race and other social characteristics) resulting (at least in some cases) in the application of an identifiably male standard to a female

---

27 *Glasgow Corpn v Muir* (1943), *supra* n 21 at 457.

28 See, for example, C K Allen, *Legal Duties and Other Essays in Jurisprudence* (1931) Clarendon Press at p 72; B Hepple and M Matthews, *Tort: Cases and Materials* (1991, 4th edn) Butterworths at p 247.

29 P S Atiyah, *Accidents, Compensation and the Law* (1980, 3rd edn) Weidenfeld and Nicolson at p 42.

30 *Supra* n 17; see also C Forell, 'Reasonable Woman Standard of Care' (1992) 11 *University of Tasmania LR* 1.

31 *Hall v Brookland Auto Racing Club* [1933] 1 KB 205 *per* Greer LJ at 224.

32 Martyn *supra* n 4 at pp 347–48.

defendant. Lucinda Finley[33] highlights the decision in *Tucker v Henniker*,[34] where an appellate court expressly addressed the question of whether a teenage girl involved in an accident while driving her father's carriage should be held to the standard of reasonableness of 'ordinary persons like herself' or whether she should be bound by the standard of 'mankind' in general, that is the standard of competent and experienced carriage drivers, most of whom were male. The appellate court, not surprisingly, opted for the latter (anticipating the modern decision of *Nettleship v Weston*[35] which coincidentally also involved a woman defendant) but, as Finley observes, the result of the decision in *Tucker* was to hold women to a standard which they were less likely to acquire by virtue of the social consequences which flowed from their sex, from which Finley concludes: 'If women are unaccustomed to doing an activity, it would appear inherently unreasonable for them to attempt it.'[36]

Similarly, Robyn Martyn[37] points to the absurdity of a male judiciary assessing the reasonableness of Mrs Sayers' attempt to escape from a public toilet in *Sayers v Harlow UDC*:[38]

> Three elderly judges were called upon to put themselves in the position of a woman, dressed in a tight skirt and high-heeled shoes, locked in a lavatory while her impatient husband waited for her at the bus stop.[39]

The court's conclusion that Mrs Sayers was contributorily negligent in attempting to climb out of the lavatory cubicle is, Martyn argues, a prime example of the application of a male standard in circumstances where a reasonable woman might well have evaluated Mrs Sayers' conduct rather differently.

However, feminist scholars go further than simply highlighting the gender composition of the judiciary and its likely impact on the decision-making process. Feminists further assert that the legal attributes of the reasonable man – particularly his ability to detach himself from the specific circumstances of a situation and weigh up the costs and benefits of action without recourse to 'emotional' or 'sentimental' considerations – are male, in the sense that they rely upon characteristics conventionally attributed to, and applauded in, men and contrast with features typically associated with women, such as a lack of detachment, a passionate or emotional nature and a tendency to engage with aspects of a situation not necessarily relevant to rational calculation.

---

33 *Supra* n 4.

34 (1860) 41 NH 317.

35 *Supra* n 25.

36 Finley *supra* n 4 at p 59.

37 *Supra* n 4.

38 [1958] 1 WLR 623.

39 Martyn *supra* n 4 at p 348.

In what sense can it be said that the legal attributes of the reasonable man are male? Certainly it may be argued that such a gendered characterisation of reasonable behaviour bears some correspondence to popular perceptions of gender difference. Indeed it is a recognisable, if regrettable, feature of legal culture to associate men with certain 'natural' qualities – reason and detachment, strength and courage – and to perceive women in terms of their opposites – emotion and sentiment, delicacy and timidity.[40] This feature of legal culture is humorously captured by Sir Alan Herbert's depiction of women in his classic parody of the common law:

> There exist a class of beings illogical, impulsive, careless, irresponsible, extravagant, prejudiced and free for the most part from those worthy and repellent excellences which distinguish the Reasonable Man.[41]

Herbert's picture presents women as emotional and frivolous beings, not capable of rational consideration of the weighty matters of importance which more appropriately preoccupy men. While widely acknowledged as a caricature, it retains its humour (and therefore its power) because it continues to draw on prevailing perceptions of gender difference in respect of rationality.

Historically, such perceptions of women's 'irrationality' have been a source of their exclusion and disempowerment.[42] Yet, perhaps surprisingly, feminist engagement with the question of women's rationality has not necessarily sought to deny the existence of gender differences in this context. Rather the strategy has been to challenge conventional understandings of what is rational (and therefore what is irrational) with a view to redefining rationality to include modes of analysis, forms of argument and approaches to decision-making typically deployed by women.

Such an approach derives in particular from Carol Gilligan's articulation of 'a different voice' in the context of her empirical exploration of moral reasoning.[43] Focusing on the limits of existing psychological evaluations of moral development (particularly the work of Kohlberg),[44] Gilligan highlights and explores different approaches to the resolution of moral questions, at the same time revealing a significant gender dimension. In this respect, Gilligan points out that previous empirical work relied on observations of male rather than female children and she sets about re-examining conclusions about human development by exploring the differences between the way in which boys and girls approach and resolve moral dilemmas.[45] Her results are controversial but strongly

---

40 See in particular the classic judgment of Bradley J in *Bradwell v Illinois* (1873) 83 US (16 Wall) 130 denying women the right to practise law discussed in A Sachs and J Wilson, *Sexism and the Law: A Study of Male Beliefs and Judicial Bias* (1978) Martin Robertson at pp 97–101.

41 A P Herbert, *Uncommon Law* (1969, 8th edn) Methuen at p 6.

42 Sachs and Wilson *supra* n 40.

43 Gilligan *supra* n 3.

44 L Kohlberg, *The Philosophy of Moral Development* (1981) Harper and Row.

45 Gilligan *supra* n 3 at pp 24–63.

suggestive: they have been interpreted by many as evidence that women approach and resolve moral questions differently from men[46] and that furthermore, 'feminine' approaches to dispute resolution (Gilligan's 'different voice') have been typically, but wrongly, characterised as naive and immature.

The content of Gilligan's different voice contrasts strongly with established assumptions about human moral development. While the implications of Kohlberg's work point mainly towards a developmental progression which culminates in the articulation and application of a 'language of rights' to moral dilemmas, characterised by a tendency to invoke abstract principles or hierarchies of rights to resolve disputes, Gilligan's 'voice' eschews a rights-based approach in favour of considerations which focus on the web of relationships which surround and connect the parties involved, and on modes of communication which might be deployed to resolve the conflict with minimal damage to, or disruption of, the relationships which bind the parties together.

Gilligan's argument is that such an approach, while traditionally devalued, is equally valid and no less 'developed' than rights-based reasoning. The implications of her argument include the possibility that the bounds of reason, as traditionally conceived, have been drawn too narrowly.

Gilligan's work adds considerable weight to the feminist claim that the reasonable man is male (at least empirically). From Gilligan one can recognise that the standard implicit in the reasonable man test, with its emphasis on abstract cost benefit calculations,[47] corresponds more closely with the 'male' than the 'female' voice in her work. This has led feminist torts scholar Leslie Bender to question the reliance of tort law on 'algebraic formulations to [assess] behaviour';[48] to challenge the 'language and value system [which] privileges economics and costs' and 'dehumanizes people generally' by valuing human life in largely monetary terms[49] and, ultimately, to call for the rejection of a conception of 'justice as monetary compensation for harms (achieved through win/lose resolutions of rights conflicts)'.[50] Articulating what she claims as a feminist agenda for tort law, Bender concludes:

> We need ... to help change the dominant ideology from individualist to interconnected. We need to shift from a right-based focus to a focus on both care and rights/justice, from power-over to empowering, from the prioritising

---

46 Gilligan denies that her observations establish any necessary connection between gender and particular modes of thought but acknowledges an empirical correlation. Debate about the implications of her findings produced an immediate flurry of literature: see in particular J Auerbach, L Blum, V Smith and C Williams, 'Commentaries on Gilligan's "In a Different Voice"' (1985) *Feminist Studies* 11; L Kerber *et al* 'On "In a Different Voice": An Interdisciplinary Forum' (1986) 11 *Signs* 304.

47 Expressed most famously in the celebrated 'test' of Judge Learned Hand articulated in *US v Carroll Towing Co* 159 F 2d 169 (1947).

48 Bender *supra* n 4 at p 32.

49 Bender, 'Values', *supra* n 2 at p 767.

50 Bender, '(Re)Torts' *supra* n 2 at p 861.

of the market and money to a priority of personal relationships, health, safety, and human dignity in deciding personal injury disputes.[51]

For Bender, the identifying characteristics of the current standard of reasonableness invoked by tort law are an individualistic, rights-based focus and an emphasis on markets and money. It is a standard of efficiency, a classic expression of instrumental reason, concerned with ensuring the most efficient means to particular ends. However, the concept of instrumental rationality does not stand by itself. Inevitably it relies on certain underlying assumptions about human nature, typically expressed in terms of the physical separateness of individuals and/or the pursuit of individual self-interest.[52] These are assumptions which feminist theory has challenged primarily on the grounds that they do not correspond either materially or experientially with women's lives. Robin West, for example, has argued that 'all our modern legal theory ... is essentially and irretrievably masculine'[53] because it relies on 'the separation thesis', that is, the assumption that human beings, whatever else they may be, are physically separate from each other:

> Women are not essentially, necessarily, inevitably, invariably, always and forever separate from other human beings: women, distinctively, are quite clearly 'connected' to other human beings when pregnant ...[54]

West goes on to argue that this 'material fact'[55] about women's lives, although it may result in a diversity in subjective experience, nevertheless evidences that the 'human being' of legal and political theory is male rather than female. It follows that human nature (along with the characteristics attributed to it) is a social construct shaped and informed, *inter alia*, by gender-based assumptions. By challenging the understanding of human nature which instrumental rationality reflects and revealing its gendered content, feminist legal theory further evidences the masculinity of tort law's reasonable man.

THE MALENESS OF THE REASONABLE MAN: DIFFERENT INTERPRETATIONS

Feminist tort scholars have sought to demonstrate the claim that the reasonable man is male. However, there remains a fundamental ambiguity about the nature of this claim which continues to characterise the literature: what does it mean to assert that the reasonable man is male? It is important to distinguish the different levels at which this claim may operate. The claim may be, firstly, that the conception of reason which the reasonable man expresses is biologically male in

---

51   *Ibid* at p 907.

52   Grimshaw *supra* n 12 at pp 196–98.

53   R West, 'Jurisprudence and Gender' (1955) *University of Chicago LR* 1 at p 2.

54   *Ibid*.

55   *Supra* n 53 at p 14.

the sense that only men possess the physical or intellectual attributes necessary to comply with it. Such a claim is rarely explicitly made although it is arguably implicit in judicial pronouncements such as Bradwell[56] which rely on woman's 'nature' to deny her capacity to engage in certain activities (such as practising law).[57]

Secondly, the claim may be that the reasonable man expresses a standard which is socially male in the sense that men are more likely or more able to comply with it by virtue of their gender socialisation. Such a claim assumes that gender is a social construct and that many of the commonly perceived differences between men and women, in terms of ability or inclination, are socially rather than biologically based. This idea seems to inform much of the feminist exploration of case law, for example Finley's treatment of the *Tucker* case or Martyn's account of the decision in *Sayers*, discussed above. In both instances the writers highlight the different social roles assumed by, or allocated to, men and women and the corresponding differences in skills and/or perceptions which may result. It probably also underlies Bender's critique of the reasonable man and her rejection of the instrumental rationality which he articulates. In particular, Bender's reliance on Gilligan suggests her acceptance of the (empirical) claim that men and women tend to reason differently while at the same time she frequently appeals to perceived differences between men and women's social roles to explain and justify her rejection of the concept of legal responsibility which the reasonable man test entails:

> It is arguable that law's meaning of responsibility does not include interpersonal care-giving because that kind of work has been traditionally done by women, not by the men who created and developed tort law, nor by the men who ran the business world that created all these mass torts and personal injuries.[58]

Thus Bender, Finley and others rely on differences between men and women's experiences in their efforts to identify the maleness of the reasonable man. Implicit in their claims is the assumption that experience can be identified and demarcated in terms of gender, an assumption which is increasingly controversial.[59]

Thirdly, the claim that the reasonable man is male may be made metaphorically rather than biologically or socially. Thus, for example, popular representations of rationality as 'male' and 'irrationality' as female may invoke a cultural understanding whereby 'male' and 'female' are deployed hierarchically,

---

56 *Supra* n 40.

57 See also Susan Okin's excellent discussion of Rousseau, 'The Natural Woman and Her Role' in *Women in Western Political Thought* (1979) Princeton University Press at pp 106-139. Feminists are rightly wary of making claims which attribute perceived gender differences to biological rather than social sources. However, there remains a regrettable ambiguity in some of the literature exploring gender differences; see, for example, E Wolgast, *Equality and the Rights of Women* (1980) Cornell University Press.

58 Bender, 'Values' *supra* n 2 at p 771.

59 *Supra* n 18.

operating to include (male) or exclude (female), to approve (male) or disapprove (female), to render secure (male) or insecure (female). In this context gender functions symbolically, that is as a metaphor which carries particular meanings not necessarily biologically or socially derived.[60] Perhaps then the reasonable man is metaphorically male; that is, the attribution of maleness carries a particular cultural meaning which reinforces the legitimacy of the standard of care which he expresses and at the same time renders illegitimate alternative formulations. This is not a dimension which feminist tort scholars have sought to explore, yet it may be that the reasonable man is best understood in these terms, particularly given certain inherent weaknesses in socially-based claims. In any case it must be recognised that any evaluation of feminist responses to the perceived maleness of the reasonable man must be informed by an understanding of the basis of the perception under scrutiny. It does not appear that such an understanding is fully apparent in the literature to date. To what extent can it help to clarify the dilemma for feminists which the reasonable man creates?

THE REASONABLE MAN DISPLACED: ALTERNATIVE STRATEGIES

The reasonable person

Feminist preoccupation with the maleness of the reasonable man has inevitably cast doubts on his legitimacy even in the most traditional circles. Yet the replacement of the reasonable man with the reasonable person has been slow in coming, if the textbooks are to be taken as a measure of things. In fact, most conventional texts still refer to the standard of the reasonable man[61] although there is an increasing tendency to avoid the anthropomorphism altogether and talk instead of the 'standard of reasonable care' in negligence.[62] At one level it is difficult to see precisely what is achieved by such a change in linguistic convention particularly in the face of the feminist claim that the standard at issue is male not just in name but also in substance. It is arguable that such a change in language is dangerously misleading in attributing a false universality to what is in fact a partial and loaded standard. Hence many feminists (myself included) continue to use the language of the reasonable man in order to highlight the gendered content of the standard being applied.

---

60 For an exploration of the metaphorical deployment of gender in western political thought, see in particular Lloyd *supra* n 16. See also S Harding, *The Science Question in Feminism* (1986) Cornell University Press; L Irigaray, *Speculum of the Other Woman* (1985) Cornell University Press.

61 See, for example, W V H Rogers, *Winfield and Jolowicz on Tort* (1994, 14th edn) Sweet & Maxwell at p 125; R Heuston and R Buckley, *Salmond and Heuston on the Law of Torts* (1992, 20th edn) Sweet & Maxwell at p 226.

62 K Stanton, *The Modern Law of Tort* (1994) Sweet & Maxwell at p 61.

However, if the shift in language from reasonable man to reasonable person does not by itself ensure the gender neutrality of the standard of care, it does express the aspiration that the standard applied should be a truly universal one. Is this aspiration either attainable or desirable? Can a single universal standard governing human behaviour be devised and should feminists be a part of such a project?

The attempt to render tort law's standard of care as truly universal has inevitably focused on its underinclusiveness. The assumption is that if, for example, women's perspectives can somehow be included in a court's evaluation of reasonable behaviour, then a universal standard can emerge, rehabilitated yet relatively intact. A significant example of this strategy has been the development of the 'reasonable woman' standard in the US.[63] As a legal concept the reasonable woman has emerged, not in general competition with the reasonable man/person, but in specific instances where the wrong which is the subject of litigation has a gender dimension and perceptions of the harm done are likely to diverge along gender lines. Thus, for example, the reasonable woman has had some success in the context of sexual harassment litigation. A number of courts in recent years have applied the standard to evaluate whether or not the conduct in question is sufficiently offensive to constitute the wrong.[64] However, the standard has not met with universal acceptance even in the context of sexual harassment and some courts have rejected it in favour of the reasonable person approach.[65] In *Harris v Forklift Systems Inc*[66] the US Supreme Court declined the opportunity either to expressly endorse or repudiate the standard thus continuing to leave room for manoeuvre either way in the lower courts.

The emergence of the reasonable woman standard directly addresses the adequacy of the reasonable person test as an inclusive (and therefore universal) measure of human behaviour. Feminists have argued, both in and out of the courtroom, that as between the sexes, assessments of what is reasonable sometimes diverge (particularly where sexual behaviour is involved) and in these circumstances the application of the reasonable person standard by predominantly male judges operates exclusively by applying a male rather than a

---

63   The advent of the reasonable woman standard has spawned a voluminous literature; see, for example Finley *supra* n 4; Forell *supra* n 30; D Brennan, 'Commments: From a Woman's Point of View: The Use of the Reasonable Woman Standard in Sexual Harassment Cases' (1992) 60 *University of Cincinnati LR* 1281; N Cahn, 'The Looseness of Legal Language: The Reasonable Woman Standard in Theory and Practice' (1992) 77 *Cornell LR* 1398; T Lester, 'The Reasonable Woman Test in Sexual Harassment – Will it Really Make a Difference?' (1993) 26 *Indiana LR* 227.

64   *Ellison v Brady* (9th Circuit 1991) 924 F 2d 874; *Robinson v Jacksonville Shipyards* (1991) 760 F Supp 1486.

65   *Rabidue v Osceola Refining Co* (6th Circuit 1986) 805 F 2d 611; *Caleshu v Merrill Lynch, Pierce, Fenner and Smith* (1990) 737 F Supp 1070.

66   (1993) 114 S Ct 367.

female perspective.[67] Such a claim is well-illustrated by the contrasting opinions of the majority and minority of the court in *Rabidue v Osceola Refining Co.*[68] At issue was the question of whether or not a 'hostile' working environment which included sexually offensive posters, persistent obscene and sexually explicit language and personal sexual insults constituted sexual harassment in relation to the plaintiff.[69] In concluding that the environment was not sufficiently offensive to constitute sexual harassment, the majority relied on the expectations of the 'hypothetical reasonable individual' in the plaintiff's situation. By contrast, Keith J dissented from the majority view and criticised the court for failing 'to account for the wide divergence between most women's views of appropriate sexual conduct and those of men'.[70] Urging the adoption of a reasonable woman test in order to evaluate the nature and degree of harm, he concluded that the environment in question was sufficiently offensive to the plaintiff to constitute sexual harassment.

Keith J's dissent formed the basis for future more successful appeals to a reasonable woman standard in sexual harassment litigation. At the same time the differing conclusions reached by the judges in *Rabidue* (and in subsequent cases) as to the nature and degree of offence required to establish sexual harassment, clearly evidences the divergence which feminists identify. However, to acknowledge the existence of different perspectives as to what constitutes reasonableness is to further throw into doubt the feasibility and desirability of a single universal standard. Not only does it suggest that the claim to impartiality and objectivity upon which such a standard would rely could not be sustained, but the implications go further still by demonstrating that the process of presenting as objective and universal what is in fact subjective and partial can produce disturbing political and moral results. This is well evidenced in feminist discussion of the reasonable person standard. For example, Finley argues that the standard is reductive because, in seeking to articulate a single perspective, it denies the possibility of a multiplicity of perspectives.[71] In a similar vein Robin Martyn laments the relentless 'search for a common denominator' which the reasonable person standard requires.[72] Leslie Bender goes further, arguing that the standard is oppressive because, by claiming objectivity, the reasonable person standard empowers some and silences others: 'Like the notion of America as a

---

67   To illustrate the way in which gender perceptions diverge on sexual matters, Toni Lester cites a recent study of federal government employees showing that men felt that the problem of sexual harassment in the workplace was greatly exaggerated while women did not: Lester *supra* n 63 at p 227.

68   *Supra* n 65.

69   Contrary to Title VII Civil Rights Act 1964, as applied in *Meritor Savings Bank v Vinson* (1986) 477 US 57.

70   *Rabidue supra* n 65 at 626.

71   Finley *supra* n 4 at p 63.

72   Martyn *supra* n 4 at p 358.

melting pot, the reasonable person standard encourages conformism and the suppression of different voices.'[73]

In an interesting exploration of the doctrine of foreseeability as applied to the question of property manager liability for third party rapes of residents, Bender (with Perette Laurence) shows how tort doctrine, both on its face and as applied, reflects a perspective which is experientially male in terms of its assessment of the risk of rape thereby ignoring or marginalising women's perspectives and denying them their needs (in this case a rape victim's need for a remedy in the context of third party carelessness).[74]

The strongest account of the way in which the claim to objectivity is implicated in women's oppression is found in the work of Catharine MacKinnon. MacKinnon argues that objectivity, the idea of the 'nonsituated, distanced standpoint',[75] is a method by which men's point of view is privileged and women's silenced:

> Male dominance is perhaps the most pervasive and tenacious system of power in history ... its point of view is the standard for point-of-viewlessness, its particularity, the meaning of universality.[76]

It is also the means by which women become objects of men's desire and satisfaction:

> Objectivity is the epistemological stance of which objectification is the social process, of which male dominance is the politics, the acted-out social practice.[77]

So viewed, objectivity, expressed through the articulation of universal standards, plays a principal role in constructing and maintaining hierarchical and oppressive gender relations.

However, despite the potency of MacKinnon's arguments the feminist rejection of objectivity is far from absolute. The idea that there exists a concept of universal reason guiding our way toward what is right and good is still attractive even in the face of post-modernist/feminist attack. Such a desire to reclaim the universal can be found within feminist philosophical thought. Martha Nussbaum, for example, has recently and persuasively challenged what she characterises as 'the feminist assault on reason', arguing that reason is a weapon of resistance to oppression not a mode of oppression:

> Convention and habit are women's enemies here and reason their ally. Habit decrees that what seems strange is impossible and 'unnatural'; reason looks head on at the strange, refusing to assume that the current *status quo* is either immutable or in any normative sense 'natural'. The appeal to reason and

---

73 Bender *supra* n 4 at p 23.

74 L Bender with P Lawrence, 'Is Tort Law Male? Foreseeability Analysis and Property Manager's Liability for Third Party Rape of Residents' (1993) 69 *Chicago-Kent LR* 313.

75 MacKinnon *supra* n 16 at p 50.

76 C MacKinnon, 'Feminism, Marxism, Method and State: Towards Feminist Jurisprudence' (1983) 8 *Signs* 635 at pp 638–39.

77 MacKinnon *supra* n 16 at p 50.

objectivity amounts to a request that the observer refuse to be intimidated by habit and look for cogent arguments based on evidence that has been carefully sifted for bias.[78]

Nussbaum acknowledges that appeals to reason and objectivity have often been used to disempower and exclude women but such appeals, she claims, are not really grounded in reason, but constitute 'a claim of objectivity ... used as a screen to mask mere prejudice'.[79] Thus they do not necessitate the abandonment by feminists of the notion of objectivity itself. In this context, Nussbaum rejects the arguments made by many feminist philosophers that universal standards necessarily lead to the exclusion and/or oppression of some groups and the privileging of others. For Nussbaum a belief in the possibility of objective knowledge runs hand in hand with a commitment to the idea of some fundamental human essence. While she is prepared to recognise that gender differences are, by and large, socially constructed and oppressive, she retains a belief in the idea of a 'fixed human essence' which she sees, moreover, as a source of women's liberation:

> On the whole the rationalist idea of a fixed human essence, far from promoting human oppression, helped to advance their equality. For if we are not more than we are made to be by society, and women appear to be different, then they are different.[80]

Thus, unless we acknowledge some 'inalienable rational core'[81] in ourselves, we are what we appear and only that. Gender differences become no less real because they are socially constructed as the only reality is that which is socially forged.

Looking at the different approaches of Nussbaum and MacKinnon, perhaps the most striking contrast lies in the way in which they perceive social relations. MacKinnon sees social relations in general, and gender relations in particular, in terms of hierarchy and domination.[82] It is power which defines how women stand in relation to men and the differences between them. The role of reason in this process (MacKinnon uses the term 'objectivity') is to construct/ reflect/reinforce power relations not to penetrate or transcend them. For MacKinnon, the political and epistemological are inextricably bound up: knowledge becomes a means by which power can be exercised in favour of the powerful.

On the other hand Nussbaum's perception of the role of reason seems entirely located in the realm of the ideal. This is evidenced by her emphasis on the power of reason to cut through 'convention and habit', as if oppressive gender relations were simply the result of an intellectual error, or a wilful failure

---

78 Nussbaum *supra* n 16 at p 59.

79 *Ibid.*

80 Nussbaum *supra* at p 62.

81 *Ibid.*

82 MacKinnon *supra* n 76.

to address the question with proper impartiality. Her distinction between claiming objectivity and objectivity itself, while valid at some level, presupposes that a nonsituated, distanced standpoint is possible; that the individual is able to step outside the social relations of which he forms a part and the epistemology which underpins them. At bottom the differences between MacKinnon and Nussbaum reflect a fundamental disagreement within feminism, and beyond, as to the possibility of objective knowledge within the context of oppressive social relations, a disagreement which is based in turn upon differences about the way in which knowledge is produced and mediated.[83]

Articulating an ethical standard of care

One result of feminist disillusion with claims to objectivity has been a much closer scrutiny of the moral and ethical assumptions which underlie allegedly neutral positions. Thus, for example, in the context of tort law, this has led some feminist legal scholars to forsake the pursuit of an objective (in the sense of value-free) standard of care in favour of one which is ethically defensible. The leading proponent of such an approach is American feminist Leslie Bender who has adopted an explicitly moralistic approach to the articulation of a standard of care in negligence.

Bender starts from a position which views law as playing an important role in 'encouraging and improving our social relations'.[84] Pursuant to this, Bender questions whether the moral premises which currently underlie the standard of care in negligence properly serve this purpose: 'Have we gained anything,' she asks, 'from legally condoning behaviour that causes enormous physical and mental distress and yet is economically efficient?'[85] The tendency of tort law to reduce human tragedy to efficiency calculations is, she claims, 'inconsistent with our core values', being, 'violative of human dignity and equality'.[86]

Calling for the rejection of the moral preferences which currently inform tort law, Bender seeks to articulate an alternative ethical vision. This vision has a number of interrelated strands. Of central importance is her suggestion that the conduct of the tortfeasor be measured 'by the care that would be taken by a "neighbour" or "social acquaintance" or "responsible person with conscious care and concern for another's safety"'.[87] Bender views this standard as imposing

---

83 These issues have been extensively explored within feminist theory generating a greater range of positions (in relation to the role of reason) and considerably more complexity (as to the relationship between knowledge and power) than is reflected here. See, in particular, the work of Luce Irigaray explored in M Whitford *Luce Irigaray: Philosophy in the Feminine* (1991) Routledge.

84 Bender *supra* n 4 at p 31.

85 *Ibid.*

86 Bender, 'Values' *supra* n 2 at p 767.

87 Bender *supra* n 4 at p 25.

a higher duty of care on the tortfeasor, one which is consistent with an appreciation of 'every individual's special humanity'.[88] Bender also focuses on the disparities of power which often characterise tortious disputes in which injured plaintiffs with few resources find themselves up against highly-organised and well-resourced corporate defendants. She argues that tort doctrine should specifically recognise such inequalities of power; for example, by placing both the initial economic loss and the burden of proof on the corporate defendant.[89] Finally, in the context of remedies, Bender makes her most controversial proposal: calling for a concept of legal responsibility as 'taking care of', she suggests that this should include, where appropriate, a requirement that the tortfeasor engage in interpersonal care-giving in relation to the tort victim.[90] This ensures a legal meaning of responsibility which recognises our interconnectedness as human beings and reflects the social understanding of responsibility played out in women's daily lives.[91]

Bender self-consciously locates her ethical position within Gilligan's 'different voice',[92] clearly relating the values she expresses to women's experience.[93] Thus her articulation of a feminist ethics is one which is socially female, that is, one which she derives from a perception of women's social role. It follows that it is not an ethical position which men are precluded from holding. Indeed it is Bender's aspiration that the merits of the position will attract it to all by virtue of the values it espouses.

Bender's arguments are appealing particularly in their willingness to challenge taken for granted assumptions about the nature of legal responsibility for others. However, her espousal of the values reflected in Gilligan's 'different voice', is far from unproblematic. In particular not all feminists agree that she is articulating essentially feminine values. Catharine MacKinnon, for example, is wary of attempts to revalorise allegedly 'feminine' attributes. Observing that 'women value care because men have valued us according to the care we give them',[94] MacKinnon questions whether the different voice which Carol Gilligan articulates is really women's, 'rather than what male supremacy has attributed to us for its own use'.[95] Thus while women may be socialised to nurture and to care, they do so, MacKinnon argues, in compliance with men's perceptions of how they should behave.

---

88 *Supra* n 86.
89 Bender, '(Re)Torts' *supra* n 2.
90 Bender, 'Values' *supra* n 2.
91 *Ibid* at pp 770–71.
92 Bender *supra* n 4 at pp 28–30.
93 *Supra* n 91.
94 MacKinnon *supra* n 16 at p 39.
95 *Ibid*.

A further point raised by Bender's position is whether or not the commonality of experience upon which she relies can be said to exist. Do not such appeals to a unified female experience make the same false claims to universality that feminists attribute so frequently to men, resulting moreover in the same oppressive consequence, namely, that those who do not share the privileged experience are thereby excluded and their experience denied? This possibility has been recognised by some feminist legal theorists in the context of the reasonable woman standard. For example, Finley acknowledges the dangers of invoking gender stereotypes, hitherto deployed to disempower and oppress women, in order to promote their interests. She is also sensitive to the difficulties involved in expanding the standard of reasonableness to take account of women's perspectives without at the same time broadening her concern to include the perspectives of all those who have been defined as outside the standard traditionally invoked.[96] The strength of these concerns has led some feminists to call for the abandonment of the reasonable woman standard. In a comprehensive exploration of the deployment of the standard, Naomi Cahn argues that, despite some gains, the 'theory and practice of the reasonable woman standard further stereotypes and disempowers'.[97] Cahn calls for a new 'context-based standard' which recognises and gives voice to multiple perspectives and diverse subjective experiences in the assessment and resolution of disputes.[98] However she is, to say the least, vague as to how such a standard could be effectively deployed given its indeterminate content. Indeed, it may be that the implication of recognising a multiplicity of perspectives and conflicting subjective accounts in place of an 'objective' understanding of a particular interaction precludes the articulation of any standard at all, in the sense of operating as a norm, a call for compliance, a prohibition of deviance.

Moreover, it is arguable that the same insights render problematic any attempt (such as Bender's) to articulate a public realm, in the sense of a set of standards which govern community life, because such standards inevitably operate to privilege particular viewpoints and suppress others.

CONCLUSION

The increasing philosophical and political focus on diversity, as opposed to commonality, in human experience raises grave doubts about the viability and direction of the feminist project itself. In particular, serious questions have been raised about the meaning and implications of the category 'woman' in the context of radical political strategy. Judith Butler has argued that, once

---

96   Finley *supra* n 4 at p 64.

97   Cahn *supra* n 63 at p 1402.

98   *Ibid* at pp 1435-45. Cahn is addressing the reasonable woman standard in the context of sex-related wrongs such as spousal abuse, sexual harasssment and rape.

understood as 'a set of values or dispositions', that is, in terms of a fixed conception of identity based on gender, the category 'becomes normative in character and hence exclusionary in principle'.[99] This renders problematic (and potentially oppressive) any attempts to pursue the interests of women as a group because the group in question is 'built upon the denial of a decidedly more complex cultural identity or non-identity, as the case may be'.[100] Recognition of this insight has produced a theoretical shift away from a focus on gender *per se*, towards a preoccupation with the manifold streams which flow into the formation of cultural identity. In political terms, it requires at the very least a sensitivity to the fluidity of identity (as opposed to its fixedness) and an awareness of the way in which gender, race, class, (dis)ability and other features of social and cultural life intersect and inform a particular political moment. Some writers have gone further to argue that the recognition of diversity compels a fundamental reassessment of radical political ideals. Iris Marion Young calls for a rejection of the ideal of community because it '... presumes subjects can understand one another as they understand themselves. It thus denies the difference between subjects'.[101] She argues instead for the pursuit of 'the politics of difference', based upon recognition and affirmation of differently identified groups and the celebration of distinctive cultures and characteristics within and among them. Such an approach inevitably precludes political strategies based upon particular metanarratives, accounts of social/sexual/racial oppression which rely upon some coherent theoretical unity, and directs political energy instead into localised struggles based on securing the recognition and representation of different groups (reflecting a variety of social and cultural configurations) in the political realm.

The full implications of such insights for radical political practice have yet to be worked out. What is their significance in the context of debate about the standard of care in negligence? Certainly they cast doubt on the political and legal value of such doctrinal innovations as the reasonable woman, although it may be that the answer to this dilemma lies not in a principled adoption or rejection of the 'reasonable woman' standard but in the careful and pragmatic consideration of its desirability and application in particular contexts. Such a pragmatic and strategically focused approach to its deployment may help to avoid the exclusionary tendencies inherent in the standard and at the same time give recognition to those instances where gender is a dominant interpretive and allocative factor. Moreover, such a focus avoids the 'all or nothing' approach which conventional reasoning compels, in favour of a solution which depends less on the articulation of abstract principle and more on the consequences of concrete application.

---

99   Butler *supra* n 18 at p 325.

100   *Ibid* at p 338.

101   I M Young, 'The Ideal of Community and the Politics of Difference' in Nicolson *supra* n 18 at p 302.

Bender's attempt to reconstruct the standard of care in accordance with a feminist ethics is perhaps more problematic. Not only does such a project run into difficulties in the context of theoretical trends towards anti-essentialism but also, in seeking to articulate universal (in the sense of being generally applied) standards, she runs the risk of assuming a homogeneity in outlook which is not reflected in individual experience, thereby compelling conformity through the suppression of difference.

The seeming impossibility of articulating standards without attracting such consequences has led one writer, Robin Martyn, to call for legislative definition of tortious responsibility in the context of particular harms.[102] This avoids the articulation of a general principle (beyond the acceptance that legal responsibility entails liability) and places the question of particular standards in the hands of a democratically-elected body which, while it cannot claim objectivity in its decisions, can at least profess to be representative of a multiplicity of viewpoints and concerns (although given the weaknesses of western systems of democracy, such a profession does not necessarily tally with actuality!).

Martyn's suggestion might be a neat and practical way round some of the difficulties to which the reasonable man standard, and the feminist critique of it, give rise. However, practical problems aside, one thought which emerges from this exploration of the feminist critique of the reasonable man, within the broader contours of the feminist critique of reason, is a consideration not of what it addresses but rather of what it ignores. For example, Bender's discussion of the standard of care appears to be completely ahistorical. No effort is made to trace its emergence or the factors which contributed to its ascendance, whether doctrinally or socially. It follows that no perspective which sheds light on, for example, the relationship between tort law and particular economic processes, is addressed or even acknowledged. Thus, the feminist emphasis on context appears to be selective in the sense that the debate about the desirability of the reasonableness standard takes place almost entirely outside any historic or economic context.

This, I think, leads to certain fundamental mistakes. For example, Bender, in company with other feminist commentators on the tort system,[103] assumes that the standard of care, the test of legal liability, should determine the question of compensation. Yet there is no necessary reason why this should be the case. The social and legal process of articulating and enforcing standards to govern individual behaviour and the degree to which society assumes a responsibility for the misfortunes of its members do not have to precisely coincide. Certainly a case for linking them must be made.

---

102 Martyn *supra* n 4.

103 Martyn *supra* n 4; see also S Wildman, 'Enlightened Insurance in a World Made Safer' (1990) 44 *University of Miami LR* 877.

A further problem which besets the feminist critique of tort law's reasonable man (and indeed the feminist critique of reason generally) is a tendency to understand oppression as some sort of intellectual error (or 'inadvertence').[104] So, for example, Bender's arguments proceed on the basis that tort law is a misrepresentation of 'our core values'[105] which, if more generally realised, would make the case for change unanswerable. Likewise much of the feminist/post-modernist preoccupation with the oppressive consequences of operating categories male/female; reason/passion; individual/community presupposes that oppression derives from the categories themselves (in the sense that their repudiation is a commonly prescribed recipe for liberation) rather than from the practices which engender and effect the oppressive relations in the first place.

Such reflections are likely to lead towards a very different terrain from that which is addressed in this essay; they are, perhaps, for another time and place. Yet it remains the case that, despite the power of the feminist critique of reason to entrance and captivate the mind, the political consequences which flow from it are deeply troubling. For this reason, the time for radicals to address a growing fissure between political and intellectual visions must come soon.

---

104 Bender, 'Values' *supra* n 2 at p 771.
105 *Ibid* at p 767.

CHAPTER FOUR

A FEMINIST CHALLENGE TO TORT LAW

*PATRICIA PEPPIN**

Among the traditional first-year law school subjects, tort law seems to be relatively well situated to reflect the diversity of individuals' lives, as it takes into account the social context within which private disputes occur. Its core subject matter includes injuries to people's bodies, the right to physical integrity, and bodily inviolability. With the expansion of the modern law of negligence, tort law has gained a means by which relationships between actors can be analysed to determine whether the behaviour of the defendant within the relationship conforms to societal expectations. Negligence, in contrast to the intentional torts, requires analysis of the relatedness of people, or of people and institutions, and requires the imaginative process of placing oneself in various real and hypothetical positions.[1] Negligence law exhibits a more complex form of reasoning, which explains why it has acquired a greater potential to respond to the cultural pluralism of the late 20th century. As Ann Scales argues:

> Feminism brings law back to its purpose – to decide the moral crux of the matter in real human situations ... Finding the crux depends upon the relation among things, not upon their opposition ... It would also seem obvious that relational reasoning is law's soul, that law's duty is to enhance, rather than to ignore, the rich diversity of life.[2]

---

* I would like to thank the editors of the *Texas Journal of Women and the Law* for their contribution to the article from which this paper has been drawn, 'Power and Disadvantage in Medical Relationships' (1993) 3 *Texas Journal of Women and the Law* 221, and for permission to reproduce these portions of the article. I would like to acknowledge the contribution of many people who assisted in the development of this article: Mary Jane Mossman and Sanda Rodgers who organised the panel discussion, *Feminist Analysis: Challenging Law and Legal Processes*, at the Canadian Bar Association – Ontario Institute of Continuing Legal Education, Toronto, Ontario, January 1992, where a part of this paper was presented; the participants at the Health Law Teachers Conference of the American Society of Law and Medicine session, *Teaching the Doctor-Patient Relationship from a Feminist Perspective*, Seattle, Washington, May 1992, who made comments and suggestions; Sheila Noonan, Elaine Carty, Martha Bailey, Jackie Duffin, Karen Rothenberg, and Jerry Bickenbach with whom I discussed aspects of the research; Jane Koster who provided creative research assistance; Sandy Tallen who very capably prepared the manuscript; the Law Foundation of Ontario and John D Whyte, former Dean of the Faculty of Law, Queen's University, who provided the financial support which made this project possible; and Lisa Fong and Rachel Ariss, who transcribed the manuscript.

1 For instance, the action for breach of the doctor's duty to disclose medical treatment information to the patient requires an examination of the communication between the parties, a comparison of the actual disclosure with a standard, and an assessment of what the hypothetical reasonable patient in the patient's shoes would have done if the standard had been met. See eg *Reibl v Hughes* [1980] 2 SCR 880 at 899 (noting that the objective standard of negligence requires consideration of the patient's input in the determination to undergo surgery as a crucial counterweight to the force of the doctor's recommendation); *Canterbury v Spence* (DC Cir 1972) 464 F2d 772 (defining the disclosure standard as reasonable under the circumstances, and finding jury issues on the physician's duty to disclose, the occurrence of a negligent operation, and negligent care of the patient by the hospital).

2 Ann C Scales, 'The Emergence of Feminist Jurisprudence: An Essay' (1986) 95 *Yale LJ* 1373 at p 1387.

Does tort law, and negligence law in particular, take account of the social reality of women's situations in society? Does it handle constructively, or merely reflect, the unequal nature of society? Negligence law continues to be problematic from a feminist point of view. The goals of tort law do not include the achievement of equality or distributive justice. The more modest goals are compensation and deterrence, sometimes accompanied by punishment.[3] Accepting these goals for the moment, one can analyse how well tort law achieves its goals for members of disadvantaged groups.

Elements of negligence, such as recognition of harm, duty, and the standard of care, need to be construed in a manner sensitive to historic disadvantage. Hierarchy, dominance, and disadvantage characterise relationships in life; awareness of this dimension should enter into the determination of liability and compensation. Acknowledgment of a power imbalance can assist a court in reaching doctrinal conclusions.

A legal standard that merely reflects the dominant view in society, while asserting its own value-neutrality, provides no room for alternative experiences. For instance, the 'reasonable man' test for the standard of care, the 'reasonable person in the shoes of the plaintiff' test of causation in informed consent cases, and the doctrine of reasonable foreseeability, all require the plaintiff to prove conformity to a norm. Writing on the reasonableness standard in tort law, authors such as Lucinda Finley, Leslie Bender and Martha Chamallas have demonstrated that reasonableness is judicially constructed, has a history of bias in favour of white male, middle-class, able-bodied values, and resonates with the perceived dichotomy between reason and emotion.[4] The mythical reasonable man is exemplified in England by 'the man who rides the Clapham omnibus' and in the United States by 'the man who takes the magazines home and in the evening pushes the lawn mower in his shirtsleeves'.[5] The 'reasonable person' standard might be 'false gender neutrality'[6] and function merely as a mask for the

---

3   W Page Keeton *et al*, *Prosser and Keeton on the Law of Torts* (1984, 5th edn) at p 3 ('Protection of the interest in freedom from intentional and unpermitted contacts with the plaintiff's person extends to any part of the body, or to anything which is attached to it and practically identified with it').

4   See Lucinda Finley, 'Laying Down the Master's Tools: A Feminist Revision of Torts' in *Women, Law and Social Change* 53 (1990) T Brettel Dawson (ed) [hereinafter Finley, 'Laying Down'] (describing her classroom use of A P Herbert's fictitious *Fardell v Potts* case, which holds that the reasonable man standard could not apply to a woman because a reasonable woman does not exist, to demonstrate that the stereotype of woman 'as unreasonable and overly emotional could actually infect judgments about a woman's conduct'); and Leslie Bender, 'From Gender Difference to Feminist Solidarity: Using Carol Gilligan and an Ethic of Care in Law' (1990) 15 *Vermont L Rev* 1 at p 19 (questioning the idea that white male perspectives are considered neutral while women's and minorities' viewpoints are 'biased and political'); and Martha Chamallas, 'Feminist Constructions of Objectivity: Multiple Perspectives in Sexual and Racial Harassment Litigation' (1992) I *Tex J Women & L* 95 (arguing that the reasonable person standard should be modified to include multiple perspectives to partially explain reasons for the exclusions of certain groups); and Lucinda M Finley, 'A Break in the Silence: Including Women's Issues in a Torts Course' (1989) I *Yale JL & Feminism* 41 at pp 57-58 (discussing how '"objective" rules are too often formed by a collection of male perspectives' and noting that judgments may be affected by the perception that women are overly emotional).

5   Finley, 'Laying Down' *supra* n 4 at p 53.

6   Susan Moller Okin, *Justice, Gender and the Family* (1989) at pp 10-13.

gendered standard underneath. If so, the reasonableness standard is an invitation to decision making based on hidden values. The concept of reasonableness may be given explicit content, as is done in the analysis of the standard of care by the consideration of risks and benefits.[7] Even risks and benefits, however, are subject to the imagination of judicial interpreters and legal advocates.[8] To the extent that the individual's own experiences, political situation, and life expectations are taken into account in a contextual analysis, individual autonomy and equality may be better achieved.[9]

Since the avoidance of harm is desirable, concern about the lack of effective deterrence through tort actions in informed consent and products liability is appropriate. In actions by injured patient consumers against the pharmaceutical industry, tort law appears insufficient to control an industry with such massive potential to create risk and the resources to wage litigation.[10] The major pharmaceutical disasters of the 20th century, including DES and the Dalkon

---

7   For instance, in the evaluation of the doctor's disclosure of treatment information to a patient. See *supra* n l; see also Keeton *et al supra* n 3 at pp 171–73 and n 46. Judge Learned Hand set out his famous theory of risk-benefit analysis in *United States v Carrol Towine Co*:

   '[T]he owner's duty, as in other similar situations, to provide against resulting injuries is a function of three variables: (1) the probability that [the moored vessel] will break away; (2) the gravity of the resulting injury, if she does; (3) the burden of adequate precautions. Possibly it serves to bring this notion into relief to state it in algebraic terms: if the probability be called P; the injury L; and the burden B; liability depends on whether B is less than L multiplied by P; ie whether B [is less than] PL' (2d Cir 1947) 159 F2d 169, 173.

8   For example, in *Eve v Mrs E*, Justice La Forest, in his judgment for the unanimous court, could not imagine that any benefit would result from allowing a developmentally handicapped woman, incapable of consenting herself, to have a contraceptive sterilisation. See *Eve v Mrs E* [1986] 2 SCR 388 p 390 (Can) (stating that sterilisation should never be authorised for non-therapeutic purposes in the absence of consent, since it can never be determined that it would be done for the woman's benefit). The court took this position in spite of the extensive use of sterilisation as a contraceptive worldwide. This example shows the failure of imagination that can occur at the conceptual level with respect to risks and benefits, as well as the failure to imagine on an individual level what the sterilisation or lack of sterilisation would mean for Eve's own life. The judgment exemplifies a limited form of rights analysis – one made without elements of context. I have developed this analysis in 'Justice and Care: Mental Disability and Sterilisation Decisions' (1989–90) *Canadian Human Rights Yearbook* 65.

9   For an analysis of gender bias in judicial decisions with respect to death and dying, see Steven H Miles and Allison August, 'Courts, Gender and "The Right to Die"' (1990) 18 *Law Med & Health Care* 85 (concluding that it is more likely for a court to find and allow evidence of men's desires to continue or eliminate life support systems, because courts tend to view men's opinions as rational and women's as less authoritative); and see also Leslie Bender, 'A Feminist Analysis of Physician-Assisted Dying and Voluntary Active Euthanasia' (1992) 59 *Tenn L Rev* 519 p 527 (suggesting that current approaches to voluntary euthanasia would be improved by the infusion of 'feminist' values such as caring, responsibility, and responsiveness).

10 For a discussion of the aggressive and unremitting litigation tactics used by the A H Robins company in the Dalkon Shield litigation, see the comments of Chief Justice Miles Lord on the settlement of the case, which were stricken from the record as a result of the company's attempt to have the Chief Justice reprimanded; 'The Dalkon Shield Litigation: Revised Annotated Reprimand by Chief Judge Miles Lord' (1986) 9 *Hamline L Rev* 7.

Shield, involved pharmaceutical products for women's reproductive systems.[11] Countless women and children worldwide have been injured by these products.[12] Neither the tort system nor the regulatory systems in place at the time prevented these harms. Adequate warnings about risks, which would enable the consumer to decide whether or not to use a product, are needed. Most importantly, safe products must be created.

In analysing the negligent infliction of nervous shock, Martha Chamallas states:

> The law of torts values physical security and property more highly than emotional security and human relationships. This apparently gender-neutral hierarchy of values has privileged men, as the traditional owners and managers of property, and has burdened women, to whom the emotional work of maintaining human relationships has commonly been assigned. The law has often failed to compensate women for recurring harms – serious though they may be in the lives of women – for which there is no precise masculine analogue.[13]

Chamallas demonstrates that historically, women who suffered physical injuries as a result of fright were disadvantaged by the classification of these injuries as emotional harm.[14] The suffering that women experienced after miscarriages or harm to their children was viewed by judges as unreasonable, because the injury was too remote and unforeseeable.[15] A transformation of the law that incorporates relational interests (with a child, a foetus, or a family member) into one's own physical integrity creates 'the beginnings of a feminisation of tort law'.[16]

---

11 See eg Roberta J Apfel and Susan M Fisher, *To Do No Harm: DES and the Dilemmas of Modern Medicine* (1984) at pp 19-20 (reporting that Diethylstilbestrol (DES), a synthetic estrogen, was approved for use in pregnant women by the Food and Drug Administration without any research to prove it was safe or effective for pregnant women or their foetuses); and Diana B Dutton, *Worse Than The Disease: Pitfalls of Medical Progress* (1988) (discussing the problems and uncertainties associated with four areas of medical innovation including drugs, medical devices, public health, and genetic engineering); and Richard B Sobol, *Bending the Law: The Story of the Dalkon Shield Bankruptcy* (1991) at pp 1-22 (describing the consistent refusal by the A H Robins company to acknowledge repeated evidence and indications of the Dalkon Shield's potential for causing non-fatal and fatal septic abortions). It also occurred with the breast implant. See Nicholas Regush *Safety Last: The Failure of the Consumer Health Protection System in Canada* (1993) at pp 73-105 (noting how little doctors and government regulators knew about the risks of breast implants for years following their release and discussing how doctors, manufacturers, and the US and Canadian governments ignored and downplayed the harms associated with breast implants).

12 See eg Apfel and Fisher *supra* n 11 at p 1 (stating that DES had been used in a variety of medical conditions from 1940 to 1971, exposing millions of women and children to harm during pregnancy). Because registers of drug and device-induced injuries do not exist, and because of inadequate post-marketing surveillance in North America, we have no way of knowing with any degree of accuracy the extent of injury caused by even the most seriously harmful products. Litigation provides one source of data, but significant deterrents to bringing lawsuits exist. For instance, DES was prescribed widely in Canada; however, no lawsuit has been brought by a DES-injured plaintiff in Canada.

13 Martha Chamallas with Linda K Kerber, 'Women, Mothers and the Law of Fright: A History' (1990) 88 *Mich L Rev* 814 at p 814.

14 *Ibid* at p 816.

15 *Ibid*.

16 *Ibid* at p 862.

Leslie Bender has suggested that the idea of relationship and responsibility should incorporate the notion of caregiving, or 'taking care of', in the area of mass torts.[17] Bender has proposed that tort law base its perceptions of human beings on their interconnections and mutual dependency, and that it refashion remedies to correspond to this understanding.[18] In her opinion, payment of money is insufficient as a remedy for mass harms because the tortfeasor is not required to provide any care, which is exactly what the tort victim needs, and because victims live with the harms every day, while the defendants have no comparable experience.[19] She has proposed new kinds of remedies comparable to community service that require corporate defendants who have engaged in mass torts to act as caregivers.[20]

Elements missing from tort law include: power, connection and mutuality as aspects of the concepts of autonomy and relationships, remedies that respect emotional harms and interrelationships, and doctrinal remedying of inequalities. Feminist theory helps legal analysts explore the biases in seemingly neutral doctrines. Many doctrines value characteristics deemed important by some men and ignore or devalue women's particular experiences and views, including the political contexts of the lives of the members of nondominant groups in society. Legal doctrine has failed to take account of the systemic disadvantage of such groups in society and has failed to acknowledge that the power imbalance exists and is both reflected and amplified through the institutions of power in society, including the law.

APPLICATION: SEXUAL ABUSE

In this section, a reconceptualisation of the legal framework for dealing with sexual abuse between a doctor and a patient will be presented. *Norberg v Wynrib*,[21] a case involving a sex-for-drugs deal between a doctor and his patient, posed a doctrinal dilemma for the Supreme Court of Canada.

In 1978, Laura Norberg became addicted to the prescription drug Fiorinal, a painkiller given to her by her sister when she was experiencing pain from an

---

17 See Leslie Bender, 'Feminist (Re)Torts: Thoughts on the Liability Crisis, Mass Torts, Power, and Responsibilities' (1990) *Duke LJ* 848 at pp 904–06 (arguing that tort law should recognise emotional, physical, and spiritual harms and that tort remedies should require corporate tortfeasors to perform physical and emotional caregiving work).

18 See *ibid* at pp 904–05 (arguing that tort law's definition of responsibility is financial and should be expanded to reflect the amount of caregiving required for the injured and should require the tortfeasor to play a role in the caregiving).

19 *Ibid* at pp 905–07.

20 See *ibid* (proposing that corporate defendants compensate their tort victims with caregiving services and continual care for the duration of the victim's harms, while focusing on 'health, safety, and human dignity in deciding personal injury disputes').

21 [1992] 2 SCR 226.

abscessed tooth, which was not diagnosed by medical and dental professionals.[22] In order to feed her addiction, Ms Norberg first obtained the barbiturate from her sister and later obtained it through a medical doctor who prescribed Fiorinal for her broken ankle, until his retirement.[23] In 1982, she approached Dr Wynrib and obtained Fiorinal from him by telling him about her ankle injury and other health problems requiring painkillers.[24] Later the same year, Dr Wynrib, after identifying her chemical dependency, confronted her with her addiction and offered a sex-for-drugs deal.[25] When Laura Norberg's other sources for the drug became unavailable and she became 'desperate' near the end of 1983, she returned to Dr Wynrib and engaged in sexual activities in return for access to the drug.[26] During this time, Dr Wynrib also acted as her general practitioner, referring her to a gynaecologist and ordering diagnostic tests; he did not, however, recommend a drug addiction program.[27] When she discussed her addiction with him, he told her simply to quit.[28] Ultimately, she was investigated, charged, and pleaded guilty to the offence of 'double doctoring' under s 3.1(1) of the Narcotic Control Act.[29] Ms Norberg stopped seeing Dr Wynrib and enrolled in a drug rehabilitation programme.[30] She commenced an action against Dr Wynrib on the grounds of sexual assault, breach of fiduciary duty, and negligence.[31] The defence pleaded *ex turpi causa* successfully at trial and in the British Columbia Court of Appeal.[32] This controversial doctrine, requiring that no action proceed from an illegal or immoral cause, prevents plaintiffs from using the courts to profit from their own wrongdoing.[33] When the British Columbia Court of Appeal applied this defence to prevent Ms

---

22   *Ibid* at 237–38.

23   *Ibid* at 238

24   *Ibid*.

25   See *ibid* at 238–39 ('[Appellant] testified that [the doctor] told her that "if I was good to him he would be good to me" and he made suggestions by pointing upstairs where he lived above his office').

26   *Ibid* at 239–40.

27   *Ibid* at 313–15 (Sopinka J concurring in the judgment). Justice Sopinka considered these facts important to the analysis of negligence based on a breach of the duty to treat. *ibid* at 315.

28   *Ibid* at 240.

29   *Ibid*. See also Narcotic Control Act, RSC 1970, c N-1, amended by SC 1985, c 19, s 198.

30   *Ibid* at 241.

31   *Ibid* at 241–43.

32   *Ibid* at 243–44. The trial court and appellate court also found that the appellant consented to the sexual assault and dismissed the battery claim. *Norberg v Wynrib* (1990) 66 DLR (4th) 553 at 556 (BCCA). Although the trial judge found that the doctor breached a duty of care to the appellant, he dismissed her negligence claim because the harm suffered was emotional distress rather than physical injury. *Ibid* at 557. Unlike the trial court, the appellate court would have allowed her negligence claim, finding the harm in her continued addiction, but would have limited damages to the period during which the doctor knew of her addiction. *Ibid*. The three appellate judges rejected the fiduciary duty argument. *Ibid* at 553, 566, 569. The majority believed that disclosure of confidential information or something of that nature was necessary for a breach of fiduciary duty. *Ibid* at 556. Justice Locke, in his dissent, asserted that no equitable rule disclosed a duty when the individual had neither breached confidentiality nor used undue influence. *Ibid*. Ultimately, the majority dismissed her appeal. *Ibid* at 559.

33   *Hall v Hebert* [1993] 2 SCR 159 at 169. In *Hall*, Justice McLachlin, with three justices concurring, found that *ex turpi causa non oritur actio* operates as a defence rather than as an element negating a ...

Norberg's recovery, Justice Locke dissented. He found that no common purpose and no common criminal act had existed, that immorality was not sufficient to raise this bar, and that any sexual immorality was not relevant to the wrongful supply of drugs.[34]

During the year in which the case was before the Supreme Court of Canada, the issue of sexual abuse by doctors became the subject of considerable media attention, largely as the result of a task force which had been established by the College of Physicians and Surgeons of Ontario – the governing body of the medical profession. The Task Force on Sexual Abuse, chaired by Marilou McPhedran, a feminist lawyer, held public hearings (sometimes *in camera* at the request of speakers) and established a phone-in line for people to talk in confidence about sexual abuse.[35] The task force received an overwhelming response from abused women, and a number of abused men, who came forward to talk of their experiences.[36] In its report, the task force proposed, and the College of Physicians and Surgeons adopted, a zero tolerance policy for sexual abuse: 'Due to the position of power the physician brings to the doctor-patient relationship, there are NO circumstances – NONE – in which sexual activity between a physician and a patient is acceptable ... It is ALWAYS the doctor's responsibility to know what is appropriate and never to cross the line into sexual

---

33   ... duty of care. *Ibid* at 185. She also noted that the purpose of the doctrine is to preserve the integrity of the legal system. *Ibid* at 178-79. The court concluded that *ex turpi causa* should be used only in rare circumstances, and its use is not justified when the plaintiff's claim is for compensation for personal injuries as a consequence of the negligence of the defendant. *Ibid*. Modern cases have assessed whether the act required must be criminal, otherwise illegal or immoral, whether a causal connection is necessary between the turpitude and the harm, and whether a common purpose and act must be shared by plaintiff and defendant. Lewis N Klar, *Tort Law* (1991) at pp 331-33; and Allen M Linden, *Canadian Tort Law* (1977) at pp 439-43 (examining the rebirth of the doctrine and its application in tort cases); and G H L Fridman, *Introduction to the Law of Torts* (1978) at pp 71-73 (summarising the application of the doctrine to tort cases). Courts also have considered whether the doctrine's basis is the unwillingness of the courts to bring the system of justice into disrepute or an imposition of standards of illegality or immorality to counter otherwise tortious behaviour. Klar *supra* at pp 326-30; and Linden *supra*; and Fridman *supra*. Even though the modern doctrine has looked to the law, rather than to morality, to define the standard, the *ex turpi* doctrine has been criticised for preferring wrongdoing defendants to base plaintiffs, for importing a contract-based notion into tort law, and for imposing a nebulous standard rooted in 19th century views of wrongdoing. Linden *supra* at pp 439-43; and Fridman *supra* at pp 71-73; and see also Ernest J Weinrib, 'Illegality as a Tort Defence' (1976) 26 *U Toronto L Rev* 28 (assessing the appropriateness of *ex turpi causa non oritur actio* application in tort cases).

34   *Norberg v Wynrib* (1990) 66 DLR (4th) 553 at 567-68 (BCCA).

35   Task Force on Sexual Abuse of Patients, College of Physicians and Surgeons of Ontario, *The Final Report of the Task Force on Sexual Abuse of Patients* (1991) 10 [hereinafter Task Force]; and Marilou McPhedran, 'Investigating Sexual Abuse of Patients: The Ontario Experience' (1992) 1 *Health L Rev* 3 (analysing the policy process in which the Task Force on Sexual Abuse of Patients had been engaged). The Ontario Regulated Health Professions Act 1991 SO 1991, c 18, has been amended by the Regulated Health Professions Amendment Act 1993 SO 1993, effective 31 December 1993, to incorporate a definition of sexual abuse and to include particular orders available to the governing body when a member of one of the health professions has committed an act of professional misconduct by sexually abusing a patient.

36   Task Force *supra* n 35 at p 10.

activity.'[37] The report was clearly influential in the court's interpretation of the nature and social unacceptability of the harm.[38] In its final report, the task force concluded that 'the strongest basis for challenging a doctor who has taken advantage of an unequal relationship lies in the law of fiduciary relationship'.[39]

The *Norberg* case raises questions about the legal conceptualisation of the doctor-patient relationship, which is conventionally analysed in terms of battery, negligence, fiduciary duty, contract law and professional regulation. The doctrine of informed consent in battery and negligence law goes to the heart of the legal regime governing the relationship, but normally consensuality concerns treatment alternatives. In this case, the prescription drug, to which the doctor controlled access, became a commodity in a prescription drug-for-sex transaction. The lower courts reached differing conclusions on which principles applied. Norberg's arguments based on breach of fiduciary duty were successful initially at trial,[40] while her negligence argument succeeded in the British Columbia Court of Appeal.[41] The defendant's successful defence of *ex turpi causa*, however, precluded recovery at both levels.[42]

The Women's Legal Education and Action Fund (LEAF) intervened in *Norberg* to make arguments based on the condition of disadvantage of the plaintiff, the nature of addiction, abuse of persons with disabilities, and the intolerable harm of doctors abusing patients.[43] In its *factum* to the Supreme Court of Canada, LEAF attempted to restructure the court's perception of drug addiction, identifying it as a disability and a condition of disadvantage.[44] LEAF named sexual assault as a sex equality issue and argued that consent to sexual

---

37   *Ibid* at p 12.

38   See eg *Norberg v Wynrib* [1992] 2 SCR 226 at 297 (McLachlin J) (examining the effect of the sexual exploitation on Ms Norberg's self-esteem).

39   Task Force *supra* n 35 at p 80.

40   *Norberg v Wynrib* (1988) 50 DLR (4th) 167 at 172 (BCSC).

41   *Norberg v Wynrib* (1990) 66 DLR (4th) 553 at 557.

42   *Norberg v Wynrib* [1992] 2 SCR 226 at 243-45; and see *supra* n 32-33 and accompanying text.

43   *Norberg v Wynrib*, Application for Intervention [1992] 2 SCR 224, *Factum* of the Intervenor, Women's Legal Education and Action Fund (No 21924) at pp 2-6 [hereinafter Intervenor's *Factum*]. A *factum* sets out in written form the argument, with supporting authorities, to be made by the party or intervenor.

44   See Intervenor's *Factum* at pp 10-11 (noting that chemical dependence is a recognised disability under the Canadian Human Rights Act); and see also Sherene Razack, *Canadian Feminism and the Law: The Women's Legal Education and Action Fund and the Pursuit of Equality* (1991) (analysing LEAF's political action and litigation). Canadian constitutional jurisprudence has examined the relatively disadvantaged positions of groups and individuals in order to find a breach of equality rights with discrimination under the Canadian Charter of Rights and Freedoms (s 15 Canadian Charter of Rights and Freedoms, Constitution Act 1982, Pt I).

battery should be seen in the context of abuse of power in order to respect women's right to the equal protection and benefit of tort law.[45]

Arguing that other areas of the law recognise and control relationships of power and vulnerability, LEAF provided examples from contract law – including unconscionability, undue influence, and duress – and from other relationships, such as those found in sexual harassment violations, criminal law, and prohibitions against sexual contact with children.[46] LEAF argued that the court should find no consent at all where free choice has disappeared in the face of the 'power, trust and authority' of the defendant.[47] Because of the power differential between doctors and patients, the responsibility for avoiding sexual battery should rest with the doctor, certainly where the patient is a member of a group enumerated in the equality section of the Canadian Charter of Rights and Freedoms.[48]LEAF also argued against application of the *ex turpi* bar, stating that chemical dependence should not preclude recovery for a plaintiff; to do so would 'blame the victim and invite exploitation of chemically-dependent women'.[49]

The Supreme Court of Canada divided on the question of which doctrine to apply to these circumstances. All six judges decided in Ms Norberg's favour and agreed that *ex turpi* did not apply.[50] Three judges found for the plaintiff in

---

45 Intervenor's *Factum* at pp 1, 12. LEAF provided data on the particular vulnerability of women with disabilities:

'Some women are more vulnerable than others:

(a) People with disabilities are at least 150 per cent as vulnerable to sexual abuse as individuals of the same age and sex who are not disabled. Recent research showed that 27 per cent of the offenders were special service providers and that the more severely disabled the victims were, the more likely they were to be abused by a service provider.

(b) American studies have shown that black women are substantially overrepresented in rape statistics of victims.

(c) It is increasingly acknowledged that women who consult professionals are at risk of sexual exploitation. This makes it dangerous for women to seek help. Just as sexual harassment is a barrier to sex equality in the workplace, the threat and reality of sexual assault are barriers to sex equality in access to medical and other professional services.

(c)[sic] Young women are particularly vulnerable to sexual assault, especially by those known to them' *ibid* at pp 3-4.

Equal protection and equal benefit of the law are two of the four equality rights protected under s 15 of the Charter. *Ibid*.

46 *Ibid* at p 9. LEAF noted:

'Similar insight should inform the distinction between consent and coerced submission in the tort law of sexual assault. Achieving equality requires the recognition of social hierarchies. In this case, the factors to be recognised are sex, disability, and the confidential relationship (here between doctor and patient), factors which combined and interacted synergistically' *ibid* at p 10.

47 *Ibid* at p 12.

48 *Ibid* at p 13.

49 *Ibid* at pp 14, 16.

50 *Norberg v Wynrib* [1992] 2 SCR 226 at 262-63 (plurality opinion, La Forest J) at 284-88 (McLachlin J) at 316 (Sopinka J). Justice McLachlin stated her view most succinctly: 'She was not a sinner, but a sick person ...' *ibid* at 285.

battery, two found a breach of fiduciary duty, and one found a breach of the duty to treat.[51] Five of the six judges agreed that equitable doctrines applied.[52] Three of the judges found that her consent was vitiated and three judges found that she had consented to the sexual contact.[53]

In the plurality judgment, Justice La Forest, with the concurrence of Justices Cory and Gonthier, reconceptualised the idea of consent by incorporating the power dynamic between the parties to the relationship. He asserted that unconscionability, an equitable doctrine from the law of contracts, needed to be applied to consent to take account of the imbalance in the power relationship between the parties and the illegitimate use of that power.[54] The analysis of the effect of unconscionability on consent is a two-step process. First, inequality is found in the imbalance of power between the parties and the ability to dominate and influence.[55] This usually occurs in the context of a 'power dependency' relationship.[56] Second, exploitation must be found; usually, the type of relationship provides some evidence of this, as do 'community standards of conduct.'[57] Finding unconscionability leads to the conclusion that either the consent was not voluntarily given or that the ability to consent existed, but relief is to be provided on the basis of unconscionability, in the same way the doctrine operates in contracts. Justice La Forest approached the issue from the perspective of voluntariness, but thought that it mattered little which method operated.[58] Justice Sopinka rejected the use of unconscionability in tort law, taking issue with the act of importation from contracts into torts and pointing to a deficiency in its inability to reach the true issue – consent – if it were to operate as it did in contracts.[59] In contracts, unconscionability acts to establish a standard of fairness for setting aside the contract, rather than to vitiate consent.[60] Justice Sopinka also asserts that the idea of community standards, drawn from the commercial area, is irrelevant to the issue of consent.[61]

---

51 *Ibid* at 246-61, 271-93, 311-16.

52 Three justices applied unconscionability to the issue of consent *ibid* at 246-61. Justice McLachlin, with Justice L'Heureux-Dubé concurring, based her judgment on fiduciary duty *ibid* at 268, 271-93. Justice Sopinka found that a doctor-patient duty existed, but declined to characterise the relationship in fiduciary terms or to find a battery *ibid* at 312-13.

53 *Ibid* at 261, 290, 306-07.

54 *Ibid* at 247-48.

55 *Ibid* at 255.

56 Phyllis Coleman, 'Sex in Power Dependency Relationships: Taking Unfair Advantage of the "Fair" Sex' (1988) 53 *Alb L Rev* 95 at p 95. Coleman states that '"[c]onsent" to a sexual relationship obtained in ... a power dependency relationship is inherently suspect and therefore should be legally ineffective' *ibid* at p 96. See also *Norberg v Wynrib ibid* at 256 (stating that evidence of a power dependency relationship provides strong indication of exploitation).

57 *Norberg v Wynrib* [1992] 2 SCR 226 at 256.

58 *Ibid* at 250.

59 *Ibid* at 309-11.

60 *Ibid* at 307-08.

61 *Ibid* at 311.

Applying this analysis to the facts, the plurality judges found that inequality existed, primarily on the basis of Norberg's disability.[62] They also focused on the doctor-patient relationship, which they said was often characterised by an unequal distribution of power.[63] In this case, Dr Wynrib's knowledge of Ms Norberg's vulnerability, his medical knowledge and his authority to prescribe created an imbalance of power.[64] The second element, exploitation, was present because Dr Wynrib failed to treat her addiction and because 'he abused his power over her and exploited the information he obtained concerning her weakness to pursue his own personal interests'.[65] The sex–for–drugs deal diverged from community standards of conduct. The court noted that some, including the task force, view sexual conduct between doctor and patient as inherently exploitative, but held that this situation was a doctor-drug addict case which involved not only sex, but sex-for-drugs.[66] The judges dismissed the argument that Dr Wynrib was a 'lonely old man' who had himself been exploited by the plaintiff by acknowledging that, though Wynrib had his own vulnerabilities, he was the person who had initiated the transaction.[67] *Ex turpi* did not bar recovery because no causal link existed and public policy would not absolve the doctor of liability. In addition, recovery and denial should not operate on the same basis.[68] The plurality judges awarded $20,000 in aggravated compensatory damages and $10,000 in punitive damages; Justice Sopinka concurred only in the award of $20,000 in compensatory damages.[69]

Justice McLachlin, with the concurrence of Justice L'Heureux-Dubé, applied the equitable model of the fiduciary duty to find liability. In their opinion, the breach of the trust between doctor and patient was the quintessential feature of the case.[70] They would have awarded more extensive damages: $20,000 for prolonging the addiction, $25,000 for sexual exploitation, and $25,000 in punitive damages.[71]

Fiduciary duty analysis begins with a structure of inequality within which specific obligations are assessed. Justice McLachlin analysed the fiduciary relationship as one in which the dependency is not all-embracing, but is limited to a specified area. She suggested the entrusting of power over legal affairs or over one's body as examples.[72] Typically, but not invariably, the duty arises out of

---

62   *Ibid* at 257.

63   *Ibid* at 258.

64   *Ibid* at 258-59.

65   *Ibid*.

66   *Ibid* at 260.

67   *Ibid* at 260-61. Perhaps the portrayal of the 70 year old doctor as a lonely old man was nothing more than a stereotypical characterisation of the younger woman as a sexual predator.

68   *Ibid* at 262-63.

69   *Ibid at* 268, 317.

70   *Ibid* at 290-91.

71   *Ibid* at 296, 298, 301.

72   *Ibid at* 272-73.

a voluntary agreement and is dependent upon the undertaking by the fiduciary to act in the beneficiary's best interests.[73] She adopted the influential analysis of Justice Wilson, in dissent in *Frame v Smith*, in which she set out three elements of fiduciary duty: '(1) [t]he fiduciary has scope for the exercise of some discretion or power; (2) [t]he fiduciary can unilaterally exercise that power or discretion so as to affect the beneficiary's legal or practical interests; (3) [t]he beneficiary is peculiarly vulnerable to or at the mercy of the fiduciary holding the discretion or power.'[74] Justice McLachlin said that the doctor-patient relationship 'shares the peculiar hallmark of the fiduciary relationship – trust, the trust of a person with inferior power that another person who has assumed superior power and responsibility will exercise that power for his or her own good and only for his or her good and in his or her best interests'.[75] She went on to say that recognising this fiduciary relationship provides an analytic model to hold physicians to the high standards that trust requires, asserting that '[t]his point has been well made by Jorgensen and Randles in "Time Out: The Statute of Limitations and Fiduciary Theory in Psychotherapist Sexual Misconduct Cases."'[76] She preferred the fiduciary analysis to the application of negligence or contract, which she saw as founded on the assumption of 'independent and equal actors, concerned primarily with their own self-interest'.[77] In contrast, the fiduciary undertakes to act in the best interests of the other: 'The fiduciary relationship has trust, not self-interest, at its core'.[78] Justice McLachlin thought fiduciary duty captured the essence of the harm to the plaintiff while tort and contract law did not[79] – an arguable point.

The most significant aspect of the *Norberg* analysis may be the adoption of a power analysis. Five of six justices concerned themselves with inequality. They recognised that a power imbalance existed for the plaintiff because of her addiction – a socially constructed condition of disadvantage – and because of the structural framework of the doctor-patient relationship and the interactions within it.[80] Three judges laid primary emphasis on the condition and secondary emphasis on the structure, while two others reversed the emphasis. In this way, a

---

73 *Ibid* at 273.

74 *Frame v Smith* [1987] 2 SCR 99 at 136. For the recent history of the Supreme Court of Canada decision making on fiduciary duty, see *ibid* at 271, 274 (McLachlin J); and *ibid* at 312 (Sopinka J); and *McInerney v MacDonald* [1992] 2 SCR 138 at 139 (finding that a patient has a right of access to her own medical records, including those from a third party doctor, based on the fiduciary nature of the physician-patient relationship).

75 *Norberg v Wynrib* [1992] 2 SCR 226 at 272.

76 *Ibid*; and see Linda M Jorgenson and Rebecca M Randles, 'Time Out: The Statute of Limitations and Fiduciary Theory in Psychotherapist Sexual Misconduct Cases' (1991) 44 *Okla L Rev* 181 (recommending that fiduciary theory be employed as the basis for the statute of limitations in cases of psychotherapist sexual misconduct).

77 *Norberg v Wynrib* [1992] 2 SCR 226 at 272.

78 *Ibid* at 274.

79 *Ibid* at 272, 290-91.

80 *Ibid* at 257-58, 292-93.

majority of the court took account of the non-egalitarian dimensions of relationships which affect the behaviour of vulnerable participants, concluding that legal doctrine should recognise these factors. Both judgments are concerned with the exploitation of power. In the minority judgment, vulnerability in the circumstances of the relationship is more important as the source of inequality. Justice McLachlin's nuanced examination of the doctor-patient relationship pointed to the physical vulnerability of exposing one's body, the privacy needs of the patient which create the opportunity for abuse, the patient's lack of expertise, the necessary element of 'submission', the effect of illness, and societal urging to trust doctors.[81] The minority also noted that patients may be vulnerable in other ways, citing with approval Kathleen Morgan's study for the Task Force on Sexual Abuse of Patients.[82] The plurality judgment clearly owes some of its understanding to equality thinking under the Charter of Rights and Freedoms, as it has considered the impact of Laura Norberg's disability on the legal relationship. The concern for equality on the part of five judges is a significant step in the evaluation of doctor-patient transactions. If the consent and battery portion of the judgment achieves acceptance in other courts, it will make an important change in tort law. While tort law is particularly well suited to a recognition of personal circumstances, egalitarian values are not at its core. Incorporation of equality reasoning legitimises consideration of the political and power-related dynamics of context. In spite of the intersection of three conditions of disadvantage – disability, gender and race – however, the plurality judgment focuses on only one. As Mary Eberts, one of the 'founding mothers' of LEAF, has pointed out, the case proceeded on a 'race-neutral basis'; nowhere in the reported judgments is it evident that Laura Norberg is an aboriginal woman, a further and intersecting condition of disadvantage.[83] The plurality judgment is useful in its focus on the undermining of consent through unconscionable use of power. The acknowledgement that autonomy can be undermined by misuse of power has itself considerable potential to reshape consent analysis in battery. Efficacy, the power to effect one's own decisions, is at issue in this judgment. An important limitation on this method of analysis is its declining to adopt zero tolerance.[84] Clearly, some forms of sexual activity in the relationship seem to be permissible under tort law, even with unconscionability. In addition, the incorporation of the imprecise notion of community standards creates the potential for arbitrariness.

---

81 *Ibid* at 278-80.

82 *Ibid* at 279-97. The study indicated that these other factors, such as the position of women, may exacerbate the power imbalance between doctor and patient. Task Force *supra* n 35 at p 12. Justice McLachlin quoted and underlined for emphasis the portion of Professor Morgan's analysis that linked stereotypical gender norms of behaviour to the paternalistic model of the doctor-patient relationship. *Ibid* at 280.

83 Mary Eberts, 'Emerging Legal Issues in Health Care', Presentation to the Third International Conference on Health Law and Ethics in Toronto, Ontario (20 July 1992).

84 *Norberg v Wynrib* [1992] 2 SCR 226 at 260.

The fiduciary analysis has a significant tactical advantage for the plaintiff because consent is not a defence. Any assertion that the patient concurred in the activity is irrelevant and the fiduciary analysis, by implication, adopts something closer to zero tolerance. Justice McLachlin declined to adopt the 'bright, bold line approach' but stated that even though she was taking a more cautious approach as to when sufficient imbalance in power exists, she agreed that, 'where such a power imbalance exists it matters not what the patient may have done, how seductively she may have dressed, how compliant she may have appeared, or how self-interested her conduct may have been – the doctor will be at fault if sexual exploitation occurs'.[85] Once the relationship is identified as a fiduciary one, the doctrine operates to permit recovery without concern for such possible counterforces. This analysis has the ability to capture the dynamics of the relationship. It focuses on power and the abuse of power most clearly. Laura Norberg suffered all of the harms identified by the various judges: violation of her physical integrity and dignitary interest, breach of the trust relationship, and loss of early access to addiction treatment. Whether the most profound loss to her was the violation of her physical integrity and dignitary interest, or the more metaphysical loss in the breach of trust, which led to other harms, is arguable. Justice Sopinka's focus on the loss of the treatment opportunity, in contrast, seems to miss the essence of the transaction entirely, and cannot, as Justice McLachlin pointed out, be related causally to the harm.[86] The fiduciary relationship usefully focuses on the lost benefit, the failure to act with the utmost good faith with respect to the object entrusted, and the breach of the unilateral reliance, but does not focus on the violation of the body, except as the mechanism for power abuse and locus for the harm.

It may be argued that the traditional paternalistic model – that of the doctor benefactor entrusted with responsibility for providing benefits and acting in the best interests of the patient – bears an uncomfortable resemblance to the fiduciary model of interaction. As long as the fiduciary model does not become the archetype, it can play a useful role in patient actions against doctors, leaving room for recognition through other doctrines of more egalitarian and autonomous relations when they occur. As models, these views of the relationship need not be mutually exclusive; instead, they may continue to operate concurrently. The fiduciary model of the transaction, however, does not capture the potential for autonomy in the doctor-patient relationship, ignores the element of decision-making control with which the law empowers the patient, and, in Justice McLachlin's version, cedes too much power to the physician in asserting that, 'a physician takes the power which a patient normally has over her body, and which she [sic] cedes to him [sic] for purposes of

---

85 *Ibid* at 287.
86 *Ibid* at 290-91.

treatment'.[87] It would be preferable to state that patients retain decision-making power over their bodies throughout the transaction, while granting the physician permission to perform a particular treatment.

Laura Norberg's submission to sexual activity to obtain a prescribed product is perhaps atypical, but it does share common elements with other medical transactions. Her situation involved exploitation of power and coercion. Coercion involves denial of choice – that is, determining 'whether it would be fair to insist that someone put up with, or overcome, this kind or degree of psychological pressure'.[88] Ms Norberg's dependency and desperation for a form of physical relief controlled by her doctor is characteristic of the treatment paradigm. In her case, the alternatives were somewhat more foreclosed by the fact that the drug was illegal, but in many medical relationships the doctor is the sole source of treatment; second opinions are uncommon.[89] To most patients, the doctor controls access to medical treatment or potential cure, and vulnerability and dependency exist in both situations.

CONCLUSION

Consider the following example from a short story by Lynne Sharon Schwartz entitled 'So You're Going to Have a New Body!'[90] The woman in the story has agreed to have a hysterectomy for a benign fibroid tumour but has not decided

---

87 *Ibid* at 292-93. In *Hodgkinson v Simms* (1995) 117 DLR (4th) 161 (SCC), the Supreme Court of Canada considered the question of fiduciary duty where an accountant had given financial advice to a client. Justices Sopinka and McLachlin, writing for the three dissenting judges, would find a fiduciary duty only when one party cedes power to the other; vulnerability, in this context, implies dependency and total reliance by the beneficiary on the fiduciary. Where decision-making power is retained, no fiduciary obligation would arise (at 218-19). They noted that a category of relationship, such as the doctor-patient relationship might have fiduciary aspects, without the obligation arising for every act. Justice La Forest, with Justices L'Heureux-Dubé and Gonthier concurring, and Justice Iacobucci concurring in the result and much of the reasoning, found that a fiduciary relationship arose because of the trust, confidence, parties' reasonable expectations, reliance and vulnerability to harm in the relationship, *inter alia*. He commented on the *Norberg* case, stating that:

'Because of the particular context in which the relationship between the plaintiff and the doctor arose in that case, I found it preferable to deal with the case without regard to whether or not a fiduciary relationship arose. However, my colleague Justice McLachlin did dispose of the claim on the basis of the fiduciary duty, and whatever may be said of the peculiar situation in *Norberg*, I have no doubt that had the situation there arisen in the ordinary doctor-patient relationship, it would have given rise to fiduciary obligations: see, for example, *McInerney v MacDonald* (1992) 93 DLR (4th) 415, [1992] 2 SCR 138, 12 CCLT (2d) 225. As is evident from the different approaches taken in *Norberg*, the law's response to the plight of vulnerable people in power-dependency relationships gives rise to a variety of often overlapping duties' (at 178).

88 Jerome E Bickenbach, 'Critical Notice' (1990) 20 *Can J Phil* 577p 598 (reviewing Alan Wertheimer's *Coercion* (1987)).

89 See Perri Klass, *A Not Entirel Benign Procedure. Four Years as a Medical Student* (1987) at pp 146–51 (describing how doctors' power issues lead to territorial treatment of patients).

90 Lynne Sharon Schwartz, 'So You're Going to Have a New Body' in *The Melting Pot and Other Subversive Stories* (1987) 42.

whether to allow the surgeon to remove her ovaries at the same time. In response to her indecision, her doctor advises:

> The decision is entirely up to you. However, I like to take the ovaries out whenever I can, as long as I'm in there, that way there is no danger of ovarian cancer, which strikes one in a hundred women in your age group. There is really nothing you need your ovaries for.[91]

She thinks to herself that, according to his logic, 'he could cut off my head to avert a brain tumour'.[92] Later, he shows her a colour photo of benign fibroid tumours. She nods, and leaves to throw up.[93] Before surgery, he describes the terrible death one has with ovarian cancer and points out a beautiful but ravaged woman with ovarian cancer.[94] The next morning, in a 'Demerol haze', in answer to the doctor's, 'Well?' she says, inevitably, 'Take them, they're yours'.[95]

Lois Nixon and Delese Wear, discussing Schwartz's story, conclude:

> What we've witnessed is not coercion, exactly. But the doctor's subtle barrage of 'facts', always wedged between repetitions of 'It's your decision', of course, hit the target of her vulnerability and fear. In her drugged state where her ovaries were equated with a 'horrible death', what other decision could she have made? Schwartz's fiction reminds readers of the often subtle, sometimes wily, and always powerful influences of the words that pass between doctor and patient.[96]

The doctor seems to have disclosed the material risks of not proceeding, and a court might well find that a reasonable patient in her shoes would have accepted this option. The vulnerability of the patient facing pain, the unknown and an invasion of part of her body that affects her identity as a woman is set in counterpoint to the sophisticated manipulation by the doctor – perhaps well intentioned, but certainly insensitive – that undermines true consent. Instead of informed consent, we see acquiescence, submission, bowing to pressure and gender inequality in a relationship of power.

In the legal governance of medical relationships, I suggest that the feminist goals of equality, affirmation of difference, control of our bodies, and avoidance of harm can and should catalyse doctrinal change. In the area of sexual abuse by doctors of patients, I have examined the decision in *Norberg v Wynrib* to illustrate how such doctrinal change can occur.

---

91   *Ibid* at p 43.

92   *Ibid.*

93   *Ibid.*

94   *Ibid* at p 44.

95   *Ibid.*

96   Lois LaCivita Nixon and Delese Wear, 'They Will Put It Together/and Take It Apart: Fiction and Informed Consent' (1991) 19 *Law Med & Health Care* 291 at p 292 (recounting Lynne Sharon Schwartz's story and advocating the use of fiction to examine the relationship of communicating and caring between the doctor and patient).

The law must recognise that equality underpins freedom of choice. Without equality, autonomous decision-making and control of our own bodies will remain a myth.

CHAPTER FIVE

BEING HERE – WHAT A WOMAN CAN SAY ABOUT LAND LAW

KATE GREEN

INTRODUCTION

Starting

I first started writing this chapter when I was at a theoretical seminar in London. The two papers – on feminism and law – were both given by women. I sat there in a chair which was too big for me, the table too high for me to write on with comfort. My feet did not reach the ground. We were surrounded by gold-framed portraits of dead white men. I saw myself there as the Ultimate Feminine Article. In the 'Are there any questions?', I heard men speak first, and almost exclusively thereafter, about their ideas about the papers, and to me the discussion tended to centre on what the men had said, rather than on what the women had said. I recognise that my whiteness and my Englishness empower my voice – not all my lives are marginal – but I ran away at the break for tea.

Some days after that, Hilary came into my room at work on her way to a meeting with the man next door. We talked about what we were each thinking and writing towards this book, and during our conversation she looked around the door to our male colleague and called out to him, 'I'm here!'

I'm here too! I want to focus on the fact that I know that I can speak, that I can speak what I know as a woman, and on what I know when I pass as a man. Even though I and my knowledges may be devalued, ignored, stolen, I am here and speaking. Yes, I know I am caught – and I catch myself – in the glass cage of being a woman in His world but still I know that I know. I can inhabit an unknown land and it is one from which I can write:

> *... women are both inside and outside gender, at once within and without representation ... Feminism has produced, at least for feminists, a political-personal consciousness of gender as an ideological construct which defines the social subject; in thus en-gendering the subject and in en-gendering the subject as political, feminism understands the female subject as one that ... is not either 'in ideology' or outside ideology (eg in science), but rather is at once inside and outside the ideology of gender, or, as I have used the terms, is at once woman and women. In other words, woman is inside the rectangle, women are outside; the female subject is in both places at once.[1]*

---

1   Teresa de Lauretis, *Technologies of Gender: Essays on Theory, Film and Fiction* (1987) Macmillan at p 14. See too Marilyn Frye, *The Politics of Reality: Essays in Feminist Theory* (1983) Crossing Press at p 167: 'Women's existence is both absolutely necessary to and irresolvably problematic for the dominant reality and ... those committed to it, for our existence is *presupposed* by phallocratic reality, but it is not and cannot be *encompassed* by or countenanced by that reality. Women's existence is a background against which phallocratic reality is a foreground.'

I am here and elsewhere. I know/write/speak both inside and outside masculine knowledge and academic life. I have many choices: for example, I can choose to write as a Man; or speak from a Woman's place. I can also be in both places at once: for example, if I choose to speak like a Man, I can choose at the same time not to care if my words are passed over or if my ideas are translated or appropriated without my consent. Being in more places than one, I have more choices. Even in a space where the potential violence of competition and ownership appear to dominate, I still can make choices: 'Here again we revert to the task of decolonising the mind through negotiating with structures of violence'.[2]

At the same time I know the possibility of choosing to fight.

Land law may be claimed to be made in Man's image in its construction and self-conception, in its aims, methods and understanding of the world. In this light, in order to 'be a land lawyer', I must be disembodied pure intellect floating in space, my end in life to provide certainty to self-interested Men of Property. This may seem to be a land where women (I) do not and cannot exist beyond His definition of them (me). Nevertheless, I'm enjoying being here.

Questions

Can I say anything? Or write? Or know anything? Sometimes I feel I am breathing in an end of century and recessionary aimlessness, hopelessness, powerlessness, and breathing out Nothing. The echoes of the voices of Dead Masters ultimately can create in me a deathly silence. So, for today, I have decided that I don't want to talk with the corpses: today I'm going to write with and for women. It may be that, if I choose not to enter the deathly conversation, it will be as if I am not speaking: 'the objection to leaving male theory behind expresses a real fear of being silenced: unless you read/write/speak [like] the boys, no one will listen to you'.[3] So be it: Mary O'Brien quoted E M Forster's comment that 'squirrels might be in tune with the universe but are intelligible only to other squirrels'. Today squirrels. Tomorrow the world.[4]

Essentially (ha!), I am choosing a different place in which to speak today because I do not feel sure that I can say anything new using His Masters' Tools, which, as Audre Lorde has pointed out, may only be able to reproduce themselves:

> For the master's tools will never dismantle the master's house. They may allow
> us temporarily to beat him at his own game, but they will never enable us to

---

2   Gayatri Chakravorty Spivaks *Outside in the Teaching Machine* (1993) Routledge, in her essay 'French Feminism Revisited' at p 171.

3   Somer Brodribb, *Nothing Mat(t)ers: A Feminist Critique of Postmodernism* (1992) Spinifex Press at p xxviii. See too Dale Spender, 'The Gatekeepers: a Feminist Critique of Academic Publishing' in Helen Roberts (ed), *Doing Feminist Research* (1981) Routledge at p 186, who refers to 'the structural exclusion of those groups whose values and beliefs do not always coincide with the values and beliefs of the gatekeepers' at p 190.

4   Mary O'Brien, *Reproducing the World: Essays in Feminist Theory* (1989) Westview Press at p x.

bring about genuine change. And this fact is only threatening to those women who still define the master's house as their only source of support.[5]

I may use the occasional screw from his box of tricks if I feel so inclined, but I have not, Reader, I married him. (I stress that this is just my choice today; on other days I have made and probably will make other choices.)

Can I say what I know? A woman? Do I only know/write/speak in a glass cage of my sex, gender, bearing in mind that: 'The construction of gender is the product and the process of both representation and self-representation'?[6]

Since at least the time of Descartes, Woman – that is, I, me, myself – is by His definition unable to know anything: Man's rational self-cognition is based on His belief in Woman's irrationality.[7] Therefore, Man's knowledge is what is worth knowing: 'Men come to consciousness, but women come to nothing'.[8]

I do not think: therefore I am not. They know I know nothing, so their conversations render me speechless, make sure 'feminist thinking' is:

> ... 'always already' inscribed in the 'political unconscious' of dominant cultural discourses and their underlying 'master narratives' ... and so will tend to reproduce itself, to retextualize itself ... even in feminist rewritings of cultural narratives.[9]

Even if women do find a way to speak themselves, they will be subordinate to man's judgment. Cynthia Hill quoted a typical comment: 'We've gone through the logical arguments, let's have the feminist perspective'.[10]

As a result, as Mary O'Brien concluded: '... the litany of great names is too often allowed to set the limits of what can be known.'[11]

Masculine knowing characterises itself as rational, self-interested, hierarchical and, above all, abstracted from His emotional life and physical body, being concerned with the fittest ideas in a competitive market. In His book, feminine (un)knowing is inevitably His converse: intimate, natural, material, emotional. (Of course, this only refers to one feminine: that attributed to the wives of the Masters. Servants, women of other races and sexualities are beyond the two sides of the modern coin of knowledge). Evelyn Fox Keller describes how scientists – the most rigorous and masculine of all western 'knowers' – perceive their

---

5   Audre Lorde, 'His Master's Tools Will Never Dismantle His Master's House' in Cherrie Moraga and Gloria Anzaldua (eds), *This Bridge Called My Back: Writings by Radical Women of Color* (1981) Kitchen Table Press at p 99.

6   de Lauretis (1987) *supra* n 1 at p 10.

7   See for example, Deborah L Rhode (ed), *Theoretical Perspectives on Sexual Difference* (1990) Yale University Press; Moira Gatens, *Feminism and Philosophy: Perspectives on Difference and Equality* (1991) Polity Press; Genevieve Lloyd, *The Man of Reason: 'Male' and 'Female' in Western Philosophy* (1984) Methuen.

8   Brodribb (1992) *supra* n 3 at p 72.

9   de Lauretis (1987) *supra* n 1 at p 1.

10   Quoted by Cynthia Hill, 'Sexual Bias in the Law School Classroom: One Student's Perspective' (1988) *Jo Leg Ed* at p 603.

11   (1989) at p 252.

knowledge: 'Having divided the world into two parts – the knower (mind) and the knowable (nature) – scientific ideology goes on to prescribe a very specific relation between the two ... Not only are mind and nature assigned gender, but in characterising scientific and objective thought as masculine, the very activity by which the knower can acquire knowledge is also genderized. It is that between a subject and an object radically divided ... masculine ... connotes, as it so often does, autonomy, separation and distance.'[12]

'I' is never there. 'I' – or I – become not only a non-knower, but inevitably the far away object of His knowing as He floats, distantly, above the earth.[13] Roberto Calasso, from a different perspective, writes of the modern 'capacity for control', the readiness 'to take advantage of any opportunity that presents itself' implicit in this view of the world.[14]

In one of the most popular novels of the 19th century,[15] the path of true love finally runs smooth in the lives of Ellen and John. This is how they react to their newly developed consciousness of a shared love:

> Ellen sat down, and bowing her head on the arm of the sofa wept with all the vehement passion of her childhood, quivering from head to foot with convulsive sobs. John might guess from the outpouring now how much her heart had been secretly gathering for months past. For a little while he walked up and down the room; but this excessive agitation he was not willing should continue. He said nothing; sitting down beside Ellen on the sofa, quietly possessed himself of one of her hands; and when in her excitement the hand struggled to get away again, it was not permitted. Ellen understood that very well and immediately checked herself.[16]

He knows Himself as above and beyond me in the strength of his Intellect. Ironically, however, it is perhaps the weight of His great intellect which pulls His skull downwards, bowing His back under its brainy burden. His head is forced down towards His knees. What does He see then? There, before His eyes, hangs His sexuality: the over-weighted head causes His gaze to be fixed on His penis. How interesting. And I am supposed to be dependent on His obsession with this organ for my writing/knowing/speaking, His pinned butterfly?

---

12 Evelyn Fox Keller, *Reflections on Gender and Science* (1985) Yale University Press at p 79. See too her explanation of the social hierarchy which results at p 92.

13 See Donna Haraway for her description of the spaceman floating knowledgeably above the earth in *Simians, Cyborgs and Women: The Reinvention of Nature* (1991) Free Association Books. Also: 'One of the most resistant features of scholarship is the division between object and subject: the absence of the language of subjectivity, and in particular the "I" from "serious" scholarly work ... We employ all sorts of circumlocutions in order to ensure that our persons do not invade our work ...', Margaret Davies, 'Feminist Appropriations: "Law, Property and Personality"' (1994) *Social and Legal Studies* 365 at p 366. (It may be that men are able to be simultaneously disembodied and sexed male because they take their bodies for granted as the norm: the body is so forgotten as to become invisible. Alternatively – and more plausibly – they are so fearful of their bodies' decay that they repress all consciousness of it.)

14 Roberto Calasso, *The Marriage of Cadmus and Harmony* (1994) Vintage at p 230. He continues: 'But for all this 360-degree field of vision, there remains a black speck, a point that the eye cannot see – itself.'

15 Susan Warner, *The Wide, Wide World* (1987) The Feminist Press, first published 1850.

16 At p 560.

In His world, power is produced by His knowledge, and negativity produces nothing,[17] so I am silent and ignorant and ever the object of His power:

> Once satisfied to control her body and her movements, once pleased to create images of her and then order her body to conform, the Master of Discourse now aspires to the most divine of tasks: to create her in his image, which is ultimately to annihilate her.[18]

Am I annihilated?

Sometimes I speak gruffly in order to sound like a man, but I know that I am often patted on the head and then ignored. Gillian Rose remarked of her 'fellow' geographers:

> ... feminism remains outside the project of geography. Feminists have engaged with several of the key debates in the discipline since the late 1970s ... I have had to represent these encounters not as a series of conversations between equals, but more as a series of brush-offs ... Feminism's concerns are never wholly acknowledged by the geographical arguments with which it engages, and geography continues virtually to disregard feminist theory ... there is hardly ever a sustained engagement with feminist work.[19]

Alternatively, what I say may be adopted without acknowledgement by a masculine knowledge which has no respect for my copyright.[20] If a woman gives a seminar paper, I observe Man listening. At the end, the 'Are there any questions?' opens a masculine space in which He takes over the 'conversation', and I seem merely to respond to His words, with a proper deference.

Annihilated as Woman and made to disappear as Man.

Can I say anything about the law, the ultimate abstract truth? Some legal scholars feel they live on the margins of the law. For Peter Goodrich not much has changed perhaps since the time of medieval legal anti-intellectualism:

---

17   de Lauretis (1987) *supra* n 1 at p 35. And see too Julia Kristeva: 'On a deeper level, however, a woman cannot "be"; it is something which does not even belong in the order of *being*. It follows too that a feminist practice can only be negative at odds with what already exists so that we may say, "that's not it", and, "that's still not it"' in Elaine Marks and Isabelle de Courtivron (eds), *New French Feminisms: An Anthology* (1981) Schocken Books at p 137.

18   Brodribb (1992) *supra* n 3 at pp xvi and xviii. See too her comments on modern French philosophers at p 81.

19   Gillian Rose, *Feminism and Geography: the Limits of Geographical Knowledge* (1993) Polity Press at p 3.

20   See too Beverley Thiele, 'Vanishing Acts in Social and Political Thought: Tricks of the Trade' in C Pateman and E Gross (eds), *Feminist Challenges: Social and Political Theory* (1986) Allen and Unwin at p 30. And Frye (1983) at p 165: '... the concept of the species [man] ... is one according to which there are no females of the species ... Man understands his own perception as simultaneously generating and being generated by a point of view. Man is understood to author names; men have a certain status as points of intellectual and perceptual origin. In so far as the phallocratic scheme permits the understanding that women perceive at all, it features women's perceptions as passive, repetitive of men's perception, nonauthoritative'. As Calasso remarked, 'The eye cannot see itself' (1994) *supra* n 14 at p 230.

> The lawyers hated the 'fine university men'; they explicitly denied that a good scholar could ever make a good lawyer ... There is, in other words, no room or place ... for an independent scholarship of law ...[21]

Especially unlikely must be a legal scholar in a 'new' university: a concept as suspect to the great owners of knowledge as new money buying up the land in previous centuries. As a woman I am even less plausible, suspended in the margins of the margins. If I write law I must do so as a male scholar, from the 'God's eye-view'[22] for law is claimed to be a science. The inheritors of Bentham's legacy of legal positivism, immaculately conceived out of his legal science, today's law teachers are born and grow into a masculine concept of what it is to write, speak or know the law:

> In this traditional representation the discipline of law is always, in the last instance, an enterprise in strict reason or logic, and human social behaviour is correspondingly, in its most basic principles at least, to be viewed legally as the consequence of reasoned intentions and explicitly formulated goals.[23]

Law judges, it is said, from an objective and rational standpoint; similarly, law is judged from this standpoint, according to its fitness for its purpose. In the modern world, judging means a rational masculine testing and nothing else. In addition, rational judgment is reinforced by a penetrating academic style in which there is never a hint of uncertainty (oh no!): it permits no inconclusive endings, and very few controversial conclusions. It accretes layer upon layer of rule and exception and lists of examples.[24] As Evelyn Fox Keller knows, this seems to pose an impossible problem to a woman (in the following quotation I have changed 'scientist' to 'lawyer'):

> ... any [lawyer] who is not a man walks a path bounded on one side by inauthenticity and on the other by subversion. Just as surely as inauthenticity is the cost a woman suffers by joining men in misogynist jokes, so it is, equally, the

---

21 Peter Goodrich, *Languages of Law: from Logics of Memory to Nomadic Masks* (1990) Weidenfeld & Nicolson at p 22.

22 Sandra Harding remarks on this: 'I am arguing for politics and epistemologies of location, positioning and situating, where partiality and not universality is the condition of being heard to make rational knowledge claims ... I am arguing for the view from a body, always a complex, contradictory, structuring and structured body, versus the view from above, from nowhere, from simplicity. Only the god trick is forbidden', *The Privilege of Partial Perspective* (1988) F S 575.

23 Peter Goodrich, *Reading the Law: a Critical Introduction to Legal Method and Techniques* (1986) Blackwell at p 209. See also Ngaire Naffine, *Law and the Sexes: Explorations in Feminist Jurisprudence* (1990) Allen and Unwin, and Lynne Henderson's review of Eisenstein, MacKinnon and Smart (1991) 25 *Law and Soc Rev* 411.

24 See for example, E H Burns, *Cheshire and Burns' Modern Law of Real Property* (1994, 15th edn) Butterworths who deals at p 372 with the *Prudential* decision ([1992] 3 WLR 279, and see below) as a simple restatement of an ancient principle (but compare Gray's treatment in *Elements of Land Law* (1993, 2nd edn) Butterworths at pp 687-96). Other typical examples are lists of leasehold covenants which do, or do not, touch and concern the land, or of easements which 'lie in grant'. In practice too, the method of law seems masculine: see, for example, Leslie Bender, 'A Lawyer's Primer on Feminist Theory and Tort' (1988) *Jo Leg Ed* 3 at p 7, or Rand Jack and Dana Crowley Jack, *Moral Vision and Professional Decisions: the Changing Values of Women and Men Lawyers* (1989) Cambridge Universiy Press.

cost suffered by a woman who identifies with an image of the [lawyer] modelled on the patriarchal husband ... Her alternative is to attempt a radical redefinition of terms.[25]

So, if I don't write/know/speak law as He does then, according to the legal geographers, I am not on the map. And if I speak law like a Man, where am I?

Can I say anything about land law? Of all academic law pigeonholes, property law (and its exemplar, land law) is the epitome of a masculine knowledge. It is perceived as one of the most difficult of the core subjects, one of the most rigorous, that requires a love of maths, an aptitude for chess;[26] the abstract play of interests in land is a war-game for minds.

Writing as a woman academic land lawyer, from the margins of the margins, I am very aware of land as a subject at the core of the law, but, like Gillian Rose, I note my invisibility everywhere in the field. I do not exist as a land owner: there are no official statistics on the ownership of land by women, or on the value of their shares in land, their dispossessions or evictions.[27] Women are hidden in the shadows of their fathers, husbands or sons. When women creep out from these shadows, they find themselves trapped by property law: if they choose to be (as in fact they often are) financially dependent and unknowing of the market place, they will be treated as Woman (and not fully human). If they choose to appear as land owners, then they are judged as Men. Thus, from the recent decisions in *Barclays Bank plc v O'Brien*[28] and *CIBC Mortgages plc v Pitt*,[29] it seems that I must be either Woman, and protected by the courts for child-like ignorance and weakness, or Man, judged as having acted as an autonomous and self-interested individual. Neither of these recognises the experiences of many women or their partners or mortgagees.

Commentators have seen land law's function as providing the 'certainty' essential to the smooth running of the market: conveyancing must be facilitated so that rational men know where they stand.[30] Reason is seen to demand that the needs of property owners, self-interested and rational individuals in the

---

25 (1985) *supra* n 12 at pp 174-75.

26 ' ... a game of chess, even if played by dilettantes, is an austere metaphor of life and a struggle for life, and the chess player's virtues – reason, memory and invention – are the virtues of every thinking man. The stern rule of chess, according to which the piece that was touched must be moved, and it is not permissible to re-do a move of which one repents, reproduces the inexorability of the choices of the living', Primo Levi, *Other People's Trades* (1991) Abacus at p 133.

27 I can find no statistics on the presence of women as directors of building firms or building societies. I can think of several explanations for this, all of them demonstrating the invisible exclusion of women.

28 [1993] 4 All ER 417, HL.

29 [1993] 4 All ER 433, HL.

30 For example, in *Ashburn Anstalt v Arnold* [1989] 1 Ch 1, CA: 'The vice of uncertainty in relation to the duration of a [leasehold] term is that the parties do not know where they stand. Put another way, the court does not know what to enforce ...', *per* Fox LJ at 12. See below for more on this case.

market place, override the needs of those who are different: weaker or poorer, or in a different way defined as Other.[31] Thus, the effect of the cases in the last paragraph, for example, is not merely the chance result of case law, for, as Margaret Davies argued:

> ... the law constructs itself precisely by excluding that which is considered non-legal; the right of property is founded primarily on the right to control and exclude; and 'right' itself – the right way of doing things ...

> The 'rightness' of objectivity, rationality, scientificity and independence ... obtains its force from the exclusion of a culturally devalued 'feminine' or wrong way ...[32]

Anyone who is not seen by land law to be an autonomous, self-interested actor in the market place is thereby excluded. The notion of 'property' requires that a hierarchy of inside and outside is created and maintained. As Woman, I'm improper, excluded by the very foundations of land law.

Land law's method is also, inevitably, described as a scientific analysis, an ordering of the raw materials of the law into a hierarchy of 'interests in land'; it has been labelled by John Dewar as 'conceptual formalism'.[33] I am excluded both by method and content.

Land law's perception of the real world is also masculine:

> Concepts of place and space are implicitly gendered in geographical discourse. Place is understood by humanistic geographers in terms of maternal Woman – nurturing, natural, but forever lost. In stark contrast, the discourse of time-geography depends on a transparent space, which refers only to the public space of Western hegemonic masculinity'.[34]

'The land' in land law has been transformed from a local, physical and emotional or spiritual understanding of *place* to alienated, intellectual information about *space* – a 'transparent' 'infinitely knowable', 'real, natural and unproblematic' space[35] reduced to paper both in the form of maps and of documents of title, now the land register.

From a different starting point, Alain Pottage refers to alienation (or 'delocalisation') by bureaucratisation:

---

31 In this light, in *Williams & Glyns Bank Ltd v Boland* [1981] AC 487 and the subsequent cases, the building societies/banks etc always won because they are the rational individuals in the market, while the occupiers are other.

32 (1994) *supra* n 13 at p 376. I like the quotation, but I do have problems with the notion of 'law' as a person which constructs itself: 'the law' is just an idea in my head, our heads, which we build by adding or subtracting here and there, by describing bits of it in different ways.

33 John Dewar, 'Licences and Land Law: An Alternative View' (1986) 49 MLR 741.

34 Rose (1993) *supra* n 19 at p 62, argues convincingly that, in geography, both these senses of space and place are the tools of masculine knowing: even the apparently feminine *place* arises from a masculine definition of the feminine.

35 Rose (1993) *supra* n 19 at p 38.

Registration extricated land from the network of relations and understanding which formed the 'local knowledge' of different communities, relocated it on an abstract geometric map, and deciphered it according to a highly conventionalised topographic code. This process marked a transformation of the idea of land in law: property ceased to be a contractual construct and became a bureaucratic artifact.[36]

Whereas, at an earlier time:

Titles could be traded as commodities only because purchasers persuaded themselves to trust in local knowledge. The continuity and coherence of this resource of memory was an undeclared presupposition of many conveyancing contracts. What was presupposed was a necessarily local sense of where rights began and ended, a local sense of place and property.[37]

Pottage's identification of land law's transformation from local to bureaucratic knowledge can equally be seen as a distancing from the material and subjectively known (feminine) *place* to an intellectual and objective (masculine) *space*.

Thus, even if the landscape be conceptualised as feminine, land law creates a space in which my only place is in the shadows, excluded from what is proper as the silent, irrational wife of the properly logical land lawyer.

THE MASCULINE IN LAND LAW

Introduction

From the above, it is clear that land law can be represented as a typically masculine pursuit. The land lawyer's object is to provide certainty by manipulating scientifically derived and maintained classifications of 'interests in land'. This certainty, predictability, is necessary to facilitate the activities of rational, autonomous actors in the market place. The purpose of studying land law is to become a conveyancer, laboratory technician to Men of Property. Each of these 'scientific' classifications – whether leases, mortgages, or easements – has its own sets of definitions, exceptions and examples. Beyond and before these are the rules relating to their creation and transfer, for alienability is one of the necessary characteristics of 'property': that is, being the object of bargains in the market is the essence of that which is proper. The rules governing creation and alienability are the closest academic land law comes to conveyancing: they include the rules about contracts and deeds, land registration and the registration of charges. The physical land itself is far remote from these rules, whether they are of the 'creative/transferring' kind or 'definitional'. It is on all these rules that the land lawyer's conclusions as to hierarchy in any given situation depend.

---

36 Alain Pottage, 'The Measure of Land' (1994) 57 MLR 361 at p 363.
37 At p 364.

Herein lies the analogy with chess, for an interest in land is only as powerful as its position in relation to the whole space.[38]

I have chosen two examples of land law's masculine pursuit of certainty. Both concern temporal certainty: the moment of sale of an interest in land and the predicted date of death of a lease. My first is s 2 Law of Property (Miscellaneous Provisions) Act 1989, setting out the primary conditions necessary for the transfer of any interest in land. My second is the rule that a lease must be of maximum certain duration from the moment of its birth, recently restated in *Prudential Assurance Co Ltd v London Residuary Body*.[39] Section 2 is part of the formal regulation of the market in land, a general policing of buying and selling, while the rule concerning the end of a lease is a paradigm of Dewar's conceptual formalism.[40]

It can be argued that much of land law is merely an extension of the law of contract, and that the rules analysed here are no exception. Section 2 can be seen as a part of the rules relating to the formation of contracts and a lease is merely a particular form of contract.

Buying and selling land

Contracts for the sale of land come into being gradually. Traditionally, there is first the offer, followed by negotiation of the terms, and then the coming-together in contract, and finally the relief of completion. It is the moment of the coming-together in contract which is governed by s 2.

The section was passed following a Law Commission Report which concluded that the then existing law (s 40 Law of Property Act 1925, supplemented by the equitable doctrine of part performance) was too confused and uncertain effectively to govern the market in land, and contained the potential for injustice.[41]

The section states:

(1) A contract for the sale or other disposition of an interest in land can only be made in writing and only by incorporating all the terms which the parties have expressly agreed in one document or, where contracts are exchanged, in each.

(2) The terms may be incorporated in a document either by being set out in it or by reference to some other document.

---

38 Brodribb *supra* n 3 (1992) argues that 'the will to certainty is a denial of castration' at p 127. Castration is not frightening to *me*.

39 [1992] 3 WLR 279.

40 *Supra* n 33.

41 'Formalities for Contracts for Sale etc of Land' *Law Com No 164* (1987) para 1.10. For an academic lawyer, it is hard to think of any rule of which this could not be said.

(3) The document incorporating the terms or, where contracts are exchanged, one of the documents incorporating them (but not necessarily the same one) must be signed by or on behalf of each party to the contract.

The section thus requires a certain distance and formality: the whole agreement concerning an interest in land is to be put in writing and signed by both sides. Without this, there is no contract, no matter what the parties may assume.[42] Within the frame of reference of the Law Commission, this extremely formal rule offered the advantages of certainty and simplicity and (therefore) justice. It would thus appear to demonstrate that land law does indeed require a masculine distance – formality – and certainty.

All the cases decided on the section have interpreted it restrictively; in each of them, the contract in question was deemed not to be subject to the rule. In the first, *Spiro v Glencrown Properties Ltd*,[43] the contract was the result of an option to purchase. Hoffmann J held that the *grant* of the option was the relevant contract for s 2; the exercise of the option was a unilateral action, and there was 'no conceivable reason why Parliament should have required … additional formality'.[44]

In the next case, *Record v Bell*,[45] there was a contract in writing and signed as required by the section, but then a further written agreement was made in order to speed up completion. By this later agreement the seller guaranteed his title to the buyer. However, it failed to incorporate all the terms of the contract, and so, when the buyer tried to avoid completing the sale, he relied on failure to comply with s 2. Judge Paul Baker QC held that this later agreement was a 'collateral contract' which did not in fact directly concern any 'interest in land' (although it directly concerned a contract for such an interest). For this reason, there was no failure to comply with s 2 and the buyer could not escape.

In the third case, *Pitt v PHH Asset Management Ltd*,[46] Pitt and the seller orally agreed, that in order to end what was effectively an auction for a house, the seller would 'lock out' any other buyers for two weeks. In exchange, Pitt would exchange contracts within that period. The seller nevertheless sold to another buyer at a higher price, and pleaded failure to satisfy s 2 as a defence to Pitt's action for damages. Both the county court and the Court of Appeal held that this was a 'lock-out' agreement which did not concern any 'interest in land' and therefore was not subject to s 2. Pitt gained his damages.

---

42 The section does not apply to contracts for the sale of land which have been completed (*Tootal Clothing Ltd v Guinea Properties Ltd* (1992) 64 P & Cr 452) and, of course, equitable doctrines (the creation of trusts being excluded from the operation of s 2) may resolve hard cases.
43 [1991] 2 WLR 931.
44 At 933.
45 (1991) 62 P & CR 192.
46 [1993] 4 All ER 961, CA.

All three cases, explained thus, demonstrate the clarity and simplicity of the section. Wherever a contract for any interest in land is claimed, writing of all the terms and all signatures are essential. However, some contracts are outside the section (those which do not directly concern an interest in land, although they may enable such a contract to be created). The chaos of the market is logically, predictably and – therefore – justly ordered.

Death of a lease

A lease enables the sharing of enjoyment of land for a 'slice of time': it formally divides the physical use and the investment potential of the land for a limited period. As with s 2 of the 1989 Act, the rules assume that rational individuals dealing in the market need formal, arm's length rules in order to co-exist. The 1925 legislation restricted leases to those for 'a term of years absolute',[47] which are defined (or rather, described) in s 205(1)(xxvii):

> 'Term of years absolute' means a term of years ... either certain or liable to determination by notice, reentry, operation of law or by a provision for cesser on redemption, or in any other event (other than the dropping of a life, or the determination of a determinable life interest) ...

This was expressed more clearly by Lord Greene MR in *Lace v Chantler*:

> A term created by a leasehold tenancy agreement must be expressed either with certainty and specifically or by reference to something which can, at the time when the lease takes effect, be looked to as a certain ascertainment of what the term is meant to be.[48]

In that case, the parties believed they had created a term of years 'for the duration of the war'. The Court of Appeal held that this could not be a term of years absolute, since the date of the war's ending could not be predicted when the lease came into effect.[49] However, since the tenant was occupying the premises and paying a weekly rent, the court held that the parties had, rather, created an implied legal weekly tenancy.

This case was distinguished by the Court of Appeal in *In Re Midland Rly Co's Agreement*.[50] Here the lease was a half-yearly periodic tenancy, with provision for three months' notice. However, the lease stated that the landlord could not give notice unless it required the property for its own use. The question of whether this was a term of years absolute arose when the landlord gave notice, not in

---

47 Leases for lives, effectively freehold estates rather than leaseholds, were specially provided for in the new regime, see s 149(6) Law of Property Act 1925.

48 [1944] 1 KB 368 at 370.

49 This inconvenient result was reversed by Parliament in the Validation of Wartime Leases Act 1944: under s 1(1), such a lease 'shall have effect as if it granted ... a term of 10 years, subject to a right exercisable either by the landlord or the tenant to determine the tenancy, if the war ends before the expiration of that term, by at least one month's notice in writing given after the end of the war'.

50 [1971] 1 Ch 725.

order to use the property itself, but in order to obtain a higher rent than that agreed originally 50 years before.[51]

The Court of Appeal here stated that *Lace v Chantler* only applied to a term expressed to be for a period, but did not apply to a periodic tenancy:

> If *Lace v Chantler* had been a case in which there was simply a periodic tenancy with a proviso that the landlord would not give notice during the continuance of the war, this court might not have concluded that such an agreement, which would of course have left the tenant free to determine on notice at any time, was inoperative to create a leasehold. There is nothing in the reasoning of the judgments to lead to the necessary conclusion that such must have been so.[52]

He explained that in the case of periodic tenancies, the maximum duration will never be known at the outset: a weekly tenancy may last 50 years. For this reason, the rule about 'terminal certainty'[53] 'cannot have direct reference to periodic tenancies'.[54] The parties had therefore successfully created a periodic term of years absolute and, further, the proviso against the landlord giving notice was also valid.

This was followed in a more recent decision: *Ashburn Anstalt v Arnold*.[55] The parties created what they called a licence without payment of any rent, but the court held that this was a lease without rent because the 'licensee' had exclusive possession of the premises.[56] Further, they had created a lease despite the fact that the term in some lights appeared uncertain: the landlord could give a quarter's notice but only when it required the land for redevelopment. The court held that there was sufficient certainty here: there was a quarterly lease, but the landlord was simply prevented from giving notice unless certain conditions were met:

> The result in our opinion, is that the arrangement could be brought to an end by both parties in circumstances which are free from uncertainty in the sense that there would be no doubt whether the determining event had occurred ... We do not see why the mere absence of a formula referring to a periodic tenancy or occupancy should alter the position.[57]

---

51   The real problem in this case, as in others, was the failure originally to provide for rent reviews.

52   Russell LJ at 732.

53   Gray (1993) at p 687 n 4. Also: 'The certainty of term principle is fundamentally the expression of a property-oriented view of the leasehold relationship; it articulates the concern that property rights should be both discrete and defined' at p 688.

54   Russell LJ at 732.

55   [1989] 1 Ch 1, CA. *Birrell v Carey* (1989) 58 P & CR 184, CA presents somewhat similar facts. There was a lease without rent, originally 'until the company ceases trading' but later amended to a twelve year period. The original agreement could not have been a lease, as it was uncertain, but the amendment brought it within the rule. Interestingly, the case might have been lost because of the absence of writing (under the precursor of s 2 Law of Property (Miscellaneous Provisions) Act 1989), but it was not pleaded (at 187).

56   Following *Street v Mountford* [1985] AC 809, HL.

57   Fox LJ at 12.

The House of Lords in *Prudential* disapproved of both these latter cases.[58] Here, a strip of land was let in 1930 to the defendant on a yearly rent. The only provision for notice was that the landlord could end the lease by two months' notice if it required the land for a road-widening project. (As in the *Midland Rly* case, the real reason for wishing to end the term was to increase the rent.) The House of Lords concluded:

> The term expressed to be granted by the agreement in the present case does not fall within this definition ... When the agreement in the present case was made, it failed to grant an estate in the land.[59]

It was however held that, as in *Lace v Chantler*, there was an implied *periodic* tenancy since the tenant was in occupation and paying a regular (here, yearly) rent. The House held that to enforce the provision that the landlord could not give notice except for road widening would 'make nonsense' of the certainty rule; further it was incompatible with a yearly tenancy, the 'essence' of which was that both sides could give six months' notice.[60] Here, therefore, the House implied a yearly tenancy with six months' notice by either side.

This decision thus reinstates the 'ancient rule'. Lord Templeman saw no difference between leases for a term and periodic leases. He stated that the latter pass the certainty test because, at any one time, it is possible to state the maximum duration (for example, the year's end). Any promise which, by restricting the giving of notice, purports to make the period of the lease indeterminate is therefore not possible in a periodic lease:

> ... principle and precedent dictate that it is beyond the power of the landlord and tenant to create a term which is uncertain. A grant for an uncertain term does not create a lease. A grant for an uncertain term which takes the form of a yearly tenancy which cannot be determined by the landlord does not create a lease.[61]

P F Smith concludes:

> It is impossible from now on expressly to create any leasehold term for a period not fixed in advance, and terminable by the landlord on an uncertain future event, with a proviso that a landlord could not put an end to the occupation of a half-yearly tenant until he required the premises for the purposes of his own undertaking ... To conclude: there is much to commend a certainty rule which is simple and which penalises carelessness in drafting of leasehold agreements, especially since the policy of the 1925 legislation is to favour the security of titles.[62]

---

58 Lord Templeman at 286 said bluntly that they were 'wrongly decided'.

59 Lord Templeman at 282, 283.

60 Lord Templeman at 283.

61 Lord Templeman at 285, 286. In fact this lease *could* be determined by the landlord, but only in limited circumstances.

62 P F Smith, 'What is Wrong with Certainty in Leases?' (1993) *Conv* 461 at pp 463, 465.

However, at the end of his (assenting) opinion, Lord Browne-Wilkinson expressed his dissatisfaction with the rule:

> It is difficult to think of a more unsatisfactory outcome or one further away from what the parties to the 1930 agreement can ever have contemplated ... This bizarre outcome results from the application of an ancient and technical rule of law which requires the maximum duration of a term of years to be ascertainable from the outset. No one has produced any satisfactory rationale for the genesis of this rule. No one has been able to point to any useful purpose that it serves at the present day.[63]

Kevin Gray, having identified five possible justifications for the rule, in the end agrees with Browne-Wilkinson that its operation is 'both arbitrary and artificial'; he also refers to it as 'brutally simple'.[64] Susan Bright,[65] argues that the decision is an illustration of the tension between two alternative views of the leasehold relationship: either as a 'contract' (where the role of the courts is to clarify and enforce bargains) or as 'property' (where the actions of the parties must be fitted into pre-existing shapes, 'conceptual formalism').[66]

Certainty, distance and justice. And let the bad draftsman be damned. If only controlling human death were as easy.

The masculine face of land law

It would seem from the above that land law is incontrovertibly a masculine knowledge. The rules maintain their logic and predictability for rational men; distance and a certain ruthlessness are also persuasive of land law's masculine world view. Thus, some 'arrangements' relating to land are recognised and allowed 'inside', and others fail the test and are excluded. The rules appear to operate to create and maintain a hierarchy, in order to include the valid – interests in land successfully created or transferred – and, at the same time, to exclude the invalid, the Others. Cases in these two areas also illustrate land law's precise and scientific method: statute is objectively interpreted, cases followed or distinguished. There is no doubt about what the conclusion is.[67]

All the rules are judged rationally, according to their fitness for their purpose: the test is whether they render the market more or less efficient. Thus, the

---

63 At 287.

64 (1993) at pp 689, 690.

65 Susan Bright, 'Uncertainty in Leases – is it a Vice?' (1993) 13 *Legal Studies* 38; Gray (1993) *supra* n 24 at p 690.

66 The rational solution to its perceived irrationality is, they say, to convert by statute all uncertain leases into certain terms, subject to a provision for notice on a specified event, as with leases for lives under s 149(6) Law of Property Act 1925.

67 Not only is the content, aim and method of land law masculine, but all the players seem to be too. This is partly due to the convention of companies being 'he' – not an empty convention either, since a company is, as a rational player in the market, hardly to be conceived as female. All the litigants and judges in the s 2 cases were men. In the lease cases, all were referred to as male: although Lace was a woman, her sex was rendered invisible behind the court's references to her as 'the landlord'.

debate on the value of the 'death foretold' rule in leases depends on whether a 'simple' technicality is more effective in the market than making sure – from case to case – that bargains are enforced.

THE FEMININE IN LAND LAW

I have reached the age when I have to wear glasses to read my 'A to Z' or file my nails. This new view of the world from behind an artificial aid is challenging, but it makes me think about looking at everything differently. That seminar and my body misplaced. But. Outside, I could see the chaos of branches against the sky and men and women passing by. Even inside, I could see women and hear their voices. I have become so conscious of my oppression that I note it with a head count on entry to each room. And it disempowers me. So now I wish to affirm my presence, voice, knowledge. And to be heard, seen and acknowledged.

I don't believe that land law is simply Masculine. Woman, I, can be found in every case. In the past I have tended to see the common law as Jung's masculine subject, who has a female soul, his *anima*, in equity, still capable of child-bearing. In this view, s 2's harshness is mitigated by the flexible and caring proprietary estoppel, daughter of equity's part performance, which may when necessary also supplement the law of leases with discretionary remedies for contractual licences.

However, I find I do not need the argument that the masculine common law has a soul to bear the necessary female burden of compromise and flexibility: Woman is, I am, present in the common law. Land law can certainly (ha!) look like a man, but that is exactly how a masculine analysis would describe it: if I look at the world through His glasses, of course I will see only what He recognises. In fact, *the law is more complicated than that.* Woman/women are present in the content, method and aims of, and as actors in, land law, and not just hiding behind false beards.

To say that the law – whether the common law or any other – is not merely a neutral, rational arbiter between reasoning subjects is hardly new. I seem to be joining the chorus from Fraunce[68] to Marx, from realists to practitioners of race critique.

> In short, lawyers have always been indecently zealous to reduce behaviour to rules and, in constructing the abstract world of the doctrine and science of law, have tended to be forgetful both of the irrationality and chance embedded in social life as well as of the instability and change intrinsic to human purpose and human personality.[69]

Law comes from the whole of human life, not only from a disembodied intellect. But I am saying something different too. My argument is that land law

---

68   See Goodrich (1990) *supra* n 21 for the story of Abram Fraunce.

69   Peter Goodrich (1981) at p 209.

is concerned not only with a simple masculine mastery of the natural world but also with a feminine negotiation, informality and compromise in face of the reality of the whole mystery of human action. First, land lawyers pay lip service to concepts of certainty, logic and distance, but in practice they adopt a less tidy and more flexible approach. There is an overt recognition that land law is dealing with a dynamic process, with uncertainties as well as certainties. Thus, the s 2 decisions all enabled the contracts in question to be enforced despite the stringent wording of the statute. The Law Commission's report preceding s 2 remarked:

> Any reform should simplify or at least not complicate conveyancing ... certainty and reliability are often essential in dealings with land and *may* call for extra formalities.[70]

As Judge Paul Baker commented in *Record v Bell*, the situation is a very common one:

> ... especially where there is some pressure to get contracts exchanged, as there frequently is, and one often finds that at exchange not all the loose ends are tidied up and it is necessary to have some last minute adjustment of the contract which takes the form of side letters ... It would be unfortunate if common transactions of this nature should nevertheless cause the contracts to be avoided. It may, of course, lead to a greater use of the concept of collateral warranties than has hitherto been necessary.[71]

Similarly, all the cases on prospective certainty of leases[72] ensured that one way or another a fair result ensued. Angels may have been dancing on the head of a pin, but that should not be allowed to distract the eye from a far more material view of the world. As remarked by Susan Bright, the real issue in most of these cases is that of updating the rent in a lease where there is no provision for rent review:

> ... the rule [in *Prudential*] is being used by the courts to free the landlord from a manifestly disadvantageous contractual arrangement ... [T]he courts have in fact been able to achieve relatively sensible (and reasonably fair) results by resorting to the ancient rule in property law requiring certainty in relation to leasehold terms. By declaring the lease void or terminable upon service of common law notice it is, in fact, opening up the relationship to be renegotiated to reflect the current property values'.[73]

The doctrine of certainty is being used to facilitate negotiation and compromise even though the process takes place behind a rigorous and logical facade. Even

---

70 Law Com No 164 'Transfers' above para 1.11, quoting the working paper para 5.2 (emphasis added). V Gersten's ('Nightmare on Main Street' (1993) LS Gaz 2) nightmare about s 2 may, as the cases so far decided show, be unlikely in waking life.

71 At 194, 201. There was also an overt recognition of this in regard to the rules preceding s 2.

72 Except *Lace v Chantler*, and that is why Parliament stepped in with the 1944 Act – see above.

73 (1994) *supra* n 65 at pp 47, 52, 74.

then, the facade occasionally cracks. As Peter Sparkes commented on *Prudential*: '... Lord Templeman has *intuitively* adopted the lease analysis'.[74]

Lord Templeman might not agree, but that is what it looks like to me too.

Further, just as the judgments in these lease cases are not purely 'rational', the 'traditional representation'[75] that human behaviour is reasoned, with 'explicitly formulated goals' is also not apparent. The parties agreeing their 'leases' in these cases made informal, convenient arrangements which were totally irrational in the long-term (although, as I write, my grasp of what rational behaviour might be becomes increasingly slippery). In any event, their agreement does not seem to have been based on that prudent foresight of what could well happen in the future which – I would assume – rational men must employ in making their arm's length bargains.

In addition, to claim that the growing list of exceptions from s 2 and the technical solutions to the technically created problem in leases make law more certain and predictable is a will o' the wisp. The more words judges use, the more exceptions and examples that appear, the less possible becomes a transparent knowledge of land law and of title to the land itself. (The gradual accretion of case law is exactly what caused the Law Commission to propose reforms to the old s 40 Law of Property Act 1925, precursor of s 2.) Smith concluded on a s 2 case, for example:

> If nothing else, *Record v Bell* serves to demonstrate that the 1989 Act fails to remove the problems inherent in the requirement of writing. As commentators have observed, and *Record* illustrates, it has introduced its own problems.[76]

Bright and Gray's suggestion that the *Prudential* problem represents a tension between the property and contract understanding of leasehold relationships may also be relevant to the 1989 Act. Smith refers to the contract function of s 2:

> ... the full extent of the terms of the agreement need not be in writing. Against the risk of invalidating contracts must be weighed the policy of certainty embodied in the 1989 Act.[77]

In the light of my arguments, it looks as though, as regards these rules, land law is the rigid, abstract and intellectual masculine voice, and contract the pragmatic, flexible, informal feminine. However, of course this depends where you are standing on the continuum of male-female: from the viewpoint of family law, contract may appear more masculine. Taking the simplistic view here, in the current interpretations of s 2, the feminine (contract) is on top; in *Prudential*, the

---

74 Peter Sparkes (1993) 109 LQR 93 at p 110 (emphasis added). However, he returns to a more orthodox analysis on the next page. Another rare example of the overt rejection of reason can be found in *In Midland Rly Agreement* where Russell LJ commented that the prospective certainty of leases 'has an air of artificiality, of remoteness from practical considerations'. He concluded that the courts should be 'unwilling to be moved by *some process of logic*' to go further than precedent demanded at p 732 (emphasis added). On the following page, he referred to his '*instinct*' to give effect to the parties' bargain.

75 Goodrich (1981) at p 209.

76 (1992) *supra* n 62 at p 220.

77 (1992) *supra* n 62 at p 219.

masculine (property) is, but nevertheless achieves what look like feminine (pragmatic, intuitive) results. However, whether or not the property-masculine and contract-feminine analysis is worth pursuing, all but one of the cases cited here (*Lace v Chantler* is the exception) illustrate the flexible, contingent – feminine – aspect of law.

Land law may be claimed to offer a masculine – rational and distant solution – to the problems of Men of Property, but in reality masculine and feminine negotiate, collaborate, and give birth to a child whose nature reflects the characters of both its parents. Sometimes, Woman is disguised as Man, or hidden in His shadow, but She does exist, active and visible to those who have new glasses. The feminine is not *always* excluded by a male property law as the other: I am not *always* 'culturally devalued' or 'wrong'.[78] Sometimes the boundaries are redrawn to include Woman because She is present and visible.

The most interesting example of this recently is to be found in *London Borough of Hounslow v Hare*.[79] Here the local council had, contrary to trust law, sold a long lease to a sitting tenant, Miss Hare, under 'right to buy' legislation. When the mistake was discovered, the council sought rectification of the register against her. Knox J quoted s 82(3)(c) Land Registration Act 1925, which, naturally, is couched in masculine terms, and remarked: '"Him" of course, has to be altered to "her" in this case'.[80]

In the event, he refused to order rectification against her:

She has been in possession for a very long time. She went in, on her evidence, in 1972 ... it seems to me that when one is dealing with a person's home the change from the near equivalent of freehold that a 125 year lease gives to somebody of the age of nearing 40 to that of a tenant, assured or not, is one of very considerable significance. That feature does, in my judgment, far outweigh any financial considerations that there may be the other way.[81]

This is an explicit recognition that land law is concerned not only with the space of the intellect in abstract 'interests in land', but also with physical and emotional place: land law is both space *and* place. (There are also the feminine elements in land law's relating to spatial certainty: exclusive and adverse possession. In both of these can be identified feminine characteristics of judgment.)

There is, of course, a need for more knowledge here. How do the conversations between Her and Him work? When will one inspire or colonise the other? But these are questions for another time.

---

78 Despite the argument of Davies (1994) in *Boland* (above), the House of Lords did recognise that a married woman is not a mere shadow of her husband. Cases since then might demonstrate that, as property law includes what is proper and excludes the Other, so the proper, rational players in the market (building societies) have won all their cases against private, occupiers of land. Nevertheless, *Boland* remains as a landmark: she *is* still here.

79 (1991) 24 HLR 9.

80 *Supra* n 79 at 27.

81 *Ibid.*

WHAT I CAN SAY

Teresa de Lauretis, having noted the constant tendency of male narratives to reproduce themselves and exclude women, stresses the vital feminist effort to rewrite the narratives 'from elsewhere':

> I think of it as spaces in the margins of hegemonic discourses, social spaces carved in the interstices of institutions and in the chinks and cracks of the power-knowledge apparati. And it is there that the terms of a different construction of gender can be posed – terms that do have effect and take hold at the level of subjectivity and self-representation: in the micropolitical practices of daily life and daily resistances that afford both agency and sources of power or empowering investments; and in the cultural productions of women, feminists, which inscribe that movement in and out of ideology, that crossing back and forth of the boundaries – and of the limits – of sexual difference(s) ...[82]

Unless I, a woman, write the law from here and elsewhere, I am silenced, and others, even further outside, will also not be heard. I know I can begin to speak from elsewhere, and that: 'Everything will be changed once woman gives woman to the other woman'.[83]

The law is – lawyers are – more complicated and paradoxical than I used to imagine. The productive tension between differences, between masculine and feminine in my examples, ensures that people are not always simply inside or outside the law. The boundaries are constantly shifting, and it is because of this dynamic and open nature of law that I may enter it.

I see that land law is not solely a masculine order seeking to impose a ruthless distance and certainty on autonomous and self-interested actors in the market. There are two separate points here. First, the feminine – Woman – is present in legal decision-making. She probably always has been, although overlooked in modern times, for, as I have shown, this law is not merely a masculine, but a human project. Second, as in the seminar where I started this article, women are – like me – present in the law: we speak in our words and in our silences even if, at times, we feel constrained, see other women translated, speak like men. More women are present in the law than formerly, at every level and in every forum:

> We are no longer pleading for the right to speak: we have spoken; space has changed; we are living in a matrix of our own sounds; our words resonate, by our echoes we chart a new geography ...[84]

---

82   (1987) *supra* n 1 at pp 25, 26. She continues, '... to inhabit both kinds of spaces at once is to live the contradiction which, I have suggested, is the condition of feminism here and now; the tension of a two fold pull in contrary directions – the critical negativity of its theory and the affirmative positivity of its politics – is both the historical condition of existence of feminism and its theoretical condition of possibility' at p 26.

83   Spivaks (1993) *supra* n 2 at p 157.

84   Susan Griffin, *Woman and Nature: The Roaring Inside Her* (1983) Harper Colophon at pp 93-94.

I change the space by my sense of place, by being here. Despite what I might see as the nihilism all around me, the obsession of theorists with their sex and death, the invisibility of woman in science and the science of the law; despite land law's relegation of me to the shadows as the Other of husbands, fathers and sons – I am here and I know I can speak, even if only squirrels read me.

Being here is always a beginning.

CHAPTER SIX

FIGURES IN A LANDSCAPE:
FEMINIST PERSPECTIVES ON LAW, LAND AND
LANDSCAPE

ANNE BOTTOMLEY

My intention ... is not iconoclastic, to smash the aesthetic surface of landscape images, to describe some deeper, more authentic world of social relations. Rather I wish to amplify the eloquence of these images ... rendering their meanings more mutable and ambiguous ... I will emphasise the fluency of landscape, not its fixity, its poetics as well as its politics. An apparently simple picture may yield many fields of vision.[1]

In so many small, and sometimes seemingly insignificant, ways we catalogue information, give definitional headings and draw distinctions between areas of study. We find a focus, construct boundaries and limit horizons; a way to organise and try to make sense of our work. We cannot avoid using such strategies; we require maps to organise our material and bring into relation sets of ideas. But we need to recognise not only the many contingent factors which lie behind these acts of mapping but also the power of the consequences of such decisions. Too often what are actually fluid boundaries become portrayed as immutable. Loosely constructed sites become burdened with coherence. Acts of mapping take on a form which suggests that they have an internal logic which transcends space and time, the contexts in which they were constituted. What was, or indeed is, simply messy, and the best one can do, appears beautiful as order, offering, it seems, certainty in its conformity and completeness. We can feel safe. Safe in the knowledge that knowledge itself is safe.

In Heffers[2] I walk, with a heavy sense of duty, to the shelves labelled 'law'; yet again I wonder, as I view shelf after shelf of heavy text and then move to the small section on theory, why anyone would choose, as a curious intellectual, to study law. I move on to the other sections: classical studies, history, literature etc to find the books which I want. Over and over again I am faced by the same evidence. Even in books which clearly, in their title for instance, indicate that they are concerned with 'law'; when they can be placed under sociology, history, classical studies or other definitional headings that is where you will find them. Not on the law shelves. These books are not for lawyers. Are these books simply 'about law' rather than 'law'?

Torn from geographies of law, as law is torn from the geography of other academic subjects; it leaves few routes into other areas for students to easily follow. Were such paths to become more clearly marked they would not only

---

1   Stephen Daniels, *Fields of Vision* (1993) Polity at p 8
2   A Cambridge bookshop.

alert the student to work which would illuminate our own subject area, but would also begin to raise questions about the seeming fixity of the subject categories themselves. Difficulties of definition, movements across subject boundaries, horizons of possibility, moments of tension as well as moments of fruitful conjuncture; all would become more visible. We should read maps not only for the guidance they offer but also for the closures they effect.

The separation of 'law' from other academic disciplines, and the consequent decisions to place books 'on law' elsewhere, reproduces a narrative of law-learning which presumes that academic law is subject-to-itself. If it needs a rationale for existence it is, of course, the operational nature of law out-there, the actual practice of it, and the presumption that most undergraduate students are undertaking the degree with purely vocationalist aspirations.

If the landscape of law in the academy is boundaried by the limited horizons of presumptions made about legal education, that lawyers are engaged in training lawyers rather than sharing an academic enterprise with the rest of the academy, then access to information (knowledges and practices) which might help us read not only our maps but our acts of mapping are denied us. An act of faith is required of us; that our maps will not only make sense but the best sense. That they are the best possible maps for our purposes. What is never open to us is to study their construction and to question the presumption that this is the only way to map our object of study.

Most mapping of law for undergraduates is predicated on textbooks; for many what is defined as a secondary source (the primary source material being the text of law found in statutes and cases) becomes not merely routes through the territory, maps of 'law', but 'the law' itself. Extracting from the practices of law significant elements into textbooks and rendering these elements into the conventions of chapters, obviously opens up the question of how far the maps offer good guidance through the territory. There are clearly cases of texts which, for many reasons, do not include important areas of the terrain within their maps. These acts of exclusion may have important consequences both in conveying a picture of the world-out-there and therefore in preparing students to be part of that world. But if we limited our critique to this we would be simply saying that the act of mapping should be essentially passive; reflecting a reality of the world-out-there as approximately as possible. This would be to make a number of presumptions. Firstly that the world-out-there is easily identifiable; secondly, that the world-out-there is simply a series of practices ('the law') which legal education is limited to preparing the student for; thirdly, and most importantly, that 'the law' is limited to being understood as what is practised as law, rather than what is thought of as law. If we take this final point seriously what it means is that the very acts of mapping are part of 'law'; part of our understanding of the meanings of law, and therefore of the possibilities of law. The construction of the map is therefore both an act of attempting to render visible a territory called law and, at the very same time, constructing that territory. The map is therefore not a simple, passive device, a reflection of a fixed object, but part of that object; because the object is only rendered visible through our constructions of it. The significance of this is reflected in the difference between the idea of 'legal discourse' and the 'discursive practices of law'.[3] What we call law, what we understand by it and what we say of it, is constructed not merely by what is 'done' in the world–out–there but also by what is taught, thought and written in the academy. The mistake is to think of 'law' as simply the practice of law, and to presume that the academy, and therefore legal education, is only about rendering visible an externality. It is a, the, constant reference point for us; but it is not the whole picture. Therefore the textbook must be looked to, read, as a dynamic practice in itself; as not simply an act of mapping the practices of law but as a struggle to impose sets of meanings, and, through that struggle, to construct 'the discourse' of law.

We require a kind of double vision. We need to understand the working presumptions we utilise, and need to utilise, but to realise their limitations in the very act of using them. We need to continue to use a reference to 'law' as presuming that it is something which we can know (identify, describe, critique and sometimes explain); for most of us nowadays that reference to 'law' is found by identifying it with the practices of law. However, when we turn to textbooks, or other commentaries on law, it becomes clear that the very act of writing on law involves a series of moves away from these practices. Every engagement with the practice of law requires a disengagement; there are decisions to be made about which practices are written up, which cases reported and commented upon; a process of selection, of choice. Some of those choices are made within the practices of law, others are made within the academy. The process of selection, when examined, tells us something of the values, the operative presumptions, used by those making that selection. Values of coherence or certainty, for instance, are often quite visible.[4] Therefore the commentaries read the practices in particular ways; giving meaning to them which can influence not merely how they are read but how they are, in the end, made.

An important aspect of the language used by many commentators, and by many students, is the idea that 'law' is sometimes not what it is meant to be; that the judges have interpreted something 'wrongly' for instance. Therefore we often find an idea that 'law' is distinctive, in the sense that it is not finally reducible to the practices which seem to produce it; they simply put it into operation. This is a useful working myth; an important act of displacement which has been utilised in different ways over many generations. When Coke said, in the 17th century, 'It is not I who speaks, but the law'; he was involved in an act of displacement which we can all recognise. But we can also recognise its political importance. Coke, as an extremely powerful and significant judge, derived a great deal of his power from this myth of common law. Law was simply to be found, revealed, and then spoken; and when spoken revealed as a

---

3   Based on M Foucault, *The Archaeology of Knowledge* (1972) Tavistock.

4   Anne Bottomley, 'Production of a Text: *Hammond v Mitchell*' (1994) *Feminist Legal Studies* 83.

rational, unitary system.[5] The powerful tug of this myth is still found in many law students today; which speaks to its power rather than to their/our naivety. Revelation in the academy is not, however, fixed simply on the judges; it is fixed on the textbook writer. Indeed many commentators feed this myth by critiquing the judges when they 'go wrong'. So the double vision we require is one which allows us to, on the one hand, judge the textbook writer by his/her fidelity to law (legal practice) and, on the other hand, be crucially aware of their construction of law; that it goes beyond mere commentary and becomes a text of law.

Of course the particular power of any individual text will be greatly dependent on qualities of authorship; the authority deemed to derive from the author and his/her power of exposition of the area of study. For instance:

> ... is the classic work on land law, and has been relied upon by practitioners and students alike for over seventy years. This new edition maintains all the traditions of the work; namely, clarity, accuracy and erudition ... Since the last edition there have been major developments in this area of law. The text has been brought fully up-to-date ...[6]

What could be simply dismissed as 'publicity' actually contains important clues on constructing authority. This is, of course, Cheshire: the first major text to be published after the 1925 legislation. The authority of history is presented by the juxtaposition of '70 years' with being, by the publication of the 15th edition, 'fully up-to-date'. Continuity is represented in the continuation of authorship as accredited to Cheshire, but now as title to the book, and by addending 'Burn', the present author, in the title but also sourced as author. The assertion that the book has 'been relied upon by practitioners and students alike' importantly suggests authority granted by the profession and shared with students; this is more than simply a teaching text. The significance of Cheshire to the building of what has become the orthodox exposition of land law has been well documented; the division of text into family and commercial interests and the predominance given to issues of conveyancing have formed the basis for many, if not most, modern land law courses.[7] However a weird displacement operates. Cheshire becomes not merely a book but an authoritative book; what is lost is the man and his enterprise in writing the book and the consequent genealogy in choosing others to continue the book in his name. For students it becomes simply a way of citing the text they use rather than thinking about the construction of it; in that sense the first figure we need to restore to the landscape is the figure of the author. The very loss of that figure as anything but name seems to be crucial in finally becoming 'authoritative'; what is at stake is

---

5   See, eg, Nicholas Blomley, *Law, Space, and the Geography of Power* (1994) Guildford ch 3 (a book shelved in Heffers under geography but not under law).

6   E H Burn, *Cheshire and Burn's Modern Law of Real Property* (1994, 15th edn) Butterworths, quotation taken from the back cover.

7   Stuart Anderson, *Lawyers and the Making of English Land Law* (1992) Clarendon.

the creation of a tradition; the tradition of the text. The text which is at one and the same time powerful because of the named authority and yet not reducible to that authorship.[8] It becomes part of the canon. Aspiring to become part of the canon, making claims to authority, requires the author to become subsumed to the text itself. How is this authority constructed? The answer to this question is made up of a number of contingent factors; some of which derive from the building of images of the area of law covered.

THE IMAGE(S) AND THE TEXT(S)

I am still surprised when I first meet new land law students by the fear they have of the subject, a heavy tradition of it being 'difficult and dull'. But I am also surprised when I meet a common resistance, on their part, to thinking of it as being related, in a very concrete way, to the world in which we live; as constitutive of, as well as being constituted by, the visible landscape within which we live our lives. A sense of place, and therefore the place of law. A sense of time and of space; and therefore of the time and spaces which law both inhabits and constructs.

The absence of a spatial dimension is, of course, consistent with not only the expectations most students have of the study of law, and perhaps, ironically, land law in particular; but also of the orthodox presentation of the subject to law students. On the surface the subject is, seemingly necessarily, presented as an abstract account of rules:

> ... the essence of the law is always understood as disembodied rather than formed in material and historical conditions; it follows that the law can be interpreted only at the highest level of spatial abstraction. Legal knowledge, by definition, must be true to the law alone.[9]

To present as disembodied the subject must be, as Berman reminds us, 'disembedded'; torn from context.[10] The production of the academic subject, the text of law, is constituted by an intersection of different narratives, formed in different historical periods and from different imperatives, but all of which feed upon, and reproduce, a landscape which is framed within law and through which other landscapes may be viewed, merely glimpsed or basically hidden. However, the maps we are to be offered are simply of 'law'; not through law to other landscapes but to law as *the* landscape. The only geography we are concerned with and one which will stand on its own. The consequence is a

---

8   Gillian Rose notes of the style of writing texts in geography: ' ... unobtrusive prose style works to deflect attention away from the author, and the effect is to invest the writing with the authority of rational men. The style attempts to erase the specifity of the author and to represent his writing as an objective expression of reason', *Feminism and Geography* (1993) Polity at p 8.

9   Blomley (1994) at p 76.

10   Harold Berman, *Law and Revolution: the Formation of the Western Legal Tradition* (1983) Harvard University Press.

presumption that we can understand, make sense of, this law-world without need for any other referents. Students who fail to 'understand' have simply either not worked hard enough or are not bright enough to share our knowledge of 'the law'. What, it is too often thought, is then required is simply more concentration on the subject. More law. Perhaps the aid of a simpler textbook before returning to a more authoritative text.

Material about the 'context' of law and legal developments seems a diversion, an overburdening of tasks on already confused students. Simplicity calls for abstraction; for cutting away the unnecessary. It feeds on and into desires for coherence and answers, and fears confusion and questions. It depends on being able to presume the authority of the text. Overall the working presumption is that any fault in lack of understanding lies simply with the student.

But we could take a different starting-point. We could take seriously the student fear of land law. Rather than dismissing this fear, we could ask what it represents and reproduces. What makes the subject 'difficult'? Drawing on Murphy and Roberts[11] we could point to the very incoherence of the area; that it has no clear conceptual core or clearly defined boundaries; rather it is a loosely held together series of ideas and practices used and developed by lawyers in relation to dealings with 'land'.

Its origins within legal education are very pragmatic; it is, perhaps pre-eminently, a subject originally conceived of as preparation for practice.[12] The first stage to conveyancing. If understanding is not achieved in the classroom it is simply because the final picture will only be, can only be, revealed later in the lawyer's office. In the actual practices of law. Therefore the pleasures of the subject must be, necessarily, deferred. 'Pleasure' is often associated with a kind of mastery; of feeling in control of the subject. If the mastery is only a possibility elsewhere, then both student and, even more so, academic operate within a *lacuna*. A *lacuna* which they must attempt to fill in order to give themselves some satisfaction. The academic, faced with a needy student, is likely to utilise a number of approaches to attempt a satisfactory presentation. They could be thought of as a series of narratives:

1   The narrative of the subject as an account of legal practices. But this is not very satisfactory as anything but a reference point; although conveyancing, Land Registry practices etc, can be taught and examined, another narrative tends to intervene;

2   The narrative of the subject as an aspect of common law teaching. Here there is a tendency to try and fit with expectations derived from other subjects, to focus on statutory provisions and case law and to construct problem-solving questions as central to the 'mastery' of the subject. This is in

11   W Murphy and S Roberts, *Understanding Property Law* (1994, 2nd edn) Fontana.

12   Anderson *supra* n 6.

tension with the first narrative but fits more comfortably with the traditional practices of undergraduate legal education. It also begins to offer a seemingly more 'academic' approach to the material. Which moves towards the third narrative;

3   That the subject can be conceptually organised, rendered not simply understandable but coherent, through the organisation of key conceptual ideas.

The problem is that whilst each of these narratives has a value and can be used constructively to engage with the area, they are too often utilised without being thought about. Students often receive them as one garbled story; shifts between them become slippages, possible plays simply dissonance. What is missed is that it is the interplay between these three narratives, the tensions between them, the gaps and the fits, that construct 'the subject', land law. In this sense, and importantly, it is not 'a subject' but merely an area constituted through a series of narratives and made available for study. Into this landscape we need to place the figure of the academic.

In recent years, both because of changes within the academy and changes in relation to professional exemptions, there has been a great deal of discussion about the 'place' of land law in the undergraduate curriculum. Should it be taught with equity and trusts? Before? After? Should it be taught as part of a broader 'property' course? Behind many, if not all, of these discussions has been a concern to make land law more palatable to students and more intellectually stimulating. There seems to be a widespread concern to 'do something' with the subject as well as the overall need to try and rationalise the increasing demands which have accrued on the undergraduate curriculum. For the academic this can be an exciting, if demanding, time. A number of imperatives impact on this scenario. Shifts are occurring in legal education, in what is taught and why. Academics are under increasing pressure to publish. Students are under increasing pressure to succeed as places within the legal profession become more scarce. The possible tensions between the academic project and student reception of it are manifest. The textbook becomes a site where this tension is played out. So much is invested in it: an academic's career and reputation, a student's sense of knowledge and understanding.

For the student the 'law' is disembodied through two thresholds: law from the world-out-there and law from the text-in-here. Reified through text, law is sought as an object rather than understood as a narrative. Text displaces our own sense of the world. The student does not look up from the text, look around and seek to ask questions of the landscape. The visible patterns of rural development and urban growth, of developments and changes in domestic architecture; these too often are simply assumed rather than explored for what they tell us about their (and our) histories. We flatten the landscape, use it simply as a backdrop to our lives, and ignore the many signs and clues that would render more visible perspectives of time and space. To be blind to these visible clues to our histories is to miss the primary opportunity we have of beginning to map those aspects which have both formed and been formed by that landscape ... and which include law. To not add the dimensions of space and time to reading our environment is to lose vital information which would help situate our reading of the text of land law. It also misses the chance to use the landscape as a source of informed metaphors which can give body to land law and help us to visualise it. We lose history and we lose imagery; we have no tools to give form and substance to the text we are presented with. It must remain as words. And our dependence on it is absolute.

CONSTRUCTIONS OF LANDSCAPES

The vogue which has recently developed for illustrating the covers of books with reproductions of art (texts published by both Butterworths and Sweet & Maxwell; Stevens now offer attractive covers) is not, I suspect, to entice the student to buy one text rather than another, but possibly is an attempt to make more palatable the increasing cost of the texts and, perhaps, to suggest a more conducive introduction to the material. It could be taken as a visible mark of a genre which is concerned to place the study of law in the context of the world-out-there. If we considered this possibility an interesting double–imaging is involved. The cover becomes the frontier between two territories: a window into the text and a window from the text on to the world.

The particular circumstances of selection obviously vary: in some texts it is quite clear that the author was instrumental in making the selection; in others any reference to the cover is omitted; indeed, frequently the image is not even sourced. In this sense we should not read too much into the choice of a cover as a process of careful selection. We must recognise the many contingencies which may lie behind a final selection, from the availability of a chosen image (who holds copyright?) to simply what looks good on the cover. The sun, for instance, in Gray's second edition of *Elements of Land Law*, published by Butterworths in 1993, is placed to operate primarily so as to underline the title and author of the book. Cleverly, one's eye is drawn not simply to the sun but beyond that to the new horizon of the title. This context to the placing of the sun is important in that it underlines the many purposes for which the image may be used. The picture becomes no more than a resource to be utilised; it has a minor, support role to play. There are no pretensions to authenticity, we are not in the realms of art or art history: these are texts on law. Indeed the marginality of the image in itself is emphasised by the number of students I have spoken to all of whom denied any memory of the covers and certainly were not initially interested in them as objects in themselves. They were simply packaging to the text. I expect that most of us would simply say that it is more aesthetically pleasing to see a pictorial representation rather than a block of colour with a title, and really go no further. However, intriguing patterns do emerge and do lend themselves to a reading of the covers themselves as a kind of text of law.

Real property books are characterised by a focus on landscape. Indeed landscape in the sense in which it is most often and most evocatively used in this country – rural landscape. Other images could have been chosen; they are available. Instead the dominant iconography has utilised not only rural landscape but also the major English artists who have been themselves melded into a tradition of 'Englishness': Turner and Constable in particular. The latest edition of Cheshire uses Constable's *Brightwell Church and Village*.[13] Blue skies, poppies, ripe corn and green trees present England in high summer. The village is glimpsed beyond the foreground of a well-beaten track which evokes age in use. All is rather sleepy; two figures walk along another track towards the horizon; but they seem to be casual not only in their size but also in their suggested demeanour. There is no bustle or hurry here, no hard labour or sense of time as measurement. Rather sun and sleepiness.

What brings together the iconography of landscape with a text on real property? The use of such imagery might not be consciously invoking narratives associated with national identity but is surely reproducing them. Their use may also tell us something of the landscape of land law.

Daniels argues in his preface:

Landscape imagery is not merely a reflection of, or distraction from, more pressing social, economic or political issues; it is often a powerful mode of knowledge and social engagement. Running through many of the images I discuss are a variety of discourses and practices, from engineering to political economy. Not all of them were put there by the artists. They are often activated, or introduced, by the various contexts in which the images are displayed, reproduced and discussed.[14]

Pausing to think about the covers of these books, of the images they utilise, before we open the solid mass of the text (in the case of the second edition of Gray 1,168 pages of it), may seem to students of law a strange diversion. There are no other illustrations in the text, there are a few diagrammatic renderings of 'basic rules' but, essentially, these texts, as in the majority of basic law texts, are characterised by the very absence of visual representations. Words are the currency here; this is a book of law. Yet playing with evocations of landscape, questioning the utilisation of the national iconography of rural nostalgia may help us situate the text and provide us with imagery we can deploy in an interrogation of the text. It might help us unpack the narratives deployed in the text, as well as those lost or marginalised. It might help us recover something of the figure of the author.

The first edition of Gray[15] takes a Turner landscape for its cover. These are the notes I wrote when first thinking about the painting:

---

13   John Constable (1776–1837). The picture is hung in the Tate, London.

14   Daniels (1993) at p 8.

15   Kevin Gray, *Elements of Land Law* (1987) Butterworths. The picture is *A Scottish Lake Scene* by J M W Tutner (1779–1851) and is hung in the Tate, London. The 2nd edn (1993) uses another Turner from the Tate: *A Town on a River at Sunset*.

Misty, colour washed, detail is hard to discern and scale is conveyed by broad sweeps of muted tones which evoke a mood as much as a place.

Two figures are placed in a landscape which emphasises their smallness and impermanence, in contrast to the overwhelming presence of hills and lakes. It is romantically misty; they seem to be walkers, resting in contemplation and awe, as they marvel at the mysteries of nature. The atmosphere is silent and still. In repose. No other element of human habitation or activity is visible. This is romantic, escapist art at its most compelling. Man contemplates a landscape in which the evidence of man's impact on landscape is nil.

These walkers would be carrying Wordsworth in their pockets.

On first sight it seems such an incongruous image to utilise – not even rural development, let alone the urban landscape, is on view here. Instead we have a direct evocation of 'nature'. I did once fantasise using it as the basis for a collage: a hint of factories or a new town from behind the hills, notices saying 'Keep Out' or 'No Fishing'; some representation of control, development or exploitation. Some sense of the issues of modern property law. The disjuncture between the image and the text seems further amplified in Gray's introduction:

> ... the law of the land often appears to have a strangely enduring quality ... The sense of stasis or permanence is, however, largely illusory: modern land law is not the slow moving subject it is commonly supposed to be.[16]

It may not be 'slow moving' but, as we move into the text, we find that it is only to be understood through certain enduring qualities:

> English law cannot be properly understood except in the light of its history, and it is in the doctrines relating to tenures and estates that the historical roots of English land law are to be found.[17]

And there we are back in the medieval period but, crucially, being introduced to:

> ... a highly artificial field of concepts, defined with meticulous precision, with the result that the interrelation of these constructs is not unlike a form of mathematical calculus. The intellectual constructs of land law move, as Professor Lawson said, 'in a world of pure ideas from which everything physical or material is excluded'.[18]

A double-distancing, historical and at the same time ahistorical, in that not only will these ideas be actually situated as a 'history' but that they still have a presence for us now, in a shared abstract universe. And then the Turner can begin to represent something much closer to the text; a sense of permeance, of presence and continuity, indeed of being out-of-time.

Gray also tells us that:

---

16 Gray (1987) *supra* n 15 at p v.

17 *Ibid* at p 55.

18 *Ibid* at p 55.

... even quite complex problems of modern land law can be explained in simple terms which start from underlying 'elements' or first principles.[19]

The promise is then of a map, a map which is built up from an introduction to basic ideas and moves then into 'complex problems'. We are offered mastery of the subject; this goes beyond being simply a map to offer routes to a map of control. The figures in Turner's landscape 'gaze' at the hills, hills that can be owned. Even in their contemplation of the landscape they lay claim to it as being under their gaze, their view, their interpretation. Just as Turner frames the landscape for us and offers us the pleasure in participation of the gaze. For landscape as a genre is the representation of the controlling gaze, the power of the disembodied eye over the viewed. Nature is for the pleasure of the viewer:

> ... images of the countryside evoke deep and pleasurable emotional responses which can empower: and this pleasure is described in Berger's words, as 'a going further than he could have achieved alone, towards a prey, a Madonna, a sexual pleasure, a landscape, a face, a different world'. This conflation of hunting, a virgin and the singly male orgasm can stand as a summary of the pleasure of landscape.[20]

To Rose, landscape is a 'visual ideology' replete with cultural codes embedded in social power structures. As the development of landscape art required an understanding of spatial techniques so also were:

> ... these spatial techniques ... implicated in relations of power and ownership ... geometrical skills were being developed contemporaneously, especially by the urban merchant class, and these too involved the accurate representation of space: calculating the volume of goods and thus the value of packaged commodities; map-making to guide the search for goods and markets; and surveying techniques to plot the estates that the bourgeoisie were buying in the countryside ...[21]

Not simply what is placed in the frame to view, but how it is made possible and, in certain ways, why it becomes necessary. Spatial techniques, new forms of mapping and measurement, are fundamental to the development of modern law, making both possible and necessary the role of law in the construction of ownership.

> And the ground, which had hitherto been a common possession like the sunlight and the air, the careful surveyor now marked out with long-drawn boundary-line.[22]

---

19 Gray (1987) *supra* n 15 at p v.

20 Rose (1993) *supra* n 8 at p 99. See also Pamela Shumer-Smith and Kevin Hannam, *Worlds of Desire, Realms of Power* (1994) Edward Arnold. For the power of landscape imagry see, eg, Simon Schama, *Landscape and Memory* (1995) HarperCollins.

21 Rose (1993) *supra* n 8 at p 90. See also Blomley (1994), David Harvey, *The Condition of Postmodernity* (1989) Blackwell and Alain Pottage, 'The Measure of Land' (1994) *Modern Law Review* 361.

22 Ovid, *Metamorphosis,* translated by Frank Miller (1984) Loeb at p 11.

Measurement, organisation of resources into units of ownership and exchange; control and mastery. For Coke the surveyor's measure became a metaphor for law: 'the golden metewand of law':

> In trying to exemplify the certainty and security to property offered by a systemised common law, Coke borrows from the lexicon of the geographer. Individual obligations and rights, he argues, should 'be measured by the golden and straight metewand of the law, and not the incertain (sic) cord of discretion ...'. This is a metaphor that Coke uses repeatedly, evoking the certainties provided by the new cartography.[23]

Blomley argues that:

> Coke's legal treatises ... can be thought of as a judicial atlas in which any datum of knowledge can be exactly located according to a complex system of rational coordinates, and then surveyed as a component part of a larger unified totality. Similarly, the chorographs and maps of the day ... speak both of continuity, land, property, and of a formalised rationality and the individual. This closure ... is related to a form of disembedding in which legal and spacial knowledge is increasingly removed from the localised settings of social and economic life. As the measurement of space becomes fixed and invariant, so legal knowledge became measured by the unitary 'metewand' of artificial reason.[24]

This was not simply the control of land but an attempt at the control of law; the beginning of the long struggle against local custom and practice, against rights in common, against the less formal claims to use, and privileging an increasingly formalised and formalistic form of law. Gray, in common with other authoritative texts, does not track this genealogy of land law; it is left to such historians as E P Thompson to recover these lost histories.[25] Indeed Gray, inheriting in many ways Coke's project, instead offers his form of academic mastery over a complex history and a complex present by offering his 'elements' of land law which, we are told on the cover of the second edition of his book, reveal the 'rational evolution of English law'. Not struggle, not partiality, not messiness but 'rational evolution'. The academic masters the law; the landscape is set for us.

And yet there is a terror and a pleasure which continues to play through these acts of mastery: they are only ever attempts at final mastery; there is always some excess, something which escapes. As the weather might suddenly change and the clouds come down upon the mountains, so the figures in Turner's painting may themselves become the victims of nature; of the unpredictable forces of nature. Nature may be beautiful but it may also be terrible. It cannot be finally mastered. As nature is imaged as woman; so both become the paradoxical place of security/stability (origin) and threat/fear (future).[26] A seductive pleasure

---

23   Blomley (1994) at p 93.

24   *Ibid* at p 104.

25   E P Thompson, *Customs in Common* (1991) Merlin.

26   See, eg, Rose (1993) *supra* n 8 and on shifts in the use of metaphor, Page duBois, *Sowing the Body* (1988) Chicago University Press.

so much more pleasurable because of the risks. Knowledge of law, mastery of law, can also be spoken in the same kind of way. In Hackney the metaphor of the chase is clearly imbued with sexuality; yet the object is given as the mastery of law.[27] In an article written by Gray:

> With private property, as with many illusions, we are easily beguiled into the error of fantastic projection upon the beautiful, artless object we think we see. We are seduced into believing that we have found an objective reality which embodies our intuitions and needs. But then, just as the notion seems reassuringly three-dimensional, the phantom figure dances away through our fingers and dissolves into a formless void.[28]

There can be no doubt that this figure is 'woman' and the searcher 'man'. And so one final reading (but in no sense do I mean this as the best, the deepest or the 'final' in any other sense than my final look at it in this paper) of the Turner might be to contrast the paradoxical evocation of nature. On the one hand as a representation of:

> ... law (as) even more 'natural'. Law and land locked together for all time, divorced from the contingencies and politicizing vagaries of social life. This suturing of nation, land and common law ... remains a powerful ideological force in contemporary English life.[29]

And yet, at the very same time, the very impossibility of a final act of mastery of law.

FIGURES IN A LANDSCAPE

The heady experience of the chase or of encounters with 'nature', may be replaced by the more benign image of the pastoral. This imagery plays on themes of a rural idyll lost, or rather almost lost; a time of accord, of the presence of figures in the landscape but figures which seem attuned to the rhythms of nature, the passing of the seasons and the fruitfulness of productivity. Signs of agricultural practices and rural habitation suggest productive co-operation rather than exploitation. Constable's picture of Brightwell used on the latest edition of Cheshire is a wonderful example of the pictorial art of the pastoral.[30] Images of stability, the slow rhythms of organic patterns of change, growth and decay belie any fear of rapidity of change or irrevocable loss; instead underpinning change and making us feel safe in a changing world we:

---

27 Jeffery Hackney, *Understanding Property Equity and Trusts* (1987) Fontana at p 10: 'The student becomes the hunter ... As the sense of participation increases, so does the pleasure; with the pleasure comes added motivation ...'

28 Kevin Gray, 'Property in Thin Air' *Cambridge Law Journal* (1991) 252 at p 305.

29 Blomley (1994) at p 75.

30 More precisely the use of certain pictures to build a narrative of, in this case, the English rural idyll. See Daniels (1993) on the construction of Constable as articulating national identity.

... live in an institutional temporality of repetition, of the immemorial coming around again, returning eternally ... [31]

This is 'the rational evolution of English law' rather than the history of struggle, of the interests of some groups triumphing over others, of people dispossessed or disadvantaged by law; instead we are invited to share in a common history of advantage and a promise that if all is not quite well now, balance will again be achieved.

The particular power of this narrative is a sense of place; of being a part of something which is enduring. The rural idyll is always just on our margins; never quite lost but a presence to be invoked both as a reminder of patterns which are enduring and as a warning against their loss. Nostalgia in this sense is not simply for a past but for the need, and possibility, of evoking that past as part of the present.[32] The geography of the rural idyll, the pastoral scene, is a geography of a moral and cognitive universe in which we are offered a place; knowledge of that place, acceptance of that place, offers the security of an identity. The identity offered, the geography offered, is however, in the dominant discourse, one of fixed identities and of limited horizons.[33] 'Knowing ones' place' is an acceptance of the *status quo*, an acceptance that security and certainty are the bulwarks against the fears and threats of change.

So a student in approaching an authoritative text is not only presented with images of the subject, of the continuities of land and law, but of their place in relation to that text. As the author is simply giving voice to an already constituted landscape, his own map being simply the best he can offer of a vision of that landscape, so the student is situated simply to receive the knowledge of that landscape. By accepting this passive stance the student may hope to come to see, to hear, what is being revealed. This place can only be secured by accepting the moral and cognitive universe which constitutes the landscape. Land, law, text become 'sutured' to construct 'land law'. Values of continuity, rationality, and indeed the working presumptions of necessity and relevance, construct the landscape and provide the contours of a map in which all information must be placed, examined and brought into relation as part of a whole. A whole which promises not simply beauty but mastery over the unruly.

The author, father, guide and mentor, is invested with the power of text and law. The student, child-like, must accept the authority of author as text and law. For the student then, to look up from the text, to ask questions about other landscapes and other maps, most transgressively to consider their own

---

31 Peter Goodrich and Yifat Hachamovitch, 'Time Out of Mind: An Introduction to the Semiotics of Common Law' in Peter Fitzpatrick (ed), *Dangerous Supplements: Resistance and Renewal in Jurisprudence* (1991) Duke University Press, at p 165.

32 See eg Dennis Klink, 'This Other Eden: Lord Denning's Pastoral Vision' (1994) *Oxford Journal of Legal Studies* 24.

33 Lee Davidoff *et al*, 'Figures in a Landscape' in A Oakley and J Mitchell (eds), *The Rights and Wrongs of Women* (1976) Penguin.

landscapes, is to face the fear of the loss of 'place', and therefore of the values of certainty and coherence, the promises of knowledge and mastery. Dissonance in text, or between text and law-in-world-out-there, or between text and reader; must be either silenced or simply received as an awful echo of what might be if we lose 'place'. Author of text and reader are placed within a simplistic relationship; in one is placed the trust of full explanation and in the other the fealty of deference. It is as difficult for one author to say 'I do not understand' in the sense that I cannot explain, or fit this into my map, as it is for the reader to say 'This does not make sense to me'. We require texts to offer guides and maps to us; but do we need to continue to invest them with such authority? Can we afford to? Can we allow them to construct our landscape of law without thinking more carefully about the narratives of law, the ideologies, they convey in the very way in which they are constituted? To need patterns, clusters of ideas, by which to make some sense of our world is not moot. To aspire to 'knowledge' is necessary. But to ignore the value-laden enterprise of the construction of landscape through text, is to presume that this is the only way of 'knowing' law, that law is rational, coherent and marked by patterns of change underpinned by continuity. It is to ignore struggle, loss, the pragmatic response to messiness, the violence of trying to impose one order over many interests. It is to presume that those things which do not fit are 'wrong' or not worthy of attention. It is to presume that the only values which are worthwhile are those which are in accord with the dominant ideology of the 'golden metewand'.

As 'Woman' has so often been used to represent the unrepresentable, that-which-does-not-fit, so women's own experiences of law can be utilised to challenge both the representation of the landscape as a logical whole and the predominance given to the ethical, and academic, values of coherence and certainty[34] to the exclusion of all others. Hearing dissonance, finding problem places in the landscape, indeed seeking that which has been hidden, lost or excluded; this may render not merely a better reflection of law-out-there, a more honest map, but also provide a sense of the limitations of the horizons we have been forced to work with and a sense of other horizons, other possibilities. To raise our eyes from the text and try to look more clearsightedly at the 'law' is not to dismiss it but to use it:

> The very images of dominion, of power in the land, may be identified as such, then reclaimed or reconstituted.[35]

However such a project necessitates an understanding of the act of 'viewing'. Rose, in examining possibilities for feminist geography, explores geographies focused on relationships, a mode of engagement which challenges the dominant masculinist gaze:

---

34 See eg Anne Bottomley, 'Self and Subjectivities: Languages of Claim in Property Law' in Anne Bottomley and Joanne Conaghan (eds), *Feminist Theory and Legal Strategy* (1993) Blackwells.

35 Daniels (1993) at p 7.

A network of interaction replace(s) the individualised and domineering view of the single point of the omniscient observer of landscape: they placed themselves in a contingent position defined in relation to friends and neighbours.

Other feminists have stressed not so much the position of the viewer of the land, but the focus of the gaze which re-presents the land ... 'the rearticulation of traditional space so that it ceases to function primarily as a space for the sight for a mastering gaze, but becomes the locus of relationships'. All these accounts posit a feminine relationship to landscape, yet all refuse to see an essential femininity.

They offer a 'feminine' resistance to hegemonic ways of seeing which dissolves the illusion of an unmarked, unitary, distanced, masculine spectator, but which also permits the expression of different ways of seeing among women. They suggest that strategies of position, scale and fragmentation are all important for challenging the particular structure of the gaze..Their task is to develop 'the conditions of representability of another social subject'...[36]

It is perhaps not surprising that images of cartography, acts of mapping, have been so productive in feminist thinking.[37] Visual metaphors, land and body, are sites of and give sight to, the contingencies of 'self' and the many locations of landscapes of relationships, meanings, dreams of change and horizons of desire. Giving body to law, land to land law, landscape to text, are strategies for not simply trying to make more sense of our world but of seeking to imagine, to image, other landscapes of possibility.

---

36 Rose (1993) at p 112.

37 See eg Alice Jardine, *Gynesis: Configurations of Women and Modernity* (1985) Ithica; Rosi Baidotti *Patterns of Dissonance* (1991) Polity, *Nomadic Subjects* (1994) Columbia. See also Green, Lim and Mackenzie in this volume.

CHAPTER SEVEN

MAPPING EQUITY'S PLACE: HERE BE DRAGONS

HILARY LIM

'This one is thought to be the best, Holiness,' the keeper said. The map showed Jerusalem in the middle, haloed and marked in red ink on the dark brown, stained parchment ... the map was annotated with blocks of writing in a meticulous tiny hand. The world was a great disc, surrounded by a river running round its rim; the corners of the vellum were filled up with angels. Within the ring, in every country depicted, swarmed beasts and birds of fabulous appearance.[1]

INTRODUCTION

In 1954 Lord Evershed could safely state that in only one case since the Judicature Acts 1873-75, the *Winter Garden Theatre*,[2] had the phrase 'fusion of Law and Equity'[3] been used in a House of Lords' decision. More recently there has been a fundamental change in judicial rhetoric and references to the 'fusion of law and equity' have become almost commonplace.

The most obvious example of this change is the deceptively simple statement by Lord Browne Wilkinson in *Tinsley v Milligan* that: 'More than 100 years has elapsed since law and equity became fused.'[4] That case involved a claim by the defendant to an equitable share in property under a resulting trust; a decision from within equity's discursive heartlands. Similar pronouncements may be found, however, within the 'new territories'. Hobhouse J, considering a dispute between a bank and a local authority which had been involved in an *ultra vires* swaps transaction, declares that: 'Since the Judicature Acts in the last century the systems of law and equity have been fused and must now be regarded as a single system.'[5] Both statements are examples of how law operates as an authoritative discourse, in that 'fusion' is presented as a self-evident truth requiring no further justification.[6]

The dominant academic response to this rhetoric has been to revive the old procedural/substantive divide and debate whether fusion is 'real' or a 'fallacy'. Proponents of the former position tend to view the process as a logical

---

1   Jill Paton Walsh, *Knowledge of Angels* (1994) Colt Books Ltd at p 229.

2   *Winter Garden Theatre (London) Ltd v Millenium Productions Ltd* [1948] AC 173.

3   'Reflections on the Fusion of Law and Equity After 75 Years' (1954) 70 LQR 326 at p 335.

4   [1993] 3 WLR 126 at 147.

5   *Westdeutsche Landesbank Girozentrale v The Council of the London Borough of Islington, Kleinwort Benson Ltd v The Borough Council of Sandwell* [1993] 2 Bank LR 159 at 176.

6   See P Goodrich, *Reading the Law* (1986) Blackwell ch 6.

rationalisation of legal and equitable principles and consider means by which fusion might be hastened. Birks, for instance, in a discussion about one aspect of the law of restitution, the recovery of misapplied funds, remarks:

> ... the recognition of the independence of the law of restitution, based on unjust enrichment, which, though it has its own additional internal complications, may in turn be seen as part of the larger task of unifying law and equity.[7]

Those writers, like Jill Martin,[8] who fall within the 'fallacy camp' seek to argue that doctrinal coherence is compatible with law and equity existing as separate entities. The two spheres are 'proximate' but not symmetrical. In this version the remarks in *Tinsley v Milligan* are read as just 'one example of an attempt to develop equitable principles by reflecting upon the position at common law'.[9]

In this article a different approach is taken to 'fusion'. A question is posed: what is, and will be, the effect of this change in rhetoric upon those who seek to use the law strategically to improve the position of those subject to oppressions? This question is underpinned by two interrelated, but contested, assumptions: (a) that law and legal discourse are not monolithic; and (b) that law can be used strategically and should not be abandoned as a site of resistance.

LAW AS A PLURAL INSTITUTION

There has been a tendency in legal theory to assume that legal discourse, specifically in its relations with other professional discourses, is unitary. Law is viewed as impervious to penetration by other knowledges, its legitimacy fed by every such encounter with alternative discourses. By way of illustration in Goodrich's discussion of legal discourse and its interface with other professional discourses[10] he details how the former is authoritative and rhetorical, thereby enabling it to control its reception whilst excluding challenges to its 'truth'. He suggests that law will consume other discursive lexicons and remake them in its own image. All discourses are presented as subject to law's greedy imperialism.

Although writing from a somewhat different perspective, King's analysis of law as an autopoetic system[11] has some features in common with Goodrich's depiction of the law as authoritarian. Drawing upon the work of Teubner, he argues that law's self-referential and autopoetic nature is apparent from its failure

---

7   'Trusts in the recovery of Misapplied Assets: Tracing, Trusts, and Restitution' in Ewan McKendrick (ed), *Commercial Aspects of Trusts and Fiduciary Obligations* (1992) Clarendon Press at p 165. See also M Lunney 'Towards a Unified Estoppel: the Long and Winding Road' [1992] Conv 239 at p 244.

8   'Fusion, Fallacy and Confusion; A Comparative Study' (1994) Conv 13.

9   *Ibid* 30.

10   Peter Goodrich, *Legal Discourse: Studies in Linguistics, Rhetoric and Legal Analysis* (1987) St Martin's Press.

11   See M King, 'The "Truth" About Autopoesis' (1993) 20 *J of Law and Society* 221; M King, 'Child Welfare Within Law: The Emergence of a Hybrid Discourse' (1991) 18 *J of Law and Society* 303. See also M King and C Piper, *How the Law Thinks About Children* (1990) Gower.

to deal with the world outside itself. He comments, in his book with Piper, that law 'can only reconstruct that world in a form that is acceptable as legal communication accessible to other legal communications in the network of legal communications'.[12]

Goodrich anticipates that he will be criticised and stresses that his is 'only a preliminary analysis, an attempt to characterise and exemplify in a schematic fashion certain of the peculiarities of legal discourse without ... claiming to be comprehensive or complete'.[13] Nevertheless, in emphasising that legal discourse manifests the characteristics of authoritarian or autopoetic discourse, both writers are in danger of delineating law's interface with other discourses as a simple one-way, all enveloping relation meeting little or no resistance.

In the discussion about 'fusion' presented below it will not be denied either that law has an immense power both to distort and exclude, or that each engagement with law by those from the outside may serve to invest the legal order with greater legitimacy. Neither is it denied that it is law's monopoly on sanctioned violence which is at the root of legal discourse. Law may disqualify, repress and absorb counter-discourses. Moreover, law's claim to have a unique affinity with justice, means that it sets itself above other knowledges and excludes other truths. Nevertheless, it will be argued that law, and in particular equity, can be both empowering and disempowering. Necessarily, this implies a view of law and legal discourse which challenge the monolithic visions.

LAW AND RESISTANCE

Limited support for the notion that law may be used strategically and should not be abandoned as a site of resistance comes from an initially surprising source. From a feminist viewpoint, Smart has argued that law is phallogocentric.[14] One of her main purposes in writing is to construct 'a warning to feminism to avoid the siren call of law'.[15] Mirroring Goodrich, she explains how the law deals with everyday, human experiences which are edited and rewritten into legal stories for processing through the system. Law stands, therefore, at a safe observation point, above the quagmire.

For Smart this separation of law and reality makes it possible for law to disqualify alternative knowledges, thereby feeding its status as the faucet of dispassionate justice. Moreover she sees law as phallogocentric because it excludes all discourses which run counter to the masculine world view.

---

12 *Ibid* at p 23.

13 *Op cit* at p 169.

14 The concept is derived from a combination of phallocentric – (the masculine, heterosexual imperative) and logocentric – the fact that knowledge is not neutral but produced under conditions of patriarchy.

15 Carol Smart, *Feminism and the Power of Law* (1989) Routledge at p 160.

However, she admits that to take her discussion to its logical conclusion would lead to 'total inactivity and political paralysis'.[16] Elsewhere she states:

> [F]eminist socio-legal scholarship [should] ... grasp the nettle that law is not simply law ... not a set of tools which we can bend into a more favourable shape ... We must, therefore, remain critical of this tendency without abandoning law as a *site* of struggle ... Law is ... productive of gender difference and identity, yet this law is not monolithic and unitary.[17]

Using law in the attempt to achieve social change may be hazardous, but it must be acknowledged that it remains attractive to those struggling under oppression.

Kingdom too asserts that Smart's warnings about law should not make it a no-go area for feminists:

> My view is that, just as analysis and activism with regard to economic struggles do not automatically accord economy the privileged status which monetarists claim for it, so writing about and participating in legal struggle is not automatically to cede legal ground to antifeminist institutions and practices.[18]

Smart does note that there are occasions where the law has explicitly deferred to other discourses, for instance, medical knowledge/power. Thus, at the meeting places of law and other discourses, '[in] some instances we may see a coalition, in others a conflict and we cannot assume a pattern of clear signposts which will point us to an inevitable future'.[19]

Further, she is prepared to state that 'we cannot know in advance whether a recourse to law will empower women, children or men'.[20] As Kingdom argues, feminists have to decide whether or not to intervene on specific legal issues. Their decisions will be 'a matter of deliberation and calculation, paying attention to the specifics of the legal political issue to hand'.[21]

This article aims to contribute towards an understanding of the specifics of equity which will enhance such calculations. However, there is a problem with even imagining a feminist politics of equity, let alone the notion of creative feminist lawyers devising strategic interventions in this area. Beyond the specialised field of cohabitation and the family home, equity is scarcely a vibrant area of feminist campaigning. Debates around the law and pressure for law reform have generally been concerned with sexual harassment, rape, new reproductive technologies and so forth.

Initially equity's potential to empower or disempower the marginal must be examined not at the boundary between legal and professional discourses but in a

---

16 *Ibid* at p 49.
17 Carol Smart, *Law, Crime and Sexuality* (1995) Sage at p 198.
18 Elizabeth Kingdom, *What's Wrong With Rights* (1991) Edinburgh University Press at p 148.
19 Carol Smart (1989) at p 19.
20 *Ibid* at p 138.
21 *Op cit* at p 148.

different space. King's attention is directed to how law thinks about science, or more specifically what he delineates as 'child welfare science'. In contrast, Smart is interested not simply in what happens when law meets science, but with the interface between law and various discourses of rebellion, especially feminist discourses. More crucially she is concerned with the 'little narratives' of individual litigants as they encounter the system. For there is a form of resistance which is much more difficult to grasp than the psy-discourses. As Smart indicates 'much more work needs to be done in tracing how women have resisted and negotiated'[22] the power of law.

Legal discourse may well be in the business, as Goodrich asserts, of sealing its challengers' lips and filtering out any alternative visions of the world. However, the opposition, if it is an opposition in the accepted sense of the word, may not necessarily accept its fate. Thus we find Smart acknowledging that in spite of a number of discursive practices which may render litigants mute, 'of course parties are not always silenced'.[23]

Smart could simply mean by this that the maverick or eccentric individual occasionally breaks through the comfortable and cosy atmosphere of legal technocrats – judge, defence lawyer and prosecutor – in her attempt to make her voice heard. However, Smart is touching upon something which goes beyond the actions of the non-conformist, important though these may be. Dews has described this as 'the burgeoning plurality of the languages of rebellion ...';[24] feminisms, black knowledges and other discourses of resistance, struggle and dissent.

I am concerned here with this multiplicity of languages, the little narratives, specifically of women, and their meetings with law. Only through an understanding of what might happen to the individual litigant and her story would it be possible even to begin to develop a politics of equity. It is argued that the space of the courtroom does provide the possibility for a conversation that might not otherwise be held, the possibility for a story to be told which otherwise would have been confined to the domestic sphere.

This conversation and the story may be distorted as it is translated into legal language, but the very act of translation establishes a claim to have a place in the public, to be able to share in the discourse of law. Having one's day in court, making one's voice heard, even if it does not finally win that day is better than having no voice at all. As Douzinas and Warrington have recently stated:

> [There is] ... a key area of law that seems ... to acknowledge the importance of alterity. The law recognises within its own procedures and attempts to impose to a certain extent upon decision-makers and judges the principle ... let the other speak, before judging another give her a hearing ... [T]he audi rule shows

---

22 Smart (1992) at p 198.

23 Smart (1989) at p 11.

24 Peter Dews, 'The *Nouvelle Philosophie* and Foucault' (1979) 8 *Economy and Society* 147 at p 149.

the law concerned to hear the concrete person who comes before it, rather than to calculate and adjudicate the general qualities and characteristics of the abstracted legal person.[25]

It will be suggested that in equitable discourse the 'audi rule' is particularly well–developed. The demand to be heard as a full and unique person, rather than as a representative of a broad legal category can, upon occasion, be made in Chancery.

A 'PLACE' FOR EQUITY?

Mason, writing in a recent issue of the *Law Quarterly Review* poses a question: is there a 'place' for equity in the contemporary common law world?[26]

He celebrates equity's extension 'beyond old boundaries into new territory where no Lord Chancellor's foot has previously left its imprint'.[27]

The new lands consist of what Mason broadly describes as the fields of 'business' and 'commerce' where the introduction of equitable doctrines and relief have raised standards of conduct. In addition he perceives a dynamic interplay between law and equity, specifically in the areas of restitution and estoppel, leading to 'greater symmetry'.

For Mason, therefore, equity has an assured place in the common law world and is capable of marching out beyond its traditional borders to permeate the old bastions of its historical rival. Equity's strength is derived from 'its concern with standards of conscience, fairness, equality and its protection of relationships of trust and confidence'.[28] As a consequence, according to Mason, equity has a peculiar flexibility when compared with law. Its incursions into the commercial world secure a thriving future for this jurisdiction based upon the values of good conscience.

At one level the above assessment of equity's position on both the current and future maps of the common law sphere of influence provides one of the more subtle interjections to the debate about 'fusion'. Mason admits to a convergence between some equitable and legal principles and uncovers a certain overlap between damages and equitable compensation. However, the most useful aspect of his discussion, for present purposes, is Mason's choice of the metaphor of the map. The metaphor is one which has been utilised recently in attempts to examine power relations, and in particular, the power of law.

---

25 C Douzinas and R Warrington, *Justice Miscarried: Ethics Aesthetics and the Law* (1994) Harvester Wheatsheaf at p 176.

26 Anthony Mason, 'The Place of Equity and Equitable Remedies in the Contemporary Common Law World' [1994] *Law Quarterly Review* 238.

27 *Ibid* at p 239.

28 *Ibid.*

Space has always had a particular resonance within feminism and this is particularly obvious in discussions about the public/private divide and its connection with masculinist power. As Rose states:

> When feminists talk about experiences of space, very often they evoke a sense of difficulty. Being in space is not easy. Indeed, at its worst this feeling results in a desire to make ourselves absent from space; it can mean that 'we acquiesce in being made invisible, in our occupying no space. We participate in our own erasure.[29]

Within feminism women are often seen as confined by space, bumping against 'glass ceilings', excluded from male inscribed territory, whether in the street or at a discursive level.

However, in the post-Foucauldian world spatial metaphors have become ubiquitous in the struggle to theorise power in the context of multiple oppressions. A list of the most commonly used terms includes 'position, location, situation, mapping; ... centre-margin, open-closed, inside-outside, global-local; liminal space, third space, not-space, impossible-space; the city'.[30] At the same time, feminist maps have become multi-dimensional, as the 'cartographers' struggle to account for differences between women arising out of multiple (often intersecting) oppressions or micro-aggressions connected with race, class and sexuality.

Spatial metaphors have also played a specific role in the critique of universalist/essentialist feminisms by women of colour. bell hooks' writings on the centre-margin provide the most obvious example of the use of such a metaphor.[31] Her template is the southern US town in which she grew up, where the black community was divided territorially from the white town by the railway tracks. Spatially the white town was clearly a geographical centre, with the black community existing in its economic and social margins. However, the centre of the town was not a separate entity, but dependent upon the service workers living in its margins.

bell hooks locates herself in the margins which are for her both real and metaphorical. However, the margin does not simply exist as a function of the centre, defined only by reference to that centre. The map is much more complex and permits the imagining of a different geography elsewhere. The marginal black community of bell hooks' childhood was also a place of resistance. The pain and suffering of those black people who fought the hegemony of the centre and their silencing by that centre was immense and resistance was not easily achieved. Nevertheless, bell hooks argues that location in the margins is dangerous but necessary:

---

29 Gillian Rose, *Feminism and Geography* (1993) Polity Press at p 143.

30 Michael Keith and Steve Pile, 'The politics of place ...' in M Keith and S Pile (eds), *Place and the Politics of Identity* (1993) Routledge at p 1. As Keith and Pile point out at the end of their list these concepts are often used quite loosely and it may be difficult to discover whether such words are being used as literal metaphor or whether the 'space' referred to is in some sense perceived as 'real'.

31 bell hooks, *Feminist Theory: From Margin to Center* (1984) South End Press.

Our living depends on our ability to conceptualize alternatives, often impoverished. Theorizing about this experience aesthetically, critically is an agenda for radical cultural practice. For me this space of radical openness is a margin – a profound edge.[32]

Margins are therefore the place for resisting the hegemonic power of the centre, they are the place for building strategy. They are also the space with the openness to imagine new geographies and new communities. They are the place of the dragons and the place of the angels.

A MAP OF LAW?

The concepts of spatial politics have also been used by writers concerned to examine more directly the power of law. De Souza Santos has used the metaphor of the map in a sustained way.[33] Although this is not openly expressed De Souza Santos's argument reveals that the metaphor of the map is capable, as some spatial metaphors are not, of 'maintaining a critical awareness of the translations connecting material and metaphorical space'.[34] He considers, as do those legal theorists discussed earlier, the way in which legal discourse distorts the narratives of the 'real' world:

> In my view, the relations law entertains with social reality are similar to those between maps and spatial reality. Indeed laws are maps; written laws are cartographic maps; customary informal laws are mental maps.[35]

His primary concern, as indicated above, is to explore the striking resemblances between legal distortions of reality and those within cartography. Maps are projections and the map maker has to make decisions about which specifics of the real world to distort in order to render them suitable for production. These decisions are based partly upon the technical requirements of the specific map but also upon the ideology of the cartographer – not always in immediately obvious ways. He points out that during the cold war the western mass media would enlarge the Soviet Union, in their maps, to exaggerate the size of the 'Communist Threat'. Similarly, maps produced under British imperialism grossly deflated the size of the whole continent of Africa.

De Souza Santos argues that the process of ideological projection can be detected in legal systems, as well as the production of maps such that 'each legal order has a centre and a periphery'.

The centre of bourgeois state legality is, for De Souza Santos, clearly occupied by contracts. Both theoretically and conceptually, he asserts that

---

32   bell hooks, *Yearning: Race, Gender and Cultural Politics* (1991) Turnaround at p 149.

33   See De Sousa Santos, 'Law: A Map of Misreading: Toward a Postmodern Conception of Law' (1987) 14 *Journal of Law and Society* 279.

34   Neil Smith and Cindi Katz, 'Grounding Metaphor', in Keith and Pile (eds) *supra* n 30 at p 68.

35   *Op cit* at p 282.

contractual principles have dominated legislation, legal training and legal ideology:

> Here the space is mapped in greater detail and absorbs greater inputs of institutional resources (legal professions, courts, etc) and symbolic resources (legal science, legal ideology and culture, etc).[36]

The techniques and ideologies of the centre are frequently exported to the periphery with little thought for their appropriateness. Peripheral needs are 'interpreted and satisfied from the point of view of the centre.[37]

It is easy to locate areas of law such as welfare law, housing law and family law on the periphery of this map. Situating equity is a little more difficult. Equity's traditional discursive subjects are women and children and this makes it at least in some degree marginal. However, the idea of 'fusion' would in this model be an inevitable absorption of the margin by the centre. Equitable concepts derived from notions of unconscionability would be displaced by those from the contractual centre, such as unreasonableness, with different distortions of social reality.

Mason, in his discussion about whether there is a place for equity in the common law world, does not explore his mapping metaphor with De Souza Santos' depth or theoretical rigour. However, it is certain that he regards equity's break-out from its former 'Bleak House' stronghold, protecting 'widows and orphans', into realms dominated by common law contractual concepts as evidence of both convergence and the seeds for equity's continued survival. Not surprisingly, like many other academics, he seizes upon the so-called *Quistclose*[38] cases as exemplary of a new kind of equity. For instance, he quotes approvingly Gummow J's remarks in *Re Australian Elizabethan Theatre Trust* (1991) 102 ALR 681.

> ... the striking feature of the *Quistclose* litigation ... that whilst previously it might have been thought that debt and trust were distinct and disparate norms, it was thereafter clear that in a given case the transaction under analysis might bear a dual character.[39]

Equity, formerly on the periphery, thus seems to be making important interventions on the centre of legal power and thereby enhancing its authority. Other obvious examples of a collusion between contract and equity include the

---

36 *Ibid* at p 292.

37 *Ibid*.

38 This line of cases takes its name from *Barclays Bank Ltd v Quistclose Investments Ltd* [1970] AC 567, although authority stretches back at least to *Toovey v Milne* (1819) 2 B & Ald 683. They have been described as 'new model commercial trusts', see Graham Moffat, *Trusts Law: Text and Materials* (1994) Butterworths at p 526. Certainly, Lord Wilberforce who gave the unanimous judgment of the House of Lords in *Quistclose* saw in this analysis the 'flexible interplay of law and equity'. For a useful review of the recognition of *Quistclose* trusts in England, Australia and New Zealand see Rickett (1991) 107 LQR 60.

39 *Ibid* at 693.

underpinning of the fiduciary relationship with contractual principles in pension fund trusts and the involvement of charitable trusts in the 'contract culture'.[40]

There is a contrast between Mason's military map of equity's barbarian hordes visiting the marketplaces of the Legal Empire to participate in an exchange of norms before returning to the hinterland and De Souza Santos' map of law dominated by the contractual centre. Neither picture is, of course, more 'true' than the other and by employing the mapping metaphor both provide a way out of the somewhat sterile 'fusion' debate. However, the interface between the legal and equitable discourses gives a more complex and cloudy picture than that suggested by Mason. It is easy to point to judicial statements about fusion, but the convergence of legal and equitable principles is still slow and uneven.

Similarly, the other component of the relationship referred to by Mason, that is the increasing invasions by equity into contract, may be overemphasised. It is too convenient to see the story of equity in developments within the 'big' trusts. Pension fund trusts and charitable trusts, although of huge importance to the wider economy, are increasingly coming under administrative regulation through legislation. The Chancery courts are giving way to enhanced roles for the Charity Commissioners and Pension Fund Ombudsman.[41]

At the same time equity's heartlands may seem to be shrinking. A parallel may be drawn with family law. Recently Eekelaar has argued that this is a jurisdiction in search of a mission.[42] He suggests that with the advent of the Children Act 1989, the courts have been marginalised in family matters such that they have lost their traditional role of protecting the welfare of the child and now only deal with 'exceptional' cases. One could add that the Child Support Act 1991 and proposals to resolve divorce through conciliation marginalise the courts still further in this field. Chancery Courts, not least through their inherent jurisdiction to protect and control persons with disabilities have made

---

40 On the overlap between contract and equity in pension funds see *Imperial Group Pension Trust Ltd v Imperial Tobacco Ltd* [1991] 1 WLR 589 where Browne-Wilkinson V-C indicated that pension fund trusts were underpinned with an 'implied obligation of good faith' owed by the employer to the employee. For a more general discussion of the importance of a contract analysis in a variety of trust contexts see R Cotterell, 'Trusting in Law: Legal and Moral Concepts of Trust' (1993) 46 CLP 75.

41 Even this movement to administrative regulation is uneven. Recent reforms in 1992 and 1993 to the law of charities have led to a wider role for the Charity Commissioners but at the same time there has been a progressive reduction in the powers of the Official Custodian for charities. Since 1961 the Official Custodian had been responsible for approximately £1.25 billion of shares and unit trusts belonging to some 40,000 charities. Changes made in the Charities Act 1992 require trustees of these charities to administer their own funds or find professionals to manage them on their behalf.

42 J Eekelaar, 'A Jurisdiction in Search of a Mission: Family Proceedings in England and Wales' (1994) 57 MLR 839.

incursions into, and played a part in constructing, the family.[43] Equity's role in constituting the family is declining and may decrease further if the Law Commission proposes legislation to deal with *de facto* relationships.

Returning to the metaphor of the map, one can see equity's realm as distant from the centre of power. Yet it has embassies in many discrete states. Moreover, there is an exchange of norms between equity and law in the discursive field of commerce and business, although the borders are fluid. This exchange may be the basis for equity's survival or it may be the source of its absorption or destruction. It may be that:

> ...the centre itself is the true nomad, it is where all cultures come to exchange their moments and to lose themselves. Come, then, in order to raid that nomadism, in order to carry off potency.[44]

OPENINGS AND CLOSURES IN EQUITY

Whatever the eventual outcome of fusion, this article poses a question: Does this exchange of norms matter for those subject to micro-aggressions? Mason, for example, whilst he is certain that, '[t]he underlying values of equity centred on good conscience will almost certainly continue to be a driving force in the shaping of the law',[45] warns that: '[b]ecause the concepts employed are not susceptible of sharp definition, there is a risk of some erosion in the apparent distinctions which have been maintained hitherto between equitable concepts such as "unconscionable" and "inequitable" and common law concepts such as "unfair" and "unreasonable".'[46]

This erosion, however uneven, it is argued, disadvantages those located in the margins who seek to get their stories heard in the legal theatre. For it is suggested that equity's relative openness, which arises in part from its peripheral location on the map of law makes it easier for 'little narratives' to penetrate legal discourse. Perhaps the most useful aspect of talking about law as a map, is that maps have boundaries and they can admit that some areas are unmappable. The template is the medieval map, with the religious centre, the clearly marked 'known world' and the areas outside its circle filled with angels or simply marked 'Here Be Dragons'.

---

43 See also A Bottomley and J Roche, 'Conflict and Consensus: A Critique of the Language of Informal Justice', in R Mathews (ed), *Informal Justice* (1988) Sage at pp 87-107. In particular they argue: 'Family law is a modern amalgam of traditions derived from the ecclesiastical courts, the courts of equity and statute law' at p 95.

44 Jean Francois Lyotard, '*Le Mur du Pacifique*' in A Benjamin (ed), *The Lyotard Reader* (1989) Basil Blackwell at p 62.

45 *Op cit* at p 258.

46 *Op cit* at pp 258-59.

A concern with the discourses of rebellion and the little narratives of litigants, arising out of the challenge to monolithic visions of law, can be added into this metaphorical map of law. It is useful to turn to Bottomley and Roche's discussion of family law in which they challenge the notion that conciliation processes necessarily offer an 'alternative' to a formal, courtroom and adversarial process.[47] They argue that family law has never been 'law-like' in the sense of a simplistic characterisation of the formal legal system. Family law has been produced from diverse ingredients which give it a unique flavour and its methods of enquiry and the considerable discretion given to its judges do not 'rest easily alongside the imagery of adversarial proceedings'.[48] On the map of law, therefore, many areas will be far from the authoritarian centre and many parts are unmapped. In bell hooks' margins of social reality there lie the possibilities and dangers of radical openness. Translated onto the legal map one can see in 'peripheral' family law, as described by Bottomley and Roche, a discursive openness which it is argued can also be found in the field of equity.

Equity's openness arises in a number of ways, including its marked interest in narrative. It has been argued that the audi-principle is highly developed in equity, allowing the other to be heard prior to the making of a decision. As in any area of law, there is a sifting of the facts into those which are 'relevant' and therefore of legal import and those which are not. However, equitable case law provides detailed readings of 'realities', albeit through stories which distort those realities.

This focus upon 'the facts' relates closely to the high degree of indeterminacy in equity's concepts and principles. The common law as a whole is essentially dynamic and indefinite, but equitable concepts built around the notion of unconscionability are markedly inexact and capable of re(formation). The recent revival of *donatio mortis causa* in *Sen v Hedley*[49] is just one instance of the possibilities equity offers to the creative lawyer. The doctrine had disappeared from view, warranting only the most cursory of references in equity textbooks. Mrs Sen's counsel brought *donatio mortis causa* back to visibility and thereby secured for her a £300,000 house. The judicial rhetoric in the Court of Appeal is a source of delight with Nourse LJ declaring that: 'certainty of precedent, while in general most desirable, is not of as great an importance in relation to a doctrine which is as infrequently invoked as this.'[50]

In other areas of the common law, alongside decisions like *Sen v Hedley*, one finds cases which demonstrate the 'will to certainty'. Nourse LJ may say of the constructive trust that it 'has been a ready means of developing our property law in modern times and that the process is a continuing one'.[51] However, Saville LJ

---

47 A Bottomley and J Roche, 'Conflict and Consensus: A Critique of the Language of Informal Justice' in R Mathews (ed), *Informal Justice* (1988) Sage.

48 *Ibid* at p 95.

49 [1991] 2 All ER 636.

50 *Ibid* at 647.

51 *Ibid*.

in *Guardian Ocean Cargoes Ltd and Others v Banco Do Brasil*[52] equally firmly resisted the attempts by the trial judge to extend the scope of constructive trusts. One basis for which Hirst J had permitted the plaintiff in this case to recover three payments, made by it as part of a financing deal which ultimately failed, was a *Quistclose* analysis. In this analysis, the trial judge had seen a clear example of the remedial use of trusts. Saville LJ rejected this extension of constructive trusts. He chose to take a pure trusts law approach and exclude the use of trusts as a remedy:

> In my judgment it is quite impossible to spell out of the transactions between the parties any trust relationship at all ... there is nothing to indicate that there was any intention that the Bank should become a fiduciary in respect of the payments, or that it would be unconscionable were the Bank not to be treated as such ... to my mind there is neither room nor need for a trust in this case.[53]

Upon occasion the fear that some judges have of equity is almost palpable. Judge Baker QC in *Re Stapylton Fletcher*, clearly sees equity as something of a 'loose cannon' when he argues that '(t)he court must be very cautious in devising equitable interests and remedies which erode the statutory scheme for distribution on insolvency';[54] Equity's loose discursive weave is, therefore, accompanied by examples of closure.

The accessibility of equity is simultaneously exciting for, and dangerous to, alter-discourses. As Patricia Williams has stated there is also 'openness as a profane relation. Not communion, but exposure, vulnerability, the collapse of boundary in the most assaultive way'.[55] She has argued, together with other members of the Race Critique, that any resolution of a dispute which provides wide discretionary power to the decision maker puts those who are marginalised at a great disadvantage.[56] In particular it is suggested that this type of discretion may foster racial and ethnic bias. They are primarily concerned that a lack of procedural rules, specifically rules of evidence, lead to an intimacy in informal systems of justice which is detrimental to the less powerful.

In Chancery there is of course no particular lack of procedural guidelines and the court is loaded down with the full panoply of theatrical techniques. However, at the concrete level of decisions within equity, disputes over the family home between cohabitees provide a warning of a danger inherent in equity. As an example, Bottomley points out that in the well-known case of *Eves v Eves*.[57] Lord Denning constructed two women-subjects as Janet the innocent

---

52 [1994] 2 Lloyd's Rep 152.

53 *Ibid* at 159-60.

54 [1995] 1 All ER 192 at 213-14.

55 P Williams, *The Alchemy of Race and Rights: Diary of a Law Professor* (1991) Harvard University Press at p 199.

56 See R Delgado *et al*, 'Fairness and Formality: Minimizing the Risk of Prejudice in Alternative Dispute Resolution' (1985) *Wisconsin Law Review* 1359.

57 [1975] 1 WLR 1338.

damsel in distress and her counterpoint Gloria the glamorous scarlet woman.[58] The open texture of equity permitted Lord Denning to produce this patriarchal narrative, to make this choice of detail and turn the realities of these women's lives into both caricature and stereotype.

The simultaneous risks and opportunities presented to women by equity will be explored in the discussion of a particular case: *Nestlé v National Westminster Bank plc*.[59] It was chosen for three reasons. First, it is a case from within equity's traditional realm, for it is concerned with the management of a small family trust. Second, it is not about the imposition of constructive trusts in cases of cohabitation. Not surprisingly it appears to have become the practice for writers, specifically from feminist standpoints, to analyse the role of equity within the field of *de facto* families. It may be worth breaking the mould. Third, the woman litigant did not 'win' her case against the bank either in the court at first instance or in the Court of Appeal. It is therefore a challenging site in which to examine whether equity's openness can be used strategically by those within the margins.

TALES OF HOFFMANN

The decision of the High Court in *Nestlé v National Westminster Bank plc* with respect to the duty of trustees to invest, was unreported, yet it made surprising appearances within academic writing throughout the common law world. In a major Australian trust law text it was claimed that: 'Modern portfolio theory has recently been recognised as providing a desirable investment strategy for trustees by Hoffmann J in the English Chancery Division.'[60]

Similarly, in the reports of those involved with the redrafting of the US Restatement (Third) on Trusts the decision is cited at length in the review of portfolio theory and its application to trusts.[61] Part of this enthusiasm may be attributed to the few sentences specifically on portfolio theory. Hoffmann J stated:

> Modern trustees acting within their investment powers are entitled to be judged by the standards of current portfolio theory, which emphasises the risk level of the entire portfolio rather than the risk attaching to each investment taken in isolation ... an investment which in isolation is too risky and therefore in breach of trust may be justified when held in conjunction with other investments.

---

58 See A Bottomley, 'Self and Subjectivities: Languages of Claim in Property Law', in Anne Bottomley and Joanne Conaghan (eds), *Feminist Theory and Legal Strategy* (1993) Blackwells.

59 (1988: Lexis) (Transcript: Barnett Lenton); [1993] 1 WLR 1260 CA.

60 Ford and Lee, *Principles of the Law of Trusts* (1990) The Law Book Co Ltd at p 480.

61 The definition of the trustee's standard of care in the Restatement (Third) now reads: 'a trustee is under a duty to invest and manage the funds of a trust as a prudent investor would ... this standard requires reasonable care, skill and caution, and is to be applied to investments not in isolation but in the context of the trust portfolio'. For a discussion of the deliberations over the redrafting see E C Halbach Jr (1992) 77 *Iowa Law Review* 1151.

Discussions of this theory have concentrated the minds of academics considering proposals for reform of the rules on trustee investment.[62] However, there may also be interest in the case for its novelty value.

The gradual case-by-case modernisation of trustee investment law has been a process dominated by litigants connected either with charities[63] or – to a lesser degree – pension funds.[64] Even these steps towards change have been faltering. A similar picture is painted by Gordon in the United States:

> A significant factor in the development of the common law is the decision of particular litigants to contest rules adverse to their interests ... What is surprising, even stunning, is the paucity of recently decided cases that take up the question of investment prudence'.[65]

For, as Gordon further argues, beneficiaries of large trusts may be able to bear the financial cost in challenging existing investment rules, but a peculiar characteristic of trust law reduces the likelihood of legal action: settlors are permitted to contract around the standards and duties required by law of trustees through the use of exclusion clauses in trust instruments.

The case of *Nestlé v National Westminster Bank plc* was, therefore, a most unusual occurrence since it involved a challenge by the remainder beneficiary – Georgina Nestlé – upon the trustee of a relatively small family trust fund. She claimed that the National Westminster Bank plc (formerly the National Provincial Bank) as sole trustee mismanaged the fund over a period of many years. It was contended that, but for this poor administration, she would have had a portfolio of investments worth £1,800,000 rather than the £269,203 which she received in 1986. In short, she argued that the bank were in breach of trust and that the bank's behaviour amounted to negligence. Her claim did not succeed because Georgina Nestlé was, in the opinion of the Court of Appeal, unable to prove any actual loss to the fund as a consequence of the actions or inactions of the trustee bank.

Hoffmann J states that Georgina Nestlé's conduct is not relevant to assessing whether her claim for breach of trust is well-founded. However, he precedes this statement with a construction of the plaintiff which surpasses Lord Denning's old-fashioned stereotypes and borders upon misogyny:

---

62 It is open to discussion as to what Hoffmann J intended to mean by the phrase 'portfolio theory'. It seems unlikely that he was referring to the notion of portfolio theory as devised by economists. It seems more probable that he was in Pozen's words simply referring to 'the principle of diversification [which] is that the overall construction of the portfolio, rather than the selection of individual securities, should be the focus of investment decisions, R Pozen 'Money Managers and Securities Research' (1976) 51 NUYLR 923 at p 940.

63 See for example: *Trustees of the British Museum v AG* [1984] 1 WLR 418; *Steel v Wellcome Custodian Trustees Ltd* [1988] 1 WLR 167 (where an application by trustees of a charity with funds of approximately £3,200 for a wide degree of discretion in exercising their duty to invest was sanctioned, incidentally by Hoffmann J); and *Harries v Church Commissioners* [1992] 1 WLR 1241.

64 See *Cowan v Scargill* [1984] 2 All ER 750.

65 Jeffrey N Gordon, 'The Puzzling Persistence of the Prudent Man Rule' (1987) 62 NY Univ LR 52 at p 75.

> If ever anyone was born with a mission in life, it was Miss Georgina Nestlé. The mission was to wreak vengeance on the National Provincial Bank Trust Department for the supposed wrongs inflicted on her family. She was brought up from infancy in her mother's unshakeable belief that the Bank had tried to destroy their lives ...

Despite Judge Hoffmann's denial of psychoanalytic skills he describes Georgina Nestlé using the bank as a 'surrogate victim on which to be revenged for the pain caused by parental rejection' The behaviour is said to be marked by its 'intemperance and irrationality'. The 'evidence' for this includes Georgina's conviction that the Bank was a conspiracy of freemasons and in league with her one-time solicitor, the fact that she called in the City of London Fraud Squad and the demonstrations she organised with her mother in which they 'paraded through the City carrying sandwich boards inscribed with suitably uncomplimentary texts' about the bank. Nor does the BBC escape criticism by the trial judge. The accusation against that body being that 'the good offices' of its investigative journalists permitted 'Miss Nestlé ... to broadcast her grievances to the nation'.

Georgina Nestlé, in Hoffmann's narrative, features as a demented spinster, with echoes of Dickens' Miss Flite.[66] Her action 'is and always has been hopeless', 'not because of any technicality or deficiency in the law but because it is entirely without merit'. The bank on the other hand figures in Hoffmann J's account as either the supplicating victim of Georgina Nestlé's, and to some extent her mother's, madness or the tolerant father of a recalcitrant child. The bank therefore attempted to 'appease' the plaintiff by paying her solicitor's bill while her behaviour was such that she was a 'thorn in their flesh'. The bank appointed an internal inspector to investigate and answer all her questions, which he did very patiently but the 'steady drizzle of abusive letters continued'.

This is by no means the only example of Hoffmann J's storytelling capabilities. In the recent case of *Walton v Walton*[67] Lord Justice Hoffmann considered a first instance decision in which the plaintiff's claim to a farm, legally owned by his mother, based upon equitable estoppel had been rejected. The Court of Appeal reversed that decision and Hoffmann LJ's is the only substantial judgement.

A variety of stereotypes of woman usually exploited by the cartoonist are employed by the judge to lampoon three generations of women in the Walton family. In the first paragraph he describes the plaintiff's mother, a woman whom

---

66 'We looked at one another, half laughing at our being like the children in the wood, when a curious little old woman in a squeezed bonnet, and carrying a reticule, came curtsying and smiling up to us with an air of great ceremony. "O!" said she."The wards in Jarndyce! ... It is a good omen for youth, and hope, and beauty when they find themselves in this place, and don't know what's to come of it". "Mad!" whispered Richard ... "Right! Mad, young gentleman ... I have the honour to attend Court regularly. With my documents. I expect a judgement. Shortly ... "', Charles Dickens, *Bleak House* (1853) Penguin at p 81.

67 (1994: Lexis) (Transcript: John Larking).

he only 'knows' through the transcript of evidence and by this time deceased, as 'a capable, dominating and manipulative woman'. Elsewhere he recounts that '[a]s she grew older, Mrs Walton became more difficult' and 'her friends lost patience with her overbearing behaviour and ... she developed a fantasy life'. Hoffmann LJ reads 'choice' pieces from the transcript, much of it pertaining to descriptions of Mrs Walton. This includes the following statement from a school teacher about an incident in which he had questioned the plaintiff, (her son), about his earnings from work on the farm:

> she tackled me in the middle of the main street ... she was about 40 or 50 yards away when she decided to have a conversation with me. She had a very loud voice and it was very embarrassing, but basically telling me that it was none of my business as to what Alfie earned and to keep away from her family.

Nor is Mrs Walton the only woman in the case subjected to Hoffman LJ's translation. Her daughter in law, described by the judge at first instance as 'a woman whom I wholly trust ... a completely reliable witness' becomes in Hoffmann's version of the story an embittered ex-wife. As in *Nestlé* an aspect of his narrative which is admitted to be 'peripheral to the legal issues', here the breakdown of the marriage of Mr and Mrs Walton (the younger), is 'important background to the evaluation of the evidence'. Her views as regards discussions between her husband and his mother have to be discounted because her resentment against her former spouse 'emerges from the transcript' and she is 'far from a dispassionate witness'. Hoffmann LJ makes similar remarks about Miss Amanda Walton who, although the 'judge made no comment on [her] ... credibility' cannot be 'regarded as a reliable witness' because her 'dislike of her father emerges too strongly'. Elsewhere he avers that she 'has clearly taken her mother's side in the bitter feelings arising from the break up of the marriage', and describes her 'evidence' as 'altogether too frail a vessel ... to be relied upon'. Her sin is therefore loyalty to another woman. One begins to wonder if any woman, in a 'Hoffmann narrative', can be anything other than mad, bad or dangerous to know.

A defence against simple misogyny could be made on the grounds that the expert witnesses which Georgina Nestlé called in her support – both men – were deemed to have an equally tenuous grip upon reality. Yet the rhetorical devices utilised in their damnation are somewhat different and it is difficult to banish the thought that for Lord Justice Hoffmann they are 'guilty by association with' and most importantly for misguidedly supporting this irrational, single-minded, old maid.

The investment analysis of Professor Briston, Chair of Accounting at the University of Hull, is likened in disparaging tones to that of a bizarre religious dogma. He is said to be a believer in the 'cult of the equity'. His change of opinion concerning appropriate forms of investment from those which he published in 1974 prove, according to Hoffmann J, that 'he has embraced the true faith to such an extent that he now thinks that the fund should be invested exclusively in equities'. Indeed he goes further and describes the Professor as a 'recanted heretic'.

Georgina Nestlé's second witness, Mr Peter Harris, an investment consultant, is quickly sketched by Hoffmann J as a man in love with statistics and out of touch with the decision-making of participants in the real world. Harris argued that there was a standard, accepted within the investment field, by which the competence of fund managers could be tested: had they exceeded, or at least been in line with, the average performance of unit trusts? He presented statistical data which, to his mind, showed the bank to be grossly negligent. In dismissing the notion that the trustees of a family trust could be judged by the above test, Hoffmann J stated:

> In my judgment Mr Harris has erected a standard which not only requires a gift of prophesy rather than ordinary skill and care but is completely divorced from the background of real life against which the Bank had to make its investment decisions.

The male protagonists in *Walton v Walton* however are continuously associated with the voice of reason if only because of the absence of derogatory statements about their evidence. Mr Walton told the court that when his mother said 'You'll get the farm one day' that that was 'enough for him'. He also stated that his mistake was not to get something in writing. Hoffmann LJ repeatedly comments that he finds Mr Walton 'convincing'. Similarly the plaintiff's son, who had remained close to his father, Mr Charlton, a retired fertiliser salesman, and the aforementioned teacher – Mr Hutton – are all treated as giving evidence which can be relied upon for its truth.

Through the tales of Hoffmann, woman is firmly located as an outsider and a hysteric excluded from the realm of male rationality. In these stories most of the women are represented as having 'transgressed lines of gender, territoriality, sexuality, familiarity'; subverted oppositions of 'culture/nature, active/passive, father/mother, man/woman'.[68] At the same time it is curiously both fascinating and refreshing to read judgments spattered with such free commentary and transparent manipulation of the characters. It is necessary to ask whether this reading is anything other than a demonstration of the oddity, bias and prejudice of a single judge. Furthermore is the *Nestlé* case anything more than the story of a relatively rich, white woman whose experience is highly specific to her class and race?

As already discussed, feminist writers have deconstructed legal discourse and shown it to be phallogocentric. From this standpoint Hoffman's tales reveal yet again law to be 'a discursive field which disqualifies women's accounts and experiences'.[69] Lord Justice Hoffmann's judgments stand out only because of the ease with which such a reading can be made. It is not necessary to delve and discover the secret ways in which law and masculinity overlap.

---

68   A Young, *Femininity in Dissent* (1990) Routledge at p 63.

69   Smart (1989) *op cit* at p 86.

This case is also a demonstration of the contribution legal discourse makes to the constitution of woman as other; law as a gendering strategy. In *Nestlé* and *Walton* this is revealed to even the most casual reader. Smart[70] has isolated two distinct aspects to this strategy which operate symbiotically: (1) the discursive production of a type of woman; for instance the unmarried mother, the prostitute, the shoplifter; and (2) the discursive construction of woman in contradistinction to man. Modern woman, she argues, is 'mired in this double strategy'. It is, of course, a strategy of the legal method and not of a particular author – even Hoffmann LJ.

Both aspects of this strategy are present in the above narratives. The division between insider and outsider within the dominant discourse is, however, never permanent. This representation of woman must therefore be constantly reinscribed and reinforced within law and elsewhere. There may be value in simply pointing to these recurrent images. The construction of woman as other has been analysed most frequently in the field of criminal law. It is interesting to show that the gendering strategy is also at work in the more esoteric area of trustee investment law.

Moreover these judgments reveal the openness of equity which allows these caricatures of women litigants and witnesses. The discretionary power of the judges, the fluidity and flexibility of equitable principles and concepts allows the tales of Hoffmann to emerge not just in the sphere of conflict around private family property, but in discussions about the fiduciary duty of a public institution. Common law is as a whole both dynamic and indefinite. In equity, this uncertainty is found to a marked degree and the role of 'facts' in decision-making is enhanced.

This is both the strength of equity and its danger for both the woman litigant and the feminist lawyer. The waters of the legal discourse are navigable, although they may be both treacherous and unpredictable.

SIGNIFICANT OTHERS

The accessibility of equity to the individual litigant and the creative lawyer may be demonstrated by turning again to the Nestlé chronicle. In the Court of Appeal 'Miss Nestlé' the spinster with a mission no longer appears. She is displaced by a plaintiff concealed behind her lawyer, Mr Lyndon-Standford QC, who claims albeit unsuccessfully, that the Bank failed in its fiduciary duty. Miss Nestlé's behaviour is not at issue. The Bank on the other hand is presented in quite another way. On the 'facts' it demonstrated symptoms 'of incompetence or idleness'[71] and its 'management ... of the Nestlé funds ... seems to have been

---

70 Smart (1992) *op cit* at p 191.

71 *Supra* n 59 at 1276.

weak, with much correspondence and discussion but no one clearly having the responsibility to make decisions'.[72] Leggatt LJ goes furthest in the general condemnation when he states that: '[n]o testator, in the light of this example, would choose this Bank for the effective management of his investment.'[73] Staughton LJ more gently states that Hoffmann J, 'took the view that "the Bank had acted conscientiously, fairly and carefully throughout the administration of the trust" but adds that he "cannot join in that accolade".'[74]

Gone also is the 'religious fanatic' whom Georgina Nestlé called as an expert witness, replaced by Professor Briston who may have 'overstated his case' but whose evidence should not, in Staughton LJ's view, be rejected. Indeed Staughton LJ does not find the Bank's experts to be 'immune from criticism'.[75] It is difficult for the reader to believe that the two courts were dealing with the same actors. However, a similar disparity of views between the courts of first instance and appeal can be perceived in *Walton* where it is evident, even from the selected excerpts in Hoffmann LJ's judgment, that the trial judge represented the facts, the evidence and the characters differently. As detailed above, he regarded Mrs Walton the younger as an absolutely reliable witness and it was her version of the story – that Mrs Walton had made no promise, binding in equity, to her son – which was given the stamp of judicial authority.

A question slips into the mind: So what? Does it matter that equity is sufficiently flexible and open to allow for the writing of any number of stories? For, in the final event, Georgina Nestlé lost her case in the Court of Appeal. Although subject to censure, the Bank was not found to have breached the 'undemanding standard of prudence'[76] required of trustees.

Whilst I would not deny the importance of winning cases, to concentrate upon simple success and failure is perhaps to miss the point. The judges themselves view an appearance in court as the final, if not the only, chapter in every saga. Hoffmann J, for example, speaks of Ms Nestlé's activities with the BBC, the City of London Fraud Squad, at the Bank's AGM and in her demonstrations against the Bank in London as little more than an overture to the court case:

> It has for many years been plain to the Bank that this action was virtually inevitable. Its record for the guidance of officers administering the trust have been marked with a warning ... 'contentious'. The Bank has acted in the knowledge that sooner or later it would very likely have to account for its actions in legal proceedings.

---

72   *Op cit* at 1274.
73   *Op cit* at 1284.
74   *Op cit* at 1281.
75   *Op cit* at 1278.
76   *Op cit* at 1285.

There is a danger in legal theorists falling into the same trap of regarding the importance of law and the courtroom as self-evident and paramount.[77] Schneider in her account of the development of women's self defence work at the Center of Constitutional Rights[78] clearly shows that the appearance on the legal stage may be only one part of a political strategy. The case of *State v Wanrow*[79] exemplifies this for Schneider. Lawyers involved in the appeal of a Native American woman convicted for murder made a highly specific reading of the transcript from the jury trial. Their analysis was from within the context of the emerging political activity and theory of feminism. It 'reflected ... women's groups' concern(s) with violence against women, the treatment of women within the criminal justice system, and the work of defense committees organising around particular women'[80] defendants. The legal argumentation used in the appellate court emerged, therefore, from political experience. That, however, was not the end of the story:

> The particular legal focus on sex-bias in the law of self defense, and on the absence of a women's perspective in the courtroom, clarified feminist analysis of the problems facing women who kill.[81]

Furthermore, from this case women's self defence work grew. Most notably the concept of 'battered wife syndrome' was created and became an established means of defence for women who, in an earlier period, would have been deemed guilty of premeditated murder. What this shows is that 'the legal theory emerged from political experience; the legal theory in turn served to refine and sharpen political insights and clarify tensions in the political struggle'.[82]

Schneider challenges any simple assessment of success and failure in the courtroom. She argues that as the work of the Center continued in some cases what appeared to be a backward step was taken, since 'unwittingly the very sex stereotypes of female incapacity that women's defense work was intended to overcome' were recreated. This apparent constriction of political progress Schneider feels however, can be turned to good effect, in the long term, as experience again reshapes the legal theory: 'In short, the rights claims grew out of politics and then turned into politics'.[83] What Schneider reveals through this story is that a strategic engagement with legal discourse can have a creative role independent of whether cases are won or lost.

---

77   On the tendency for lawyers to overstate the importance of law see M Cain, 'The Symbol Traders' in M Cain and C Harrington (eds), *Lawyers in the Post-modern World* (1994) Open University Press at pp 15–48, esp p 15.

78   E Schneider, 'The Dialectic of Rights and Politics: Perspectives From the Women's Movement', (1986) 61 *NY Univ LR* 589.

79   88 Wash 2d 240.

80   *Op cit* at 608.

81   *Op cit* at 609.

82   *Op cit* at 609.

83   *Op cit* at 610.

Strategy can also be employed at a different level than that discussed by Schneider. Georgina Nestlé's appearance in Hoffmann J's courtroom can be read not as the high point in her dispute with the Bank, but simply one stage in her campaign. Far from being the inevitable conclusion to her narrative, her presence in court may have been relatively insignificant when compared to broadcasting on the BBC.

To take as another example *The Satanic Verses*, bringing the book into the courtroom and claiming it as blasphemous was not solely, or primarily, about an attempt to win the legal argument. Rather it was a means of bringing an Islamic viewpoint on to the centre stage. It was irrelevant whether the story was accepted by the court: in simply having an encounter with the discourse which claims to fashion truth, another truth got its airing in public. Campaigners against *The Satanic Verses* probably found themselves on television night after night partly because their case was being treated seriously by the upper echelons of the legal system, and partly because of the 'newsworthy' style of the extra-legal demonstrations.[84]

For Georgina Nestlé, the courtroom could have been just another public forum in which to publicise her arguments against the Bank, and in that sense no different from parading through the streets wearing sandwich boards. Nor was it necessarily the end of her epic. Failure in the courtroom may have dissipated her campaign, equally it may just have invigorated it. She might have simply cut her losses, or she could at this moment be honing her sword for a further encounter with the National Westminster Bank.

At the same time in emphasising the openness of equity and its location on the periphery of law, one could be effectively denoting it as in some way a 'feminist' discourse, a second-class law. Frug in her reading of various texts on impossibility doctrine in American contract law appears to come quite close to such an analysis.[85] She juxtaposes the work of Posner/Rosenfield with that by Hillman. The former present a new standard for the situations in which contract performance should be excused: that is, whenever the promisee is the 'superior risk bearer'. Frug describes the claims for the new standard concept as 'like a phallus ... singular, daunting, rigid and cocksure'.[86] Hillman's texts on the other hand ground his proposals 'in a pluralistic, context-sensitive model of contract relations'.[87] She states that the 'structure, tone and language of the Hillman articles have feminine overtones'.[88]

---

84   Playing with the media is, however, like playing with the law; hazardous in the sense that it may hijack and rewrite the protagonists' stories, but simultaneously attractive because of its power to make visible.

85   M J Frug, *Postmodern Legal Feminism* (1992) Routledge at pp 111-24.

86   *Ibid* at pp 115-16.

87   *Ibid* at p 116.

88   *Ibid* at p 117.

Frug associates what she suggests is Hillman's critique of the male model with his *equitable approach* and contrasts this with the other texts which she is reading:

> By rejecting an equitable approach, with its attendant uncertainty, Posner and Rosenfield refuse an open solution ... their response exhibits the weaknesses stereotypically associated with masculinity: they are arbitrary, rigid and authoritarian.[89]

In this article it is not suggested that equitable approaches either to the reading of texts, or to decision-making, are 'reminiscent of typical feminine criticisms of masculinity'.[90] Equity's marginality on the legal map does not mean it is 'with' the discourses of rebellion, or 'with' those who exist in society's margins. It is merely that the judicial rhetoric of equity, its concentration upon factual detail, the concepts derived from unconscionability and its values steeped in ecclesiastical tradition, together with the discretionary nature of its remedies, can render it important to those who make claims from the margins.

CONCLUSION

Does the prospect of a rhetorical fusion of common law and equity matter to those who attempt to use the law strategically? I would answer my own question in the affirmative. As already argued legal discourse is not monolithic and the erosion of equitable concepts limits the chances of pushing the 'stories of outsiders ... through the objectivist barricades'.[91] At the same time I have a certain hesitation in making this answer, which arises from a fear of overstating the possibilities for empowerment within equity.

The number of litigants with the means to enter on to the stage of equity is small and this represents a further limitation upon equity's qualities of empowerment. However, it would be wrong to deny the openings in the theatre of Chancery for the alter-discourses. In the case of *Chhokar v Chhokar*,[92] for example, a woman subject to the double-oppression of race and gender got her voice heard in equity. Mrs Chhokar's husband, who was the legal owner of their

---

89   *Ibid* at p 119.

90   *Ibid* at p 117. Perhaps equitable approaches are associated with the feminine because of the concentration upon facts and therefore upon detail. As Schor has argued in her analysis of Reynold's *Discourses*, 'the unchallenged association of women and the particular spans not only cultures, but centuries, extending from antiquity to the present day', see N Schor, *Reading in Detail: Aesthetics and the Feminine* (1987) Methuen at p 17.

91   Kim Lane Scheppele, 'Foreword: Telling Stories' (1989) 87 *Michigan Law Review* 2073. There is, of course, a further danger from the collapse of equitable concepts inside equity's traditional realms. It is possible to detect, alongside the revival of a doctrine like *donatio mortis causa*, the increasing imperialism of equitable estoppel. The perceived overlap between estoppel and constructive trusts in the field of cohabitation and the family home is well documented. In more subtle ways other doctrines have been remodelled in the image of estoppel. See, for example, the interpretation of the doctrine of part performance, albeit of limited application, in *Morritt v Wonham* [1993] NPC 2.

92   [1984] FLR 313.

matrimonial home, in which she had an equitable interest, 'sold' the house for considerably less than its market value to a Mr Parmar. Her argument, that she was entitled to live in the property with her children, prevailed. Moreover, throughout the judgment she is presented as a woman of resource whose words should be preferred to those of both her husband and Mr Parmar.[93]

Such instances are by no means numerous but they are still important. The struggles of Mrs Chhokar and Georgina Nestlé are powerful illustrations of human resistance which demonstrate that there must remain a place for equity on the map of law and that fusion would limit the potential of such resistance. Whilst the equitable jurisdiction may develop diplomatic sites near the centre of legal power, its heart should always be on the periphery, amongst the dragons.

---

93 A similar argument can be raised with respect to *Grant v Edwards* [1986] 2 All ER 426. In *Passee v Passee* [1988] 1 FLR 263 there was also at least some recognition by the courts of a variety of family formations.

CHAPTER EIGHT

BEAUTY AND THE BEASTLY BANK:
WHAT SHOULD EQUITY'S FAIRY WAND DO?

ROBIN MACKENZIE

Once upon a time, a wealthy merchant, a widower with many children, lost his fortune suddenly and was forced to retire to the country with his family to live in sadly straitened circumstances. His children loudly bemoaned their fate, save for Beauty, his youngest daughter and favourite child, who uncomplainingly performed the tasks of their former servants. One day the merchant had news that one of his ships had perhaps survived shipwreck, so that his fortunes might be restored. Before he set off, his heart filled with hope, he asked his children what gifts they would like him to bring back for them. All save Beauty wished for gold, silk or precious stones, but Beauty asked only for a rose. The merchant left, then found to his sorrow that his hopes of saving his business were unfounded. Musing sadly upon his misfortune, he lost his way, and found himself at nightfall in a strange place by a sumptuous mansion. Hungry and tired, he knocked on the door, entered, and came upon a meal waiting to be eaten, and a bedchamber prepared for a guest, but no sign of any inhabitants, no matter how he called and searched. He ate, drank and slept. Next morning, about to leave, he wandered in the garden, then caught sight of a splendid rose-bush. Resolving at least to bring Beauty what she desired, he plucked a rose.

A fearsome roar terrified the merchant. A loathsome Beast stood before him, accusing him of theft, and threatening to end his life unless that which was most precious to him was surrendered in his stead. His daughter Beauty was to be handed over to the Beast in exchange for the merchant's life. The merchant, despairing, agreed, and was sent back by the Beast with chests of gold. On his return, Beauty agreed to save her father. At the mansion, the Beast treated her with courtesy and provided her with a luxurious way of life. He asked her repeatedly whether she could love him, and if she might consent to become his wife. Beauty, however, found his appearance abhorrent, and refused him, asking instead if he would allow her to visit her family. The Beast said sadly that he could refuse her nothing, and that she might visit them, provided that she returned at the appointed time or that he would die of grief. He gave her a magic mirror in which she could see him from afar, and sent her to her family with splendid gifts. Beauty, glad to see her family restored to their former way of life thanks to the Beast's generosity, forgot the Beast, and failed to return at all. One day, coming across the magic mirror, she remembered her promise. Looking into the mirror, she saw the Beast lying thin, wasted and silent upon the ground. Stricken, she sped to his side, recalling all his past kindnesses. When she came upon him, she wept over his lifeless form, bitterly regretting the way in which she had taken him for granted in the past. Cradling him in her arms, she called to him that she loved him, and would gladly be his wife. At these words, the Beast was transformed into a handsome prince, who explained that he had been under a spell since he had treated a woman of powerful magic with arrogant disrespect. As a punishment, he had been forced to appear as a loathsome Beast until a damsel of her own free will agreed to be his bride. Weeping with joy, they embraced, and were shortly wed amid much rejoicing, and lived happily ever after.

What is wrong with this story? Why has this story, or variations of it, survived for hundreds of years? And why should we, as feminists and lawyers, care? I propose to answer these questions with a reading of the story of Beauty and the Beast which marries the fairy tale to the legal stories surrounding equitable intervention into non-commercial third party secured transactions in order to argue that the present state of the law reflects none of the possible 'happily ever after' endings. I shall consider the place of fairy tales in our lives, then draw together feminist theorising about rhetoric, allegory and myth-making in post-modern times with similar analyses of legal stories. I want to use these thoughts as a basis for evaluating possible legal alternatives in the classic situation where typically a woman, who may be a wife (*Barclays Bank v O'Brien*[1]), a mother (*Clark Boyce v Mouat*[2]), or a lover (*Massey v Midland Bank*[3]), agrees to security being placed over the family home to support credit being offered to a failing businessman.

LOW TALES AND HIGH THOUGHT

Fairy tales, like legal stories, are cultural products, capable of being read, and told, in many ways. They have always been treated as a rich natural source for universalising hypotheses. Critical theorists have analysed the development of the oral folk tale into the literary fairy tale of the propertied classes as a colonising process whereby the utopian dreams of the disenfranchised become subordinated to the culture industry. Fairy tales here thus become commodities divorced from the experiences and needs of most people: imagination is constrained by the shackles of consumerism, and fantasy and rational thought are instrumentalised to curb and depoliticise criticism.[4] Four Psychoanalytic schools treat the fairy tale as providing a crucial symbolic map of the soul, along with dreams. Freudians such as Bettelheim have argued that fairy tales allow children to name, experience and deal with conflicts which would otherwise be repressed in a psychologically damaging way.[5] Jungians see fairy tales as embodying the universal themes and archetypes through which people all over the world conduct a search for meaning in life, pass through initiations and reach spiritual integration.[6] Psychoanalytic claims to universal explanatory power are today often more modestly restricted to the formation of modern western (and male)

---

1 [1993] 4 All ER 417.

2 [1993] 1 WLR 1021.

3 [1995] 1 All ER 929.

4 Jack Zipes, *Breaking the Magic Spell: Radical Theories of Folk and Fairy Tales* (1979) Heinemann, provides a helpful critical analysis of the work of the Frankfurt School and subsequent developments in critical theory, especially at pp 93–128.

5 Bruno Bettelheim, *The Uses of Enchantment: the Meaning and Importance of Fairy Tales* (1991) Penguin.

6 Marie-Louise von Franz offers the classic Jungian perspective in *The Feminine in Fairy Tales* (1993) Zdreved Shambhala.

subjectivities but fairy and folk tales appear to constitute a bedrock of narrative elements which are held in common worldwide.[7] In Ireland, Cinderella and her sisters are called Fair, Brown and Trembling; in Iraq, Cinderella wears golden clogs and a pearl comb; in 9th century China, a kingfisher blue cloak.[8] Scholarship following Vladimir Propp's *Morphology of the Folktale*[9] has tended to confirm his thesis that traditional fairy tales are made up of discrete narrative segments which are combined according to the demands of the time, cultural background and audience of the storyteller.[10] Modern formalist writers of fairy tales have even written source books of these fragments of stories to invite us to make up our own tales, or demonstrate how this is done.[11]

Why should anyone want to make up a fairy tale, or to tell it? Where fairy tales differ from other types of symbolic narratives such as myths, sagas and legends is that there is usually a guaranteed 'happily ever after' ending: hence in these magical realms anything is possible and all transformations positive. This inherently hopeful quality, combined with their easy access to the hearts and minds of most people, together have favoured their adoption as a means of persuasion.[12] From the end of the 17th century, fairy tales have been explicitly formulated for didactic purposes: to protest against arranged marriages and suggest strategies of deliverance;[13] to encourage children to conform to aristocratic or bourgeois values;[14] or to portray the Other as bestial (Hitler loved fairy tales).[15] Writers who use fairy tale motifs today such as Michael Ende, author of *The Neverending Story*[16] and *Momo*,[17] and Terry Pratchett of the *Discworld* saga do so to conjure up 'dream worlds as personally idealistic, as politically and socially contentious, and often as spiritedly wary and iconoclastic, as their more apparently sophisticated precursors, Erasmus, Voltaire and Swift'.[18] And nightmares are equally conjured up in the use by various factions in the

---

7   Angela Carter, for instance, justifies a life-long interest in fairy and folk tales when she points out that at least two thirds of the literature of the world has been created by the illiterate; see Marina Warner's Introduction to Angela Carter, *The Second Book of Virago Fairy Tales* (1992) Virago at p xi.

8   Angela Carter, *Expletives Deleted: Selected Writings* (1992) Chatto & Windus at pp 20–23; Marina Warner, *Managing Monsters: Six Myths of Our Time: the 1994 Reith Lectures* (1994) Vintage at p 87.

9   Vladimir Propp, *Morphology of the Folktale* (1968, 2nd rev edn) Indiana University Press.

10   *Cf* Angela Carter (1992) at pp 9–16.

11   See, for example, Milorad Pavic, *Dictionary of the Khazars* (1989) Collins; Italo Calvino, *Invisible Cities* (1979) Collins.

12   Zipes (1979)

13   Marina Warner, 'Beauty and the Beasts' (1994) *Sight and Sound* at pp 6–7.

14   Zipes (1979) at pp 1–19; Warner, Introduction to Carter (1992).

15   Marina Warner, 'The Uses of Enchantment' in Duncan Petrie (ed), *Cinema and the Realms of Enchantment* (1993) British Film Institute at pp 13–19.

16   Michael Ende, *The Neverending Story* (1991) Penguin.

17   Michael Ende, *Momo* (1989) Penguin.

18   Marina Warner, *From the Beast to the Blonde: on Fairy Tales and Their Tellers* (1994) Chatto & Windus at pp 411–12.

former Yugoslavia of folklore and fairy tales in the present civil strife, or in Salman Rushdie's use of fairy tale motifs in *The Satanic Verses*,[19] and his account of this as seen through *The Arabian Nights, Haroun and the Sea of Stories*.[20]

Fairy tales, then, are cultural texts in which who is doing the telling and to whom the tales are told cannot be separated from the tale itself.[21] This rhetorical perspective is generalised to the whole of language by some modern scholars. Helen Haste argues that metaphors and analogies act as bridges between individual thinkers and their social contexts. Underlying schemata which describe how the world works are negotiated in conversations to arrive at what she describes as 'lay social theories'. The rhetorical process consists of a persuader who begins with shared assumptions and beliefs, then refines definitions and interpretations by using metaphors and analogies to change the perspective of the listener to arrive at a new shared understanding. This then becomes part of a repertoire of schemata and lay theories with which members of that culture explain the world. She gives the example of how the metaphor of Man the Hunter provides, 'a script, a set of rules for male behaviour, motives, skills and – most importantly – relations with others. This script is understood by all members of the culture; any male who chooses to adopt that persona will be interpreted accurately. The metaphor does not only make an analogy, it provides an explanation for the behaviour'.[22]

Powerful metaphors provide frameworks which resonate across varying social contexts to explain the unknown or anomalous in terms of what is perceived as normal or natural: the evil of cancer or AIDS may be used as an image to evoke a perception of race riots as an unnatural disturbance of the body politic.[23] Different frameworks or images shape lay social theory, and indeed 'objective' scientific theorising, in ways which are culturally specific: Darwin's version of evolution as the survival of the fittest resonated with 19th century Britain's Malthusian fears whereas the geographic isolation and sparse population of Russia at the beginning of the 20th century rendered it more hospitable to Kropotkin's vision of evolution as based on cooperation rather than competition.

Haste argues that since all communications are based on shared images, seeking truth is a social process. She cites the work of Michael Billig on the history of rhetoric to argue that the tools of rhetoric can be used to categorise conversational components as that which may be taken for granted, that which is a problematic anomaly, and that which is new and must be explained. In other words, social change can be monitored by decoding texts in relation to cultural lay social theories. Billig contrasts the Platonic search for essences, or absolute

---

19 Salman Rushdie, *The Satanic Verses* (1988) Viking.

20 Salman Rushdie, *Haroun and the Sea of Stories* (1991) Granta.

21 Helen Haste, *The Sexual Metaphor* (1993) Harvester Wheatsheaf.

22 Haste (1993) at p 36. These ideas are presented at greater length with persuasive subtlety at pp 1–59.

23 Susan Sontag, *AIDS and its Metaphors* (1990) Penguin.

truths and values, with the view of another contemporary philosopher, Protagoras, that since there were two sides to every question, the logos and anti-logos, truth could only be arrived at through debate. All communication can therefore be decoded in terms of what it is against, and what it is for, or what can be seen as being able to be taken for granted and what instead is perceived as problematic so that it needs to be justified or explained.[24] Haste argues that the sexual metaphors of gender in our culture prove resistant to change because they are embedded within a series of unhelpful dichotomies: masculine/feminine, light/dark, rational/irrational, culture/nature and so forth. Many scholars have pointed to this tendency to describe the world in binary oppositions. Haste's contribution here is to point to gender as an epistemological device, a metaphor we use to understand the world as part of our cultural lay social theories. She explains that we are over inclusive: 'Since gender is a primary category for differentiation, other dualities map on to metaphors of masculinity versus femininity'.[25] Hence where masculinity is embedded in our lay social theories as hierarchically superior to femininity a male who eschews dominance over women can no longer be perceived as a 'real' man. Changes in the description of differences require changes in metaphor so that we can alter what is perceived as the essence of a category or move the boundaries of what is included in that category.[26] Haste sees feminism as an anti-logos which must put forward new ways of looking at actual differences and at difference itself.[27] Feminism, in fact, must put forward an alternative logos which provides cultural space for a schema which is not simply based on the (male) Self/(female) Other; the A/not-A dichotomy. In other words, where is the B, the C, and the XYZ?

THE EMPIRE OF THE SAME

Many feminists have couched this project of representing multiplicity in non-hierarchical ways in terms of finding a space which does not replicate the masculinist closures and exclusions of the Same and Other but acknowledges the differences of others.[28] This is allied to the feminist epistemologies which portray ways of knowing as linked to our geographic, historic, ethnic, economic and other characteristics.[29] What I am interested in here is the use of spatial images to represent ways of being in the world for women. Gillian Rose in her

---

24 Michael Billig, *Arguing and Thinking* (1987) Cambridge University Press.

25 Haste (1993) at p 60.

26 Haste (1993) gives the example of the boundaries of criminal law's being extended by the criminalisation of rape within marriage; *ibid* at p 57.

27 Haste (1993) at pp 101-105 provides an example of how one might go about this.

28 See, for example Gillian Rose, *Feminism and Geography: the Limits of Geographical Knowledge* (1993) Polity; Rosi Braidotti, *Nomadic Subjects: Embodiment and Sexual Difference in Contemporary Feminist Thought* (1994) University of Columbia Press.

29 *Cf* Sandra Harding and Merrill Hintikka (eds), *Discovering Reality* (1983) Reldell.

critique of academic geography cites as typical Teresa de Laurentis on the feminist search for an 'elsewhere' beyond patriarchy:

> ... the elsewhere of discourse here and now, the blind spots, or the space-off, of its representations. I think of it as spaces in the margins of hegemonic discourses, social spaces carved in the interstices of institutions and in the chinks and cracks of the power-knowledge apparati.[30]

Rose associates feminists' use of spatial imagery in part with the general response of contemporary theory to nationalisation, globalisation and space-time compression but also with feminism's focus on the everyday.[31] Many women feel threatened in some everyday spaces, alien in others and safe only in relatively small domains. Public spaces may prove restrictive for women as it is easy to feel confined, entrapped and judged unkindly as the object of the male gaze. As S Lee Bartky puts it, 'In contemporary patriarchal culture, a panoptical male connoisseur resides within the consciousness of most women'.[32] Donna Haraway states simply that: 'Location is about vulnerability'.[33] Feminists then often picture themselves at the margins of the spatial imagination of the universalising disembodied white male knower, attempting to create a geography which allows for multiple subjectivities and positionings; a space where women need not be victims. Gillian Rose describes this project as paradoxical in that:

> ... it must imagine the position of being both prisoner and exile, both within and without. It must locate a place which is crucial to, yet denied by, the Same; and it must locate a place both defined by that Same and dreaming of something quite beyond its reach. Paradoxical space, then, is a space imagined in order to articulate a troubled relation to the hegemonic discourses of masculinism.[34]

NOMADS OR DISPOSSESSED IMAGERY AND APPROPRIATION

The problem for feminists picturing themselves as clustering in the margins is that there is simply no room there any more. All theorists who wish to disassociate themselves from Enlightenment thought valorise the margins as offering space for resistance. Isomorphically, the feminine, Derrida's differance or Lyotard's differand, can become divorced from the material conditions of actual women, and claimed as territory by brave (male) resisters, who thereupon

---

30 Teresa de Lauretis, *Technologies of Gender: Essays on Theory, Film and Fiction* (1987) Macmillan at p 25; cited by Rose (1993) at p 139.

31 *Ibid* at pp 141–42.

32 S Lee Bartky, 'Foucault, Femininity and the Modernisation of Patriarchal Power' in I Diamind and L Quinby (eds), *Feminism and Foucault: Reflections on Resistance* (1988) Northeastern University Press at 72; cited by Rose (1993) at p 145.

33 Donna Haraway, *Simians, Cyborgs and Women; the Reinvention of Nature* (1991) Free Association books at p 196.

34 Rose (1993) at p 159.

continue the practice of describing this feminine in terms of now rejected masculinised Enlightenment.[35] Rosi Braidotti sees this notion of the feminine functioning as a powerful vehicle for conveying the attempts to redefine human subjectivity across the spectrum of contemporary continental philosophy.[36] At the same time, it is a metaphor for the metaphysical cannibalism of psychoanalysis which casts the question of origins in terms of the silencing exclusion of the power of the feminine by the necessary imposition of the authority and law of the father. Men, whom she refers to as pheminists, are thus enabled to act out their womb envy and to continue the metaphorisation of women without addressing women's historical victimisation and oppression.

How are women to explore notions of difference between men and women and among women without hierarchical dominance and exclusion of the other or metaphysical appropriation? Braidotti proposes that feminists create new figurations, politically informed images of alternative subjectivities which include the complex interactions of the axes of class, race, ethnicity, gender, age and so forth, in order to invent new ways of thinking, imagining and being outside old dualistic impositions of sameness. She sees political fictions as more effective here than theoretical systems. Braidotti favours the figuration of the nomadic subject, 'the kind of critical consciousness that resists settling into socially coded modes of thought and behaviour'.[37] She argues that nomadic consciousness 'is akin to what Foucault called countermemory ... Feminists – or other critical intellectuals as nomadic subject – are those who have forgotten to forget injustices and symbolic poverty: they enact a rebellion of subjugated knowledges'.[38] She favours developing, 'a nomadic type of feminist theory, where discontinuities, transformations, shifts of levels and locations can be accounted for, exchanged and talked about. So that our differences can engender embodied, situated forms of accountability, of story-telling, of map-reading. So that we can position ourselves as feminist intellectuals – as travellers through hostile landscapes, armed with maps of our own making, following paths that are often evident only to our own eyes, but which we can narrate, account for and exchange'.[39]

---

35 For a detailed discussion of the implications for feminism of post-modern theory's valorisation of the feminine, see Rosi Braidotti (1994).

36 *Ibid* at p 140.

37 *Ibid* at p 5.

38 *Ibid* at p 25.

39 *Ibid* at p 172.

ALLEGORICAL LORE AND LEGAL STORIES

How does all this resonate with analyses of our legal system? Law possesses its own mythologies which must be deconstructed to disempower their paralysing effect on our imaginations: the excluded other of legal narrative has been revealed as the feminine, the irrational or the so-called primitive.[40] And what of reconstruction? Drucilla Cornell urges feminists to build on contemporary theory's fascination with the feminine to construct new stories: myths and allegories which use the utopian or redemptive vision of the not-yet 'to translate the feminine into an ideal which represents a better way of being human'.[41] Cornell wishes to establish an ethical feminism which uses Lyotard's notion of the differand, that which has been excluded from traditional legal discourse, to bring into being legal systems which both recognise women's suffering and redress it. She gives the example of injuries to women which could not be perceived as injuries since they could not be represented as injuries within the law: such as wife-battering, sexual harassment and rape within marriage. Cornell deals with the issue of how the figurations of woman and the feminine relate to women by agreeing with Lacan that there are no such objects as men and women in any theoretically pure sense.[42] All human beings are both masculine and feminine since there cannot be a pure referent outside contingent systems of gender representation. As a consequence, the reality of woman or the feminine cannot be detached from the fictions in life and theory which represent her. Feminist theory, then, cannot be separated from fiction since reality cannot be separated from the metaphors which constitute language. Thus the best weapon against the extant unhelpful myths of women is the creation of artificial myths and allegories. Cornell argues that Carol Gilligan's claims that men and women care for others in different ways, and that both ways are valuable, may indeed be part of just such an artificial mythology, but that telling that story begins to create a reality within which the feminist not-yet may be manifested.

Drucilla Cornell's contentions are clearly allied with Rosi Braidotti's figuration of the nomadic subject and of her vision of countermemories of suffering. Peter Goodrich shares Braidotti's Deleuzian image of the nomad and the emphasis on what is forgotten or repressed in his analyses of the common law.[43] His approach to reading the law is that of legal hermeneutics: a detailed analysis of legal rhetoric.[44] Goodrich charts the refusal in 1588 of the common law to accept the suggestions of Abraham Fraunce:[45]

---

40   Peter Fitzpatrick, *Mythology of Modern Law* (1992) Routledge.

41   Drucilla Cornell, 'The Doubly Prized World: Myth, Allegory and the Feminine' (1990) 75 *Cornell LR* 644.

42   *Ibid* at p 672.

43   Peter Goodrich, *Languages of Law: From Logics of Memory to Nomadic Masks* (1990) Weidenfeld and Nicolson, although Goodrich treats nomadism in ways which are not identical to Braidotti's.

44   Peter Goodrich, *Reading the Law* (1986) Blackwell.

45   Abraham Fraunce, *Lawier's Logike* (1588). *Cf* Goodrich (1990).

> ... an attempt to introduce to the common law an historical and comparative dimension of criticism, an attempt to link law to knowledge, to contemporary philosophy, to a non-dogmatic reason or dialectic ... an attempt finally to open a knowledge that is distinctive precisely by virtue of being presented – and lived – as closed, as final and axiomatic, a matter of custody and not of critique, of mystery and not of knowledge.[46]

This 'short history of failure' presents both a forgetting of the excluded, a repressed subject matter, and a vision of the not-yet, an allegory of the law which does not exist but which might come to be through this revelation of possibility. Goodrich analyses the use of rhetoric, myth and allegory in law in order to uncover what he terms 'a feminine genealogy of common law, an origin and a telos of legal judgement, in a lost or future gynocratic polity'.[47] He sees rhetoric as the pre-modern form of psychoanalysis: a reading of legal texts describing anomalies can thus be used to trigger an institutional memory which will reveal a repressed element. His analysis of the anomaly involved in the postal rule, whereby contracts, which purport to rest on consensus and communication between the parties, may be considered to be complete once an acceptance is posted, reveals what he calls the 'allegory of the privileged offeree ... the allegory of law's admittedly limited protection of women'.[48] Forgotten borrowings from civil law incorporated this rule in order to ensure that women responding to an offer of marriage could not suffer through its revocation: had the borrowing, and the protective attitude to women, not been repressed, the rule would not have seemed anomalous. Analyses of other anomalies also reveal repressed institutional memories of how the common law treats actual women.[49] Goodrich repeatedly criticises the common law for its tendency to refuse to look behind or beneath, but instead seek to 'smooth out the surface of the institution, to deflect criticism, to forget, to repeat and so to further repress'.[50] English common lawyers' nationalism here, like Hitler's, has relied on fairy tales and folklore to assert a purity belied by investigation or thought.[51] Alternate sources for the mystified origins upon which he draws tend to be from the civil law.

I wish to focus instead here on equity as a source of English law which has a history of being perceived by common lawyers as equally threatening to its

---

46 Goodrich (1990) on pp 18-19.

47 Peter Goodrich, 'Gynaetopia: Feminine Genealogies of Common Law' (1993) 20 *J Law & Soc* 276 at p 277.

48 Peter Goodrich, '*Jani Angolorum*: Signs, Symptoms, Slips and Interpretation' in Costas Douzinas, Peter Goodrich and Yifat Hachamovich (eds), *Politics, Post-modernity and Critical Legal Studies: the Legality of the Contingent* (1994) Routledge at pp 107-24.

49 *Ibid.*

50 *Ibid* at p 136.

51 See, generally, Goodrich (1990).

purity (or sameness read as certainty).[52] The common law and equity have had a tempestuous relationship, with common lawyers such as Coke seeing equity as outside the law and conflicting with it.[53] This relationship may now be seen as having been legally solemnised by the Judicature Acts 1873-75, which fused the administration of equity and the common law and provided that in the event of conflict between their rules, those of equity were to prevail.[54] Nonetheless, cases where judges attempt to use those equitable principles of conscience to adjust legal rules to the needs of today's society are frequently attacked or overturned as too uncertain.[55] To some extent, this is an inevitable tension between the rigidities of precedent based legal rules and a necessary admission that ideas of justice will change with social needs. Appeals to some originary values, like those of conscience and equity, must underpin efforts to adapt legal rules to a changing world, whether the rules be those of the common law or of equity.[56] In psychoanalytic terms, these originary values are mapped, as the maternal body, at the beginning of the law's linear time: they are at once the ultimate precedent yet part of the pre-symbolic imaginary which stands outside the law of the fathers. The desire to know them is inevitably subject to a lack of certainty. Such obscure objects of desire are particularly prone to being lost in institutional memory.

The model I wish to use in the analysis that follows, then, places the common law, purportedly authoritative as precedent based, rational, objective and certain, as hierarchically superior to another strand of our law, equity, which is frequently marginalised as elusive, uncertain, irrational, subjective, quintessentially feminine.[57] Images of equity are consistently those of a woman engaged in sexual acts who brings forth offspring variously characterised as

---

52 Equity's origins, like those of common law, are unclear and contentious: Blackstone, for instance, sees equity as derived from Roman and canon law, but Maitland considers that he greatly overrates their influence; cf F W Maitland, *Equity and the Forms of Action at Common Law* (1932) Cambridge University Press at 14. See also Peter Stein, 'Roman Law, Common Law and Civil Law' (1992) 66 *Tulane LR* 1591. On the other hand, Adams considers that the common law and equity were identical for many years and indeed the former can be said to have originated in the latter; cf George Burton Adams, 'The Origin of English Equity' (1916) 16 *Columbia LR* 87.

53 *Cf* J H Baker, 'The Common Lawyers and the Chancery' 1616 (1969) 4 *Irish Jurist* (ns) 368.

54 Lord Denning, before he became Master of the Rolls and set about reviving equity, saw this fusion as regrettable, since it resulted in both jurisdictions becoming fixed and immutable; *cf* Sir A Denning, 'The Need for a New Equity' (1952) 5 *Current Legal Problems* 1.

55 *Cf*, for example, the Court of Appeal's attempt in *Tinsley v Milligan* (1992) Ch 310, subsequently disapproved by the House of Lords [1993] 3 All ER 65, to establish a legal standard related to the public conscience in order to remedy legal rules seen by their Lordships as unjust, as well as the sorry stories of efforts to protect the property rights of women in *de facto* marriages.

56 As in Charles Dickens' *Bleak House* (1853) Gresham, a frightening portrayal of the catastrophic human effects of the ossification of equitable rules in the Court of Chancery.

57 Examples here range from Maitland who seeks to do away with any controversy by feminising equity as a (dangerous) supplement, a collection of appendices to a self sufficient common law; *cf* F W Maitland (1932) at p 11, to the latest edition of *Hanbury and Martin's Modern Equity* (1993) Sweet & Maxwell, where Jill Martin at p 330 approvingly cites a quotation from an Australian case, *Allen v Snyders* (1977) 2 NS WLR p 68 at p 701: 'The legitimacy of the new model [of constructive trust] is at least suspect; at best it is a mutant from which further breeding should be discouraged.'

monstrous or illegitimate; the debate in the courts over whether she is past the age of childbearing echoes that in the mass media today over the propriety of postmenopausal women's using reproductive technology to give birth.[58] This portrayal of female desire disrupting the weighty and static law of the fathers has obvious psychoanalytic and deconstructive isomorphisms. It is the preceding resonances between fairy tales and legal stories, however, which I wish to foreground in the analysis which follows.

EQUITY, WOMEN, HOMES AND MONEY

In *Barclays Bank v O'Brien*, the House of Lords reformed the law relating to third party non-commercial securities placed over family homes. The typical legal story here is that a businessman whose enterprise is failing, and so cannot support a loan, persuades a wife, parent or lover to place a security over their home in order to support further extension of credit. The business fails, the bank seeks to enforce its security, and the security provider attempts to prevent this, alleging that the businessman has misrepresented the situation to her, or has exerted undue influence in order to obtain her agreement, so that she should retain the home. In the Scots legal system, which is heavily influenced by civil law, the situation is quite simple. There is no obligation on the bank to consider anything other than its own interests: if the security provider cannot protect herself, then she should lose out.[59] In the English legal system, equity intervenes. Since *Barclays Bank v O'Brien*, under the doctrine of notice, the bank must take reasonable steps to ensure that the security provider is advised to take independent legal advice so that the transaction might be seen to be unable to be challenged as tainted by any wrongful acts of the businessman. Previously a security provider could obtain relief only if she could prove that the businessman acted as the agent of the bank, as well as actual or presumed undue influence by him to procure her agreement to the security.[60]

The earlier decision of the Court of Appeal in *Barclays Bank v O'Brien*[61] attempted to base a changed approach here on a rereading of earlier cases following *Chaplin & Co Ltd v Brammall*[62] and *Turnbull v Duval*[63] and on the

---

58 Maitland seeks to do away with any controversy by feminising equity as a (dangerous) supplement, a collection of appendices to a self-sufficient common law; *cf* F W Maitland, *Equity and the Forms of Action and Common Law* (1932) at p 11.

59 *Cf* two recent Scots cases where counsel tried unsuccessfully to argue that Scotland, despite the lack of an equitable jurisdiction, should follow *Barclays Bank v O'Brien*: *Helen McCabe v Skipton Building Society* (1994) Inner House Cases; *Elizabeth McNulty or Mumford v Governor and Company Bank of Scotland; Kathleen Smith and Same* (1994) Outer House Cases.

60 *Cf* the line of cases following *Kingsnorth Trust v Bell* [1986] 1 All ER 423 and *Coldunell Ltd v Gallon* [1986] 1 All ER 429.

61 [1992] 4 All ER 983.

62 [1908] 1 KB 233.

63 [1902] AC 429, PC.

analysis of Dixon J in *Yerkey v Jones*.[64] Their Lordships concluded that the cases established two possible roads: one where either the debtor acted as the creditor's agent or the creditor had actual knowledge of misrepresentation or undue influence on the part of the debtor; and one where the 'special tenderness to married women' which they saw as characterising equity rendered independent legal advice essential instead if the transaction was to be seen as untainted. On the second road, married women, and others where the relationship between surety and debtor rendered reliance and influence likely, were thus to be treated as a special class of protected security providers whose informed consent must be guaranteed by independent legal advice if the transaction were to be seen as untainted. The Court of Appeal saw both options as justifiable in terms of binding authority. They favoured the second path on the grounds that there was still a tendency for husbands to take business decisions, for reliance on husbands and influence over wives in these unevenly emancipated times.

The House of Lords could find no basis in principle for affording special protection to a limited class in relation to one type of transaction only.[65] Instead, their Lordships favoured a solution that they saw as principled, fitting the current requirements of society and enabling certainty. This was to rely on the doctrine of notice. A creditor would be put on notice where an emotionally or sexually vulnerable person provided security for a debtor when this was not on the face of it to that person's financial advantage. Creditors could enforce the security provided that they took reasonable steps to ensure that the security provider was advised to take independent legal advice, ideally at a private meeting where she was told of the extent of her liability and warned of the risk involved.

Subsequent cases have delineated what these reasonable steps might be. The results have derogated from the ideal considerably, and place immense weight on independent legal advice, which I have argued elsewhere is presently too nebulous a concept to bear this protective burden.[66] The warning to take independent legal advice, as well as the advice itself, need not take place in the absence of the debtor;[67] there is no obligation on the bank to ensure that the solicitor who acts for the security provider is not also acting for the debtor or the bank itself (since solicitors can deal with conflict of interest situations)[68] and the bank need not concern itself with the nature or extent of the advice.[69] As a

---

64 (1939) 63 Commonwealth Law Report 649.

65 At p 428.

66 Robin Mackenzie, 'Vulnerable Providers of Security, Risk Management and Moral Hazard: Independent Legal Advice after *Barclays Bank v O'Brien*, *Massey v Midland Bank* and *Clark Boyce v Mouat*'. Paper presented at the W G Hart Legal Workshop 1995; Liability, Regulation and Risk Management: Reorientating the Legal Rebate (forthcoming).

67 *Midland Bank v Massey*.

68 *Midland Bank v Serter* (unreported, 1 February 1994, Ferris J Lexis); *Allied Irish Bank v Byrne* [1993] 2 FLR 342; *Northern Bank Ltd v McCarron and McCarron* (unreported, 8 February 1995, Carswell LJ Lexis).

69 *Massey v Midland Bank*; *Banco Exterior Internacional v Mann* [1995] 1 All ER 936.

consequence, security providers may now lose their homes without either having had the risk involved explained to them, nor the fact that they have a choice in the matter made clear. This has, in fact, taken place.[70]

LAW'S REPRESSED MEMORIES AND MARRIED WOMEN'S REPOSSESSED PROPERTIES

I will now consider these developments using Goodrich's proposal of rhetoric as a tool to undo institutional repression of memories and Haste's notion of lay social theory. In *O'Brien* both the Court of Appeal and the House of Lords based their decisions on opposing rereadings of the earliest leading case, *Turnbull v Duval*, which had been previously accepted as anchoring the doctrine of agency. In *Turnbull v Duval*, a wife gave security over her property to secure her husband's business debts to Turnbull & Co, whose representative, a Mr Campbell, was also a trustee of her father's will under which she was a beneficiary. Campbell and Duval arranged that Campbell would prepare a document giving Turnbull & Co security over Ms Duval's beneficial interest under the will and that Duval would get his wife to sign it. She knew nothing of the security document until her husband pressed her to sign it. She did not read it, nor have it explained to her, nor receive any independent advice. She thought that it would cover his debts for beer, but in fact it extended to all his debts. The Privy Council judgment, delivered by Lindley LJ, was not prepared to say whether the fact that she had had no independent advice would suffice to impeach the security, but held that stronger grounds were that the wife had been pressed by her husband to sign a document whose true nature was very different from that which she supposed it to be. Lindley LJ did not elaborate or explain further the equitable principle or principles upon which the Privy Council then declined to uphold the security, simply stating that: 'It is impossible to hold that Campbell or Turnbull & Co are unaffected by such pressure and such ignorance. They left everything to Duval, and must abide by the consequences'.[71]

Scott LJ, delivering the principal judgment for the Court of Appeal in *O'Brien*, stated that Lindley LJ nowhere referred to agency, and that there was no finding that Duval had made a misrepresentation to his wife, nor that the pressure to sign constituted undue influence. His Lordship therefore characterised the equitable principle or principles on which the judgment was based as 'somewhat elusive'.[72] Browne-Wilkinson LJ, delivering the judgment in the House of Lords in *O'Brien*, described the basis on which *Turnbull v Duval* was decided as, 'to say the least, obscure'.[73] The pleadings before the Privy

---

70 Most notoriously in *Banco Exterior Internacional v Mann*.

71 (1902) AL 427 at 435.

72 [1992] 4 All ER 987 at 992.

73 At 425.

Council had alleged neither undue influence nor misrepresentation and the trial judge's decision had been based on Campbell's breach of fiduciary duties. His Lordship considered that the Privy Council must have erred, either by considering that Duval had committed a wrongful act against his wife when he had not, or by assuming that a presumption of undue influence existed between husband and wife when this had not yet been definitively pronounced against, or by mistakenly following Lord Romilly's heresy that when one person makes a large voluntary disposition to another, that other must show that it was made fairly and honestly and in full understanding of the nature and consequences of the transaction. Since the wife could not be said to be able to set aside the transaction as against the husband, there could be no grounds upon which she could set it aside against the creditor unless there was some obligation on creditors taking security from married women for their husbands' debts to ensure not only the absence of undue influence or misrepresentation but also that the wife had an adequate understanding of the nature and effect of the transaction.[74]

Browne-Wilkinson LJ saw the doctrines of agency and of the special protection for married women to ensure their informed consent as equally erroneous, since they were based on the unsure foundations of *Turnbull v Duval*. In his Lordship's judgment, the special equity for wives was to be rejected for four reasons: (i) he could find no basis in principle for affording special protection to a limited class in relation to one type of transaction only; (ii) to require the creditor to prove wives' knowledge and understanding was in effect accepting either the rejected hypothesis that there was a presumption of undue influence between husband and wife or the Romilly heresy; (iii) the only two cases which supported the special equity theory specifically were *Yerkey v Jones* and the Court of Appeal's decision in *Barclays Bank v O'Brien*; and (iv) the proper protection of the legitimate interest of wives could be ensured by the existing doctrine of notice properly applied.[75]

After the Privy Council's decision in *Turnbull v Duval* there followed a series of cases whereby wives who provided security to underwrite their husbands' business debts in the absence of explanation, independent advice or understanding of the transaction, were afforded equitable protection, regardless of the fact that no misrepresentations or undue influence by the husbands were alleged, and two cases where this was denied. I wish to consider these early 20th century cases, rather than the more modern series resting explicitly on the idea of agency, in order to investigate the formation of a legal anomaly. In *Chaplin & Co v Brammall* the court applied *Turnbull v Duval* to hold that since the debtor husband had been left by the creditor to obtain his wife's signature without his explaining or her understanding they must take the consequences. In *Howes v*

---

74 *Ibid* at 425–27.
75 *Idem.*

Bishop[76] a wife who understood what she was doing but had no independent advice signed a joint and several promissory note for the amount of a judgment obtained against her husband's debts. The Court of Appeal held that she was bound by it: although she had been influenced by the husband to sign there had been no undue influence. Alverstone LJ, handing down the judgment for the Court of Appeal, held that although the court did not wish to lay down a rule stating that independent advice was unnecessary where a wife acted on her husband's instructions and under his influence, he equally did not consider that equitable rules regarding confidential relationships applied necessarily to husbands and wives.[77] This case was followed in *Talbot v Von Boris*[78] where a wife signed a promissory note as security for repayment of sums advanced to her husband. The court found that she had done so under duress, but that the creditor had not known of this. The Privy Council considered the matter again in *Bank of Montreal v Stuart*,[79] where a wife who was described by Macnachten LJ as a complete invalid without a will of her own nor any means with which to form an independent judgment was persuaded to charge her property as security for her husband's debts by her husband and Mr Bruce, a solicitor acting for the bank who had previously acted for the husband. She insisted that there had been no improper influence or pressure or misrepresentation. The Privy Council found for the wife on the grounds that unfair advantage of the wife's confidence in her husband was taken by the husband and the solicitor. The bank's solicitor should have attempted to advise the wife of her position and the consequences of what she was doing. If she had refused his intervention, which Macnachten LJ thought most probable, then he should have insisted to the husband that she be separately advised. Similarly in *Shears & Sons v Jones*,[80] a debtor's wife signed an unregistered bill of sale over her property to prevent the creditor instituting bankruptcy proceedings over her husband's debts. The court found for the wife on the grounds that the bill of sale was unregistered, but also that the document could not stand, as although she understood its general nature the plaintiff had failed in its duty to ensure that she had separate and independent advice.

Dixon J, in the High Court of Australia decision in *Yerkey v Jones*, another wife-as-surety case, analysed these cases as demonstrating that although there was no presumption of undue influence between husband and wife the relationship had 'never been divested completely of what may be called equitable presumptions of an invalidating tendency'.[81] Dixon J argued that equity had a special tenderness towards wives based on the suspicion with which courts regarded gratuitous transactions by wives for the benefit of their husbands, even

---

76   [1909] 2 KB 390.
77   *Ibid* at 395.
78   [1911] 1 KB 854.
79   [1911] AC 120.
80   [1922] All ER Rep 378.
81   [1902] AC 427 at 675.

after the passing of the Married Women's Property Acts, and on the influence of the Romilly heresy that he who benefits from a large pecuniary gift must be able to show that the donor knew and understood what they were doing: although this was not accepted as sound law it contributed to the view that unless the wife understood the transaction, a large gift from her to her husband might be invalidated.[82] Consequently, equity could be seen as offering special protection to married women who provide security in support of their husbands' debts.

This series of cases has demonstrated the growth and acceptance, and final rejection, of a legal anomaly. The equitable principle or principles which Lindley LJ failed to specify whereby the Privy Council impeached the security in *Turnbull v Duval* have been described by Scott LJ as 'somewhat elusive' and by Browne-Wilkinson LJ as 'to say the least, obscure'. They do not appear to fit within the rather inchoate doctrine of confidence, nor come within presumed undue influence, nor within settled contemporary law placing a duty on creditors to ensure that those providing gratuitous security for another's debts understood or were independently advised over the transaction. In the absence of misrepresentation or actual undue influence, what could justify equitable intervention?

CAN THE INSTITUTIONAL UNCONSCIOUS REPRESS UNCONSCIONABLE INSTITUTIONS?

It is possible, as Browne-Wilkinson LJ suggests, that the analysis in *Turnbull v Duval* is simply mistaken, and the decisions following it merely respectfully accept the judgments of high authority. I wish to explore the idea that this might not be so, using Goodrich's notion of repressed memories in the institutional unconscious. Browne-Wilkinson LJ states as the first reason for rejecting the special equity for wives supported by the Court of Appeal and Dixon J in *Yerkey v Jones* that he 'can find no basis in principle for affording special protection to a limited class in relation to one type of transaction only'.[83] But from the 17th century until the passing of the Married Women's Property Acts, equity afforded the limited class of wealthy married women the creation of a special category of property, the separate estate of married woman, which existed only during her marriage, as its purpose was to protect her against her husband's common law rights. Lee Holcombe explains that, 'equity, generally considered to be 'the guardian of the weak and unprotected, such as married women, infants and lunatics', tended to view a woman's husband as 'the enemy' and against his

---

82   *Ibid* at 680.
83   At 428.

'exorbitant common law rights the Court of Chancery waged constant war'.[84] One of the special protections afforded this limited class of persons under the system of married women's separate property was in fact in respect of a single type of transaction only. Equitable choses in action,[85] the type of property the wife in *Turnbull v Duval* charged in order to underwrite her husband's debts, could come into the husband's possession only if he applied to the Court of Chancery and if he settled at least some of it on the wife and children as separate property. The Court of Chancery here examined the wife separately from the husband in order to ascertain what she wished to do with the property. The court in fact could order that all the property pass to the wife and children. Separate property, once established, was also commonly restricted by the restraint on alienation or anticipation, which in practice meant that a woman could not dispose of her separate property, nor charge it with her husband's debts.[86] This restraint was invented by Lord Thurlow, whom Holcombe describes as one of the great reforming chancellors of the 18th century: acting as trustee for a young heiress, he affirmed that without such a restraint on her disposing of her separate property, her husband would 'kiss or kick her out of it'.[87] Under amendments in the Conveyancing and Law of Property Act 1881, the High Court of Justice was permitted to remove this restraint when the wife consented to it and when the removal was seen as being in her best interests, so that she could use the property to her best advantage but remain protected against her husband.[88]

Even the common law, which portrayed a married women as a *feme covert*, sheltering beneath her husband's wing, offered some protection against spousal predation. From the 13th century, a husband could not dispose of his wife's real property without her consent. Under a system known as levying a fine, any disposition of a married woman's land required that she and her husband act jointly. The court examined the wife separately from the husband to ascertain whether she had freely agreed to alienate the land. In 1833, when the Fines and Recoveries Act abolished these fines and allowed the disposition of land by simple deed, it still required that the wife formally and separately give her consent. This requirement was abolished only in the Law of Property Act 1925.[89]

---

84   Lee Holcombe, *Wives and Property* (1983) Martin Robertson at p 37, footnote omitted. Holcombe records a set form of words to describe the property as 'for her sole and separate use and benefit, independently and exclusively of the said [husband] and being without in any wise subject to his debts, control, interference or engagements' at p 40.

85   According to Holcombe these might include monies in the hands of a wife's trustees, stocks standing in the name of a trustee for the wife's benefit, legacies left to a wife but as yet unpaid by the executor, and property from the estate of an intestate but not yet paid by the administrator; at p 40.

86   *Ibid* at p 42.

87   *Idem.*

88   *Idem.*

89   *Ibid* at pp 20-21.

In such a legal context, judges could be expected for some time after the passing of the Married Women's Property Acts to persist in conceiving of married women's property as in need of protection from their husbands. The strong expectation in both common law and equity jurisdictions was that married women should be examined to ascertain that they understood and freely desired that their property be disposed of in ways which could benefit their husbands, and perhaps unjustly enrich the husbands at the wives' expense. In terms of Haste's lay social theory, the judicial attitude to married women in the early 20th century cases following *Turnbull v Duval* was one that saw equity's role as basically unchanged. It was still a basic assumption that married women's property was subject to the risk of being charged with their husbands' debts, and that some equitable mechanism should exist to prevent this by ensuring that, unless the wives knew what they were doing and wanted to do it, the transactions could not stand. The strength of this assumption prevented the explicit search for appropriate equitable principles and the problematisation of the varying degrees of women's emancipation, which characterise the more searching recent judgments such as that of Dixon J in *Yerkey v Jones*, and later Scott LJ and Browne-Wilkinson LJ in the *Barclays Bank v O'Brien* decisions. By then, social changes had altered the cultural lay social theories upon which the courts could draw. Feminism and a more multicultural Britain had rendered the question of women's need of protection as far from presenting a unitary picture: in Billig's terms, it needed to be explained as incorporating both new and anomalous elements. Similarly, the question of to whom this protection might properly extend was no longer simple as marriage might now be seen as including both *de facto* and *de jure* marriages, and heterosexual and homosexual cohabitants. Economic concerns might also be openly canvassed as legitimate concerns of the law: given the prevalence of securities taken over the family home to support credit to small businesses, how burdensome might these safeguards appropriately be? My suggestion here is that the legal anomaly of the accepted but 'obscure' or 'elusive' equitable principles underlying the decisions following *Turnbull v Duval* might indicate an institutional forgetting and repression of measures designed to obtain a wife's informed consent to property transactions for her husband's financial benefit.

The rhetoric in the earlier cases had as its focus the image of woman as victim, completely dependent on her husband and without a will of her own, having to be saved from her softhearted and soft-headed misguided loyalties by equitable intervention, the very icon of the Victorian bourgeois wife. The later 20th century cases, however, tend to foreground the family home as the site of security in the legal and emotional sense. Goodrich has traced the significance of the home to the law's institutional unconscious:

> ... the home is a legal term invested with a remarkable significance. The home is autobiographically both domesticity and family, the site of an originary law, that of paternity as also in its earliest stages it is the *gynaeceum*, or maternal domain.

The home is connotative psychoanalytically of emotional security, of nurture and of the immemorial ...[90]

One of Goodrich's points here is that threats to the home, this sacred place, can incline a court to return 'unconsciously to a category of legal tradition with an extraordinary though heavily veiled affective force'.[91] Legal policy, then, is likely to reflect this. The frequent conflation of women and home, as spelled out earlier by Rose, has, however, often had deleterious effects for women.[92] And once the repressed institutional memory is remembered, can the legal problem concerned realistically be seen as solved?

How might the preceding history of wives, homes and creditors be interpreted from this perspective? The rules of the common law and equity which ensured that wives were examined by the courts to ensure that their property could not pass to their husbands without the wives' informed consent, or subject to any wrongdoing by the husbands, may be interpreted as the wealthy instituting legal rules to ensure that family property remained intact.[93] Given the centrality of property to English jurisprudence such concerns could hardly fail to have an effect. Nonetheless, equity's overriding jurisdiction as a court of conscience concerned to protect the weak from unconscionable acts must also be recognised as a basis for such equitable safeguards.

The problems for women here are clear. If one is masked by a sacred icon, one is expected to behave accordingly. Consequently, the law's ability to recognise what feminists call the problem of transition, where a previously disadvantaged group is given mandatory assistance until restitution and recovery are considered to have taken place, is strictly limited.[94] While the Married Women's Property Acts afforded women significant rights, they did not of themselves reform the institution of marriage in such a way that the perils against which equity sought to defend wives vanished. Equity's wish to protect the weak, however, has failed to empower those in this position. Legal mechanisms which ensured that a wife's transactions over her own property for her husband's benefit were based on free and informed consent, in the absence of her husband's wrongdoing, would have gone a long way towards remedying many wives' vulnerabilities. The failure of independent legal advice to be prescribed in this spirit in *Barclays Bank v O'Brien* and subsequent cases has often

---

90   (1993) at p 118.

91   *Ibid* at pp 118-19.

92   Feminist theory has documented the disempowering effects of the equation of women with the home in terms of wife-battering, the marital rape exemption, the feminisation of poverty and the general subordination of women. *Cf*, for example, Katherine O'Donovan, *Family Law Matters* (1993) Pluto Press; Martha Mahoney, 'Legal Images of Battered Women' (1991) 90 *Michigan LR* 1; C Pateman, *The Sexual Contract* (1988) Polity Press; Carol Smart, *The Ties that Bind* (1984) Routledge.

93   Lee Holcombe certainly has some sympathy for this view (1983) at pp 18-47; see also Roger Cotterell, 'Power, Property and the Law of Trusts: a Partial Agenda for Critical Legal Scholarship' (1987) 14 JLS 77.

94   Christine Littleton, 'Women's Experience and the Problem of Transition: Perspectives on Male Battering of Women' (1989) *University of Chicago Legal Forum* 23.

left family members who provide security for a businessman's debts with ostensible rather than actual protection, and has failed to encourage them to take responsibility for deciding what course of action might be in their best interests and acting on it.[95] The mapping of home/women/sacred in the institutional unconscious of the law results, then, in a deep ambivalence which offers women limited protection without the means of exercising full citizenship: advances towards independence, as in the Married Women's Property Acts, provoke an institutional repression of earlier protective measures as an unconscious backlash.[96]

In the traditional hydraulic model of psychoanalysis, the recovery of repressed memories translates into psychic health. The anomalous behaviour which signalled a repressed memory disappears once the memory reappears. Insight into one's own condition automatically accompanies recovery of a repressed memory. What might be seen as the healing process when an institutional repressed memory is recovered is less simple, and far from immediate. We may be vouchsafed the insight that all is still not well without agreeing on how things might look when healing had taken place, nor on how to get there. I do not wish to consider in depth possible limitations of the psychoanalytic model here, merely to suggest that the recovery of a repressed memory may be the first of many steps, and that insight in healing our legal system must be matched with imagination.[97]

'HAPPILY EVER AFTER' ENDINGS

What fairy tales, figurations or allegories are we as feminists to construct here? Rosi Braidotti's figuration of the nomad is clearly not meant to be emulated literally; as she states herself, she could not start thinking adequately about nomadism until she, 'found some stability and a sense of partial belonging, supported by a permanent job and a happy relationship'.[98] Nonetheless, as she also points out, 'very settled, anchored, sedentary people are among the least empathic, the least easily moved, the most consciously 'apolitical'.[99] Any

---

95　I elaborate on this argument elsewhere, cf Mackenzie (forthcoming).

96　Cf Katherine O'Donovan (1993) and C Pateman (1988).

97　I do not wish to imply here that Goodrich (1990) uses the concept of the unconscious in a simplistic way. On the contrary, he embeds his conception in the following citation from Michel Foucault, The Order of Things (1970) Tavistock p xi, 'the historian of science must also endeavour to retrace and restore that which eluded scientific consciousness: the influences that affected it, the implicit philosophies that were subjacent to it, the unformulated thematics, the unseen obstacles ... the unconscious of science. This unconscious is always the negative side of science – that which resists it, deflects it or disturbs it. What I would like to do, however, is to reveal a positive unconscious of knowledge: a level that eludes the scientist and yet is part of scientific discourse...', cited in Goodrich (1990) at p 16.

98　(1994) at p 35.

99　Idem.

retelling of the story of Beauty and the Beast must needs reflect both concerns. The tale recounted at the beginning of the article reflects prototypical patriarchal bourgeois themes: a woman pledges her only security (herself) to redeem a businessman's debts, she then repays those debts through marriage, and is happy. On a Jungian reading, this evidences psychological transformation and maturing, the sacred marriage or *hierogamos* as the holy grail of the human life. Taking Beauty as the female version of *homo economicus*, or the reasonable man whom Nadine Naffine argues is law's subject,[100] the tale could represent Beauty's initiation into the masculine economy described by Helene Cixous.[101] Beauty here separates from the unsuccessful businessman, with whom she has been kept a dependent, to enter the world of rational self-interest: she refuses to place a security over her interest in the family home and enters into a financial relationship with the bank, from whom she borrows money to pay for the home which will now be hers alone. She is now a mature legal subject, a citizen, the reasonable woman.

Is this the 'happily ever after' ending we want, or would settle for? It would require that Beauty receive equitable assistance to ensure that she could make an informed decision over whether to provide security to underwrite the debts, and to ensure that she knew that she had a choice. Can there be a 'happily ever after' ending which preserves the world of affection and connection, of giving without reserve, that Cixous has called the feminine economy? Kate Green suggests, in relation to repossessions of family homes under s 70(1)(g) of the Law of Property Act 1925, that since most creditors here are building societies, they are owned by members who would rather do without some tiny number of cents each than have women and children lose their homes.[102] She also cites a recommendation from the Law Commission that indemnities be available to creditors who were 'without any lack of proper care' and against whom an overriding interest was asserted, to be funded by all registered land owners through the Land Registry; again people who would presumably empathise with women's desires to retain their homes for their families.[103] The idea of homeowners empathising enough to help each other out has an obvious appeal.[104] How practical these proposals might be in the context of non-commercial third party security transactions, however, is a moot point.

---

100 Nadine Naffine, *The Law and the Sexes: Explorations in Feminist Jurisprudence* (1990) Allen Unwin.

101 Helene Cixous, *The Newly Born Woman* (1986) Minnesota Universtiy Press. Cixous' ideas of the masculine and feminine economies and their relation to English property law are considered by Kate Green in her 'Thinking Land Law Differently: s 70(1)(g) and the Giving of Meanings' (1995) 3 *Feminist Legal Studies* 197.

102 *Ibid.*

103 Law Commission, *Third Report on Land Registration* (1987) No 158.

104 Although it might not apply in every case analogous to Beauty's situation since some creditors will not be building societies.

PARADOXICAL ENDINGS C, D AND XYZ

If the happily ever after endings in the masculine and feminine economics represent A and not-A, where are C, D and XYZ? And how do we get to them? Or recognise them when we see them? I want to return here to Gillian Rose's description of the feminist project in terms of creating a paradoxical space wherein women need not be victims: 'a place which is crucial to, yet denied by, the Same ... a place both defined by that Same and dreaming of something quite beyond its reach'.[105] What might a paradoxical home be? A paradoxical security transaction? A paradoxical debtor/creditor relationship?

Some alternatives already exist. Under Islamic law, usury is prohibited so that creditors must share the risks of commercial projects and tie their profits to those expected to be made by the business itself: advocates of this system point out that the present problems termed third world debt could have been greatly ameliorated had such an approach been adopted by the leading banks from the outset. Women in Africa, Asia and South America now successfully set up and run their own mutual credit associations and businesses. Some alternatives could exist once certain preconditions were met: if feminist economics succeed in remedying the chronic undervaluing or marginalisation of women's unpaid work, the consequent loss of the traditional sexual divisions of labour and economic dependencies would transform the marketplace and domestic life as we know them into spaces which would permit paradoxical caring sexual and emotional partnerships without gendered hierarchy.[106] Securities taken over the family home, if they still existed, would be quite different.[107]

Other alternatives must wait. Feminists' quest to imagine into being the paradoxical home is part of a worldwide search for home as 'a place where you would like to belong, and might be allowed to stay'.[108] Marina Warner sees homelessness as the predicament of our time.[109] As refugees, exiles and their descendants hanker nostalgically after the imaginary homes of the past, reinforcing the conflation of home, women, ethnic identity and the sacred in a dangerous search for a mythical pure and simple authenticity read as redemption, the need to find a way to talk about home without implied exclusions and violence becomes increasingly urgent. My story here of Beauty and her options

---

105 Rose (1993) at p 159.

106 Nany Folbre, '"Holding Hands at Midnight": the Paradox of Caring Labor' (1995) 1 *Feminist Economics* 73; Marilyn Waring, *If Women Counted: a New Feminist Economics* (1988) Allen & Unwin. Folbre describes a recent bill introduced into Congress, the Unremunerated Work Act 1993, which is a first step towards this.

107 The Governor of the Bank of England has recently alluded to the need for banks leading to small businesses to move from 'an excessive reliance on the secured overdraft to a focus on the cashflow and performance of the business': B George, 'The Financing of Small Firms' (February 1994) *Bank of England Quarterly Bulletin* 67 at p 68.

108 Warner (1994) at p 84.

109 *Idem.*

is in this tradition. Warner wishes to persuade us that 'home lies ahead, in the unfolding of the story, not in the past wanting to be regained.'[110] Home need not represent closure and an illusory innocence but an internal dwelling place nourished by stories we held in common and with which we make and remake the world we inhabit. She ends the 1994 Reith lectures by quoting from Derek Walcott, the West Indian author who was awarded the 1992 Nobel Prize for literature: 'we earn home, like everything else'.[111] Warner explains that this does not represent having to pay the rent or the mortgage, but 'taking part in the journey, using memory, imagination, language to question, to remember and to repair, to wish things well without sentimentality, without rancour, always resisting the sweet seduction of despair'.[112] It is in this spirit that I believe that we as feminists must retell legal stories to ensure the refiguration of both the home and the law, until we can all feel at home in both.

---

110 *Ibid* at p 88.
111 *Ibid* at p 94.
112 *Idem.*

CHAPTER NINE

THE MIRROR TELLS ITS TALE:
CONSTRUCTIONS OF GENDER IN CRIMINAL LAW

SHEILA DUNCAN

THE LEGAL TEXT AND ITS DECONSTRUCTION

This paper analyses how the text of the criminal law[1] constructs gender. The central image of the study is the mirror: an image which has significance for both of the theoretical approaches which inform it.

First, drawing particularly from the work of Michel Foucault,[2] the mirror is the image for the watchful eye of disciplinary power[3] – the eye which sees but is not seen – the power which always holds out the image of the norm so that the disciplined will ensure that their own reflection mirrors that image. It is possible to find in the criminal law, a series of normalising images which form the basis of its power and around which it arbitrates.

Secondly, following Luce Irigaray's theory of sexual difference,[4] it is possible to see how in criminal law, the woman is constructed to mirror the desires of the male subject,[5] while she herself is constructed without subjectivity and without desire. As Irigaray argues, 'his' subjectivity is reflected while 'she' has no reflection. She is the substance of which the mirror is made, not the subjectivity which it reflects.[6]

The approach of this paper is deconstructive; and the central image which it uses focuses on the nature of legal discourse and its constructions of the male as subject and the female as mirror of the male subject. The study analyses the central role played by the notions of 'reason' and 'consent' in the construction of gender. It considers the nature of the power of legal discourse and the way in which this power in criminal law differentially disciplines male and female bodies.

---

1   The term 'text' is here intended to indicate statutes and precedent cases.

2   See n 13 below for details of the works of Foucault which most inform the study.

3   See Michel Foucault, *Discipline and Punish* (1979) Penguin at pp 170-77 for an analysis of visual and spatial notions of disciplinary power. See also pp 195-228 of the same text for Foucault's development of Bentham's panopticon – his image of the building which allows eyes to see without being seen.

4   Luce Irigaray's work can be complex without an initial introduction to her framework and philosophy. Margaret Whitford, *Luce Irigaray, Philosophy in the Feminine* (1991) Routledge, provides full and comprehensive access. Irigaray's own texts which are particularly relevant are: Margaret Whitford (ed), *The Irigaray Reader* (1991) Blackwell; *The Ethics of Sexual Difference* (1993) Cornell University Press; *Je, Tu, Nous: Towards a Culture of Difference* (1993) Routledge.

5   For a full discussion of the mirror image in Irigaray see Margaret Whitford, *Philosophy in the Feminine* (1989) Routledge at p 34.

6   *Ibid.*

The approach views the text of the law as based on a 'process of exclusion and hierarchies'[7] and is particularly concerned with law's gendered hierarchy. It seeks in the text not simply what is said, but also what is excluded as a result of that saying.[8] A gendered hierarchy privileges the superior term 'man' against the subordinate term 'woman'. My analysis is deconstructive[9] in that it seeks to reverse this process and stand in the place where the superior term 'man' is deprivileged. Following the path of Luce Irigaray,[10] I ask: what is excluded from the text of criminal law?

In the legal text, baggages of notions are associated with the terms 'man' and 'woman', with value attributed to the first at the expense of the second. The most significant of these attributes are 'rationality' and 'objectivity' ascribed to the male, and 'emotionality' and 'subjectivity'[11] ascribed to the female. In each instance, value is attributed to the terms associated with the male at the expense of the related term which is associated with the female.[12] This analysis wishes to pass those baggages through a deconstructive X-ray, holding up to scrutiny that which lies within and challenging the value ascribed to each.

THE DISCOURSE OF THE LAW

In its opposition to notions of absolute truth, and transcendent reason, post-modernism[13] opens up the possibility of challenging within one discourse the discourse of the law, its absolute 'truths' as gendered truths, its transcendent reason as gendered reason, and law's arbiter, the reasonable man, as a gendered and relative construction.

It is first necessary to analyse the law's discourse as it is expressed in the law's text. The law's discourse is its way of seeing, interpreting and constructing the

---

7   *Ibid* at p 26.

8   For a discussion of deconstruction see Jacques Derrida, *Positions* (1981) Athlone Press.

9   For Derrida, this deprivileging must continue in an infinite regression so that meaning is constantly deconstructed. See Derrida *ibid*.

10 For a consideration of Irigaray's notion of deconstruction in contradistinction to Derrida's, see Irigaray, *This Sex Which is Not One* (1985) Cornell University Press. See also a comparison between the positions of Irigaray and Derrida in Whitford (1989) at pp 123-34.

11 Subjectivity here denotes the inability to stand outside of the personal view and take a wider impersonal or 'truer' view. It will be clear from this article that the author challenges the very basis of this dichotomy between subjective and objective.

12 For a discussion of his notion of binary opposites see Derrida *ibid*.

13 This paper uses aspects of post-modernist theory in so far as it is concerned to deconstruct notions of truth, knowledge, reason and the subject. The theorist who has most inspired its post-modern aspects is Michel Foucault. Although the label post-modern is sometimes disputed in relation to Foucault, his work can be characterised as post-modern in so far as it conforms with the definition in the first sentence of this footnote. The Foucault texts which are most relevant to this study are Colin Gordon (ed), *Michel Foucault, Power Knowledge* (1980) Harvester Press, Foucault, *Discipline and Punish* (1979) Peregrine, and *The History of Sexuality* (1984) Penguin, first volume, published as *The History of Sexuality. An Introduction.*

world.[14] That discourse can be found both in the text and the subtext of the law. The discourse of the law is not simply one among many discourses. There are many discourses but the discourse of the law is one of the most powerful. It is a discourse which: '(is) said indefinitely, remains said and (is) said again.'[15] To this extent, the discourse of the law is one of the most powerful constructors of gender in our society.

Law's knowledge composes the 'truths' of its discourse. Law's discourse as expressed in the legal text constructs its own 'truths'. It is first necessary to ask: what are those 'truths'? The text of the law is, therefore, examined as 'one institutional regime for the production of truth'.[16] What are the 'truths' of the text of criminal law?

Following Foucault,[17] this paper starts from the point that each discourse has its own power/knowledge. Its power resides in its knowledge, its knowledge constructs its power.[18] It is important to consider both the law's knowledge and the law's power and to explore the nature of law's power.

Foucault draws a distinction between juridical power and disciplinary power.[19] For him, juridical power is expressed in the centralised power of the sovereign reinforced in the power of the state and the law – it is the power of prohibition – a power which he argues is increasingly less significant in Western society. The form of power which is increasingly more significant is disciplinary: 'a diffuse network of relationships which penetrate every aspect of modern life'.[20] This power does not forbid. It 'normalises', tracing the boundary between the normal and the perverse,[21] constructing the watchful eye and the mirror reflecting the norm, creating a complex and creative network that is disciplinary power.[22] It is important to understand the ways in which legal discourse functions as disciplinary power and in respect of the criminal law, the way that power disciplines the 'political field of the body'[23] and the way in which it differentially disciplines gendered bodies.

---

14   For a discussion of the notion of discourse, see Foucault, 'Politics and the Study of Discourse' in G Burchell, C Gordon and P Miller (eds), *The Foucault Effect* (1991) Harvester Wheatsheaf.

15   Foucault, 'The Order of Discourse', in Robert Young (ed), *Untying the Text* (1990) Routledge at p 57.

16   Lawrence D Kritzman (ed), *Michel Foucault: Politics, Philosophy, Culture* (1990) Routledge at p xix.

17   See particularly the texts mentioned at n 13 *supra*.

18   On these points see particularly, 'Truth and Power' in Colin Gordon (ed), *Power/Knowledge* (1980).

19   This is a constant theme in Foucault's work but a very full and clear exposition of it can be found in *Discipline and Punish* (1979), a text which is both exciting and accessible. On the notion of disciplinary power, see particularly *Discipline and Punish* (1979) but also *The History of Sexuality. An Introduction* (1984).

20   Sheila Duncan, 'Law's Sexual Discipline: Visibility, Violence and Consent' in (September 1995) *Journal of Law and Society* vol 22 no 3 at p 326.

21   See Duncan (1995) for a full discussion of this.

22   Foucault, *Discipline and Punish* (1979).

23   Foucault *ibid* at p 170.

It is clear that legal discourse in the criminal law does set out to prohibit certain conduct. The law of rape, for example, sets out to prohibit non-consensual sexual intercourse.[24] But the text of the law of rape only prohibits certain forms of non-consensual intercourse namely non-consensual intercourse where the man does not honestly believe that the woman is consenting.[25] It is, therefore, able to create permissions: permission to the perpetrator of non-consensual sexual intercourse outside that forbidden parameter. In this way, law's power can be disciplinary, structured around its constructions of the normal and the perverse. Only non-consensual intercourse where the man does not honestly believe the woman is consenting or is reckless as to her consent,[26] can be traced outside the normal. In these constructions of normal and perverse, the discourse of the law differentially constructs gender, and disciplines differently gendered bodies.

The discourse of the law seeks to use reason as a central part of its method yet reason is differentially used and constructed, for example in the law of rape so as to allow legitimate space for the desire of the male subject who is not tested by reason. Further, in its exclusion of reason in the law of rape, it provides a space for legitimate violence[27] – violence against the woman who does not consent although her attacker 'honestly believes'[28] that she does.

THE SUBJECT OF THE LAW

Traditional conceptions of the legal subject[29] place that subject as a clear, certain, fixed, pre-existing identity at the core of the law. For Foucault, the subject is 'scattered'.[30] His subject is de-centred, dissolving, uncertain and constructed by the discourse(s) which that subject inhabits. For Foucault, the subject is both the subject of and subject to the discourse.[31] The subject is constructed by the discourse but that subject is also able to self-construct within the discourse. As Simmons argues, Foucault's framework for interpretation moves between these poles: at one end the subject is burdened by what Simmons calls 'unbearable heaviness'[32] s/he is repressed, determined, controlled, but at the other end s/he

---

24 This issue is examined in more detail below.

25 For a full discussion of this matter see particularly the issues raised on *Morgan* below.

26 The *mens rea* for rape is either intention or recklessness, s 1(1) Sexual Offences (Amendment) Act 1976.

27 Foucault discusses the opposition between reason and reason's others, specifically madness but also violence and sexuality in 'The Order of Discourse' (1990). See Duncan, 'Law as Literature: Deconstructing the Legal Text' in (1994) *Law and Critique* vol V no 1 at p 4.

28 See discussion below particularly in respect of *Morgan*.

29 The legal subject of traditional jurisprudence.

30 Rosi Braidotti, *Patterns of Dissonance* (1991) Polity at p 49.

31 For a full discussion of these different aspects of Foucault's work see Lois McNay, *Foucault and Feminism* (1992) Polity.

32 Jon Simmons, *Foucault and the Political* (1995) Routledge at pp 3–5.

is totally free, totally without purpose, totally able to self-construct: in a state of 'unbearable lightness'.[33] It is within this interpretative framework that the subject of criminal legal discourse can be located. Subject to the repressive aspects of a law which forbids, yet provided with the self-constructing space of a differential disciplining which, in certain circumstances, allows for the free expression of his desire.

Foucault's subject is embodied, circumscribed by the disciplining of the body but with space for the fashioning of his identity.[34] The legal subject is presented as the man of reason but it is be possible to see how the subject of the text of criminal law is infused with 'reason's others',[35] with violence and desire and to see how the text of that law provides him with space for his construction as a violent, desiring being.

For Foucault, also, sexuality itself is socially constructed,[36] although part of that construction is that sexuality consists of eternal overwhelming urges and uncontrollable needs. Its social construction is that it is uncontrollably natural. Sex, he says, has not been annexed, 'to a field of rationality', rather, 'our bodies, our minds, our individuality, our history', have brought us, 'under the sway of a logic of ... desire'.[37] Legal discourse creates that space for the logic of desire but, crucially, it is the constructed desire of the male subject, following Irigaray.

Foucault's subject is embodied, constructed and self-constructing, the subject of a discourse. Foucault does not gender this subject but Irigaray challenges the notion of the ungendered subject. She is concerned with 'the sexual indifference that underlies the truth of any science, the logic of every discourse'.[38] For her, whilst sexual difference remains untheorised, what is presented as universal is, in fact, male. All theory must therefore be examined for its sexual subtext. It is that subtext which excludes woman from subjectivity. She is unrepresented in the symbolic order, she is outside that order, supporting it, *mirroring* its male subject. She is other to an order which does not and cannot recognise sexual difference.

Following the work of Irigaray,[39] it is the argument of this paper that the *legal* subject *is* gendered: gendered male. It is argued here that the legal text has no concept of sexual difference and further that what is presented as universal is, in fact, male. The universal legal subject is the male subject. The subject which the law constructs is the male subject. There is no female subject in the text of the

---

33   *Ibid.*

34   The notion of the self-constructing self is particularly developed in Foucault's later work, most notably the last two volumes of the *History of Sexuality viz The Use of Pleasure* (1985) Penguin and *The Care of the Self* (1986) Penguin.

35   Braidotti (1991) at p 52.

36   Foucault develops the details of this argument in *History of Sexuality. An Introduction.* (1984). See particularly Part 2 '*Scientia Sexualis*'.

37   Foucault, *The History of Sexuality* (1987) Peregrine at p 78.

38   Luce Irigaray, 'The Power of Discourse and the Subordination of the Feminine' in Margaret Whitford (ed), *The Irigaray Reader*, (1991) Blackwell at p 118.

39   See particularly the references at n 4.

criminal law. The woman appears only as the mirror to male subjectivity. She is constructed to mirror him and his desires, and, to this end, her body is differentially disciplined within the law to provide space for his subjectivity.

The construction of the woman as other, excluded from subjectivity, can be grasped more specifically in analyses of the law of prostitution and evidential law in respect of rape.

One of the most extreme examples of the construction of the woman as other, without subjectivity, in the criminal law may be found in the law of prostitution.[40] The prostitute is excluded as subject by legislation which effects every aspect of her life and threatens to criminalise almost everyone with whom she comes into contact.

Prostitution is not illegal *per se* but the law creates a variety of offences which can criminalise the prostitute and most of those who have contact with her in her daily life.

Her working life is fraught with possibilities of illegality. She can be charged with soliciting[41] after she has been cautioned for loitering or soliciting on two occasions.[42] She will then receive the label 'common prostitute' and any attempt she may make to obtain the protection of the criminal law against sexual or physical violence will be severely undermined. If she works with or near another prostitute,[43] she can be charged with brothel keeping.[44] Her home life is undermined by the law: if she lives but does not work with another woman, they are both open to charges of brothel keeping.[45] If she lives with a man, he can be charged with living off immoral earnings.[46] This charge has been extended by case law to effect any commercial relationship which the prostitute has directly, or even in some instances indirectly,[47] where there is any excess cost and the person demanding the excess is aware of her prostitution. Those who rent property to her are also open to criminal charges of brothel keeping[48] and

---

40 For a full discussion of this theory in respect of prostitution see Sheila Duncan, 'Disrupting the Surface of Order and Innocence: Towards a Theory of Sexuality and the Law' in (1994) *Feminist Legal Studies* vol II no 1 at p 22.

41 Section 1(1) Street Offences Act 1959.

42 In 1990, there were 10,020 convictions for this offence (Home Office's statistics provided to the author).

43 *Donovan v Gavin* [1965] 2 QB 648.

44 Section 33 Sexual Offences Act 1956 creates the offence of keeping, managing, acting or assisting in the management of a brothel. A brothel is a place where two or more prostitutes work together.

45 Either under s 33 of the 1956 Act (see n 46 *supra*) or under s 34 of the same Act which creates the offence for a lessor, landlord or agent of premises either to knowingly permit premises to be used or to continue to be used as a brothel or under s 35 which creates the offence for a tenant or occupier to knowingly permit premises to be used as a brothel.

46 Section 30 Sexual Offences Act 1956 creates the offence of living off immoral earnings.

47 For example in the case of *Ferrugia* (1979) 69 Cr App Rep 108, CA, a cab driver was convicted of a s 30 offence as a result of his engagement by an escort agency to drive prostitutes to their customers even though the fare was paid by the customers.

48 Section 34 of the 1956 Act. See n 45 above.

living off immoral earnings in the case of any excess rental where the landlord is aware of her prostitution. Her clients can be charged with kerb crawling.[49]

In each area of subjectivity, the prostitute is constructed as other: as worker, as friend, as tenant, as partner, as consumer. She is 'constructed as pariah – a legal leper who may infect all she meets'.[50] Yet the law provides just enough space to allow the prostitute to provide sexual services to satiate the desires of the male subject; for instance, a landlord can let premises to one prostitute knowing that they are to be used for prostitution and she, as tenant, may work by herself on those premises.[51]

As a rape complainant, the woman is denied subjectivity, constructed as 'other' through a variety of evidential provisions. First, she has been subject to a corroboration warning which requires the judge to tell the jury that they must be careful if they are to convict on her uncorroborated testimony because she may have ulterior motives for bringing these charges.[52] Even with the abolition of this warning under s 32(1)(b) Criminal Justice and Public Order Act 1995, it may still be given in the judge's discretion. The woman is not the subject here, her truth-story is undermined by these warnings.

Secondly, only in rape does the defendant – the male subject – retain his shield, his protection against the court's taking his previous convictions into account if he attacks the character of the complainant.[53] In any other offence, an attack on the character of the complainant leaves the defendant open to having his previous convictions put in evidence. In the rape trial alone, the complainant can be constructed as whore, as temptress, as liar, with impunity.

Thirdly, it is open to the defendant in the rape trial to apply to the court for the complainant's previous sexual history to be put in evidence.[54] Research shows that on a consent defence, the majority of defendants make this application and the majority of judges grant it.[55] If the complainant were present

---

49   Under s 1 Sexual Offences Act 1985, they can be charged with kerb crawling and under s 2 with persistent soliciting. In 1990 the figure for convictions under this offence was 100 times smaller than the number of women convicted of soliciting in the same period.

50   Duncan (1994) *op cit* n 42 at p 22 which develops the issues raised here in respect of prostitution.

51   J C Smith and B Hogan, *Criminal Law* (1988, 6th edn) Butterworths at p 459. The 7th edn (1992) does not deal with prostitution.

52   It is stated in *R v Henry and R v Manning* (1968) 53 Cr App Rep 150 at 153 that women have a tendency to invent stories.

53   The provision that the defendant should loose his protection against his previous convictions being put in evidence where he casts imputations on the character of a prosecution witness is made under s 1(f)(ii) Criminal Evidence Act 1898. *DPP v Selvey* [1970] AC 304 provides that in rape alone the defendant does not lose his shield under these circumstances.

54   Under ss 2(1) and (2) Sexual Offences (Amendment) Act 1976 the defendant must apply for the judge's leave to cross-examine the complainant.

55   A study by Zsuzanna Adler, *Rape on Trial* (1987) Routledge and Kegan Paul at p 73 showed that nearly 60% of defendants using the consent defence applied to put the complainant's previous sexual history in evidence: 75% of them were successful.

as subject, her previous sexual relationships could not possibly be relevant to whether she entered into this sexual encounter as a freely consenting and desiring subject.

The Criminal Justice and Public Order Act 1994 now extends the offence of rape to cover men who have anal intercourse forced upon them.[56] It will be very interesting to see whether, and how, the male subject victim is subjected to these legal indignities of erased subjectivity. Will his previous sexual history be applied for or put in evidence? Will attacks on his character still leave the defendant's shield unblemished? Will the test for consent remain as honest, not necessarily reasonable, belief?[57]

It is possible to see in the law of rape and prostitution how the woman is excluded from subjectivity; the mechanisms of that exclusion can be very concretely grasped by tracing the central concepts of reason and consent through aspects of the criminal law.

NOTIONS OF REASON AND CONSENT

The construction of reason is central to the construction of the male subject, both in its attribution to him, and the concomitant ascription of emotionality to the female other. It is necessary now to dig more deeply into the text of criminal law to deconstruct the notions of reason that may be found there.

The criminal law's concept of consent is one of the most central constructors of gender. Its use and construction are saturated with gender. They vary across a range of offences which differentially construct the female other and the male subject and differentially discipline their respective bodies.

Further, it will be argued that there is an important interplay between these notions of reason and consent, which further construct gender in the criminal legal text.

---

56 It also extends rape of a woman to include anal rape. Previously the offence of rape could only be committed vaginally and therefore only against a woman. See *R v Gaston* (1981) 73 Cr App R 164 in which the prosecution unsuccessfully tried to prove a charge of rape *per anum*. Until the 1994 Act, the Sexual Offences Act 1956, which defined the position, stated expressly that rape could only be done by a man against a woman.

57 Or, most interestingly, will the male complainants with *homosexual* histories find themselves open to erased subjectivity and will the case of a raped *heterosexual* man be dealt with very differently? Will the complainant's proven *heterosexuality* counter any of the defendant's claims of honest belief in consent or, conversely, will his *homosexuality* imply consent and honest belief in it? For the parallels between the construction of the male homosexual and the female other see Duncan (1995).

Reason

The role of reason in the rape trial can be illustrated by a deconstruction of *Morgan*,[58] the 1976 case which still provides the precedent test for consent in rape.

There are two aspects to the issue of consent in substantive rape law. The first is: was the woman consenting? And the second: did the defendant believe that she was consenting? This dual aspect combined with the principle established in *Morgan* that the defendant's belief in consent only had to be honest, not necessarily reasonable, creates the space for legitimate rape. A non-consenting woman can be subjected to sex with no legal redress if the defendant *honestly believed* she was consenting.[59]

What is the role of reason in the rape trial? As law's primary tool it appears in many masks in the case of *Morgan*. Defence counsel for the three younger defendants in *Morgan* argued before the House of Lords that the judgment of the reasonable man could be no guide to the beliefs of the three young men who came with Morgan to have sex with his wife, assured by him that she would be a willing partner albeit that they were told to expect resistance.[60] Under these circumstances, reason could not be an appropriate test. These were reasonable men for whom, under the circumstances, reason should be suspended.

Prosecuting counsel in *Morgan* argued that reason must set the external standard for honest belief. If the belief were mistaken, then it must be reasonable,[61] otherwise the defendant could too easily claim honest belief based on his drunkenness or his vanity.[62] Such a test of belief in consent would have narrowed the space for the male subject's legitimate desire.

In delivering their judgment on *Morgan*, the majority of the judges – Lords Cross, Hailsham and Fraser – each sidestep the reasonableness test for the defendant's honest belief. Lord Cross chooses to step outside legal discourse and into popular discourse, arguing that it is necessary to consider the ordinary *man's*

---

58 [1976] AC 182.

59 See Sheila Duncan, 'Law as Literature: Deconstructing the Legal Text' in (1994) *Law and Critique* vol 5 no 1 for a full discussion of the case of *Morgan*.

60 The facts of *Morgan* are summarised at the beginning of the House of Lords' judgment at 182: 'The defendant Morgan invited the other three defendants (McDonald, McClarty and Parker), much younger men, to his house and suggested that they should have intercourse with his wife, telling them that she was "kinky" and any apparent resistance on her part would be a mere pretence. Accordingly, they did have intercourse with her despite her struggles and protests. They were subsequently charged with rape and also, together with Morgan, with aiding and abetting rape. The wife gave evidence that she resisted and did not consent. The three younger defendants in their evidence said they had believed what Morgan had told them, that the wife resisted at first but later actively co-operated in the acts of intercourse'. Marital rape did not legally exist until 1991 (*R v R* [1991] 4 All ER 481) so Morgan could not be charged with rape.

61 The leading cases of *R v Tolson* (1889) 23 QBD 168 and *R v Prince* (1875) LR 2 CCR both establish the precedent that mistaken belief must be reasonable.

62 '... his confidence that his charms were irresistible' *Morgan* at 197.

understanding of the word rape and finds that, 'according to the ordinary use of the English language, a man (cannot) be said to have committed rape if he believed that the woman was consenting to intercourse'.[63] Even if she were not consenting.

In delivering a judgment from within legal discourse in the highest appeal court, Lord Cross finds it necessary to move from the terms of legal discourse to consider the way in which the ordinary *man* defines an offence and then to follow that definition. Lord Cross chooses to sidestep reason and he literally invests the male subject with power to determine whether his behaviour constitutes rape.

Lords Hailsham and Fraser both concur in countering reasonable belief with intention. To intend to have intercourse with a woman who does not consent or even to be reckless as to whether she is consenting is the *mens rea* for rape. Such intention or recklessness sidesteps the need for honest belief to be reasonable. Lord Fraser summarises their position:

> If the defendant believed (even on unreasonable grounds) that the woman was consenting to intercourse then he cannot have been carrying out an intention to have intercourse without her consent.[64]

On this basis, the legal text's own established principle that mistaken honest belief must be reasonable[65] is jettisoned in rape, and the space is provided for the male subject to rape legitimately.

Although *Morgan* was decided in 1976 on a three to two majority judgment, it still remains the authority for the test for consent in rape. It was further shored up in the case of *Satnam and Kewal*[66] where Lord Hailsham's position on intention was quoted with approval. Public outrage after the judgment on *Morgan* led to the passing of a provision in the 1976 Sexual Offences (Amendment) Act requiring that reasonableness was one factor to be taken into account in determining whether the defendant had an honest belief in consent. A major criminal law textbook calls this a 'public relations exercise'.[67]

A further exclusion of reasonableness from rape trials occurs as a result of the decision that *Cunningham*[68] rather than *Caldwell*[69] recklessness would apply in the case of reckless rape. In *Cunningham* recklessness, the defendant simply has to know that there was a risk that the complainant was not consenting. In *Caldwell* recklessness, he would have the necessary *mens rea* if he failed to consider a risk

63   *Morgan* at 203.
64   *Morgan* at 237.
65   See note 61 *supra*.
66   *R v Satnam S and Kewal S* [1983] 78 Cr App Rep 149.
67   Smith and Hogan, *Criminal Law* (1992, 7th edn) at p 452.
68   *R v Cunningham* [1981] 2 All ER 863.
69   *R v Caldwell* [1980] 71 Cr App Rep 237, CA.

which the reasonable person would have considered. Again, the rape defendant is provided with an expanded space in which to construct the consent of the female other.

Constructing consent

Two related issues flow from the construction of consent in legal discourse. First, constructions of consent construct the male as subject and the woman as other in aspects of the text of criminal law. Secondly, differential notions of consent result in differential disciplining of the male and female bodies.

What must be focused on here is the space in which the woman is not consenting to sexual intercourse but the law does not acknowledge that what is happening is rape: the male subject's honest belief in consent where none exists. In this space, the woman is rendered powerless and unprotected; she is obliged to *mirror* his desires, she is constructed as other. The *Morgan* and *Caldwell* tests, the possibility of her sexual history being put in evidence, the defendant's unassailable shield, the remnants of the corroboration requirements – all these construct her as other and him as subject.

Morgan, both as precedent and as symbol, creates the possibility that even in the extremes of gang rape using all forms of resistance open to her and with her children present in the wings, the word of her husband as to her consent could have exonerated the three younger defendants and Morgan by default[70] if only they had stuck to their story of resistance and not argued that Mrs Morgan was enjoying and participating in these activities.[71] This is the literal and symbolic construction of the female as other and the man as desiring subject. Mrs Morgan was not consenting, the jury and both appeal courts accepted that, but the defendants were allowed to legitimately construct consent on the word of her husband and there was *nothing* she could do to undermine this.[72]

The construction of the male subject's space for the legitimate expression of his sexual appetite with a non-consenting woman extends beyond the issue of non-consent to the issue of consent induced by fraud 'as to the nature and quality of the act'. Here there are two issues: first, the nature of sexual

---

70 Morgan was charged with aiding and abetting rape because until 1991 (*R v R* [1991] 4 All ER 481) it was not possible for a man to be charged with raping his wife. If the other three had been successful in their appeal, it is possible that Morgan's own conviction would also have been quashed on the basis that the accessory cannot be convicted where there is no principal offender. However *Cogan and Leek* [1976] QB 217 which was decided at the same time and where no principal offender remained convicted, still left the accessory's conviction unaffected.

71 *Per* Lord Cross at [1976] AC 204.

72 Under s 2(1) Criminal Appeal Act 1968, the appeal court 'may, notwithstanding that they are of the opinion that the point raised in the appeal might be decided in favour of the appellant, dismiss the appeal if they consider no miscarriage of justice has occurred'. The House of Lords in *Morgan* chose to use their proviso and the defendants remained convicted despite winning on the point of law. They failed to establish that they were relying on Morgan's word as to his wife's consent.

intercourse which was being consented to, and, secondly, consent by the female other to a non-sexual act which is sexually motivated and conducted by the male subject to the ontological degradation of the female other.

In the case of *Clarence*,[73] Mrs Clarence consented to sexual intercourse with her husband although he knew and she did not know that he suffered from venereal disease. The legal issue was whether there was fraud as to the nature and quality of the act. The court held that there was not. The act to which Mrs Clarence consented was constructed by the law as it was constructed by the male subject. Mrs Clarence's subjectivity in consent is disregarded. She did not knowingly consent to intercourse with a diseased man. She did not consent to the grievous bodily harm which she sustained and which was foreseeable to her husband, but, although the issue here is exclusively *her* consent, her consent is constructed as consent to the act which *he* desired, ignoring the consequences of which only he was aware. Her consent has been constructed to mirror what the court established to be his primary purpose: the satiation of his desire.

Consent to non-sexual acts which are sexually motivated revolve around medical circumstances where the body of the female other, in these situations of vulnerability, is still constructed by the law for the pleasure of the male subject: through a notion of consent which denies her subjectivity.

In *Bolduc and Bird*[74] a doctor conducting a vaginal examination secured the presence of a friend by passing him off as another doctor. The court held that there was no fraud as to the nature and quality of the act. It was still a medical examination, even if done for the prurient sexual pleasure of the doctor's friend and, possibly, the doctor himself.

In *Mobilio*,[75] the defendant penetrated a number of his female patients with an ultrasound transducer.[76] This was for no medical purpose, without medical authorisation and entirely for the defendant's sexual gratification. Again, the court constructed consent against the female other to exonerate the male subject. There was held to be no fraud.

The male subject's legitimate space for non-consensual sex is further underlined by the law of incest. Section 10 Sexual Offences Act 1956 forbids a man to have vaginal intercourse, irrespective of consent, with his granddaughter, daughter, sister or mother. In practice the great majority of incest is committed

---

73 *R v Clarence* (1888) 22 QBD 23.

74 *R v Bolduc and Bird* [1967] 63 DLR (2d) 82. This case arose in British Columbia, Canada. The final appeal was heard in the Supreme Court of Canada and the case is precedent in English law. The issues were whether the 'examination' was 'consented' to and whether there was fraud as to the nature and quality of the act.

75 *R v Mobilio* [1991] 1 VR 339. This was an Australian case heard in the Supreme Court of Victoria and is a precedent in English law.

76 Because this was an Australian case, the defendant had been charged with rape. In the English legal system any charge brought against him would have been indecent assault. Even with the changes in the law of rape under the Criminal Justice and Public Order Act 1994 (see n 56 above), only the penis can be the instrument of rape.

by fathers with their daughters.[77] This area of law arguably protects the girl (possibly woman) within the family. In practice it is rarely charged and, further, it only protects where there is a blood relationship between the two parties and does not protect in the event of step or adoptive relationships.[78] The rationale for the legislation has been argued to be its attempt to prevent the production of any defective resulting progeny[79] not to protect the young girl vulnerable to the power of the male subject in the family.

Technically the issue of consent does not arise because the defendant commits the offence whether or not the woman consents. However, in practice the issue does arise in two ways. First, where the girl does not consent, the man can be charged with rape but, whatever her age, she will still have to pass all the hurdles of establishing non-consent to a rape charge.[80] It is important to stress here that for the female other in the context of the power of the male within the family, the notion of consent may be meaningless: she cannot tell her mother; her father is an all-powerful authority figure; she has nowhere else to go.

Acknowledging the space for legitimate non-consensual sex,[81] the law creates an offence under s 11 which can only be committed by a girl/woman over the age of 16 which is that of permitting a man in the prohibited degrees to have sexual intercourse by her consent. But it is possible for a man to have sexual intercourse with (for example) his daughter over 16 and for her not to be charged with a s 11 offence although he is not charged with rape. In other words, for the law she has not permitted intercourse to take place by her consent but neither can she establish non-consent for the purposes of a rape charge. The space between not permitting intercourse, and the male subject's honest belief in consent, is the male subject's space for non-consensual sex.

In his judgment in *Attorney General's Reference (No 1 of 1989)*,[82] Lord Lane gave sentencing guidelines on incest. In the first instance, he considers sex between the father and the pre-pubescent girl as a crime which 'falls far short of rape', although that girl may well have been coerced by fear of her father and silenced by the constellation of the family.[83] The girl who approaches and then

---

77 Victim/offender relationship statistics are not kept by the Home Office but the commentary on *R v Winch* [1974] Crim LR 487 states: 'The vast majority of cases of incest which come before the courts relate to sexual intercourse between fathers and teenage daughters, frequently when they are below the age to consent to intercourse.'

78 Liz Kelly states, in *Surviving Sexual Violence* (1988) Polity, that incestuous abuse other than by a biological father is overwhelmingly likely to be by an adult male relative in a 'social father' position in relation to the victim. Quoted in N Lacey, C Wells and D Meure (eds), *Reconstructing Criminal Law* (1990) Weidenfeld and Nicolson at p 355.

79 *R v Winch* [1974] Crim LR 487.

80 The man could be charged with indecent assault because, unlike in the case of rape, a girl under the age of 16 cannot consent. See *R v Satnam S and Kewal S*, n 68 *supra*.

81 Which is incest but not rape.

82 *Re Attorney General's Reference (No 1 of 1989)* [1989] 3 All ER 571.

83 For a further discussion of this issue see Duncan (1994) *supra* n 40 at pp 18-22.

reaches puberty is in this judgment increasingly constructed not merely as fully consenting but as temptress:

> The older the girl, the greater the possibility that she may have been the willing or even instigating party to the liaison, a factor which will be reflected in sentence.[84]

The equation is made between puberty and consent and the female other is constructed to *mirror* or even to create the desire of the male subject. Her absence of subjectivity is underlined in the case of *R v Ballie-Smith*[85] where the defendant successfully appealed against an incest conviction arguing that he mistook his 13 year old daughter for his wife.[86] How could such a mistake have been possible? For the court this was a female body without subjectivity.

One of the biggest dichotomies in legal notions of consent arises in the distinction between consent to offences of physical violence and consent to offences of sexual violence. This distinction in itself is problematic in that sexual violence is always physical to the extent that it has a physical dimension and physical violence may also be sexual.[87] It is easier to draw a distinction by considering specific offences which have or do not have a sexual or physical dimension to their legal definitions. Rape, indecent assault and incest all have sexual dimensions without which the offence is not committed. In the cases of rape and incest, sexual intercourse is required. The offences of common assault, assault occasioning actual bodily harm,[88] grievous bodily harm,[89] and grievous bodily harm with intent[90] do not have a sexual element as part of their legal definitions, although within any one case there may be a sexual dimension.[91] Consent is theoretically a defence in respect of all of the aforementioned offences.[92]

The great majority of these offences of legally defined *physical* violence are committed by men and the great majority of them are committed against men.[93] Just as the sexual space of the male subject is constructed by the laws relating to sexual violence, so the physical space of the male subject is constructed by the

---

84　*Re Attorney General's Reference (No 1 of 1989)* [1989] 3 All ER at 571

85　*R v Baillie-Smith* [1977] 64 Cr App Rep 76.

86　There was a second ground for the appeal but the Court of Appeal held that his appeal would have been successful on this ground alone.

87　Many forms of physical violence can have a sexual dimension particularly in the context of pre-existing personal relationships between male perpetrators and female victims; for example, in domestic violence. Misogynist murder of women as a result of their ascribed sexuality as prostitutes is another form of sexual and physical violence.

88　Section 47 Offences Against the Person Act 1861.

89　*Ibid* s 20.

90　*Ibid* s 18.

91　See n 87 *supra*.

92　Murder and manslaughter are not considered because it is not legally possible to consent to be killed.

93　Patricia Mayhew, *Summary Findings British Crime Survey* (1994) HMSO. This summary, which is based on the 1993 statistics, shows that the great majority of victims of assault crimes are males aged between 16 and 29.

law relating to physical violence.[94] It is this space which defines the male subject's possibilities for self-expression in violence, most specifically consensual violence between men/boys.

The construction of the male subject through his participation in 'manly sports'[95] is ensured through a line of cases from *Coney*[96] to *Attorney General's Reference (No 6 of 1980)*[97] which have preserved a space for that construction. It is possible to consent to visible violence[98] in the case of 'properly conducted'[99] games and sports. In other areas of violent self expression, the male subject is in more difficulties. If there is no visible, physical harm, consent can be a defence but the test here will be whether the conduct of the complainant viewed as a whole could have been considered to have constituted consent[100] – a very different test from the completely subjective one in rape.

Where an intentional assault has caused visible physical harm, consent cannot be a defence unless that harm is 'transient or trifling'[101] or if it falls into one of the categories of exceptional circumstances as set out by case law and confirmed by *Brown*.[102] These exceptional circumstances are 'manly sports',[103] 'rough but innocent horseplay'[104] and where the purpose justifies the harm, most notably legitimate and authorised medical interventions.

Brown settles that: 'It is not in the public interest that people should try to cause each other actual bodily harm for no good reason'[105] and where such good reason does not exist, consent cannot be a defence. In respect of visible violence outside of that very limited space, a male subject will not be allowed to consent, just as in the very considerable space for heterosexual male sexual violence, the law does not in its construction of rape allow the female other not to consent.[106]

---

94   A full discussion of these issues can be found in Duncan, 'Law's Sexual Discipline: Visibility, Violence and Consent' (1995).

95   This notion has been used in a number of leading cases relating to assault and consent eg *Coney* (1882) 8 QBD 534 and *Attorney General's Reference (No 6 of 1980)* [1981] All ER 1057.

96   (1882) 8 QBD 534.

97   [1981] All ER 1057.

98   Visible to the naked eye or visible by means of medical technology. The latter will usually refer to internal injuries.

99   *Attorney General's Reference (No 6 of 1980)* [1981] All ER 1057 at 1059.

100 *R v Donovan* [1934] 2 KB 498. Even for common assault, consent will not be an effective defence in the case of prize fights, presumably because they are illegal in any event.

101 *Donovan* at 509.

102 *R v Brown* [1992] 2 WLR 441.

103 *Coney* at 534.

104 Archbold, *Criminal Pleading and Practice* (1988, 43rd edn) paras 20-124 quoted in *R v Brown* [1992] 2 WLR at 449.

105 *R v Brown* at 449.

106 Duncan (1995) at pp 337-38 considers the implications of *Brown* in respect of homosexual sadomasochism.

Further, the judgment in *Brown* made it clear that not only were homosexual sadomasochistic activities[107] considered to be no good reason for the infliction of physical harm but also the House of Lords sought to extend its protection to the 'young men' who could be 'proselytised and corrupted'[108] by 'cult violence'.[109] This is protection which the law does not seek to extend to young female victims of rape in general because there is no age below which the victim cannot consent. Nor was it extended to the specific 15 year old victim in *Satnam and Kewal*[110] where rape convictions against the two defendants[111] were quashed and the court chose to reaffirm *Morgan*, leaving the honest belief test in tact and making no comment on the fact that a 15 year old can legally consent to sexual intercourse for the purposes of a rape charge although she cannot consent to indecent assault.[112]

As willing and enthusiastic 'victim' or as protesting complainant, the male subject cannot have consent constructed against him in matters of visible physical violence.[113] Of course, the same protection is extended to the female complainant but only in matters of visible physical violence where she is much less likely to be the victim and not in sexual violence where she almost always is.

DISCIPLINING GENDERED BODIES

Legal notions of consent construct gender in the law: they assist in the construction of the male as subject and the female as other. They also differentially discipline the bodies of the male subject and the female other. The mirror – the watchful eye of disciplinary power – reflects differential norms for the male subject and the female other.

The male body is disciplined by the law through the constrictions on its capacity to exert non-consensual violence on another male body but the capacity of the male body as political, sexual force is intensified by the space provided to the male subject in sexual offences and particularly in rape. The body of the female other is disciplined through the space which is provided to the male subject to construct her consent where none exists and by the complicity which that exacts from her in her own ontological degradation.

The very construction of sexuality creates the possibility for disciplining the body and the law constructs sexuality, particularly through its mercurial notions

---

107 The 'victims' were fully willing, consensual and derived pleasure from the aforementioned activities.

108 *R v Brown* at 584.

109 *Ibid.*

110 *R v Satnam S and Kewal S.*

111 In the appeal they were, of course, appellants.

112 Satnam had been charged with indecent assault as well as rape and when his rape conviction was quashed, he was convicted of indecent assault.

113 *R v Brown* n 107 *supra.*

of consent, to provide space for the sexual expression of the male subject. The space for the female other is as mirror for that desiring male subject.

It is interesting to note that where the female other is perceived to be outside the parameters of desirable female, the law does not construct her as mirroring male desire. In the case of *Kimber*,[114] the defendant was convicted of assaulting a 56 year old mental patient, 'Betty'.[115] Following *Morgan*,[116] the defendant argued honest belief in consent. The court, upholding the conviction, focused on Betty's consent and Betty's desires, although, following *Morgan*, the issue was *his* honest belief. The space for the male subject to legitimately express his sexual desires is not extended here because those desires are constructed outside the *normal* and the female other is not perceived as mirroring them.[117]

The female body is disciplined as a sexual body, disciplined to mirror the sexual desire of the male subject, to expand the space of his legitimate desire. Where her body is constructed as sexual, the space for her consent is consistently contracted; where her body is not constructed as sexual – as in the case of the ageing woman or the very young girl – that space is expanded. The criminal law disciplines the female body, as it denies subjectivity to the woman/girl.

CONCLUSION

It has been possible to see how the discourse of the criminal law constructs gender across a range of offences. Law's power is disciplinary – constructed around the mirror – the watchful eye of which also reflects gendered norms for the disciplined subject. In its disciplinary aspect, the law extends the power of the male subject to construct himself as desiring subject in respect of the female other who mirrors that desire. Concomitantly, it disciplines the body of the female other, subject to that power. The male physical body is itself disciplined in relation to the body of other male subjects.

The constructions of reason and consent in legal discourse are central to this process. Reason is constructed against the female other as it is ascribed to the male subject, although he is not tested by it. Differential constructs of consent create the power of the male subject for the legitimate space of the sexually constructed female other, as they limit the power of that subject's physical body. As watchful eye, as reflected norm, as refracted desire: the law's mirrors powerfully construct gender and in so doing, they gender justice.

---

114 *R v Kimber* [1983] 2 All ER 316.

115 'Betty' was the pseudonym given to her by the court. Although she was suffering from a severe degree of mental disorder, she was not defined as mentally defective under the terms of the Mental Health Act and, therefore, technically she was able to give consent.

116 Although this was a case of indecent assault, it was held that the consent test from *Morgan* did apply.

117 For further discussion of the issue of the non-sexual woman, see Duncan (1995) at pp 341–42.

CHAPTER TEN

BATTERED WOMAN SYNDROME: SHIFTING THE PARAMETERS OF CRIMINAL LAW DEFENCES (OR (RE)INSCRIBING THE FAMILIAR?)

*SHEILA NOONAN**

INTRODUCTION

The enterprise of legal method, as traditionally defined, operates on the basis of erasure in the quest to generate coherent content and stable categories.[1] Moreover, the established canons of reading and relevance permit the exclusionary practices of law to play a significant role in maintaining hegemony based on gender, race and sexual orientation. In short, within the legal order erasure and marginalisation are violences of the everyday variety.

Criminal law exemplifies the imposition of responsibility infused with the logic of individualism.[2] The processes of criminal law require the containment of social context, in which culturally constituted differences are transcended or bracketed;[3] both inclusions and exclusions form part of the arsenal of its achievement. Within traditional criminal law defences, the structuring of universally salient exculpatory criteria have largely operated to dramatically curtail, if not foreclose, their availability to women.

Most feminist writing in criminal law relates principally to women's experience as either victims or offenders. Yet, it is precisely the distinction between victimisation and agency, that warrants closer scrutiny. Firstly, theoretically the principal identification of the body of woman as *victim* within criminal law obscures the fact that only certain types of women may be able to bring themselves within this construct. Secondly, it masks the phenomenological experiences both victims and offenders may share. My interest lies in exploring the cases of women who have been victimised and by virtue of that victimisation offend against their abuser; such women enter court claiming the identity of both victim and offender. It is precisely because in 'domestic'[4] violence cases

---

* I would like to express my gratitude to Lisa Fong for her invaluable research assistance. I also wish to acknowledge the financial support received for this research through Advisory Research Council, Queen's University.

1   See eg Peter Goodrich, *Reading the Law* (1986) Blackwell.

2   See eg Alan Norrie, *Crime, Reason and History* (1993) Weidenfeld and Nicolson.

3   See Edward Palmer Thompson, *Whigs and Hunters* (1975) Peregrine at p 268.

4   This term is, of course, highly problematic in the manner in which it suggests that the violence is somehow of a different (and private) order. However, it is used in the vast majority of feminist research on this subject.

women's bodies are 'stretched across the divide of assailant/victim',[5] that they carry the potential to disrupt the framework within which this binary opposition of victim/offender seeks to operate.

Recently, in Canada and in England, efforts to locate domestic violence within the parameters of traditional substantive defences have been successfully made in part through juridical endorsement of a psycho-pathological model, namely 'the battered woman syndrome' ('BWS').[6] Within this context, I am particularly interested in the way in which BWS has to date affected substantive criminal defences.

At one level, the terrain it occupies within law could perhaps be characterised as a gesture toward the matrix of women's cultural situation. At the same time, BWS relies upon familiar motifs in terms of comprehending women's violence, thereby (re)producing truth claims about women's criminality and woman more generally.

Through examining recent cases, particularly those in which evidence relating to BWS has been permitted, I propose to explore the instantiation of gendered and racially-based difference the law will apprehend. At one level the paper addresses how the juridical construction of the cumulative effect of violence normalises domestic violence, trivialises fear, and polices the bounds of difference. Yet, it is the perceived choice either 'for' or 'against' the use of BWS evidence as a political strategy that I seek to complicate.

The 'dangers' attached to the legal adoption of BWS, including reliance on its dubious definition and the constitution of 'expertise' within this domain, have been exhaustively covered within extensive feminist commentary.[7] Acutely problematic is the transliteration of women's narratives which sanctions as admissible only those facets of their stories converging with medical and legal discourse. In a deep sense then, within the legal arena, all appears already authorised: the speakers, modality of expression, and site of contestation.

---

5   Alison Young, '*Caveat Sponsa*: Violence and the Body in Law' in J Brettle and S Rice (eds), *Public Bodies-Private States* (1994) Manchester University Press at p 136.

6   It is, of course, the case that the other model, that of individual responsibility, still forms the backdrop against which assessments of individual culpability are rendered.

7   Seema Ahluwalia, 'Diminished Conceptions of Women in Domestic Violence Research' in Dawn Currie (ed), *From the Margins to the Centre: Selected Essays in Women's Studies Research* (1988) Women's Studies Research Unit at p 75; Sue Bandalli, 'Battered Wives and Provocation' (1992) 152 *New Law Journal* 212; Elizabeth Comack, 'Justice for Battered Women?' (1988) *Canadian Dimension* 8; Donna Martinson, Marilyn MacCrimmon, Isabel Grant and Christine Boyle, 'A Forum on *Lavallee v R*: Women and Self-Defence' (1991) 25 *UBCL Rev* 23; Sheila Noonan, 'Strategies of Survival: Moving Beyond the Battered Woman Syndrome' in Ellen Adelburg and Claudia Currie (eds), *In Conflict with the Law* (1993) Press Gang 247; Katherine O'Donovan, 'Defences for Battered Women Who Kill' (1991) 18(2) *Journal of Law and Soc* 219; Martha Shaffer, '*R v Lavallee*: A Review Essay' 1990 22 n 3 *Ottawa L Rev* 607; Elizabeth Sheehy, 'Battered Woman Syndrome: Developments in Canadian Law After *R v Lavallee*' in Julie Stubbs (ed), *Women, Male Violence and the Law* (1994) Institute of Criminology at p 174; Elizabeth Schneider, 'Particularity and Generality: Challenges of Feminist Theory and Practice in Work on Woman-Abuse' (1992) 67 *NYUL Rev* 520; Julie Stubbs and Julia Tolmie, 'Race, Gender and the 'Battered Woman Syndrome'': An Australian Case Study' (1994) 8 *Canadian Journal of Women and Law*, forthcoming; Alison Young, 'Conjugal Homicide and Legal Violence: A Comparative Analysis' (1993) 31 *Osgoode Hall LJ* 761.

Nonetheless, this paper assumes as its starting point that criminal law, like law in general, is neither finally closed nor undifferentiated.[8] The structuring of the salience of BWS evidence may in fact reflect more fluidity than the foregoing suggests, though subject positions do so far appear relatively constant.[9] However, it may be precisely by virtue of the invocation of BWS that the inconsistencies perpetrated, or elisions occasioned, within criminal law doctrine may become more palpable, and ultimately, less stable. The paper will thus at one level reflect the way in which woman as offender is constructed within evolving criminal law defences, but also the ways in which such representations may carry the potential for disruption.

JURIDICIAL DEPLOYMENT OF FAMILIAR MOTIFS: BATTERED WOMAN SYNDROME

Legal narratives are highly coded and structured. But the stories which underlie the cases, grounded as they are 'in the everyday', and rooted in the 'particular and mundane',[10] are not easily repressed and continually challenge confinement.

The dissonances occasioned through application of simplistic binary tools to complex human experience can only rarely dissemble the artifice on which law relies. The transgressions are rarely neatly contained. Ultimately the law is forced to make manifest its strategies, and to bear witness to what is at stake.

I have elected to explore recent cases in which women have killed abusive spouses or partners. At one level, the tenor is legally familiar, examining doctrinal limitations and transmogrifications in existing defences. At a deeper level, I wish to explore, within the legal text, how it is that individual women, in their particularities, are (re)presented. What follows is a partial selection of BWS cases; I have chosen to concentrate in greater detail on those cases where women of colour are accused.

On occasion, I juxtapose truth claims about female criminality against particularised criminal cases of women who have responded violently under circumstances of abuse. My purpose is not to allege that the criminal law discourse coalesces with 'knowledges' of female offenders somehow emanating from outside law. Rather, I wish to suggest that juridical mapping of exculpatory categories, formulated through intersecting patterns of inclusion and exclusion, to some degree animates, formulates and reinscribes familiar motifs about female criminality. The recirculation carefully circumscribes, if not contains, the limits of recognition of difference within criminal law.

---

8   See Anne Bottomley and Joanne Conaghan (eds), *Feminist Theory and Legal Strategy* (1993) Blackwell.

9   The argument here is not that the 'law is male', but rather that the it is the 'masculine subject position' the law represents. For a fuller discussion of this issue, see Dawn Currie, 'Feminist Encounters With Post-modernism: Exploring the Impasse of Debates on Patriarchy and Law' (1992) 5 *Canadian Journal of Women and the Law* 64.

10   Jane Brettle and Sally Rice, *Public Bodies–Private States* (1994) Manchester University Press at p 1.

BASIC INSTINCT: VILIFICATION AND
THE AGGRESSIVE 'LESBIAN'

Positivist criminology from its inception was geared to identifying criminality.[11] It sought signs by which criminals could be discerned and classified, typically by the presence of disease, irregularities and anomalies.[12] Adopting anatomico-pathological methods, Lombroso and Ferrero sought physical markers of degeneracy reflecting a throwback to an earlier atavistic state. Female offenders physical attributes were painstakingly calculated: measuring of the crania, anklebones and middle fingers; examining handwriting; endless counting of wrinkles, tattoos, grey hairs etc was all carried out in an effort to 'render the female offender visible, and thus containable'.[13] However, while signs of anomalies were apparent among prostitutes, they were largely absent in relation to other female criminals.[14] Thus, Lombroso, in a generalised account of female offenders, contends that women are essentially conforming, not deviant.[15] Women are mere lawbreakers whose offending is not caused by their criminal nature, but rather results from external pressures.[16] Nonetheless, though few in number, Lombroso and Ferrero suggested there were also 'true' female criminals:

> We also saw that women have many traits in common with children, that their moral sense is deficient; that they are revengeful, jealous, inclined to vengeances of refined cruelty.
>
> In ordinary cases these defects are neutralized by piety, maternity, want of passion, sexual coldness, by neatness and an undeveloped intelligence. But when a morbid activity of the physical centres intensifies the bad qualities of women, and induces them to seek relief in evil deeds, when piety and maternal sentiments are wanting, and in their place are strong passions and intensely erotic tendencies, much muscular strength and a superior intelligence for the conception and execution of evil, it is clear that the innocuous semi-criminal present in the normal woman must be transformed into a born criminal more terrible than any man.[17]

In this sense, criminology posits a tautology to explain female offending: women don't commit crime unless they are, in effect, masculine.[18]

---

11 For an excellent review of Lombroso see Beverley Brown, 'Women and Crime: the Dark Figures of Criminology' (1986) 15:3 *Economy and Society* 354.

12 *Ibid* at p 388.

13 Lynda Hart, *Fatal Women: Lesbian Sexuality and the Mark of Aggression* (1994) Princeton University Press at p 12.

14 Brown (1986) at p 389.

15 Beverley Brown, 'Reassessing the Critique of Biologism' in Loraine Gelsthorpe and Allison Morris (eds), *Feminist Perspectives in Criminology* (1990) Open University Press at p 51.

16 *Ibid* at p 50.

17 Cesare Lombroso and Gugliemo Ferrero, *The Female Offender* (1958) Philosophical Lib at p 151.

18 Hart (1994) at pp 12-13, argues that Lombroso constructs the true female offender as 'not a woman'.

Physical anomalies detected in prostitutes and the few true female criminals were essentially marks of masculinity: muscular strength, a heavy jaw, and unrestrained desire. In keeping with the racism implicit in atavistic formulations, female homosexuality was initially ascribed to 'othered worlds', the lower classes, and criminals.[19]

The linking of inordinate desire and aggression is not new; both lesbianism and criminality have inextricably occupied this terrain.[20] Female aggression has historically been displaced on to lesbians; usurping masculine privilege, rather than object choice, has been a defining feature of the ascription of sexual identity.[21] Lillian Faderman's research suggests that many women prosecuted for lesbianism initiated sexual encounters, cross-dressed, used phallic prostheses or otherwise usurped male roles.[22] Havelock Ellis purported to document the significant number of cases in which female inversion 'led to crimes of violence'.[23]

Within the male specular economy, the lesbian occupies the space of man's double; precisely due to her construction as at once retaining her feminine gender but simultaneously not 'being a woman', there is no space in the logic of (in)difference which would permit her sacrificial entry.[24] In short, her association, by virtue of being lesbian, with desire and with aggression, precludes her from positioning herself in the role of the victim. Hence, in the handful of cases emerging from the United States (there are none to date in Canada, Australia or England), the courts have systematically refused to permit evidence of the cumulative effects of abuse, despite growing documentation of violence in lesbian relationships.[25]

An illustration of the displacement of aggression and violence on to those women who occupy the scopic position of lesbian is afforded by the reaction to the now infamous Canadian trial of Paul Bernardo. He stands convicted of two counts of first degree murder in the horrendous sexual slaying of two young teenage girls. Bernardo was married to Karla Homolka, who has received a 12 year sentence for manslaughter for her role in the deaths. In exchange, Homolka testified against Bernardo, providing evidence that the girls were strangled after

---

19   *Ibid* at p 4.

20   *Ibid* at p 14.

21   *Ibid* at pp 7–11, discussing the work of Havelock Ellis and George Chauncey.

22   Lillian Faderman, *Surpassing the Love of Men: Romantic Friendship and Love Between Women from the Renaissance to the Present* (1981) William Morrow and Company.

23   Havelock Ellis 'Sexual Inversion in Women' in *Studies in the Psychology of Sex* (1904) F A Davis Co vol 2 at p 124.

24   See Hart, (1994) at pp 4–11 for a thorough discussion of this process.

25   Ellen Faulkner, 'Lesbian Abuse: the Social and Legal Realities' (Symposium on Lesbian and Gay Legal Issues) (1991) 16(2) *Queen's LJ* 261. See also Claire M Renzetti, 'Building a Second Closet: Third Party Responses to Victims of Lesbian Partner Abuse' (1989) 38 *Family Relations* 160; Ruthann Robson, 'Lavender Bruises: Intra-Lesbian Violence, Law and Lesbian Legal Theory' (1990) 20(3) *Golden Gate UL Rev* 567.

sexual molestations recorded on video which included sexual assaults perpetrated by Homolka.

The Crown in an effort to bolster the credibility of Karla Homolka, as Crown witness, relied expressly upon evidence of the significant abuse she suffered at the hands of Bernardo. Homolka testified that her participation in the events which ultimately culminated in the deaths of the young women was coerced and took place against the backdrop of the terror to which she was subjected within her relationship with Bernardo. Bernardo had also repeatedly threatened to expose her role in the death of her sister, Tammy. Homolka procured drugs from the veterinarian clinic in which she worked. After imbibing alcohol laced with drugs, a tissue soaked in halothane was placed over Tammy's mouth. Tammy was first sexually assaulted by Homolka, then raped by Bernardo. These events were recorded on videotape; Tammy died from asphyxiating on her own vomit.

The 'lesbian acts' were constructed pornographically, that is as representations designed to ensure male viewing pleasure, and deployed by Bernardo as a strategy of localised control over Homolka. Nonetheless, cross-examination was directed toward uncovering the degree of 'pleasure' that Homolka may have experienced.

Even though Homolka testified that she participated in the acts under extreme fear of Bernardo, media attention and public response has overwhelmingly centred on her. Perhaps this is not only because the sexual molestation and deaths of Kristin French and Leslie Mahaffy were horrendous and recorded on tape for the jury to witness, but also because a woman was involved in planning and executing the abductions, and sexually assaulting the victims.

Somehow, Bernardo has become largely lost in this. On 4 November 1995 he was declared a dangerous sexual offender, thereby subject to indefinite incarceration. Although he still maintains his innocence in respect of the French and Mahaffy murders, he admitted responsibility for 32 charges arising out of 13 sexual assaults attributed to the Scarborough Rapist.[26] Additionally, he confessed to a further sexual assault in 1991, and to his role in the death of Tammy Holmolka.[27]

The 'facts' of the Bernardo case are among the most harrowing in the history of Canadian criminal law. They bear a decidedly surrealistic quality, from the love animating attempts to satiate Bernardo's pornographic proclivities, to the brutality of the rapes of all the women in the story. Nonetheless, Karla Homolka's actions raise hard questions both about the effects of trauma and captivity, and the degree to which actions taken in circumstances of coercion should be legally viewed as mitigating.

---

26 'Bernardo Judge Wants Him Forever', *The Globe and Mail*, 4 November 1995, A1.
27 *Ibid.*

A QUESTION OF SILENCE – THE VARIED GUISES OF THE LEXICON OF FEMALE UNREASON: SELF-DEFENCE AND DIMINISHED RESPONSIBILITY

Lombroso and Ferrero began from the basic premise that women are non-criminal for two reasons; the first relies on 'organic conservatism',[28] the female ovum is immobile in contrast to the sperm. Secondly, by virtue of child-rearing responsibilities, women are insulated from varying environmental conditions which promote individual variation; women are thus closer to their species type than male criminals who display a wealth of individual anomalies.[29] Both propositions focus on explanations for female non-criminality.[30] Female criminality becomes a contradiction in terms;[31] it is the norm of female non-criminality which makes true criminality unintelligible:

> The monster of the genuine female criminal is not just a creature from the wardrobe of ancient misogyny but a statistical and theoretical monster, since she contradicts the thesis of the female conformist nature. It is not her evil which threatens but her *unintelligibility* [my emphasis].[32]

Hence, Brown concludes that women's suitability for 'medicalizing alteration' derives from this prior characterisation of their non-criminal nature.[33]

It is the unintelligibility of female criminality, the fact that they are not really true criminals, which renders them available for mechanisms of psychiatric treatment. Hilary Allen argues that women are approximately twice as frequently given a psychiatric disposition in legal proceedings, paradoxically because they are seen as not as sick as men.[34]

Female criminality thus becomes constructed as unintelligible, and consigned to the realm of unreason. As Ingleby suggests:

> If we go back to first principles, what the 'mentally ill' have lost is not their bodily health, nor their virtue, but their reason; their conduct simply does not 'make sense'.[35]

As R D Laing observed, it is the failure to situate behaviours in the context of a person's life which creates the impression that behaviours are irrational or unintelligible. By locating oneself within another's world such actions could instead be characterised as 'a perfectly rational adjustment to an insane world'.[36]

---

28 Brown (1986) at p 390.

29 *Ibid.*

30 *Ibid.*

31 *Ibid* at p 395.

32 *Ibid* at p 395.

33 *Ibid* at p 400.

34 Hilary Allen Justice, *Unbalanced: Gender, Psychiatry and Judicial Decisions* (1987) Open University Press at p xi.

35 David Ingleby (ed), *Critical Psychiatry: The Politics of Mental Health* (1982) Penguin Books at p 128.

36 Ronald David Laing, *The Politics of Experience* (1967) Penguin Books.

In Canada, BWS evidence has afforded an opportunity for courts to contextualise assessments of culpability in the light of subjective apprehensions of fear arising within the dynamic of abusive relationships. Paradoxically, however, rather than dislodging unintelligibility, efforts to (re)assert women's rationality of response to domestic violence have been less than successful. This is perhaps attributable to the interaction between the discourses of law and psychiatry.[37]

To date, in England, there has not been a case in which a battered woman has successfully pleaded *self-defence*.[38] In part, this stems from the reluctance of the judiciary to depart from understandings of self-defence reflected both doctrinally and in the criteria articulated in s 3 Criminal Law Act 1967[39] which require a close scrutiny of the circumstances as they relate to the nature of the woman's subjective assessment of her circumstances, and an objective assessment of the reasonableness of the force deployed. In other words, even though a woman apprehended an attack, her response is assessed in relation both to the proportionality of the force she used to avert harm, and as to whether the resort to force was reasonable. At issue in relation to the reasonableness of the resort to force is whether retreat is possible, and whether an attack is imminent at the time self-defensive action was taken.

Effectively, the same doctrinal requirements existed in Canada prior to the Supreme Court decision in *R v Lavallee*.[40] Angelique Lavallee gave evidence that, at a party on the night of the killing, the deceased, Rust, had assaulted her and threatened to kill her when the rest of the guests had departed. As Rust left the bedroom where he had assaulted and threatened her, she shot him in the back of the head. Given that the fatal shot was imparted under circumstances in which a life-threatening attack was not imminent, a self-defence plea would have failed under then existing precedent.

Evidence was advanced by an expert who testified that Angelique Lavallee was suffering from 'battered woman syndrome'. Directly calling into question the requirement of imminent attack, Madame Justice Wilson endorsed an American case which argued that requiring that, 'a battered woman wait until the physical attack is "underway" before her apprehensions can be validated by law would ... be tantamount to sentencing her to "murder by installment"'.[41] Relying heavily upon Walker's concepts of 'learned helplessness' and 'traumatic bonding', the syndrome evidence was adduced to assist the jury in appreciating the woman's state of mind.

---

37 For an in-depth analysis of these interactions, see Allen (1967).

38 See eg J C Smith and B Hogan, *Criminal Law* (1992) Butterworths. The issues of provocation and necessity will be discussed later.

39 (UK) 1967 c 58.

40 [1990] 1 SCR 852. For general discussion see eg D Stuart, *Canadian Criminal Law* (1995, 3rd edn) Carswell.

41 *Ibid* at p 883.

In fact, BWS bears on the issue of subjective (mis)perceptions so as to potentially exonerate or mitigate the impact of criminal responsibility. Madame Justice Wilson in *Lavallee* stressed that masculine standards of reasonableness 'must be adapted to circumstances which are, by and large, foreign to the world inhabited by the hypothetical "reasonable man"'.[42] In her view, expert evidence of the effect of battering on women in domestic relationships was necessary to assess the individual woman's state of mind. Without it, the jury might not be able to appreciate questions such as why she would continue to live in an abusive situation. Such evidence could assist the jury in determining if the woman's subjective fear 'may have been reasonable within the context of the relationship'.[43]

In seeking to explain why an abused woman would remain within an abusive relationship, BWS stresses the woman's victimisation and paralysis; it cannot therefore simultaneously be used to assert her act of self-preservation as reasonable. Instead, by broadening assessments of reasonableness to include the situation of battered women, the focus shifts away from the reasonableness of the acts of self-preservation. It is precisely the assertion that her actions are otherwise unintelligible which assists in casting the battered woman as suffering from a form of mental incapacity.

Alison Young argues that BWS is seen to manifest itself, crucially, through a series of unreasonable decisions:

> Her victimisation, as a battered woman, makes her stay in the relationship (when she should have left the abuser). It makes her continue to believe in his promises to reform after each attack (when she should have no faith left in him). It makes her take lethal action against his violence (when she should have called the police or a neighbor, left the house, left the room). In short, 'battered women's [sic] syndrome' makes an abused woman follow the wrong course each time a choice of action presents itself. Each time, she takes the unreasonable decision.[44]

Thus, Young concludes, the reason retrieved through application of the BWS is the reason of the unreasoning.

The lexicon of unreason is entirely transparent in English decisions in which *diminished responsibility* has been pleaded. Section 2 Homicide Act 1957 permits a plea of diminished responsibility in homicide cases where an accused can demonstrate that she was 'suffering from such an abnormality of mind ... as substantially impaired [her] responsibility ...'. The *Ahluwalia*[45] decision, discussed below, was seen to open the possibility of introducing BWS evidence in diminished responsibility cases, though it has been rarely exercised in England.

---

42   *Ibid* at p 874.

43   *Ibid* at p 882.

44   Young (1994) at p 145.

45   *R v Ahluwalia* [1992] 4 All ER 889.

Though not expressly relying on BWS, the recent case of *R v Stubbs*[46] affords an illustration of psychiatric assessments of abnormality falling short of insanity. The appellant pleaded guilty to manslaughter in her killing of an abusive husband. Three years later her new partner came forward to accept responsibility for the death. At that time Ms Stubbs admitted that she had killed her former spouse after enduring years of physical, sexual and emotional abuse. On the night in question, the deceased was in the process of abusing her when she knocked him unconscious. Fearing his response, she killed him. On the basis of two psychiatric reports (which spoke to the accused's history of depression arising both from hereditary factors and on account of the abusive nature of the relationship) the court was prepared to find that her intent was impaired within the meaning of the Homicide Act. In spite of being a parent of three children, the accused was sentenced to 30 months' imprisonment.

The salience of 'unreason' at the level of doctrine would appear to function in opposite directions in these two defences. On the one hand self-defence expressly purports to render intelligible actions taken against a backdrop of abuse. In contrast, diminished responsibility posits a prior deviation from normality which is enduring at the time of the offence. In point of fact, both reason and its opposite are inscriptions of sameness: at once, a (re)inscription of male rationality (and an acknowledgement of the incomprehensibility of women's agency).

Both defences rely heavily, if not exclusively, on psychiatric assessments. The logic of the science of irrationality cannot be divorced from the history of 'psy' discourse and its relationship to the demands of punishment. In particular, the medicalisation and concomitant objectification of various forms of deviance, together with their trappings of pseudo-scientific certainty, have operated to produce the subject which justifies the object of punishment.[47] It is a discourse which at once is both saturated with and instantiates normalising power.[48]

What is normalised, and sanitised, in the process of invoking BWS is male violence against intimates. This process is particularly transparent in those cases where provocation is pleaded.

---

46 (1993) 15 Cr App R (S) 57, CA.

47 See Michel Foucault, *Discipline and Punish* (1977) Vintage Books.

48 In Foucault's words, 'The judges of normality are present everywhere. We are in a society of the teacher judge, the educator judge, the "social worker" judge; it is on them that the universal reign of the normative is based; and each individual, wherever he finds himself, subjects to it his body, his gestures, his aptitudes, his achievements. The carceral network, in its compact or disseminated forms, with its systems of insertion, distribution, surveillance, observation, has been the greatest support in modern society of normalising power' *ibid* at p 304.

CRIMES OF THE HEART: PROVOCATION: NORMALISING VIOLENCE AND TRIVIALISING FEAR

Central to criminal law doctrine is the notion of individual fault. Though there are increasing numbers of objectivist assessments of criminal responsibility, *mens rea* remains one of the enduring features of analysis. The juridical subject is assumed to exercise free will and therefore must bear responsibility for his actions. Guilt is assessed principally, though not exclusively, in relation to intentionality, foresight, motive, and reason. Nonetheless, the criminal law provides defences by way of concession to 'human frailty' so that this, under certain conditions, for example rage and involuntary impulses, can be mitigating.

Like diminished responsibility, provocation is a partial defence; it is available where an accused faces a charge of murder.[49] Under the principles articulated in *R v Duffy*[50] provocation requires a 'sudden and temporary' loss of self-control. Notwithstanding the omission of this phrase from s 3 Homicide Act 1957,[51] its legal salience has been repeatedly affirmed until the very recent decision in *R v Humphries*.[52] As in self-defence, the test for provocation is comprised of both subjective and objective components. First, the judge must assess whether provocation caused the accused to lose self-control. Secondly, the trier of fact must be satisfied that a 'reasonable man' under these circumstances would have been so provoked.

The subjective component is difficult to satisfy if there has been a lapse of time between the provocative act or statement and the killing. Lack of immediacy suggests that the accused had a 'cooling-off' period in which to reflect on the circumstances; delay raises the spectre of calculated revenge.

Prior to the *Humphries* decision there was no tendency toward recognition of the cumulative effect of violence which culminated in death. The emphasis was almost entirely localised to the 'provocative act' immediately prior to the killing. Paradigmatic examples of provocation remain acts which injure or threaten the male psyche: confessions of adultery; questioning paternity; threats to leave.

---

49 For a thorough discussion of both the defences of diminished responsibility and provocation see O'Donovan (1991).

50 [1949] 1 All ER 932.

51 Section 3 Homicide Act is as follows:

'Where on a charge of murder there is evidence on which the jury can find that the person charged was provoked (whether by things done or by things said or by both together) to lose his self-control, the question whether the provocation was enough to make a reasonable man do as he did shall be left to be determined by the jury; and in determining that question the jury shall take into account everything both done and said to the effect which, in their opinion, it would have on the reasonable man.'

52 *R v Humphries* (CA, 7 July 1995 as yet unreported).

As Alison Young explains:

> The particular versions are masculine ones, with emphasis on masculine metaphors of temperature, speed and pressure ... Provocation, in this conceptualization, lights a fuse which can ignite violence. Just as the lighting of fuses and the exploding bomb are tropes which feature in male action movies which exclude the perspectives of women, this characterisation of anger does not include the emotions experienced by many battered women.[53]

Thus, the objective component, that is whether the reasonable man would have been provoked to do what the accused did is not an easy test for a woman to meet despite its reformulation in *DPP v Camplin*[54] which requires that the reasonable man is to be infused with the same age, sex and 'characteristics' as the accused.

The *Thornton*[55] decision is perhaps the best known of all the English cases involving battered women who kill abusive partners. Sara Thornton had experienced violence at the hands of her partner on a number of occasions.[56] During an argument, she went to the kitchen, selected a knife, sharpened it, and returned to her husband who had threatened to kill her when she was asleep. She expected him to ward off the blow, but instead he died as a result of the injury. The trial judge affirmed the necessity for 'a sudden and temporary loss of self-control'. She was convicted of murder and on appeal her conviction was upheld.

It has been suggested that this decision placed undue emphasis on the 'suddenness' requirement and was not in keeping with earlier authorities where the central issue was simply whether what transpired occurred in the heat of passion:

> ... the suddenness requirement anomalously rewards with the possibility of mitigation those for whom it was natural to respond immediately with fatal violence, whilst seeming to deny it to those who may have made efforts to control their anger, but who boil over when they find they cannot.[57]

Women's groups have been vitally involved in lobbying for appeals of women's cases. In May, the Home Secretary announced that Sara Thornton's case will be referred back to the Court of Appeal.[58] Undoubtedly her appeal will transpire under considerably more auspicious circumstances given the Court of Appeal's reworking of provocation in *Humphries*.

Emma Humphries was released in July 1995 after having served 10 years for killing her violent partner, Trevor Armitage. Her murder conviction was

---

53 Alison Young, 'Conjugal Homicide and Legal Violence: A Comparative Analysis' (1993) 31 *Osgoode Hall Law Journal* 771.

54 [1978] 2 All ER 168.

55 *R v Thornton* [1992] 1 All ER 306.

56 For an intriguing discussion of the *Thornton* decision see Alison Young (1994).

57 Jeremy Holder, 'Provocation and Loss of Self-Control' (1992) *Law Quarterly Review* 193.

58 'Howard Refers Sara Thorton Case Back to Court of Appeal', *The Guardian*, 5 May 1995, Home Page.

overturned and a verdict for manslaughter substituted, on grounds of provocation. Emma Humphries began working as a prostitute at age 16 and met the deceased with whom she took up residence. He began sexually and physically abusing her. While she was remanded on another charge, he commenced relations with another woman.

In February 1985 she met Armitage in a pub where he indicated that he and two friends wanted a 'gang bang'.[59] She returned home whereupon she took two knives and slashed her wrists. He began to undress and taunted her about not having done a very thorough job on her wrists. She lost control and stabbed him. At trial she was convicted of murder, despite psychiatric evidence that she suffered from 'abnormal mentality with immature, explosive and attention-seeking traits'. In charging the jury, the trial judge instructed that they could only consider the effect of the jeer on a woman who *did not have a distorted and explosive personality*.[60]

In two extremely important rulings, the court held first, that the characteristics of immaturity and attention-seeking (though not explosive personality) were characteristics within the meaning of the *Camplin* test. The jury were entitled in light of the psychiatric evidence to consider these characteristics in assessing whether the reasonable person would have been provoked. The provocative jeer was intended to target this abnormality. Secondly, the court ruled that it was incorrect to deal with the provocative taunt in isolation from the entire history of the abusive relationship. In the court's words:

> This tempestuous relationship was a complex story, with several distinct and cumulative strands of potentially provocative conduct building up until the final encounter. Over the long term there was the continuing cruelty, represented by the beatings and the continued encouragement of prostitution, and by the break-down of the sexual relationship. On the first part of the night in question there was the threatened 'gang bang', and the drunkenness. Immediately before the killing, quite apart from the wounding verbal taunt, there was his appearance in an undressed state, posing a threat of sex which she did not want and which he must have known she did not want, thus demonstrating potentially provocative conduct immediately beforehand not only by words but also by deeds. Finally of course there is the taunt itself, which was put forward as the trigger which caused the appellant's self-control to snap.[61]

Thus, it seems that the English courts are now beginning to grapple with the threat and fear that battered women face. Provocation does not conceptually capture the profile of these cases particularly given that the central dynamic is one of anger leading to loss of self-control; research on battered women who kill suggests that self-preservation is the defining feature. The difficulty is that

---

59   *The Times*, 8 July 1995.

60   *NLJ Practitioner*, 14 July 1995 at p 1032.

61   *Ibid* at p 1033.

juridical categories have an either/or quality. Although the English courts have been unprepared to countenance self-preservation, it would seem that some of the analysis of contextualising violence has now been sanctioned by virtue of the *Humphries* case.

THE HAND THAT ROCKS THE CRADLE: PRESERVING THE MATERNAL

Formulations of motherhood typically achieve stability and coherency through reliance not only on 'a traditional heterosexual matrix',[62] but also through reinstating the constructed female subject of white, middle-class mythology.[63] Good mothers are women who devotedly and selflessly dispense love, warmth and care to their offspring. As children, these myths serve as a symbol of our loss at both an emotional and psychic level. As mothers, these accounts are internalised and form the standard according to which our failure is judged, by ourselves and others.

Iconography of 'good mothers' almost invariably depicts white women. Conversely, myths about 'bad mothers' are mapped disproportionately on to the bodies of non-white women.[64] Reliance on idealised accounts of women's caring and nurturing capacities is particularly pernicious when perceived deviation from these qualities is so differentially policed in our social order(s).

Criminality has been one of central interchangeable components of bad motherhood,[65] despite research which suggests that some women lawbreak to provide materially for their children.[66] Thus, unlike property law, where Anne Bottomley identifies the tug of the 'vortex of wife/mother/innocent',[67] criminal law is less forcefully centrifugal (and predominantly unidirectional) in cases where mothers are charged with criminal offences.

I am not suggesting that motherhood is never mitigating, but rather, that it is more difficult to fit within conventional tropes of motherhood cases where women are suspected of criminal activity. Within criminal cases, motherhood may be invoked in relation to the familial responsibility the mother bears as the primary care giver of children. In so far as her actions can be read as principally

---

62 Adria Schwartz, 'Taking the Nature Out of Mother' in Donna Bassin, Margaret Honey and Meryle Kaplan (eds), *Representation of Motherhood* (1994) Yale University Press at p 240.

63 See Madeline Henley, 'The Creation and Perpetuation of the Mother/Body Myth: Judicial and Legislative Enlistment of Norplant' (1993) 41 *Buffalo Law Review* 703.

64 *Ibid.*

65 See Dorothy Roberts, 'Punishing Drug Addicted Mothers Who Have Babies: Women of Color, Equality and the Right of Privacy' (1991) 104 *Harv Law Rev* 1149; and Dorothy Roberts, 'Motherhood and Crime' (1993) 79 *Iowa Law Review* 95.

66 See Ann Worrall, *Offending Women: Female Lawbreakers and the Criminal Justice System* (1990) Routledge at pp 141–143.

67 Anne Bottomley, 'Self and Subjectivities: Languages of Claim in Property Law' in Anne Bottomley and Joanne Conaghan (eds), *Feminist Theory and Legal Strategy* (1993) Blackwell at p 57.

aimed at fulfilling her obligations of support and protection, maternal responsibilities are most typically deployed as at least mitigating.

The former proposition is demonstrated in part by a recent Canadian decision in which evidence of battering was salient in the court's assessment of the defence of necessity. The existence of necessity as a substantive defence has historically met with reluctant acknowledgment, both in England and in Canada.

Beginning in *R v Morgentaler*,[68] and especially in *Perka v R*,[69] the Supreme Court of Canada imposed doctrinal requirements which in significant respects parallel the restrictions formerly imposed on the availability of self-defence. Until the decision in *R v Lavallee*, both self-defence and necessity shared two conceptually related elements, namely a demonstration that the peril sought to be averted was imminent, and a finding of proportionality between action taken and harm sought to be averted. The SCC in *Lavallee* acknowledged the limited and gendered construction of these requirements within the context of self-defence. However, there has been no similar reworking of the substantive principles of necessity which have remained subject to an additional and seemingly insurmountable burden, namely the requirement that no other reasonable legal alternative is available.[70]

Some reworking of these principles has recently been attempted. Lise Lalonde[71] was a mother of five children who, in a period that spanned almost 10 years, episodically lived with the father of four of the children. She was physically and verbally abused during the relationship. She was charged with fraud on the basis that she was periodically required to file forms attesting to the fact she was living alone in order to qualify for family benefits. The allegation was thus that she misrepresented her living arrangements in order to receive state benefits to which she was not entitled. The trial judge found that the male partner was an abusive alcoholic who frequently threatened to take the children. He accepted Lise Lalonde's testimony that she was afraid to receive welfare (as opposed to family benefits) because she was concerned that the cheque would be issued to him and that she would thus have no means of feeding her children:

> [T]he issue here is, was this accused justified in making the false statements that she made, in the sense that her purpose was not to defraud the public but to preserve herself and her children?[72]

The requirement that no legal alternative be available was transmuted into a stipulation 'that there must not be a reasonable alternative available'.[73] In

---

68 [1993] 3 SCR 463.

69 [1984] 2 SCR 233.

70 The practical impossibility of meeting these criteria is demonstrated by the fact that there has been only one successful necessity defence post-*Perka* and prior to *Lalonde*.

71 *R v Lalonde* (1995) 22 OR (3d) 275.

72 *Ibid* at 285.

73 *Ibid* at 287.

commenting on how the facts fulfilled the doctrinal requirements Mr Justice Trainor observed:

> In my view, the answer for Lise Lalonde, a battered wife, lies in the fact that she had, in her mind no reasonable alternative and putting food on the table for her children, in her circumstances, was pressing.[74]

However, perceived failure of maternal responsibilities may heighten juridical assessments of culpability. Where maternal care is deemed wanting, mothers have, in effect, been held responsible for failing to protect their children from the violence of an abusive partner. Punishment can thus take the form of either criminal prosecution, removal of the children from maternal care, or both.

In *R v Emery*[75] the appellant was initially sentenced to four years imprisonment, reduced on appeal to 30 months, on a cruelty charge for failing to prevent violence by the child's father, Hedman. His assault on their 11 month old daughter resulted in her death from peritonitis, occasioned by reason of a blow which ruptured her bowel. The *post mortem* revealed a large number of other injuries, including fractured ribs. Emery testified that Hedman 'routinely and severely abused not only Chanel [the child] but herself'.[76] She did not intervene to protect the child because she feared Hedman. In reducing the sentence Lord Taylor CJ commented:

> It cannot be too clearly emphasized ... that the parent's paramount duty is to protect his or her child. Failure to do so, with results such as occurred here, cannot be excused by other pressures that there may have been upon the mother, unless they were such as to render her incapable of action. Still less can such failure be excused by a mother putting her relationship with her partner, or even her own protection, before the life and health or her child, as the learned judge found was the case here.[77]

The insularity of legal 'subject matters' obfuscates the full import of instantiation within law of a given representation of women. Law's teleological tendency toward seamlessness of doctrine in the end suggests that motifs cannot be neatly hermetically contained within the domain of criminal law.

Recent developments within Canadian child welfare jurisprudence highlight the dangers of juridical entrenchment of BWS. Child protection cases frequently involve familial situations within which a woman is subjected to abuse at the hands of her male partner. In this sense it is certainly not a recent development that battered women are likely to have the abuse they have suffered deployed against them as an indication either of their emotional unavailability to parent, or their inability to adequately protect their children, either from violence or the effects of witnessing violence. The mother's incapacity in relation to protection is frequently the focus of social service practice and juridical intervention.

---

74 *Ibid*.

75 *R v Emery* 1992 14 Cr App R(S) 394.

76 *Ibid* at 395.

77 *Ibid* at 396–97.

The recognition of BWS in the criminal context has given new purchase and lent empirical 'truth' to the suggestion that particular mothers are, by virtue of this 'condition', incapable of providing adequate parenting to their children. Typically the result of such an appraisal is that an application for society or crown wardship is granted.

In *Children's Aid Society for the Districts of Sudbury and Manitoulin v T(L)*[78] a manager of a shelter for battered woman spoke of the mother's tendency to minimise the abuse to which she had been subject and her tendency to recant. She linked these traits with 'the battered wives syndrome'. On this basis, and in the face of other CAS evidence, the court concluded that it was 'abundantly clear' that the mother suffered from 'the battered woman syndrome'. The CAS succeeded in their application for Crown wardship partially on the basis of a dismal prognosis for future parenting contained in a psychological assessment which stated:

> Regrettably, only a minority of battered women end up firmly rejecting the violence and reestablishing a life on their own for the purpose of raising their children in a non-violent atmosphere (Campbell, 1990). Perhaps the majority of women (the exact number is not known) choose to believe that returning to their husbands will be in everyone's best interest over time, and that the violence will end.

It is poor women, and women of colour, who are most vulnerable to juridical intervention in the name of child protection. The impact of differential intervention, when coupled with a racial construction which is in tension with BWS, makes access to justice very difficult to achieve where women of colour are involved.

POLICING 'OTHERNESS': THE SALIENCE OF RACE

One of the most difficult facets to map of those cases which have relied on BWS evidence is the impact of race. The erasure of colour as a 'relevant' matter for inclusion in the 'facts' of the legal text renders it virtually impossible to know whether the woman accused is white or of colour. It has been suggested, for example, that Angelique Lavallee was Aboriginal, yet there is nothing in the recorded facts which would indicate this. Yet, in other cases race is clearly and centrally present.

In those cases where race is ascribed the effect of the accused's gendered and racialised 'difference' are inextricably interwoven and the impact of race cannot be neatly circumscribed.[79] In point of fact, the desire to isolate and contain the

---

78   (1991) OJ No 1118 (unreported).

79   See N Iyer, 'Categorical Denials: Equality Rights and the Shaping of Social Identity' (1993) 19 *Queen's LJ* 179 (Iyer worries especially about how legal categories conflate difference as distinction and difference as hierarchy).

impact of race and gender 'differences' is precisely the politics which relegates 'the identity of women of colour to a location that resists telling'.[80]

To date comparatively scant attention has been devoted to the impact of using BWS evidence where a woman of colour stands accused.[81] There is every reason to suspect that women of colour are not treated in a monolithic way. At the very least, a particular woman will be treated as belonging to a specific racial grouping. Each racial identity unfolds within a specific socio–historic construction with a counterpart in juridical discourse[82] which may or may not coalesce. Secondly, her particularities, both in relation to race and gender, are likely to influence the matrix within which a person is ultimately positioned.

The following discussion proceeds by examining those cases from which it is apparent that a woman of colour has been charged; therefore, what follows is likely to represent a partial sampling. For the reasons discussed above, I also distinguish the cases of Asian women from those of Aboriginal women. In doing so, it is necessary to concede that both the designations 'Asian' and 'Aboriginal' obfuscate and subsume the vast cultural and linguistic differences within these categories. However, it is imperative to begin to unpack whether particular racial categories are juridically infused with a specified logic of difference.

In *R v Tran*[83] a 32 year old woman, Yu-Ming Tran, described as a 'native of Cambodia', pleaded guilty to manslaughter in the homicide of her husband Brian Tran. Prior to her relationship with Tran, Yu-Ming had been involved with another man, described as 'the inscrutable' Kam Wu. During the early months of her relationship with Tran, she continued to maintain contact, largely by telephone, with Kam Wu. Eventually the on-going contact was discovered and in the court's words 'the duplicitous world of Yu-Ming Tran was exposed and began to unravel'. She attempted suicide, was admitted as a psychiatric patient and later continued as an out-patient in treatment for depression. From the point of discovering that Kam Wu had been an on-going presence in Yu-Ming's life, Tran became extremely controlling, abusive, and highly possessive.

Yu-Ming Tran is constituted contemporaneously as a foreigner, as 'having a personality disorder of an histrionic type and a depressive disorder', and as deceptive in her interpersonal relationships (nowhere does the text reveal

---

80 Kimberle Crenshaw, 'Mapping the Margins: Intersectionality, Identity Politics, and Violence Against Women of Color' (1991) 43 *Stanford LJ* 1242.

81 However, this literature is beginning to emerge. See, for example, Elizabeth Sheehy, 'Battered Woman Syndrome: Developments in Canadian law after *R v Lavallee*' in J Stubbs (ed), *Women, Male Violence & The Law* (1994) Institute of Criminology at p 174; and Julie Stubbs and Julia Tolmie, 'Battered Woman Syndrome in Australia: A Challenge to Gender Bias in the Law?' *ibid* at p 192.

82 This is where the work of Daina Chiu strikes me as so significant. She carefully examines the history of Asian Americans and the various patterns of exclusion and assimilation, juridical and otherwise, and brings this history to bear on her analysis of cultural defences. More of this work must be done in order to permit a full interrogation of the impact of BWS in cases where visible minority women stand accused. See Daina Chiu, 'The Cultural Defense: Beyond Exclusion, Assimilation, and Guilty Liberalism' (1994) 82 *Calif L Rev* 1053.

83 [1991] OJ No 2052 (Ont Ct Justice) (unreported).

whether the relationship with Kam Wu was sexual). The full impact of these constructions is difficult to summarise. Her 'Cambodian' heritage renders her 'not Canadian'.[84] The psychiatric diagnosis, coupled with her tendency toward deception, functions to cast doubt on her credibility as a witness. This manifests itself by way of the trivialising her accounts of the violence and the palpable scepticism with which her account of events is treated:

> It was the recollection of the accused that, during late 1988 and early 1989, the deceased's verbal and physical abuse of her continued weekly. For the most part, the physical abuse comprised slaps on the face. She was only kicked twice, and punched but twice. The verbal abuse consisted of her denigration by reference to prostitutes, animals held in no or low esteem in her culture, and limited intellectual capacity.

Scepticism in relation to her claims that the relationship was violent is apparent within the narration of those events by virtue of the passive and distanced voice the court adopts:

> Episodes of physical assault, in my respectful view, were much less frequent than as recounted to Dr Shane by the accused and as repeated in his evidence. None were life-threatening, nor could be reasonably perceived as such.

Medical records are also canvassed and found to provide scant corroborative evidence that abuse was unfolding.

The immediate events leading to the killing were that early in the morning Tran demanded food and, as she prepared a meal, he indicated that he wanted to have sex (a pattern which was often part of her descriptions of the circumstances surrounding abuse, though the court does not comment on this). When she rejected his advances he launched into verbal abuse:

> He told her that she was just a slave. There was nobody who was as dumb or stupid. She was worse than a pig ...

He went to the bedroom and she followed him carrying a pot of oil, telling him to stop insulting her or she would pour it on him. She spilled some of the oil on him, whereupon he attacked her. In fear of another beating she grabbed a kitchen knife, which happened to be in the bedroom, and stabbed him. Her evidence that he had tried to strangle her with a scarf was apparently not accepted as fact by the court. Afterwards she attempted to take her own life.

The court, while acknowledging that the provocative comments may be culturally specific, does little to unpack whether Brian Tran's words were, in fact, provocative. Ultimately, the court does not characterise the case as one of either self-defence or provocation, but rather as one of involuntary manslaughter.

---

84 Which as Leti Volpp points out in discussing cultural defences creates an image in which the dominant law and culture is portrayed as neutral and cannot be questioned. It also suggests that there is a dominant culture to which is added 'a spoonful of cultural diversity from immigrants'. Hence it presupposes that the culture of immigrants is distinct from the culture of Canadians, ie, Canada itself is not touched by 'othered' cultures. See Leti Volpp, '(Mis)Identifying Culture: Asian Women and the "Cultural Defense"' (1994) 17 *Harv Women's LJ* 57.

Yu-Ming Tran's racial construction carries a decidedly 'other' flavour. From her recounting of witnessing the atrocities of war in Cambodia during her childhood, to the cursory efforts to understand whether her husband's insults may have been provocative, the court's discomfort with knowing how to acknowledge her difference, and to what end, is apparent. At one level, there is an open acknowledgement of her difference. For example, the court is unprepared to sentence her to a federal penitentiary given the hostile environment in prisons for women toward racial minorities. At another level, her difference is subsumed in the logic of sameness. The court comments repeatedly on her ability to maintain employment. In this respect, she conforms to notions of the 'model' immigrant,[85] who is acceptable precisely because she is able to be gainfully employed.

The approach of the English Court of Appeal, in the only reported decision dealing with an Asian woman killing her abusive partner, reflects a similar approach in which racial difference is acknowledged but its 'impact' is legally circumscribed. In particular, the trial judge ascribes salience to her racial 'characteristics' in a manner which appears at its most benign to render race irrelevant, or on a less sanguine reading, entirely calculated to heighten culpability.

Kiranjit Ahluwalia, an Asian woman born in India, was charged and initially convicted of murder on the death of her husband.[86] Her marriage had been arranged and took place in Canada, whereupon the couple moved to England. From a very early date the husband was physically and emotionally abusive. His conduct gave rise to a series of court injunctions aimed at restraining his violence against her. From 1981 there was considerable medical documentation of injuries she had sustained at his hands. About two months before the incident, Kiranjit Ahluwalia learned that her husband was having an affair and her evidence was that he taunted her about this relationship.

On the night in question, the accused attempted to engage her husband in conversation about their relationship. He refused to speak to her and threatened to beat her the following morning if she could not furnish funds to pay a bill. Early in the morning she went outside, obtained some petrol, and took it, and a candle, upstairs. She threw the petrol and the lighted candle into his room and went to dress her child. The deceased sustained burns, for which he was treated, but died approximately one week later.

At trial, the defence sought a verdict of manslaughter on grounds of provocation; the jury convicted of murder. On appeal, it was affirmed that provocation required a 'sudden and temporary loss of self-control'. Nor was the court prepared to overturn the trial court judgment on the basis of failure to permit a contextualised assessment of the impact of her race:

---

85 For a discussion of the historical deployment of this representation in relation to Asian immigrants see Chiu (1994) at pp 1079–80.

86 *Supra* n 44.

The only characteristics of the defendant about which you know specifically that might be relevant are that she is an Asian woman, married, incidentally to an Asian man, the deceased living in this country. You may think she is an educated woman, she has a university degree. If you find these characteristics relevant to your considerations, of course you will bear that in mind.[87]

Thus, the court never considered whether there may have been greater reluctance to call the police, or 'a more generalised community ethic against public intervention'.[88] Nor was her mental state attributable to the abuse, a characteristic that could enter the subjective component of the provocation test:

True, there was much evidence that the appellant had suffered grievous ill-treatment; but nothing to suggest that the effect of it was to make her 'a different person from the ordinary run of [women]', or to show that she was 'marked off or distinguished from the ordinary [women] of the community'.[89]

Ultimately, the court was prepared to find on the basis of fresh evidence, including evidence relating to her mental state, that the defence should be permitted to produce evidence of diminished responsibility.

It is striking that the courts were prepared in these two cases to entertain psychiatric history.[90] In this respect, these cases have a distinctly different flavour from those Canadian cases in which Aboriginal women were accused. It is impossible to generalise from only these two cases; however, it is important that any further such cases be closely analysed to assess whether models of ultra-femininity[91] make psychiatric pathologisation a familiar motif where Asian women are charged.

ABORIGINAL WOMEN

The history of colonisation, relocation, and efforts to enforce assimilation, has resulted in the chronic impoverishment of Aboriginal peoples in Canada. Systematic efforts by the colonisers to disrupt traditional customs and economies has caused significant 'ruptures in Aboriginal peoples' social relations'.[92]

Criminal justice statistics for 1991 reveal that nearly one quarter of the female prison population was comprised of Aboriginal women, though they represent less than 2% of the population.[93] Recent studies of the rates of

---

87   *Ibid* at pp 897-99.

88   Mary Ann Dutton, 'Understanding Women's Responses to Domestic Violence' (1991) 23 *Hofstra LR* 1236.

89   *Supra* n 44 at p 898.

90   Although clearly in *Tran* the court was unprepared to attach any exculpatory significance given the scepticism with which her testimony was treated.

91   Chiu (1994) at pp 1086-88.

92   Carol LaPrairie, 'Aboriginal Women and Crime in Canada: Identifying the Issues' in Ellen Adelberg and Claudia Currie (eds), *In Conflict with the Law* (1993) Press Gang Publishers at p 237.

93   *Ibid* at p 236.

childhood abuse disclose that between 60 and 85% of Aboriginal women were victimised during their childhood or adolescence.[94]

The profile which exists in respect of Aboriginal offending generally seems of particular salience in the cases dealing with Aboriginal women who kill abusive partners. In other words, racial constructions of Aboriginal offending seem much more patently at play.

A recent study of Aboriginal homicide in Ontario suggests that Aboriginal peoples are over represented as both homicide victims and suspects.[95] In keeping with earlier work, Doob *et al* found that alcohol was more frequently recorded by police as involved in the offences.[96] Homicides were almost invariably intra-racial, and the overall picture differed little between on and off reserve populations.[97] Typically, the police characterised the homicides as an argument that escalated out of control.[98]

In the cases below, we see the 'truth' of the empirical literature (re)produced.[99] In other words, there appears to be a juridical construction of Aboriginal offending which has a hauntingly familiar quality. It is as though juridical narrations reinforce stereotypical assumptions about Aboriginal drunkenness, violence, and intra-racial quarrels. The point here is not a dispute about what 'actually' happened in these cases, but rather that the construction of relevant legal facts almost invariably invokes this information where Aboriginal women stand charged even though these same factors also feature in the criminological literature dealing with homicides committed by whites.

Perhaps due to this dynamic, Aboriginal women seem less readily included in the general characterisation of women as essentially non-violent;[100] hence it is exceedingly difficult for the models of passivity and learned helplessness to

---

94 Generally see *ibid*. The lower figures are based on studies of particular communities; the higher figures relate specifically to Aboriginal women in conflict with the law. Thus, Fran Sugar and Lana Fox, *Survey of Federally Sentenced Women in the Community* (1990) Native Women's Association of Canada found violence was experienced by 70% of the women they surveyed. Data contained in the *Report of the Task Force on Federally Sentenced Women: Creating Choices* (1990) Correctional Service Canada suggest that approximately 90% of federally incarcerated Aboriginal women reported they had been subject to physical abuse, and over 60% reported incidents of sexual violation.

95 Anthony Doob, Michelle Grossman and Raymond Auger, 'Aboriginal Homicides in Ontario' (1994) 36(1) *Canadian Journal of Criminology* 29.

96 *Ibid* at p 47.

97 *Ibid* at pp 55–58.

98 *Ibid*.

99 My argument of course, does not rely on any claim about truth at all, except that knowledges generate truth-effects.

100 See Elizabeth Sheehy, 'What Would a Women's Law of Self-Defence Look Like' (1995) Ottawa: *Status of Women in Canada*.

explain their actions.[101] An illustration of this can be found in *R v Eyapaise*,[102] where a woman was charged with assault with a weapon. Nellie Eyapaise had an extensive history of abuse, beginning in her childhood. She is identified as Aboriginal through her story of having been gang raped at age 12; she recalls her memory of the rapist being consoled and told not to worry 'because she was only an Indian'.[103] From early childhood, she had been subject to both sexual and physical abuse within her family. At the age of 16, she entered her first of four abusive relationships.

On the night in question, she was drinking with her cousin at a bar when she met the stranger. After the bar closed the trio continued drinking at her cousin's house. Over the course of the evening, she responded to two efforts by the stranger to sexually assault her by striking him. When he grabbed her on the third occasion, she escaped his grasp and stabbed him with a knife. Undue weight seems to have been attached to the accused's failure to respond passively. Mr Justice McMahon commented that, 'The accused's actions belie the feeling of helplessness or the paralysis of fear that is more typical of a battered woman in an abusive situation'.[104] The attempts to sexually assault her were also minimised in the remark that, 'there is no evidence that he was violent in the usual sense of the word'.[105] In convicting the accused of assault causing bodily harm, the judge stressed that the accused had other options available to her to preserve herself from harm:

> Her cousin Donald Ironbow was present and could have intervened, as in fact he eventually did. Mrs Ironbow was in an adjacent room and apparently sober. Boutin was a stranger. Had the accused left in a taxi as she had arrived, he could neither follow nor find her. A phone was close at hand to call the police or her husband ...[106]

The motif of Aboriginal drunkenness[107] also features in *R v Raymond*.[108] In imposing sentence for aggravated assault in relation to the wounding of her

---

101 It is unfortunate the juridical tests have focussed on these concepts. Especially since in recent work Fischer *et al* found that not all women who are battered display increasingly passive behaviour. See Karla Fischer, Neil Vidmar and Rene Ellis, 'The Culture of Battering and the Role of Mediation in Domestic Violence Cases' (1993) 46(5) *Southern Methodist Univ L Rev* 2117.

102 (1993), 20 CR (4th) 246 (Alta QB).

103 *Ibid* at pp 249-50.

104 *Ibid* at p 251.

105 *Ibid*.

106 *Ibid*.

107 See Michael Jackson, 'Locking Up Natives in Canada' (1989) 23 *UBC L Rev* 215 who concludes at p 218:

'Almost every study that has been done notes the high rate of alcohol-related offences in which native people are involved. Put at its baldest, there is an equation of being drunk, being an Indian and in prison ... The fact that the stereotypical view of native people is no longer reflected in official government policy does not negate its power in the popular imagination and its influence in shaping decisions of the police, prosecutors, judges and prison officials.'

108 [1993] NWTJ No 86 (unreported).

abusive common law partner, Taylor, Laura Raymond received a sentence of one year's imprisonment followed by two months' probation. Virtually no information appears in the text as to either the history of the abuse Laura Raymond had sustained at the hands of her partner, or the events culminating in the shooting. While she had been sent to Alberta for psychiatric assessment, the presentation of the medical evidence only tangentially relates to her history of abuse; primary emphasis is devoted to her alcoholism.

Laura Raymond who was the mother of two small children received a period of incarceration, no doubt in part due to the gravity of the offence, but also because the sentencing judge made it clear that he wished to send a message to the community of Tuktoyuktuk that this was an unacceptable way to behave:

I go to Tuktoyuktuk more often than any other judge because I am based out of Inuvik ... Unfortunately, it is a community in which there are many families that are like your family. These are families in situations where alcohol abuse is rampant and drunken, senseless violence occurs far too frequently.

The conditions of probation included terms that Laura Raymond would receive alcohol counselling and requiring her to abstain from alcohol and from possession of any illicit intoxicants.

A similar peremptory treatment of the violence within the conjugal relationship occurs in *R v Howard*.[109] On an appeal against a five year sentence for manslaughter, the court declined to admit as fresh evidence the report of a psychologist who interviewed the accused after the imposition of sentence and which contained opinions that, 'if accepted by a court could have led to a 'battered woman syndrome' defence [sic] ... ' As Marilyn Howard was not seeking to withdraw her plea, the court relied on a report from a prison psychologist which fleetingly commented on the history of violence within the 11 year relationship.

On the version of the facts adopted by the court, Marilyn Howard was in the course of arguing with her husband when he commenced hitting her. The argument related to the deceased's accusation that he was not the father of the child Marilyn Howard was carrying. She broke away, ran to the kitchen and found a knife, returned to the bedroom and stabbed him. Again, no history of past abuse is recounted by the court and the significance of the struggle which lead to the killing is not given any appreciable weight. The Court of Appeal appears to endorse the trial judge's characterisation of these events as a 'quarrel' in which 'there seemed to be a lack of real threat to the accused'. Although it certainly would seem that self-defence could have been raised, provocation and intoxication were the mitigating factors identified by the court.

Provocation, though not available as a defence to a charge of aggravated assault, was also mentioned by the judge imposing sentence in *R v Catholique*.[110]

109 [1991] BCJ No 3786 (BCCA) (unreported).
110 [1990] NWTJ No 164 (Sup Ct) (unreported).

Though suggesting that her actions were taken under 'emotional pressure sensing herself to be genuinely in real peril' he commented that '[i]t would be difficult in the circumstances of the present case, to gauge with any hope of accuracy the degree to which the 'battered woman syndrome' truly applies'. Again, almost no reference to the past history of abuse is apparent, though in one cryptic comment a previous assault on Rita Anne Catholique which required stitches is mentioned. The incident on the day of the wounding is cast within a narrative which is similar to a number of the previous cases. She and her husband were drinking, an argument flared up, and he began assaulting her:

> ... [H]er spouse ... proceeded to slap her vigorously and repeatedly with his open hand so that she reacted, or better, overreacted, with an overwhelming rage actuated as much by fear for her personal safety as by being again physically abused and by her consequent anger.

The court apparently being unwilling to clearly characterise her actions as self-preservation or anger, evidence of battering becomes significant only by way of mitigating sentence. Rita Anne Catholique received a two year suspended sentence, and probation.

A more thorough-going assessment of culpability is revealed in *R v Eagles*[111] where a woman was charged with having uttered a death threat against an abusive husband to whom she had been married for 25 years. Judge Lilles permitted testimony by Dora Eagles and her children as to the significant history of abuse perpetrated by the husband. The judge emphasized that *Lavallee* did not stipulate that expert evidence is a precondition for reception of factual testimony bearing on the accused's state of mind. The history of control and violence was such that when it was coupled with her consumption of alcohol and anger in the face of unfair and callous treatment, the court was unprepared to attach moral guilt to her actions:

> Listening to Dora Eagles give her evidence, it was apparent that her act was that of a desperate woman, cornered and barely hanging on to threads of self-esteem, and self-worth. She was powerless. Even while [she was] separated from her husband, he was significantly impacting, if not controlling her life ... The facts conjure up elements of reflex action, provocation and self-defence while not being clearly any of these three. Yet at the same time, it is with considerable certainty that I have concluded that there is a total absence of the kind of moral guilt which would justify a finding of criminal responsibility.

Dora Eagles was acquitted on the basis of a generalised lack of *mens rea*. In effect, the case may signal a willingness to undertake a cumulative assessment of the coercion inherent in abusive relationships so as to mitigate against criminal responsibility.

---

111 [1991] YT No 147 (unreported).

Though it is beyond the scope of this paper, careful attention should be paid to the development of the so-called 'cultural-defences' in the United States.[112] In some respects, the underlying claim for those who advocate greater legal recognition of cultural specificity is not unlike claims about why BWS should be admitted:

> The notion is that a recent immigrant who acts in accordance with cultural dictates should have that weighed in assessing either his or her mental state or normative culpability.[113]

There are several significant problems that warrant highlighting. First, debate around the use of cultural evidence has at one level reproduced explicitly racist ideology. Secondly, it has pitted against one another the agendas of activists and scholars involved in anti–racist and feminist work.[114] Caught in the divide are those feminists writing out of their experiences as women of colour. The use of cultural defences has been highly essentialising and often based on stereotypical assumptions about the behaviour of particular racial groups. Finally, the cases in which cultural evidence has been permitted appear to reproduce historic patterns of exclusion and assimilation.[115]

POSTSCRIPT: STRATEGIC CALCULATIONS

Subjectivity which seeks acceptance within the domain of the social relies upon the violent expulsion and destruction of those aspects of 'self' submerged in fear and horror. Kristeva's concept of abjection defines the socially configured boundaries of the clean and proper body.[116] Those cases before the courts which succeed on the basis of BWS rely upon fixing the woman in the position of victim, or the abject.[117]

The strategy of pleading BWS is appealing precisely because the results may be auspicious: acquittal; reduction of sentence; and, in some instances, release from incarceration. However, reinscribing woman as victim constrains not only our understanding of female criminality, but it encodes woman as subjectless within law.

---

112 See C Choi, 'The Cultural Defense in Criminal Law' (1986) 99 *Harvard Law Review* 1293; D Chiu, 'The Cultural Defense: Beyond Exclusion, Assimilation, and Guilty Liberalism' (1994) 82 *California Law Review* 1053; A Gallin, 'The Cultural Defense: Undermining the Policies Against Domestic Violence' (1994) 35 *Boston College Law Review* 723; N Rimonte, 'A Question of Culture: Cultural Approval of Violence Against Women in the Pacific-Asian Community and the Cultural Defense' (1991) 43 *Stanford Law Review* 1311; L Volpp, '(Mis)identifying Culture: Asian Women and the 'Cultural Defense' ' (1994) 17 *Harvard Women's Law Journal* 57.

113 For a very thorough discussion see Volpp (1994).

114 See Crenshaw (1991) and Volpp (1994).

115 Chiu (1994).

116 J Kristeva, *Powers of Horror* (1982) Columbia University Press.

117 See Young (1994) and S Noonan, 'Pertaining to Connection: Abortion and Feminist Legal Theory' in J Hart and R Bauman (eds), *Explorations in Difference: Law, Culture and Politics* (forthcoming, 1996) University of Toronto Press.

> It could be argued that, pragmatically, evidence as to 'battered woman's syndrome' represents a compromise made by defence lawyers in order to minimise the sentences their clients may suffer. This may indeed be a compromise, but it is one in the manner of the Faustian bargain, in which the bargainer loses at every turn.[118]

In a highly sophisticated piece, Alison Young argues (at least implicitly) that because of the sacrificial nature of the marriage contract, invocation of BWS as a strategy should be eschewed. Reliance on BWS in the context of either exonerating or mitigating sentence acts to 're-sacrilise her as victim', thereby positioning woman as subjectless.

The trade-off between theory and practice is starkly posed; in it, feminism finds itself at something of an impasse in the debates around legal engagement. Rhetorical styles have altered (anti-legal engagement in particular is now infused with insights from post-structuralism) but fundamentally the divisions parallel and replicate familiar positions.

On the one hand there are theorists, sometimes located 'outside' law who stress that, at least predominately, law's power to regulate daily life should be resisted, and de-centred.[119] Thus, Carol Smart characterises law quintessentially 'as a mechanism for fixing gender differences and constructing femininity and masculinity in oppositional modes'.[120]

Within feminist legal theory, few would dispute Smart's claim that law *does* this. And yet, it must be stressed that legal discourse cannot be situated as foundational. To attribute the fixing of gendered differences solely (or even predominately) to law is to consign legal discourse to the realm of metaphysical; in this respect Smart over draws the 'power of law' in the very move calculated to de-centre it. This is transparent in Smart's failure to acknowledge that other knowledges, and in particular sociology, are also implicated in (re)producing gendered difference:

> I am not suddenly trying to suggest that sociology floats above contamination by the social, or that it is a pure science which provides unassailable truths; but it does provide alternative accounts which are generated by an adherence to articulated methods. With sociological knowledge we can always see the packaging and the ingredients, it always provides the means for its own critique. Sociology always has the potential to construct subversive knowledge.[121]

Sociology has thus freed itself, by virtue of its transparent method, from the power/knowledge configuration to which all other discourses are subject.

---

118 Young (1994) at pp 149-150.

119 See for example, Carol Smart, *Law, Crime and Sexuality: Essays in Feminism* (1995) Sage. In the Canadian context, a similar position is espoused by Lorene Snider, 'Feminism, Punishment and the Potential of Empowerment' (1994) 9(1) *Can J of Law and Soc* 78.

120 Smart (1995) at p 218.

121 *Ibid* at p 230.

On the other hand, there are those for whom engagement within law carries the potential to wield (at least) small, concrete gains for particular women. Anne Bottomley and Joanne Conaghan argue that law provides space for argument, engagement and resistance. In their view law is general, is neither so uni-dimensional or undifferentiated as Smart's (re)presentation would suggest.[122] They thus conclude:

> The operation of law involves a continual use of strategies, in which one is constantly balancing the possibilities against the probabilities. Again, let us be clear in general, it is a more than uneven fight. As law is constituted in a society which still privileges sections of that society in terms of gender, race, class, and socially defined standards of ability, so it is by no means a 'free space' for equal engagement. But neither is it closed space which we must continually struggle against rather than within. When Smart states that 'the entry of feminists into law has turned law into a site of struggle rather than being taken only as a tool of struggle' we would agree, but we would add that it is [a] site within which we find tools; it was never a tool because it was not a single entity or practice.[123]

Sheila McIntyre argues that, '[a]bandoning law altogether is a luxury of theory and/or privilege from the perspective of those long abandoned by reformers and reformism'.[124]

In our preoccupation with finding the best position, negotiating the treacherous terrain of strategic calculations, the question is begged: who is to arbitrate the dispute? Some feminist theorists writing out of their position as women of colour have been criticised for the assumption that abandoning the legal, in favour of relocating to the extra-legal, is the best strategy.[125] But this is to presume there is, or can only be, one answer. While I have emphasized readings of the cases which have at one level reinscribed familiar motifs of sex and race, I want to suggest how these cases could be cast in a rather less pernicious light.

To date, only a handful of cases have been decided in Canada in which BWS evidence has been coupled with an existing substantive criminal law defence so as to serve as a basis for acquittal.[126] In actual fact in both Canada and in England, it most frequently operates by way of mitigating sentence. Though ultimately less than successful on its own terms, that is in assisting in understanding how the cumulative effects of violence may impinge on subjective assessments relevant to substantive criminal defences, BWS evidence

---

122 Bottomley and Conaghan (1993).

123 *Ibid* at p 3.

124 Sheila McIntyre, 'Redefining Reformism: The Consultations That Shaped Bill C-49' in Julian Roberts, Renate Mohr (eds), *Confronting Sexual Assault: A Decade of Legal and Social Change* (1994) University of Toronto Press at p 293.

125 See especially Patricia Williams, *The Alchemy of Race and Rights* (1991) Harvard University Press at p 146.

126 Specifically, *Lavallee*, *Eagles*, and *Lalonde*. It remains to be seen what the outcome of *Petel* (1994), 87 CCC (3d) 97 (SCC) will be once it has been retried.

could perhaps legitimately be regarded as an incursion. Within the parameters of criminal law discourse, the re-conceptualisations occasioned by virtue of the introduction BWS evidence may yet be significant.

By virtue of its effort, though rarely fully realised in practice, to contextualise action against the backdrop of coercive relationships, the door is opened to what has heretofore remained almost invisible. In particular, the recognition of BWS carries the potential for social locatedness to inform assessments of agency and moral culpability. These cases thus challenge criminal law's penchant for the separating of context from agency.[127] It is, therefore, unsurprising that BWS evidence has most frequently been used at the time of sentencing, where traditionally broader questions in relation to factors leading to individual culpability have been permitted. In other words, it may be because BWS is so potentially *subversive* to the containment of social context that the courts have been reluctant to permit it to more fully infiltrate substantive criminal defences. Thus, the potential for the door to be opened to more contingent and contextualised assessments of culpability is precisely what makes these cases so significant both at the level of practice and theory.

Practically, BWS cases have opened the door to more nuanced discussions of moral (and legal) culpability. This is evidenced by the heightened scrutiny of juridical sentencing practices. Particularly in England (but also in Australia) the imposition of lengthy periods of incarceration has attracted the attention of women's groups and the public at large. The media have played an important role in highlighting glaring examples of morally unacceptable sentencing practices. Thus, a number of women who have initially been convicted of murder have had their sentences reduced on appeal. In Canada, the Federal government has just agreed to review the cases of women currently incarcerated for having killed abusive partners.[128]

In general, it appears that women are currently receiving shorter sentences where self-preservation is at issue.[129] Mandatory life sentences for murder where an abusive partner has been killed are now the exception rather than the rule.[130]

Theoretically, the dividing line between 'criminal women' and 'woman' in general is arguably increasingly difficult for the courts to sustain. Thus, at one level the juridical failure of incomplete or inadequate contextualisation of action may speak to the very instability of the category victim/agent itself. Rather it may suggest unease about the ability of either the tropes of victimisation or unreason to ultimately safely contain female criminality.

---

127 For an argument as to how the defences of necessity and duress also challenge legal individualism in criminal law see Alan Norrie, *Crime, Reason and History* (1993) Weidenfeld and Nicolson at pp 154-171.

128 'Battered Women Who Killed Win Reviews', *Toronto Star*, 14 July 1995, A3.

129 I deliberately use the word 'appears' because criminal justice statistics on sentences for various types of homicide are so incomplete. I have interviewed women in prison over the course of the past five years. My impression is one gained from talking to women about their cases and their sentences. See generally Noonan (1993) and Sheehy (1993).

130 *Ibid.*

But lest all this assume the cast of marshalling arguments in favour of the instrumental, it should be emphasised that embracing legal pragmatism is insufficient. Geraldine Finn has convincingly argued that politics grounded purely in instrumentalism, in fine-tuning norms and procedures to include women or to redress feminist criticisms, reproduces the logic it purports to contest.[131] In other words, Young and others who have cogently argued against invoking the BWS point to a logic which, if not inexorable, cannot be easily arrested.

In relation to feminist praxis, Finn argues that it is both imperative and understandable that claims to moral (substitute, legal) goods must be articulated in authorised categories of thought. Claims are not even comprehensible as such unless authorised categories are adopted. Distinguishing between ethics and politics,[132] she emphasises that feminists must at the same time call into question 'the values of liberal individualism'[133] which underlie the categories we are obliged to invoke in seeking technical-political accommodations or modifications. The 'ethical space', ie 'the space between representation and reality, language and life' is thus that which exists outside the categories of institutionalised discourses:

> This space between category and experience, representation and reality, language and life, is, I believe, the necessary and indispensable space of judgment; of creativity and value, resistance and change. It is the ground of critical intentions and originating experiences which enable us to call the *status quo* into question and challenge the already known universe and its organization into the predicative and prescriptive categories of practical reason ...[134]

Extrapolating from her argument, feminist legal praxis should be informed by the aporia which exists outside legal representation.

Additionally, strategic decision-making needs to begin from a place of acknowledging the complexity of multiplicity: any juridical ascription of ritualised difference which is premised on a homogenous group mythologised within racist discourse must be challenged at every turn. However, an assessment of the probable impact of particularised multiplicity must inform a decision whether to use BWS in any particular case.[135] To do this, more work remains to be done in mapping genealogies of exclusion and assimilation across racial categories. Only through such work can we begin to more fully appreciate how legal discourse coalesces into projects of subordination.

---

131 Geraldine Finn, 'The Space-Between Ethics and Politics: Or More of the Same?' in Eleanor Godway and Geraldine Finn (eds), *Who Is This We?* (1994) Black Rose Books.

132 *Ibid* at p 101.

133 *Ibid* at p 106.

134 *Ibid* at p 207.

135 See Volpp (1994).

CONCLUSION

While I believe that feminist legal theory is largely self-reflexive in relation to the articulation of values inscribed within legal individualism, too often strategic choices as to use of law have failed to interrogate the impact on race. The politicisation of domestic violence, at least in North America, has largely been driven by efforts to stress that it is an offence which cuts across racial and class barriers. As Kimberle Crenshaw points out, 'the displacement of the 'other' as the presumed victim of domestic violence works primarily as a political appeal to rally white elites'.[136] Feminist strategies to combat violence against women have thus participated in conceptualisations which suggest that it is problematic because it happens to white women.

Feminist strategies have also typically coalesced with law and order political agenda(s). Calls for 'tougher' sentencing practices rely upon the elision or rejection of the experiences of women who have been subject to criminalisation and the attendant regimes of discipline. Harsher sentences thus impact on women who often have histories of dramatic subjugation, and resistance. There has been a significant reluctance within feminism to acknowledge that criminalised women, many of whom have been subjected to lives of seamless abuse but whose stories furnish richly haunting documentation of strategies of survival, are also on the political agenda. Disproportionately, it is women of colour who are affected by these occlusions.

The legal salience attached to racial difference therefore needs to be carefully mapped. In any event, the preliminary assessment of cases involving Aboriginal women suggests that their racial constructions may be in direct tension with the motifs of BWS. While so-called, 'cultural defences' have not received formal juridical attention in either Canada or the United Kingdom, recent developments in the United States also present compelling grounds for circumspection. We should be similarly sceptical of juridical construction of difference which may have the effect of leaving women of colour once again caught in the interstices of feminist and race agendas.

At this juncture, far too little is known about the impact of the strategy of adducing evidence of BWS where the accused are women of colour. Any strategic calculations as to whether there may be benefit in using BWS on behalf of particular women must interrogate the impact on race. Failure to do so may once again witness feminism embracing mechanisms of resistance that replicate racial oppression(s).

---

136 Crenshaw (1991) at p 1260.

CHAPTER ELEVEN

CRITICAL PERSPECTIVES ON WOMEN'S RIGHTS: THE EUROPEAN CONVENTION ON HUMAN RIGHTS AND FUNDAMENTAL FREEDOMS

STEPHANIE PALMER

There is growing pressure in the United Kingdom to incorporate the European Convention on Human Rights and Fundamental Freedoms into domestic law. What would a formal declaration of rights mean for women? Could the European Convention be a weapon for empowering disadvantaged groups in society, such as women? Could this strategy enable women's concerns and experiences to become a central part of legal discourse? Consideration of such fundamental questions has the potential to challenge the traditional scope of civil liberties and human rights generally.

The purpose of this paper is to discuss some possible implications of the incorporation of the European Convention into domestic law for women.[1] This analysis will be directly informed by the insights of feminist scholarship and its commitment to eliminating the subordination of women. Yet, the articulation of political demands in terms of rights raises a pressing issue that must be addressed: Is a rights-based strategy a flawed means to address social inequality?[2] This paper analyses some of the articles in the European Convention and the potential for feminist approaches. Further, given the crucial importance of the application and interpretation of a rights-based document, the role of the judiciary will also be examined. The underlying theme is the marginalisation, and even exclusion, of women's concerns in the dominant discourse. Could incorporation of the European Convention be a mechanism to allow feminist engagement with the 'mainstream' of constitutional law? Looking into the future, or possible futures, is always a rather speculative enterprise and I acknowledge that in many ways this project raises more questions than it provides answers.

---

1   Analysing women as a category directly raises the issue of essentialism. Is it possible to make any claims about women without taking into account factors such as race, class and sexual orientation? R Braidotti, *Nomadic Subjects: Embodiment and Sexual Difference in Contemporary Feminist Theory* (1993) Columbia University Press, argues the need to retain the use of the category for strategic purposes. Women do share common experiences and gender remains an important and influential factor in the lives of women. See also G Bock and S James (eds), *Beyond Equality and Difference* (1992) Routledge at pp 1–13.

2   A number of feminists have focussed on the limits of law and legal method to achieve gender reform. See eg C Smart, *Feminism and the Power of Law* (1989) Routledge at pp 144–46 and E Kingdom, *What's Wrong With Rights* (1991) Edinburgh University Press. Although E Kingdom highlights the dangers of rights discourse she concludes, in ch 8, that there may be political reasons for supporting the campaign for a UK Bill of Rights. For a discussion of why the use of law has been so equivocal for feminists see M Thornton, 'Feminism and the Contradiction of Law Reform' (1991) 19 *International Journal of the Sociology of Law* 453. The failure of rights to achieve social change has also been a theme within the critical legal studies movement, see generally M Tushnet, 'An Essay on Rights' (1984) 62 *Texas Law Review* 1363.

A RIGHTS BASED STRATEGY AND FEMINIST THEORY

Given the unwritten constitutional structure in the UK, which provides little formal protection for human rights, it is unsurprising that the idea of a Bill of Rights is seen as holding out hope for groups in society who do not hold political power. Civil liberties and human rights discourse have traditionally been dominated by men, in a world where men have struggled 'to assert their dignity and common humanity against an overbearing State apparatus'.[3] Women were excluded from the systems that created, interpreted and applied the laws.[4] As society changed and more women entered public life the 'rights of man' gradually came to include women. The increasing number of women entering the work force led to demands for equal pay and legal recognition of the rights of women. Fuelled by the women's movement which sought to achieve equality for women in a man's world, emphasis was placed on the elimination of discrimination. These legal changes sought to place women in the situation of men, to extend to women those recognised rights held by men.

Yet the participation of women in political life and formal equality in the eyes of the law has not led to social justice or real equality between men and women. Those matters of concern to women, in the field of civil and political rights, are often defined in law in such a way that women's voice is not heard. For example, the law of pornography is perceived within a framework of freedom of expression versus morality, even though it clearly affects the status and dignity of women and may even contribute to violence against women.[5] The law on abortion is regulated by the criminal law and controlled as a medical matter, rather than as an issue of women's right to choose. Thus the right to terminate a pregnancy could easily be qualified by the competing interests of the State in the welfare of foetal life.[6] Domestic violence against women is not a central part of the civil and political rights agenda. It is only very recently that the criminal law has protected women against marital rape.[7] The priority of traditional rights is the protection of men and women within the public sphere. It provides a system of rights that the individual can assert against the state. But where the harms against women are distinctive, their needs are rarely addressed.

---

3   N Burrows, 'International Law and Human Rights' in T Campbell *et al* (eds), *Human Rights: From Rhetoric to Reality*, (1986) Blackwell at pp 80-81.

4   See C Pateman, *The Sexual Contract* (1988) Polity Press, Cambridge. The franchise was extended to women in 1926.

5   See G Robertson, *Freedom, the Individual and the Law* (1993, 7th edn) Penguin at pp 211-48 and compare with C MacKinnon, *Feminism Unmodified: Discourses on Life and Law* (1987) Harvard University Press at p 195.

6   N Burrows (1986) at p 84. See also the Warnock Report (1984) HMSO Cmnd 9314.

7   *R v R* [1992] 1 AC 599. This decision has been challenged as a violation of Article 7 ECHR (freedom from retroactive criminal offence and punishment).

It is hardly surprising that some feminists should be sceptical about the difference that more rights would make to their everyday lives. They point to legislation such as the Sex Discrimination Act 1975 which has failed to deliver the promised equality between men and women.[8] Some feminists suggest that a rights-based strategy is misguided in a liberal legal world antipathetic to feminist ideals. Feminists, such as the sociologist Carol Smart, have even concluded that the use of rights discourse to achieve equality has been counterproductive; it has led to false hopes and perhaps even been detrimental to women's claims.[9] Understandably, experience of the limitations of rights-based discrimination statutes has led to doubts about the wisdom of exploiting law as the most critical strategy in achieving equality.

The feminist critique of rights has several related aspects. One facet of this critique is that rights are inherently individualistic and competitive and women's experience is not easily translated into this narrowly accepted language of rights.[10] Rights rhetoric can simplify complex power relations but it fails to overcome existing structural inequalities which are woven into women's daily lives.[11] A perverse but consistent result of rights-based strategies is the reinforcement of the most privileged groups in society.[12] Nicola Lacey observes a link between rights claims and ascribing formal equality.

> In a world in which white, male and middle-class people both have more effective access to legal forums and meet a more sympathetic response when they get there, the ascription of formally equal rights will in effect entrench the competitively asserted rights of these privileged people.[13]

Feminists have also convincingly illustrated that the ostensibly universal category of 'individual' suggested by liberal theorists is constructed on the basis of male attributes.[14] The liberal legal world ignores the gender inequalities which are built into the very definition of the system. Men and women cannot compete if the gender neutral rules are established to suit the apparent interests and needs of a man's world. Consistent with many other international human rights documents, the European Convention embodies the classical liberal position of the individual and there is an assumption that human rights discourse is gender-neutral.

---

8   See K O'Donovan and E Szyszczak, *Equality and Sex Discrimination Law* (1988) Blackwell and N Lacey, 'Legislation against Sex Discrimination: Questions from a Feminist Perspective' (1987) 14 *Journal of Law and Society* 411 for a discussion of the UK legislation.

9   C Smart (1989) at p 158.

10 See H Charlesworth, 'What are Women's International Human Rights?' in R Cook (ed), *Human Rights of Women* (1994) University of Pennsylvania Press p 58 at p 61. The Feminist critique of rights draws upon other critical inquiries including the critical legal studies movement. See R Gordon, 'New Development in Legal Theory' in D Kairys (ed), *The Politics of Law* (1990) Pantheon Books at p 413.

11 C Smart (1989) at p 144.

12 D Kairys, 'Freedom of Speech' in D Kairys (ed), *The Politics of Law* (1990) Pantheon Books at p 265.

13 N Lacey, 'From Individual to Group' in B Hepple and E Szyszczak (eds), *Discrimination: The Limits of the Law* (1992) Mansell at pp 106-7.

14 See C Pateman (1989) at p 221.

Another facet of the critique of rights rests on their inapplicability in the private sphere. The public world of state, market, politics and men is perceived as superior to the private realm of women and the family. In the USA and Canada, the public/private dichotomy has been at the centre of the argument concerning the ineffectiveness of rights. The argument is that rights discourse takes for granted that there is or should be a division between the public world, that enforces rights, and a private world of family life in which individuals pursue their diverse goals, relatively free from state interference.[15] The limitation of rights usage to the public sphere is a special disadvantage to women and children who may face oppression in the hidden private sphere.

On a more pragmatic level, many feminists fear that by diverting attention away from political reform and into legal disputes, rights-based strategies will limit aspirations by merely reframing debates within the dominant discourse and increasing reliance upon a predominantly male judiciary. Thus, this emphasis on rights will inevitably be at the expense of other aspects of women's situation. As the legal system is skewed in favour of those whose interests are already protected in the law (the prevalent norms are based on male attributes), then rights discourse is unlikely to change the structural inequalities of power.[16] Moreover, the discourse may not allow women to address the fundamental issues underlying inequality, questions of the feminisation of poverty, inequality in earnings, and the organisation of child care. A primary concern, then, is that rights may be appropriated by the powerful and women's concerns will continue to be marginalised.[17] The androcentric construction of rights as interpreted by courts in the United Kingdom has been well documented.[18] Some rights, for example the right to respect for family life or freedom of religion, have been used by both international and domestic institutions to justify the oppression of women.[19]

On the basis of this critique of rights, should feminists be equivocal about the introduction of the European Convention, or some other form of a Bill of Rights, into the domestic law of the UK? There are persuasive arguments which

---

15   See W Kymlicka, *Contemporary Political Philosophy* (1990) Oxford University Press at pp 247-62; J Fudge, 'The Effect of Entrenching a Bill of Rights Upon Political Discourse: Feminist Demands and Sexual Violence in Canada' (1989) 17 *International J Sociology of Law* 445; N Lacey, 'Theory into Practice? Pornography and the Public/Private Dichotomy' in A Bottomley and J Conaghan (eds), *Feminist Theory and Legal Strategy* (1993) Blackwell at p 93.

16   M Minow, 'The Supreme Court, 1986 Term Foreword: Justice Engendered' (1987) 101 *Harvard Law Review* 10 at pp 10-17.

17   C Smart (1989) at p 145.

18   N Lacey (1992) at p 99 The operation of the sex discrimination law is a good example: the individualisation of rights means that an individual litigant may find that evidence concerning her employer's past behaviour and attitudes towards other people in other circumstances, which may play a part in the recognition of her own treatment as discriminatory, is not admissible in proving her individual complaint. *Ibid* at pp 107-8.

19   H Charlesworth, C Chinkin and S Wright, 'Feminist Approaches to International Law' (1991) 85 *American Journal of International Law* 613 at pp 635-38.

suggest that women should cautiously support a formal declaration of rights. First, the potential to exploit the immense political power of a rights-oriented framework cannot be ignored or discarded as irrelevant. Given the power of law in society, women cannot afford to abandon law as a potential medium for change. Rights rhetoric has played an important part in improving the lives of subordinate groups in society, including women.[20] The language itself offers a recognised mechanism through which to frame political and social wrongs. Martha Minow aptly states: 'I worry about criticising rights and legal language just when they have become available to people who had previously lacked access to them. I worry about those who have telling those who do not, "You do not need it, you should not want it"'.[21] Second, rights can be an effective means of harnessing political demands for progressive change. It can influence the general terms of the political debate and potentially contribute to wider social change. Third, it could provide an opportunity to introduce perspectives and experiences into the courts which have been consistently excluded or marginalised in domestic constitutional law.

Finally the symbolic power of rights cannot be easily dismissed. Patricia Williams states that she is uncomfortable with that part of the Critical Legal Studies movement which rejects rights-based theory, in particular that part of the critique which relates to the black struggle for civil rights.[22] In a powerful statement she provides some indication of the power of rights claims: '"Rights" feel so new in the mouths of most black people. It is still so deliciously empowering to say. It is a sign for and a gift of selfhood that is very hard to contemplate restructuring .,. at this point in history. It is the magic wand of visibility and invisibility, of inclusion and exclusion, and of power and no power.'[23] The empowering nature of rights discourse is too important to overlook as one tactic, amongst others, to challenge gender subordination.

It is suggested that rights claims could be used in a strategic way to empower oppressed groups but I am not assuming that the feminist critique outlined above is irrelevant, or that feminists should not be wary of the concealed traps posed by such a tactic. Rights are a double-edged sword in that they operate within the existing discourse. In Canada, feminists fought hard to have equality rights included in the Canadian *Charter of Rights and Freedoms*. Yet more men than women have successfully resorted to this equality guarantee in order to resolve

---

20 The attack on liberalism by critical feminists has been more ambivalent than that of their critical male colleagues. They have been more willing to acknowledge that in the past liberalism has proved to be a progressive political doctrine. See D Rhode, 'Feminist Critical Theories' (1990) 42 *Stanford Law Review* 617 at p 627.

21 M Minow, 'Interpreting Rights: An Essay for Robert Cover' (1987) 96 *Yale Law Journal* 1860 at p 1910. See also M Minow, *Making all the difference* (1990) Cornell University Press.

22 P Williams, 'Alchemical Notes: Reconstructed Ideals from Deconstructed Rights' (1987) 22 *Harvard Civil Rights–Civil Liberties Law Review* 401 at p 404.

23 *Ibid* at p 431.

their equality claims.[24] There is a contradiction in using legal rights to achieve feminist goals within 'the realm of legality which is embedded within a deliberately obtuse masculinist culture'.[25] Experience of reforms suggests that entering the liberal world of legality exposes contradictions and throws up paradoxical results.

Even the meaning of equality itself has been questioned as equal rights in the law have proved unable to address the realities of women's unequal treatment. On the one hand, as long as women as a group were not considered to be eligible for equal status with men because of the perceived 'natural' difference between men and women, it was logical to challenge exclusion through demands for equal rights that were blind to gender differences. Thus, liberal feminists equate equality with equal treatment without accommodating for any difference between men and women.[26] Equality for women came to mean equality with men: the standard for comparison and the means to assess success or failure.[27] Yet norms of formal equality (that women should never be treated differently from men) have sometimes impaired, rather than advanced, the claim for equality in substantive terms. Once formal equality has been attained, gender is no longer perceived as a problem. The very success of liberal feminism has contributed to the marginalisation of women in decision-making. Formal equality in the law means that gender as an explicit category of political decision and distribution has been dismantled with the subsequent loss of its critical foothold.[28] Even programmes of equality of opportunity, such as that provided in the Sex Discrimination Act 1975, have failed to live up to their promise of empowering women. In practice certain barriers to women being treated like men in the public sphere are dismantled through prohibiting discrimination, but 'the gendered patterns and results which feminism takes as symptoms of social injustice (the manifestations of continued oppression and subordination) can be written off by equal opportunity theory precisely because of its liberal basis'.[29] The principle of formal equality has benefited women who meet male norms but not women who engage in traditional female activities. Thus, certain aspects of women's lives remain entirely unaddressed by the application of norms of formal equality as understood in the legal system. The public/private dualism inherent in liberal legalism imposes real limits on its transformative potential.

---

24 See A Petter, 'Legitimizing Sexual Equality: Three Early Charter Cases' (1989) 34 *McGill Law Journal* 358 at p 360 and A Cote, 'Canada Kills the Court Challenges Programme' in J Kerr (ed), *Ours By Right* (1995) Zed Books at pp 68-71.

25 M Thornton (1991) at p 467.

26 W Williams, 'The Equality Crisis: Some Reflections on Culture, Courts, and Feminism' in K Bartlett and R Kennedy (eds), *Feminist Legal Theory* (1991) Westview Press.

27 See eg the UK Sex Discrimination Act 1975.

28 E Frazer and N Lacey, *The Politics of Community* (1993) Harvester Wheatsheaf at p 79.

29 *Ibid* at p 80.

An alternative approach which seems to avoid the pitfalls of a collapse back into classical liberalism, is to ground the idea of equality within an explicit recognition of sexual difference. Thus, some feminists have focused on the 'differences' between men and women as the only means to redress the subordination of women. Cultural feminists, for example, draw on the work of Carol Gilligan who noted the disparity in psychological tests of moral development between young women, who received lower scores, and their male peers.[30] Most psychologists interpreted these results as showing a problem or fault with women's psychological development. Gilligan challenged this received wisdom and suggested instead that this disparity could reflect distinctive modes of reasoning.[31] Inspired by this interpretation, some feminists have drawn analogies with the legal system. '[T]raditional psychological theories have privileged a male perspective and marginalised women's voices, so, too, law privileges a male view of the universe ... The language and the imagery of the law underscore its maleness: it lays claim to rationality, objectivity, abstraction, characteristics traditionally associated with men, and is defined in sharp contrast to emotion, subjectivity, and contextualised thinking, the province of women.'[32]

Focusing on women's 'different voice' and acknowledging the differences between feminine and masculine modes of reasoning raises its own dilemmas. The strength of this analysis lies in its assertions that values traditionally associated with women be considered valuable and that it is insufficient for legal strategies to focus only on assimilating women. Societal structures must be altered to serve women's distinctive needs.[33] Yet the idea of a distinctive 'women's voice' illustrates the difficulty of 'theorising from experience without essentialising or homogenising it'.[34] It is impossible to claim that any experience can claim universal authentic status.[35]

Unfortunately, the juxtaposition between the distinctive approaches of those feminists working within the traditional framework of equality and those feminists using the 'difference approach' has resulted in a situation of impasse. Many feel that it is crucial to move beyond what might too easily become a stale debate.[36] Therefore, a rather different strand of work has emerged within

---

30   C Gilligan, *In a Different Voice: Psychological Theory and Women's Development* (1982) Harvard University Press.

31   There was a tendency for males to conceptualise moral problems in terms of rights, obligations and rules and to categorise a moral situation in abstract terms. Females tended to contextualise moral issues and analyse problems in terms of relationships and responsibilities which resulted in less clear cut decisions. See *ibid* at pp 159-67.

32   H Charlesworth (1994) *supra* n 10 at p 65. See also parallels within the work of L Irigaray, *Je, Tu, Nous. Toward a Culture of Difference* (1993) Routledge.

33   D Rhode (1990) at p 621.

34   *Ibid*.

35   See for example A Bunting, 'Theorizing Women's Cultural Diversity in Feminist International Human Rights Strategies' in A Bottomley and J Conaghan (eds), *Feminist Theory and Legal Strategy* (1993) Blackwell at p 6.

36   See for example, G Bock and S James (eds), *Beyond Equality and Difference* (1992) Routledge at pp 1-13.

feminist jurisprudence which rejects the oppositional framework of this debate and tries to find other ways forward. It seeks to move beyond difference to focus on 'the difference difference makes'.[37] This strategy requires contextual analysis: it questions whether 'legal recognition of gender distinctions is likely to reduce or reinforce gender disparities in power, status and economic security'.[38] For example, Deborah Rhode focuses on disadvantage[39] and Christine Littleton has suggested redefining the goal of equality as 'acceptance'.[40] Institutions would be required to respond to gender differences by restructuring to accommodate women and their life patterns and thus there would be no cost for difference. MacKinnon focuses on power to bypass the equality or difference debate. (The subordinate position of women can be understood as the product of sexual domination of women by men). Thus, the central issue for analysis of inequality is dominance rather than difference. Feminists should focus on whether the policy or practice in question integrally contributes to social disadvantage because of gender status.[41] The dominance approach takes MacKinnon beyond the standard focus of inquiry to include matters such as pornography, prostitution and violence against women.

Throughout all these debates, there is, however, another possibility and that is the recognition that all theory is simply an exploration of possible insights. This approach, inspired by post-modernist thinking, emphasises the need for a plurality of insights rather than the search for a 'grand theory'. Carol Smart argues that, 'the last thing we need is a feminist jurisprudence on a grand scale which will set up general principles based on abstractions as opposed to the realities of women's (and men's) lives'.[42] Such endeavours can never capture the contextualised and partial nature of our knowledge. This approach, however, still requires the adoption of an ethical standard. One such aspect of this ethical practice might simply be the continual evaluation of strategies deployed to improve the conditions of women's lives. In this strategic approach, the possible use of rights discourse is not to be simply accepted or rejected but carefully examined and cautiously adopted for its possibilities.[43]

The challenge lies in claiming rights discourse for women.[44] There is a need to give meanings to rights that are imaginative and responsive to the realities of

---

37   See D Rhode (1990) at p 622.

38   *Ibid.*

39   D Rhode, 'The Politics of Paradigm: Gender Difference and Gender Disadvantage' in G Bock and S James (eds), *Beyond Equality and Difference* (1992) Routledge at p 149.

40   C Littleton, 'Equality and Feminist Legal Theory' (1987) 48 *University of Pittsburgh Law Review* 1043 at p 1052.

41   C MacKinnon, *Towards a Feminist Theory of the State* (1989) Harvard University Press at p 232.

42   C Smart (1989) at p 69.

43   See A Bottomley and J Conaghan (1993) at pp 1–5.

44   M Minow (1987) at p 1910 and P Williams, *The Alchemy of Race and Rights* (1991) Harvard University Press at p 159. See also H Charlesworth (1994) at p 62.

women's lives and that acknowledge the gendered disparities of economic, social and political power. In Canada, women's organisations, like the Women's Legal Education and Action Fund (LEAF), have had to fight constitutional challenges by men to the rape shield laws, abortion and obscenity laws.[45] Nevertheless, Canadian feminists have been somewhat successful at using the legal forum to articulate personal accounts and to suggest alternative visions. There is no guarantee that progress will be made quickly, but that is an insufficient reason to abandon the idea of using rights claims as one tactic in seeking to transform the system and to achieve the goal of true equality.

THE EUROPEAN CONVENTION ON HUMAN RIGHTS

It is against the background of these debates within feminism that I now turn to consider the European Convention on Human Rights. There is increasing political pressure within the UK to incorporate the European Convention on Human Rights into domestic law. Both the Liberal Democrat Party and, more recently, the Labour Party believe that it should be. The language of rights has even influenced the Conservative Party who have introduced a series of 'citizen's charters'.[46] There is also considerable support for this idea amongst the senior judiciary,[47] the bar[48] and legal academics.[49] Lord Lester has introduced a Bill into Parliament that would, if passed, incorporate the Convention into domestic law.[50]

Civil libertarians have become increasingly aware of the weakness of the British constitutional structure when faced with a strong government which is willing, and able, to pass legislation contrary to the traditionally accepted tenets of liberty and freedom.[51] A Bill of Rights holds out the promise of greater recognition of human rights issues and of a judicial barrier to protect citizens

---

45 See M Eberts, 'Canadian Women's Legal Fight for Equality' in *Ours By Right* (1995) Zed Books at pp 65-67 who addresses the problem of funding in the struggle for equality.

46 *The Citizen's Charter* (1991) HMSO Cm 1599.

47 See L Scarman, *English Law: The New Dimension* (1974) Stevens; Lord Bingham MR, 'The European Convention on Human Rights: Time to Incorporate' (1993) 109 *Law Quarterly Review* 390. In the recent House of Lords debates on a Bill to incorporate the European Convention on Human Rights, Lords Ackner, Browne-Wilkinson, Scarman, Lloyd of Berwick, Simon Of Glaisdale, Slynn of Hadley, Taylor of Gosforth, Woolf of Barnes, voted or spoke in favour of the Bill. See Lord Lester, 'The Mouse that Roared: The Human Rights Bill 1995' [1995] *Public Law* 198. See also the dissenting judgment of Lord Bridge in *Attorney General v Guardian Newspaper Ltd* [1987] 3 All ER 316.

48 A Lester, 'Fundamental Rights: The United Kingdom Isolated' [1984] *Public Law* 46.

49 See, R Dworkin *A Bill of Rights For Britain* (1990) Chatto and Windus; D Feldman, *Civil Liberties and Human Rights in England and Wales* (1993) Oxford University Press; D Oliver, *Government in the United Kingdom: The Search for Accountability, Effectiveness and Citizenship* (1991) Open University Press; G Robertson (1993). But compare with K Ewing and C Gearty Freedom, *Under Thatcher: Civil Liberties in Modern Britain* (1990) Clarendon Press at ch 8 and J Waldron, 'A Rights-Based Critique of Constitutional Rights' (1993) 13 *Oxford Journal of Legal Studies* 18.

50 *Human Rights Bill* (1994/95) HL No 5 HMSO. See also Lord Lester (1995) at p 198.

51 See K Ewing and C Gearty (1990) and G Robertson (1993).

against future authoritarian behaviour. The acceptance by the British courts of European Community law as a form of fundamental law has suggested that some form of entrenchment is no longer perceived as an insurmountable problem.[52] Yet the cautious acceptance that rights claims may be an appropriate strategy to bring women into the 'mainstream', and one avenue to transform institutional and social practices does not automatically lead to the conclusion that the European Convention on Human Rights itself is the best way to achieve this aim.

The European Convention on Human Rights is a treaty ratified by the UK in 1957. It protects traditional civil and political rights such as freedom of expression and assembly, the right to life, personal liberty and a fair trial. Individuals in the UK, who claim to have suffered because of an alleged breach of the Convention, have a right to petition the Commission and may ultimately have their case heard by the European Court of Human Rights.[53] Although the Convention is not part of the domestic law of the UK the courts are increasingly taking greater cognisance of the Strasbourg jurisprudence.[54] In addition, the United Kingdom has the dubious honour of having been found by the European Court of Human Rights to have violated the Convention in a large number of cases.[55] When a claim is upheld, the UK is obliged to bring its law into conformity with the Convention and this usually requires legislation. The mechanism of individual petition has proved to be an effective method to force states to abide by the Convention. Decisions of the European Court of Human Rights have had some success in influencing human rights law in the UK and especially in protecting the rights of prisoners, mental health patients, and to a lesser extent children and immigrants.[56] Many of the beneficiaries of decisions by the European Court of Human Rights belong to groups who do not have political power and, in many of these cases, do not have the right to vote.

---

52   *R v Transport Secretary, ex p Factortame (No 1)* [1989] 2 WLR 997; *R v Transport Secretary, ex p Factortame (No 2)* [1990] 3 WLR 818. See also the *New Zealand Bill of Rights* (1990) which restricts the operation of this Bill of Rights to review of administrative action and does not extend to primary legislation.

53   The Eleventh Protocol to the European Convention on Human Rights establishes a new procedure for bringing individual petitions. See Miscellaneous Series 35 (1994) HMSO Cm 2634.

54   The general position is set out in *Derbyshire CC v Times Newspapers* [1992] 3 All ER 65, *per* Balcombe LJ at 77-78 (but note Lord Keith who reached his decision on the basis of the common law but examined the jurisprudence of the ECHR) [1993] 1All ER 1011 at 1020-21. See also *Brind v Secretary of State for the Home Department* [1991] 1 All ER 720; *R v Chief Metropolitan Stipendiary Magistrate, ex p Choudhury* [1991] 1 QB 429 and Lord Browne-Wilkinson, 'The Infiltration of a Bill of Rights' [1992] *Public Law* 397. The European Court of Justice has also referred to the European Convention and consistently held that fundamental human rights are enshrined in the general principles of Community law. See *Johnston v Chief Constable of the Royal Ulster Constabulary* [1986] ECR 1651; *International Handelsgesellschaft*, Case 11/70 [1970] ECR 1125 and *SPUC v Grogan* [1991] 3 CMLR 849. The institutions of the EU have declared that they are bound to consider the ECHR in the exercise of their powers. See Article F Title 1 of the Maastricht Treaty on European Union.

55   As of April 1995, the European Court of Human Rights has found at least one breach of the European Convention by the United Kingdom in 35 cases, with 16 cases pending. The only European state to exceed this total is Italy with 82 breaches. See HL Deb (18 April 1995), WA cols 43-44.

56   See C McCrudden and G Chambers (eds), *Individual Rights and the Law in Britain* (1994) Clarendon Press.

The Convention protects certain fundamental civil and political liberties and these rights must be protected in the countries which have ratified it. From a feminist perspective the nature of these protections is limited. The assumption is that these stipulated human rights are universal and are held by all people regardless of their gender: the rights of men have been extended to include women who are placed, theoretically, in the same situation as men in the public sphere. While civil and political rights are important for all people, the construction and interpretation of these rights papers over gender differences, based not only on biology but also on the way that are our society is structured. It neglects the socioeconomic structures in which women's subordination occurs. It is primarily women who take care of children and assume responsibility for domestic duties and that inevitably affects their economic, social and political status. The emphasis placed on the protection of individuals in the public sphere sidesteps the fact that many women spend all, or at least part, of their lives within the non-political private sphere, the realm of the family and domestic life. Traditionally, this area of private life is considered inappropriate for human rights and civil liberties protection.[57]

The public-private distinction of liberal theory is reflected in Article 8 of the European Convention: 'Everyone has the right to respect for his private and family life, his home and his correspondence'. Lack of state intervention, or scrutiny, on the basis of privacy, can conceal the inequality of power relations in the private sphere; indeed non-regulation can easily translate into male dominance.[58] Article 5 of Protocol No 7 of the European Convention extends to spouses equal rights and responsibilities in their relations with their children and in regard to marriage, its dissolution and property. Although an additional right to equality is created, it applies only to those laws of a private character and not to 'other fields of law such as administrative, fiscal, criminal, social, ecclesiastical or labour laws'.[59] Such rights may potentially contribute towards reconstructing conceptions of public and private but the UK has neither signed nor ratified this Protocol. As the private sphere and the family play a central role in maintaining sexual inequality, any system of human rights must avoid conferring legitimacy on the right of men to freedom at the expense of the oppression of women in the forgotten domestic sphere.[60]

---

57 See C Pateman, 'Feminist Critiques of the Public/Private Dichotomy' in S Benn and C Gaus (eds), *Public and Private in Social Life* (1983) Croom Helm at pp 281, 285. For a discussion of why gender has not been an issue in international law see H Charlesworth, 'The Public/Private Distinction and the Right to Development in International Law' (1992) 12 *The Australian Yearbook of International Law* 190.

58 This is not to deny that there exist some intimate areas where there should be protection from state interference. For further discussions of the public/private dichotomy see N Lacey (1993) at p 93 and W Kymlicka (1990) at pp 247–62.

59 Explanatory Memorandum to Protocol 7 Council of Europe Doc H (1984) at p 5.

60 Most complaints of gender discrimination have related to family law matters and raised Article 8 ECHR. Many of these cases have been brought by men complaining about their legal relationship with their children. See eg Application No 11418/85 *Jolie and others v Belgium*, admissibility decision of the European Commission of Human Rights, 14 December 1986, 47 D&R 243; Commission Report of a friendly settlement, 8 October 1987, 53 D&R 65.

The incorporation of any Bill of Rights into UK domestic law must provide a direct source of rights not only against the State but also as between private persons in order to overcome the shortcomings so evident in other jurisdictions. Judy Fudge provides examples where the Canadian Supreme Court has used the public/private distinction to determine the scope of Charter rights in such a way that women's substantive inequalities are not addressed.[61] Arguably, individuals in the UK have a remedy in Strasbourg when the domestic law denies them their human rights even where the violation concerns their relations with other private individuals.[62] It is clear, however, that the application of the ECHR to date has emphasised state actors, 'at the expense of concern for victims'.[63]

A second underlying assumption in the Convention is that equality means treating men and women alike. The civil and political rights set out in the ECHR promise formal equality for all people but as the previous discussion outlined the meaning of equality itself is controversial. Article 14 states that the rights and freedoms in the Convention shall be secured without discrimination on any grounds including, amongst others, sex. There are a number of severe limitations with the interpretation of this article. First, Article 14 does not establish a right to non-discrimination independent of the rights and freedoms guaranteed by other provisions of the Convention. Rather than securing additional rights, it represents a commitment to ensure the effective exercise of the substantive rights set out in the earlier provisions.[64] Unsurprisingly, this requirement, combined with the wide margin of appreciation given to contracting states, has resulted in very few cases based on gender discrimination before the European Court of Human Rights.[65]

The problem of the inequality between men and women is defined primarily in terms of discrimination but within an accepted male-dominated context. The discrimination standard demands a comparison of the victim's treatment with the 'normal', that is, male, standard. There is no avenue for challenging the accepted criteria; the successful argument is based on assimilation, on equality with men. Disadvantages suffered by women are redressed by equal treatment and the value of any specifically female life experiences is inevitably marginalised. The difficulty is that equality is promised

---

61 J Fudge, 'The Public/Private Distinction: The Possibilities of and the Limits to Charter Litigation'(1987) 25 *Osgoode Hall Law Journal* 485.

62 See A Clapham, *Human Rights in the Private Sphere* (1993) Clarendon Press. He argues that: 'The ECHR ought to be interpreted so that it is applicable where victims face abuses from private actors' at p 343.

63 *Ibid* at p 356.

64 See A H Robertson and J G Merrills, *Human Rights in Europe* (1993, 3rd edn) Manchester University Press at ch 5.

65 See *Abdulaziz, Cabales and Balkandali v UK* (1985) 7 EHRR 471. The UK then changed its immigration law so that neither the spouses of male nor female British citizens were given an automatic right to enter the UK.

only to those women who can conform to a male model. This approach, as Nicola Lacey has observed in relation to the UK discrimination laws, assumes 'a world of autonomous individuals starting a race or making free choices [which] has no cutting edge against the fact that men and women are simply running different races'.[66]

The Convention does not include any positive affirmation of equality between men and women, such as the equality guarantee in the Canadian *Charter of Rights and Freedoms*, s 15.[67] The Supreme Court of Canada has adopted a contextual approach to equality rights which requires a court to examine the historical disadvantage of a group and consider substantial inequality.[68] Through the adoption of this approach, women have a voice and their stories can be presented to the court. In a symposium on equality in Canada, it was agreed by the Women's Legal Education and Action Fund (LEAF) that: 'Women must get their stories into court to develop a body of evidence about women's poverty, physical vulnerability and social and legal inequality in order to force the courts to respond.'[69] In contrast, the rights set out in Article 14 of the European Convention dictate a role of non-interference rather than a positive guarantee by the State to promote equality. Article 14 does nothing to empower women and may even filter out women's experiences of subordination.

Without an equality clause in a Bill of Rights, it will be more difficult for women to gain a foothold in order for their perspectives to be presented and considered. When the courts come to balance up conflicting interests, those rights included in the Bill of Rights are likely to be given priority, to trump those that are excluded. For example in the United States of America, the First Amendment, which guarantees freedom of speech, has been defined to include the right to make, use and distribute pornography. In *American Booksellers' Association Inc v Hudnut*[70] an Indianapolis ordinance that restricted pornography was found to have violated First Amendment guarantees. The ordinance at issue imposed restrictions on pornography, which was defined to mean the graphic sexually explicit subordination of women, whether in pictures or in words, including one or more of the following: (i) women being presented as sexual objects who enjoy pain or humiliation; (ii) women being presented as sexual objects who experience sexual pleasure in being raped; (iii) women being

---

66 N Lacey (1987) at p 420.

67 Section 28 guarantees that the rights and freedoms under the Canadian Charter apply equally to women and men, and is not subject to legislative override, *Andrews v Law Society of British Columbia* [1989] 1 SCR 143. The Supreme Court rejected the 'similarly situated' or formal equality test. The Council of Europe is considering the inclusion in the ECHR of a provision enshrining the principle of equality between women and men. See Council of Europe *Information Sheet No 30* (1992).

68 See Andrews (1989) *ibid* and *R v Morgentaler* [1988] 1 SCR 30.

69 Leaf Equality Symposium 5 *Leaf Lines* (1992) at p 3.

70 771 F 2d 323 (1985)

presented as sexual objects tied up or cut up or mutilated or bruised or physically hurt, or as dismembered or truncated or fragmented or severed into body parts; and (iv) women being presented in scenarios of degradation, injury, abasement or torture. The legislation would have made it unlawful to traffic in pornography, to coerce others into performing pornographic acts or to force pornography on anyone in any place of employment, school, home or public place. The court struck down the ordinance emphasising that the definition of pornography had created a constitutionally impermissible viewpoint which the court likened to 'thought control'.[71] The judges were unable to accommodate these new feminist principles that addressed the status and dignity of women within their constitution and attempted to rectify an imbalance in speech.[72] Advocates of the legislation had argued that pornography silences women and prevents them from playing a full and active role in the community. This measure could then be justified as a means of empowering women in the market place of ideas.[73] But such ideas could not compete with the powerful First Amendment jurisprudence. There is no equality clause in the US constitution and attempts to obtain an equal rights amendment have failed.[74]

In contrast, when the Canadian Supreme Court, in *R v Butler*,[75] was called upon to consider whether the Canadian obscenity law contravened the *Charter* guarantee to freedom of expression, it focused on the risk of anti-social behaviour, and in particular, the threat to the integrity and safety of women. According to Sopinka J, such material was obscene not because it offends against morals but rather because it is contrary to the 'equality and dignity of all human beings', and is perceived as a social harm, in particular, to women.[76] He stated: 'If true equality between male and female persons is to be achieved, we cannot ignore the threat to equality resulting from exposure to audiences of certain types of violent or degrading material'.[77] The importance of this decision is that the *Charter* issues were approached in a manner which centrally locates harm to women, as well as addressing the threat posed to other *Charter* values, such as physical integrity and equality. The court was attempting to balance the objective of protecting freedom of expression as against securing the goals of ending victimisation and promoting substantive equality.

---

71   *Ibid* at p 328.

72   N Lacey has identified the private/public dichotomy in this decision: '... the production of pornography is seen as a matter of public right [to free expression], and hence protected, whilst its consumption is constructed as a matter of private interest, and also protected', Lacey (1993) at p 104.

73   See C MacKinnon (1987) at pp 193-95.

74   Even with an equality amendment in the US constitution, there is no guarantee that the court would have come to a different conclusion. There are significant cultural and political differences between Canada and the USA which could also be influential.

75   (1992) 8 CRR (2d) 1.

76   *Ibid* at p 20

77   *Ibid*.

In spite of the apparent willingness of the Supreme Court Justices in *Butler* to redress social and sexual inequality, some commentators have suggested that the results generally under the *Charter* regime have been, at best, ambiguous.[78] There is, for example, the fear that right-wing groups in society may 'hijack' the victory in Butler, in order to pursue their own agendas and seek to repress certain forms of art and, especially, gay, literature.[79] In 1989, the Canadian Advisory Council on the Status of Women reported on the operation of the equality guarantees in the *Charter*. They concluded, after analysing 591 decisions of the courts, that 'women are initiating few cases, and men are using the *Charter* to strike back at women's hard-won protections and benefits'.[80] Perhaps the most notorious example is the striking down of the rape-shield laws, which imposed certain restrictions on evidence concerning the sexual activity of victims in sexual assault cases.[81] Access to the law is likely to remain easier for men rather than women as litigation requires economic backing in addition to considerable emotional support. Many individual litigants report the experience as a disempowering one.[82] Litigation pursued by pressure groups, for example, the EOC, would be preferable, but the experience of LEAF in Canada suggest that 'women's groups may thus find that their limited resources are being used defensively against attacks on rights won in the democratic system rather than offensively to change conditions of disadvantage by legal rather than political means'.[83] Nevertheless, the equality guarantees in the Canadian *Charter* have provided a powerful political symbol around which feminist groups can unite. The feminist critique has engendered a political debate and it is hoped that this will lead to greater public consciousness and eventually social change.

THE ROLE OF THE JUDICIARY

There is no doubt that the introduction of the ECHR or some other form of entrenched guarantees would fundamentally change the relationship between the judiciary and the Parliament. Many critics, especially those on the left, fear

---

78 See J Fudge (1989) at p 445.

79 The first seizure authorised after *Butler* was of gay material. See *Glad Day Bookshop Inc v Deputy Minister of National Revenue, Customs and Excise* (unreported decision of Ontario Court of Justice, 14 July 1992).

80 G Brodsky and S Day, *Canadian Charter Equality Rights for Women: One Step Forward or Two Steps Back?* (1989) LEAF.

81 *R v Seaboyer* (1991) 83 DLR (4th) 193

82 See K O'Donovan and E Szyszczak (1988) and M Thornton, *The Liberal Promise: Legislation Against Sex Discrimination in Australia* (1990) Oxford University Press

83 K Ewing, 'The Bill of Rights Debate' in K D Ewing, C A Gearty and B A Hepple (eds), *Human Rights and Labour Law: Essays for Paul O'Higgins* (1994) Mansell p 147 at p 170. See also J Fudge and H Glasbeek, 'The Politics of Rights: A Politics with Little Class' (1992) 1 *Social and Legal Studies* 45.

that such a transfer of power would give too much power to unelected and unaccountable judges.[84] A Bill of Rights would oblige the judges to consider and monitor civil liberties but this would not avoid the interpretive difficulties confronting judges who must give meaning to abstract constitutional rights. Clearly, a declaration of rights, such as those contained in the ECHR, is not self-evident in its meaning. What interpretive analysis then is the court likely to use if these rights are open-ended and contain no obvious fixed meaning?

Article 2 of the European Convention is an example of a right which raises interpretive difficulties. Article 2 provides in part:

> Everyone's right to life shall be protected by law. No one shall be deprived of his life intentionally save in execution if a sentence of a court [is made] following his conviction for a crime for which this penalty is provided by law.

This right was clearly formulated in the context of the obligation of states to ensure that courts observe due process of law before capital punishment is imposed, thus exposing the androcentric structure of the Convention.[85] Pressing questions have been raised concerning the effect of this Article on abortion laws. Does 'everyone' here include the unborn? What is the relationship between Articles 2, 8 (respect for private and family life) and 12 (right to marry and to found a family)? A literal reading of the Article provides no guidance. This issue of reproductive autonomy is a central issue for women's rights: without control of their destinies women cannot hope to achieve social equality.[86]

The European Court has not specifically addressed the issue of whether foetuses have a right to life but decisions of the European Commission of Human Rights suggest that they do not. In *Paton v UK*[87] a father tried unsuccessfully to persuade the courts to prevent the mother from having an abortion. The Commission did not accept the argument that Article 2 applied to a foetus. They reasoned that to decide otherwise would mean that an abortion would be prohibited even where the life of the pregnant woman was seriously at risk, in effect regarding the foetus as of higher value than the life of the pregnant woman. Neither does the Convention confer on women a right to an abortion. In *Bruggemann and Scheuten v Federal Republic of Germany*,[88] two women claimed that the legal rules governing abortion in Germany violated Article 8 ECHR, in that they were not free 'to have an abortion carried out in case of an unwanted pregnancy'. The Commission concluded that these circumstances did not give

---

84 K Ewing and C Gearty (1990). This would depend on the nature of the measure adopted. The issue of democracy is more directly raised if the courts have the power to strike down legislation. The problem would be less acute if the adopted measures were limited in scope by operating as an interpretive guide regulating executive and administrative decisions. See for example the *New Zealand Bill of Rights* 1990.

85 See A H Robertson and J G Merrills (1993) at pp 32-34: 'This understanding of the right to life is essentially male-oriented, since men consider state execution more immediate to them than death from pregnancy or labor.' R Cook, 'International Protection of Women's Reproductive Rights' (1992) 24 *New York University Journal of Law and Politics* 645 at p 689.

86 N Burrows (1986) at p 85.

87 (1980) 3 EHRR 408.

88 (6959/75) DR 10, 100, Eur Comm HR, Report of 12 July 1977.

rise to a beach of Article 8. Pregnancy is not a wholly private matter as the mother's right to respect for privacy was bound up with the life of the developing foetus.

In a recent decision, *Open Door Counselling Ltd Dublin Well Woman Centre Ltd & Others v Ireland*[89] which arose out of Ireland's prohibition on all counselling on abortion, including the provision of non-directive information about the availability of terminations in Britain, the European Court on Human Rights unequivocally found that this ban could not be justified under Article 10(2). Nevertheless, the court left open the controversial question of the compatibility with the Convention of national laws which authorised abortions.[90] Ewing and Gearty persuasively argue that this decision is likely to embolden 'right to life' groups to challenge abortion legislation in one or other of the Member States.[91] It is very likely that the European Court would give states a wide margin of appreciation but it does open the possibility that some restrictions on abortion may be demanded by Article 2.

If the ECHR were incorporated into UK domestic law, it is conceivable that our courts may have to address a challenge to the Abortion Act 1967. The implications for women are enormous. Abortion could potentially become an issue for the courts to decide rather than an issue for Parliament and the democratic process. It is probably unlikely that the courts would strike down the abortion legislation: it is more likely that a balance would be struck between a woman's right to privacy and the rights of the foetus under Article 2. The issue would then be approached as one of conflicting rights, arguably a conflict that cannot be solved within a traditional rights framework. Nevertheless it does mean that, as in Canada, women may be forced to fight in the courts to preserve gains already made in the political system. Moreover, in fighting to retain the *status quo*, women may be forced to forego arguing for what they truly hope to achieve, namely a law based on the recognition of women's right to control their own bodies.

It also raises the possibility that women may be excluded from the decision-making process. One of the most striking aspects of the House of Lords is that all the judges are white men. Given that the freedoms articulated in the ECHR, or any other Bill of Rights, are open to varying interpretations then the role of the judiciary becomes immensely important. Our present senior judiciary are not representative of the community. There are a handful of women High Court judges, one in the Court of Appeal, and no minorities. This is hardly surprising when we consider the limitations on eligibility for those who hold high judicial

---

89   1992 Series A No 246-A.

90   K Ewing and C Gearty, 'Terminating Abortion Rights?' (1992) *New Law Journal* 1696. The issue was addressed by six of the dissenting judges.

91   *Ibid* at p 1697.

office. The process of selection is socially exclusive and effectively denies access to people from different backgrounds. It ensures that the judiciary remain a very homogeneous group.[92]

If judges are doing more than literally interpreting a document, then they will be influenced by personal values and life experience. Would it make a difference to seek judges with varied life experiences? Would they have a greater 'potential for better understanding the multitude of perspectives that are likely to be placed before them in the courtroom'?[93] Bertha Wilson, the first woman Justice of the Supreme Court of Canada, specifically addressed the question of whether women judges would really make a difference.[94] She asserted that in some areas of the law 'a distinctly male perspective is clearly discernible'.[95] She went on to say that the presence of more women judges could contribute to the judicial system by virtue of their differing perspectives on the world. It could help 'to shatter stereotypes about the role of women in society that are held by male judges and lawyers, as well as by litigants, jurors and witnesses'.[96] It would also increase the public's trust that the courts can respond to the legal problems of all of its citizens. The judgment of Wilson J in *R v Morgantaler*[97] highlights the influence that a woman's voice could have on a court. This case concerned the restrictions on the right of women to secure an abortion. In addressing the substantive issue of whether abortion should be limited under the Canadian *Charter*, she stated: 'It is a decision that deeply reflects the way the woman thinks about herself and her relationship to others and to society at large. It is not just a medical decision; it is a profound social and ethical one as well'.[98] She then added: 'It is probably impossible for a man to respond, even imaginatively, to such a dilemma not just because it is outside the realm of his personal experience (although this is, of course, the case) but because he can relate to it only by objectifying it, thereby eliminating the subjective elements of the female psyche which are at the heart of the dilemma.'[99]

Some of these misgivings could be overcome by making changes to the way that judges are appointed and trained. It is clear that adding a few token women or minorities to the Bench will not necessarily mean that the silenced

---

92 See K Ewing (1994) at pp 174-76 for an excellent discussion of the judiciary and the question of gender. This section draws upon his analysis.

93 P Cain, 'Good and Bad Bias: A Comment on Feminist Theory and Judging' (1988) 61 *Southern Cal LR* 1945.

94 Madam Justice Bertha Wilson, 'Will Woman Judges Really Make A Difference?' (1990) 28 *Osgoode Hall LJ* p 507 at p 515.

95 *Ibid.*

96 *Ibid* at p 517.

97 (1988) 44 DLR (4th) 385.

98 *Ibid* at p 490.

99 *Ibid* at p 491.

communities will have a representative. Nevertheless the selection process could be altered to ensure that more people would be eligible for appointment to the Bar and this may lead to a judiciary which is more representative of the community as a whole.[100]

Procedural changes may also provide an important mechanism to bring broader perspectives to the attention of the court. The reception of *amicus* or Brandeis briefs, expanded submissions to the court which set out wider social and economic information, could be a vital way of presenting courts with a wider range of perspectives and views. In Canada, LEAF has used briefs to tell women's stories with some success, notably in the *Butler*[101] case. Stephen Sedley has recently called for the introduction of the brief system in the UK. It would, he suggests, help escape 'the pressures, which cannot be wholly resisted, towards omnicompetent adjudication ...'. He adds that, '[t]here are no guarantees that better educated courts will get everything right, but to be sent ... on a voyage without modern navigational aids and supplies is to experience the worst of both worlds, the old and the new'.[102]

CONCLUSION

Feminist theory needs to combine its critical vantage point on gender subordination with strategies that can lead to change. The adoption of a formal declaration of rights creates an opportunity for feminist engagement with public law and new ground for theorising and strategy-making. The experience of Canadian feminists clearly shows that significant conceptual constraints exist to limit attempts at social change through a litigation strategy. Yet it is hardly satisfactory to give up on law altogether as one tactic to achieve change. Whether or not women look to law, the law will continue to have a profound effect on our everyday lives.

The incorporation of the European Convention into domestic UK law is unlikely to lead to a radical transformation of our legal system. It is already an outdated human rights instrument. It fails to cover many rights and freedoms, such as social and economic rights, which should be considered essential in a human rights document.[103] Although sex is a prohibited ground of discrimination in the Convention, the 'sameness' model adopted by the

---

100 See discussion in K Ewing (1994) at pp 176–78.

101 (1992) 8 CR (2d) 1.

102 S Sedley, 'What's to be Done About Human Rights?' (11 May 1995) 17 *London Review of Books* 13 at p 15.

103 The European Social Charter (Council of Europe) came into force in 1965 and was intended to complement the ECHR by providing for social rights such as rights to work, education, health care and rights to protection of the family, particularly for mothers and children. Unlike the ECHR, the Charter does not confer enforceable rights on individuals and it has not been particularly influential in the development of law and policy in the UK.

European Court of Human Rights renders systemic disadvantage invisible and is unlikely to bring to the forefront women's particular concerns.

Nevertheless, the introduction of the European Convention into domestic law may provide an opportunity to unsettle existing discourses. A space may be created which would allow women's perspectives and experiences to enter into the law. There could be openings to ask previously unasked questions and to reframe debates. The introduction of a formal declaration of rights will not solve political and social conflicts within a society but it can heighten awareness of the conflicts. It has the potential to mobilise movements, to influence political debate, and, perhaps, to bring about social change.

CHAPTER TWELVE

A NEW SETTLEMENT BETWEEN THE SEXES? CONSTITUTIONAL LAW AND THE CITIZENSHIP OF WOMEN

*KATHERINE O'DONOVAN**

Universal suffrage gave the vote to all adult British subjects in 1926. This should have been the last act of a political play in which women's part had been restricted, indeed almost non-existent. Research on the 'person' cases has analysed the difficulties women faced when they made legal attempts to be acknowledged as having legal personality.[1] Not only was the right to vote denied to women, with certain late modifications for women of property, but they could not enter universities, qualify for the professions, or, if married, have a legal existence independent of their husbands. All this is well-known. It is still relevant, however, in two ways. Firstly, there remain questions about women as legal subjects; questions that have been taken up anew with the late-modern examination of subjectivity.[2] Secondly, although a gradualist and piecemeal reform of women's constitutional status has occurred, it still remains the case that women are under-represented in national politics as a whole.[3] It will be argued below that gradualism and under-representation are connected.

This paper examines how feminist ideas might influence discussions of constitutional law. It is not intended to suggest that the constitutional position of men is perfect, or even good. Rather the paper's aim is to criticise the British constitutional tradition using discussion of the position of women as an illustration; simultaneously, ideas of writers interested in women's citizenship will be advanced and examined. The first part of the paper discusses the unwritten constitution in order to establish the context of the discussion. The second part analyses the feminist critique of women's legal subjectivity, and the consequent difficulty of inserting women into the British constitutional tradition. The third part looks to agenda set by feminists in citizenship debates. Finally, a reconstitution inspired by feminist writers will be offered for analysis and critique.

---

* Katherine O'Donovan is author of *Sexual Divisions in Law* (1985), *Family Law Matters* (1993) and *Equality and Sex Discrimination Law* (1988, co-author).

1 A Sachs and J Hoff Wilson, *Sexism and the Law: A Study of Male Beliefs and Judicial Bias* (1978) Robertson.

2 K O'Donovan, *Sexual Divisions in Law* (1985) Weidenfield & Nicolson ch 2.

3 The literature on women as objects, as 'other', as would-be subjects is vast. Examples are: L Irigaray, *Speculum of the Other Woman* (1985) Cornell University Press; N Naffine, *Law and the Sexes: Explorations in Feminist Jurisprudence* (1990) Allen & Unwin; C Smart, 'The Woman of Legal Discourse' (1992) 1 *Social and Legal Studies* 29; S Duncan, 'Law's Sexual Discipline: Visibility, Violence and Consent' (1995) 22 *Journal of Law and Society* 326. On women's absence from politics, see J Lovenduski and V Randall, *Contemporary Feminist Politics* (1993) Oxford University Press.

PART ONE
SUFFRAGE AND SETTLEMENT: A GRADUALIST THEORY

According to Professor Sir Ivor Jennings, whose book on constitutional law is regarded as a classic, 'the British Constitution has not been made but has grown'.[4] This gradualist theory is consonant with the evolutionary nature of the English common law. But whilst much of that law has now been written into cases and statutes, the British constitution is unwritten. This might be regarded as a paradox, in so far as the foundational text is unavailable. The effect is to combine pragmatism and form. Something which is unwritten may nevertheless be known, understood and observed. Although some politicians believe that the constitution is 'something we make up as we go along',[5] this is not the view of the professoriate. On the contrary, despite its lack of a key text, the constitution is said to exist, to evolve, to contain principles and rules against which the conduct of government can be judged.[6]

To some, however, the constitution may seem closer to the elephant as experienced by six men of Hindostan. Depending on which part one of the blind men touched, it was variously described as a wall, a spear, a snake, a tree, a fan, a rope. The poet's conclusion is:

And so these men of Hindostan
disputed loud and long,
each in his own opinion
exceeding stiff and strong,
though *each* was *partly* in the right
and all were in the wrong.[7]

It is possible to analyse the British constitution not just as indefinable, but also as a myth. To say this is more than to say that there is no physical text, such as exists with written constitutions to which one can point. For such texts may also be deconstructed as imaginary in the sense that they are not observed, but are merely statements for public relations purposes. Words on a piece of paper do not have a life of their own. They have to be implemented, interpreted. Institutions have to be created to carry them into effect. In the sense that government in Britain is institutional government, the response can be made that the constitution is not a myth but has a real existence.

The claims that are made for the existence of a British constitution are various. The constitutional tradition can be located in standard law textbooks

---

4 W I Jennings, *The Law and the Constitution* (1959, 5th edn) London University Press at p 3.
5 Professor Peter Hennessy, cited in A Barnett, 'The Empire State' p 3 in *Power and The Throne, Charter '88* (1994) Vintage.
6 K C Wheare, *Modern Constitutions* (1966) Oxford University Press. Thomas Paine wrote, in *Rights of Man*, that Britain lacked a constitution.
7 J G Saxe, 'The Blind Men and the Elephant' in *The Oxford Treasury of Children's Poems* (1988) Oxford University Press.

presented as authoritative by the professoriate to generations of university students. This is an expository rather than a critical tradition. The agenda that is set is one of description and analysis in the form of elucidation. Where critical discussion emerges from those critical of the formalist tradition, the debate becomes one of definitions. Thus, in Britain there is a constitution in the institutional sense, whereas elsewhere the constitution refers to a text.[8] A further point is that for the British courts there is no constitutional law of the *Grundnorm* kind, and for English politicians and political scientists the constitution is *practice*. 'In the absence of legal criteria that distinguish constitutional law from other laws, the definition becomes so broad that it defines nothing at all. In the context of the British legal system, the term constitutional law is thus literally meaningless'.[9] The relevance of this to feminist concerns is that arguments based on equal citizenship, justice for all and equality under the law, take on the qualities not of mercy but of mercury, and slip away.

If the constitution is accepted as existing in an institutional sense, certain consequences follow. Its existence is a matter of tradition and practice. What this means is that the past is always with us. In this context, the past is exclusionary. Women and men of the non-propertied classes were excluded from politics. This constitution, based on tradition, creates a weak democratic system, where men too are at a disadvantage. An example of the British tradition given by a senior politician and former embodiment of legal authority is the book *On The Constitution* by Lord Hailsham.[10] Amongst chapters on fundamentals: the monarchy, executive, legislature, cabinet, judiciary, there is no reference to those who are governed, the subjects of the state. The constitution is identified as resting on parliamentary sovereignty and the rule of law. Primacy is given to the House of Commons as an elected chamber. This reference to the electorate is repeated containing an assumption that once they have voted their participation ends. For Lord Hailsham, it 'is no good beginning with high-sounding generalities about inalienable rights or civil liberties or vain abstractions like "the people" or "society in general"'.[11] Tradition, stability, and the rule of law are his answers. This pragmatism may have served a homogeneous, deferential society where there was consensus over matters such as individual and group rights, a unitary state, the form of government, secrecy and the role of the subject under the state. The continued assumption that the opportunity to vote in national elections deals with public participation must be open to question.

For political scientists voting is the supreme political act. Universal suffrage not only turns the populace into citizens, but also legitimises the political order. The assumed consent of citizens is implied through the vote. When the vote was finally allowed to women, the conventional reason given was that they had

---

8   C Munro, *Studies in Constitutional Law* (1987) Butterworths.

9   F F Ridley, 'There is no British Constitution' (1988) 41 *Parliamentary Affairs* 341.

10   Lord Hailsham, *On The Constitution* (1992) HarperCollins.

11   *Ibid* at p 7.

proved themselves worthy during the first of the 20th century wars. An alternative explanation may be sought in the organic British constitution. Views about the vote and its power had changed. With the development of the party political system, the threat of the women's vote was less apparent.[12] The growth of national mass parties, with agendas offered as a package, left little opening for radical feminist views. Other changes were also taking place, including the emergence of a welfare state philosophy, where married women were incorporated into the state as dependents.[13] Thus, it is arguable that universal suffrage did not mean the placing of women's concerns on the political agenda, nor did it create a *de novo* consideration of what women's citizenship might mean. That discussion is only beginning at the end of the century.

The idea of democracy is conventionally used to justify those political arrangements current in the United Kingdom. This seems to rest on the idea of public opinion to which government is accountable. Such accountability 'entails that a government must continuously test its representativeness, that is to say whether its claim that it is 'derived from public opinion' is still valid'.[14] But being representative also includes the idea of citizens seeing their concerns presented as significant. That is why there have been feminist demands for more women in Parliament, as judges, and in other powerful places.

Writers critical of the lack of a constitution to ground British political authority, and of the formalist tradition in the teaching of constitutional law, make the point that Britain never developed the idea of popular sovereignty. Other states, such as France or the United States, justify their political arrangements in such terms. The stories that political entities tell themselves about their origins differ according to many factors, including culture and history. In Britain talk of the sovereignty of the electorate merely allows choice between political parties.[15] Authority comes from the ideal of parliamentary supremacy. Parliament can change the rules of government, prolong its mandate, alter universal suffrage, change the electoral system, and confer or withhold rights. 'If we ask where that power comes from, the answer is broadly that Parliament claimed it and the courts recognised it. The people never came into the picture'.[16] Stories can change. At present, consent of the governed, outside of revolution, is not an issue in British public law. It does not feature in the story.

---

12   C Pateman, paper delivered at the School of Social Sciences, Australian National University, 1993.

13   H Land, 'Women Supporters or Supported?' in D L Barker and S Allen (eds), *Sexual Division and Society; Process and Change* (1976) Longmans; H Land, 'Sex-Role Stereotyping in the Social Security and Income Tax Systems' in J Chetwynd and O Hartnett (eds), *The Sex Role System* (1978) Routledge & Kegan Paul.

14   S E Finer, *Comparative Government* (1970) Penguin at p 63.

15   F F Ridley *op cit* n 9 at pp 343-45.

16   *Ibid* at p 345.

The issue of consent takes many forms. It presents itself in discussions of 'an elective dictatorship',[17] in denials of mandate for a comprehensive party manifesto,[18] in criticism of the excessive power of the Prime Minister under the system of party politics.[19] Such discussion has not been influenced by feminist visions.

Consent is of cultural significance in feminist theory, if only because the consent of women in sexual relations, in marriage, in government, has been assumed. Implied consent to the will of more powerful persons is built into the structure of laws such as the law of rape, marriage and sexual relations within marriage. Deconstructing those structures has been an important part of the work of feminist legal scholars. Repeated repetition of the point that assumed consent denies the autonomy of legal subjects has produced results such as the abolition of the male marital rape exemption.[20] In constitutional law one looks in vain for such discussion. Yet it seems that implied consent is built into the British system of government as it was into sexual relations in marriage.

PART TWO
WOMEN AS LEGAL SUBJECTS: FORGOTTEN OR NOT MADE?

Recent work on political philosophy and on jurisprudence argues that women continue to be excluded as full legal subjects despite changes in the law. Pateman[21] takes us back to the origins of social contract theory, a story told in political philosophy to justify current state organisation. She indicts the notion of the free individual who contracts freely into the social contract, asserting that this hypothetical individual is patriarchally constructed. Dealing with the original exclusion of women from public life, and their location in the private sphere under the power of fathers and husbands, Pateman implicates social contract theory as omitting women's lack of freedom and as leaving a legacy of problems about women's incorporation as citizens. Some have attempted to answer this by saying that it is a historical and contingent omission which was rectified in the 20th century. But Pateman's point is that the very concepts under discussion in political philosophy are affected by this history. In particular she argues that the notion of the free individual is a male construct:

> the conclusion is easily drawn that the denial of civil equality to women means that the feminist aspiration must be to win acknowledgement for women as 'individuals'. Such aspiration can never be fulfilled. The 'individual' is a patriarchal category.[22]

---

17   Lord Hailsham, *The Dilemmas of Democracy* (1978) Collins at p 22.

18   A Barnett *op cit* n 5.

19   L Wolf-Phillips, 'A Long Look at the British Constitution' (1984) 37 *Parliamentary Affairs* 385.

20   *R v R* [1991] 4 All ER 481. See K O'Donovan, *Family Law Matters* (1993) Pluto ch 1.

21   C Pateman, *The Sexual Contract* (1988) Polity Press.

22   *Ibid* at p 184.

One interpretation of this is that, because of past history, the very concepts used in political discussion are gendered. Escaping from the past requires, not gradualism, but reconstitution of citizenship. Fitting women into the shoes of men does not guarantee a fit. Another reading suggests that the political subject is represented as an atomised person 'free' of connections with others. Feminist jurisprudence has challenged the person at the heart of liberal society, precisely because his relationships with others are represented as contractual rather than, at least for some, based on friendship or love.[23] It is not being suggested that this depiction of the 'liberal person' makes him male. The intention is to suggest that it is only a partial representation of any person. The contribution of feminist scholars has been to make and illustrate these points.

These points have been made in writings discussing a reconstitution of citizenship. Whilst on the one hand there is a search for a form of universality which citizenship must comprise, there is nevertheless a lively awareness of difficulties. As Anne Phillips has said, the danger is that real live men will be smuggled 'into the seemingly innocent and abstract universals that nourish political thought. The "individual" or the "citizen" are obvious candidates for this form of gendered substitution'.[24] Universal citizenship must encompass simultaneously embodied persons different from one another, and abstract persons with equal rights and responsibilities, with aspirations, needs and beliefs, which are connected yet separate.

Equality under the law is foundational in feminism. Yet feminist theory has been critical of how women are represented as legal subjects. With late modernity interest in subjectivity leads to questioning of whether the individual 'seen' by law has the attributes ascribed to a woman or a man. This is a problematic area, if the attribution of essentialist qualities is to be avoided. Specific studies of areas of law such as abortion,[25] sexual crimes,[26] employment law,[27] international law[28] and defences to homicide[29] have shown the absence of

---

23 R West, 'Jurisprudence and Gender' (1988) 55 *University of Chicago Law Review* 1.

24 A Phillips, 'Citizenship and Feminist Theory', in G Andrews (ed), *Citizenship* (1991) Lawrence & Wishart at p 76.

25 S Sheldon, 'Who Is the Mother to Make the Judgment? The Construction of Women in English Abortion Law' (1993) 1 *Feminist Legal Studies* 3.

26 S Duncan, '"Disrupting the Surface of Order and Innocence": Towards a Theory of Sexuality and the Law' (1994) 2 *Feminist Legal Studies* 3.

27 N Lacey, 'Legislation Against Sex Discrimination: Questions from a Feminist Perspective' (1987) 14 *Journal of Law and Society* 411; K O'Donovan, 'Labour Law's Subject: A Hidden Agender?' in Y Kravaritiou (ed), *Le Sexe du Droit du Travail en Europe* (1996) EUI.

28 H Charlesworth, C Chinkin and S Wright, 'Feminist Approaches to International Law' (1991) 85 *American Journal of International Law* 613.

29 D Nicholson, 'Telling Tales: Gender Discrimination, Gender Construction and Battered Women who Kill' (1991) 3 *Feminist Legal Studies* 185; K O'Donovan, 'Defences for Battered Women Who Kill' (1991) 18 *Journal of Law and Society* 219; K O'Donovan, 'Law's Knowledge: The Judge, The Expert, The Battered Woman and Her Syndrome' (1993) 20 *Journal of Law and Society* 24; C Wells, 'Battered Woman Syndrome and Defences to Homicide: Where Now?' (1994) 14 *Legal Studies* 266; A Young, 'Conjugal Homicide and Legal Violence: A Comparative Analysis' (1991) 31 *Osgoode Hall Law Journal* 761.

a female subject. Work on the latter has shown that the characteristics of the person able to respond rapidly, and with violence, to provocation or physical threat, are more likely to be those of a person socialised in the ability of self-defence. This criticism is not confined to areas of law which seem to require a particular type of body, or freedom from domestic responsibilities. Examples have been analysed where representations according to gender enter into seemingly neutral areas of law such as property.[30] Attention has been given to language,[31] legal method,[32] and law's insistence on categories.[33] What this work argues is that the representation of women in these areas is unsatisfactory, or even false. This is hardly surprising, given the history of law-making in Britain; but it does challenge the theory of representative democracy.

PART THREE
FEMINIST CONTRIBUTIONS TO CITIZENSHIP DEBATES

The universal model citizen, abstracted from characteristics and communities, poses difficulties for embodied women with families and relationships. A major area of difficulty concerns gender relationships. This is so not only in the sense of gender as relational, but also in so far as gender marks reproduction, family, sexuality, particular sets of interests and social relations. Sarah Benton asks whether there can be friendship when women are so often sex objects for men and not equal subjects. This applies to political discourse as much as to legal. Even if some basis can be found for the admission of 'virtuous women' to citizenship, what of sexual women, the prostitute, the lesbian, the gay man? Political man must sacrifice his self-interest, 'in the interest of creating the city, and within that city he is "public man"'.[34] He is vulnerable, his status is not secure, he can be called to account by his fellow men and exiled for betraying the brotherhood of public life. His sexual desires are problematic. So he has constructed a private space in which he can be free. There he splits the objects of desire in two: there are those over whom he has authority , his family; and there are those who are the objects of erotic fantasies, whores, sluts, children, homosexuals. In Benton's description of the *polis*, prostitutes and homosexuals are outside the law, and therefore cannot be subjects; nor can 'good women', for like nature they are non-political.

---

30 A Bottomley, 'Self and Subjectivities: Languages of Claim in Property Law' (1993) 20 *Journal of Law and Society* 56; A Bottomley, 'Women, Family and Property' in M Maclean and J Kurczewski (eds), *Families, Politics and the Law* (1994) Oxford University Press; K Green, 'Thinking Land Law Differently: Section 70(1)(g) And the Giving of Meanings' (1995) 3 *Feminist Legal Studies* 131.

31 R Martin, 'A Feminist View of the Reasonable Man' (1994) 23 *Anglo-American Law Review* 334.

32 M J Mossman, 'Feminism and Legal Method; The Difference it Makes' (1986) 3 *Australian Journal of Law and Society* 30.

33 *Ibid.*

34 S Benton, 'Gender, Sexuality and Citizenship', in G Andrews (ed), *Citizenship* (1991) Lawrence & Wishart at p 151.

The themes played by Benton can be found in other feminist writings. For example, the explanation offered by Pateman[35] for women's exclusion from political life and the public sphere draws on social contract theory. In this account patriarchy is overthrown by sons when the social contract is made. Women however remain under the power of husbands and fathers.

The idea that as objects of desire women cannot be subjects, and therefore citizens, has been used by Catherine MacKinnon to attack pornography.[36] Her argument is that freedom of speech permits the circulation of pornography, thus denying women's subjectivity as we are turned into objects in these images and texts. If this is so, women's citizenship is threatened, for as objects our personhood is denied. If liberty is a foundation of the constitution, or part of the social contract, then pornographic images and stereotypes of women restrict their freedom to be and to become. 'Women and men constitute continuous threats against each other's freedoms'.[37]

I am not convinced that these arguments have to be read in a literal fashion. Their success is in locating history and tradition that remain with us. The history and tradition of political discourse is of a brotherhood from which women and some men were excluded.[38] I do not wish to suggest a unitary brotherhood, for this has not been so. Challenging exclusion and changing the rules of the political club are part of the battle for women and excluded men. For those unhappy with the club, or who feel excluded, there are issues about what citizenship might mean to them. There is a utopian element to these issues, but they also have a practical, political dimension. From at least the 17th century a fundamental political problem has been how to draft the social contract so as to retain individual freedom and yet to agree to surrender power to the state for the commonwealth. The civil freedoms of the individual, such as freedom from arbitrary arrest, or freedom of speech, so prized by men, may not be given priority by women. Whereas men's freedoms lie in the construction of the private life free from the interference of the state, women often need the state to enter this domain to rid them of its tyrannies. Public life is imprinted with the colours of the private.[39]

The history of women's demands against the state is a history of achievement: Married Women's Property Acts, the vote, equal parental rights, divorce on equal terms and, more recently, a degree of control over sexuality and reproduction, and anti-discrimination legislation. It might therefore seem that women have changed the agenda. But closer inspection reveals that conditions of entry were set by those already in the club. The early claims by women were for the allocation of rights, privileges and power on a formally equal basis with

35   C Pateman *op cit* n 21.

36   C MacKinnon, *Feminism Unmodified* (1987) Harvard University Press.

37   S Benton *op cit* n 34 at p 160.

38   J Lovenduski and V Randall *op cit* n 3.

39   K O'Donovan *supra* n 2.

men, and not for a radical alteration of values. This has changed. Women's definitions of civil freedoms now claim priority. For example, a curtailing of men's freedoms in relation to pornography and physical and sexual abuse is primary for some groups; to 'reclaim the night', that is to make the evening streets safe for women, through a male curfew, if necessary, is a priority for others.

The problem of the private relationships of citizens presents itself in a variety of guises. Critiques that political theory ignores the domestic realm and fails to theorise the relation between family and politics have become common.[40] But what that relationship might be in the ideal world of citizenship is not clear, or agreed. A whole series of issues are open to debate. There is the problem of what is meant by family. Which relationships are recognised and legitimated; which fall outside the law? Does citizenship for lesbian and gay couples include the privileges extended to heterosexual couples? Are transsexuals to remain forever outwith the law?

Identities are presented in the literature on citizenship as a problem of abstraction from difference to universal hypothesis. What I am raising here is the problem of stigmatised identities whose differences are outwith the law. In the construction of citizenship, are these differences to be given a place? Are same-sex partnerships to be accorded the same privileges as heterosexual partnerships? Are prostitutes to accepted as full citizens? Will masculinity and femininity continue to be constructed in law as polar opposites? Will the sex/gender system continue to be reproduced in social and legal institutions?

What goes on in the home is the focus of criticism of the relationship between family and *polis*. At present we live with the sexual division of labour and constitution of the economic and domestic spheres as separate. There is nothing necessarily wrong in that. 'What is wrong is that men and women do not enter the two systems on equal terms.'[41] The family is a problem for political theorists. One does not enter a family through full consent; one is born into relationships unwilled and unchosen by oneself, where roles and power are preordained. There one learns that being born female or male will dictate the course of one's life. One may offer a daily prayer of thanksgiving that one was not born a woman. This in itself is a reflection on notions of autonomy, consent, and justice. By contrast, citizenship upholds the ideal that differences of birth are irrelevant in the *polis*. Justice in the family, and justice in citizenship have to be separated for political theory to justify itself.

For women too the family is a problem. We are taken to have chosen a role which is culturally prescribed for us. Because of what happens in the family from birth, citizens will not enter the city on equal terms. This may be one reason why political philosophy ignores the domestic realm. But as Susan Moller Okin

---

40   F Olsen, 'The Family and the Market' (1983) 96 *Harvard Law Review* 1497.

41   B Jordan, *The Common Good* (1989) Blackwell at p 30.

points out, political theorists have ignored the internal inequalities of the family because of their fundamental assumption that the patriarchal separation of the private/natural sphere from the public/civil realm is irrelevant to theories of justice and to political life.[42] What goes on in the family affects children and, subsequently, adults. Conceptions of self and life chances may be limited. This is true of all children, as models of femininity or masculinity transmitted culturally are confining.

What goes on in the family is crucial to political life, for it is there that our future citizens are produced; it is there that moral development, including development of a sense of justice, takes place. Given the gender stratification that still exists in many homes, what kind of a place is the family to bring up children? The past exclusion of women from the public/civil realm means that the practices that produced the individual are contaminated by patriarchal subordination. All may be well under the ideal constitution, but today's individual is constructed culturally, and discursively. This individual is gendered, and gender difference is a badge of inferiority for some. Past exclusions inform present practices. History has not yet ended.

In lineage, descent, the patrilineal system, inheritance, the monarchy, succession to title and nobility, men define the family. There is a nexus: masculinity, authority, the bloodline, *pater familias*, public representative of the family. This facilitates ignorance of feminist theory. In traditional political theory the public/private distinction is between state and civil society. The domestic sphere is forgotten and classified as outside politics. This accounts for the individual who is 'seen' politically as being male. In feminist theory it is otherwise. The division is between the domestic sphere on the one side as being the private sphere, with both state and civil society being perceived as public. All are considered to be political.

A NEW SETTLEMENT BETWEEN THE SEXES: FEMINIST RECONSTITUTIONS

Utopian thinking is part of feminist philosophy. Rethinking arrangements requires imagination, dreams, but also concepts and language in which to express these. The ideal and the practical are married in such discourse. It is hardly surprising to find discussions, disagreements and painful debate amongst those who wish to change the way things are. To add to the difficulty, such conversations do not start from nowhere, but from the arrangements which already exist, which are familiar. Reference has already been made to the difficulties of using a concept such as the liberal individual in feminist political argument. But how can an escape be made from established concepts and

---

42   S M Okin, *Justice, Gender and the Family* (1989) Basic Books ch 7.

language by those who wish to communicate a new vision? Some theorists talk of 'reclamation', 'reconstitution', 'reconstruction', yet others deny that this is possible.[43] An example can be taken from Nicola Lacey's critique of Luce Irigaray's proposals for special citizenship rights for women. Behind this debate lie issues about universal citizenship.

Difference is 'the joker in the citizenship pack' according to some commentators. Undoubtedly this must be recognised, yet transformed. But differences cannot necessarily be assumed to follow clearly along gender lines, with women falling to one side and men to the other. As women's lack of subjectivity has been identified as a problem, so too has the assumption that women share the same subjectivity. The construction of an inclusive legal subject raises a myriad of questions about inclusiveness within abstraction. Notwithstanding these difficulties, there is a distinctive feminist contribution to such debates.

The debate is about how differences can be recognised, how women can have their equal citizenship recognised and how this is to be realised. This is not a matter of maintaining the old structures, whilst recognising differences. Nor is it about incorporating the hitherto powerless. That those persons and groups stigmatised as 'other' in the past have a positive contribution to make based on their experiences can no longer be denied. Their experiences give them understandings denied to the powerful. Some among them have even dared to suggest that they might show the way. Feminist theorists have put forward arguments based on women's sense of justice, and on maternal thinkers. There has been considerable discussion of claims for woman-centred perspectives, ideas and beliefs. It is not possible to point to a general consensus but rather to a debate. As woman as subject has emerged, so has the realisation that not all women share the same perspective. Rather we must come to terms with subjectivities. Perhaps a more practical approach has been the drawing-up of a list of matters of importance to women, which universal citizenship will have to take into account. These discussions will be considered in turn.

Feminist jurisprudence has a history of arguments about women's conceptions of justice, contrasted to those ascribed to men.[44] Women are said to be less committed to a version of justice couched in abstract rules and to look to the context of a problem, dispute or act. Carol Gilligan advances the thesis that male reasoning adheres to a formalistic set of neutral legal principles couched in objective impersonal rules, an 'ethic of rights', whereas female reasoning is discretionary and person-oriented, couched in equitable principles, with a flexibility that looks to the spirit of the law and an 'ethic of care'.[45] Not all

---

43 S Hall and D Held, 'Citizens and Citizenship', in S Hall and M Jacques (eds), *New Times* (1989) Lawrence & Wishart at p 177.

44 C Gilligan, *In a Different Voice: Psychological Theory and Women's Development* (1982) Harvard University Press.

45 C Gilligan *ibid*.

feminist theorists accept Gilligan's typology. Some have argued that women's present values are the product of oppression and that we cannot know what women's authentic voices will be like until they cease to be subordinate.[46] It is possible for lawyers to reformulate these two 'ethics' in terms of the distinction between law and equity, both of which inform justice. So it appears that the gendered female voice identified by Gilligan already speaks in law. Yet other writers object to the presentation of two very different voices, and the attachment of gender to them, finding therein the continued reification of the dualisms of gender. It is said that so long as the male-female dichotomy remains in place the female will be constituted as inferior. This debate is now waning, and is open to a number of objections. For example, the emphasis on 'women's authentic voices' assumes an essential quality to women. The debate already belongs to an earlier stage of theory, in which theorists were still able to contrast persons according to gender. As self-conceptions have changed, particularly amongst women, these points appear to speak to a static conception of gender.

A history of drawing lessons from mothering, and from other activities gendered female, has also informed discussions of citizenship. Robin West emphasises that women's experiences of relationships are different from those of men, because of connection in pregnancy and breast-feeding, and because they are penetrated rather than penetrating in sexual intercourse.[47] However, whether this the basis for an alternative sense of justice, or for a broader standard encompassing women's experiences, or whether this corresponds to the experiences of all or many women, remains open to challenge. To this may be added the fact that girls are raised primarily by a parent of the same sex, whereas boys have to separate themselves from the nurturer to achieve their individuality.[48] On this has been built a theory of different psyches. Women's sense of self is different from, and their sense of connection to others is greater than, that of men. Therefore, the argument goes, women's sense of justice, their understanding of relationships, provides an alternative model for citizenship to men's. My own position is that these perceived differences are not essential, but cultural. Furthermore, a claim to privilege women's experiences as superior, rather than as another way of thinking, runs the danger of leaving present dichotomies and inequalities in place. Sometimes such claims are made as a way of entering an arena of debate, and are expressions of preferences. The point is that all experiences must be welcomed in political discourse where they have something to add to the conversation.

---

46 C MacKinnon in 'Feminist Discourse, Moral Values and the Law: A Conversation' (1985) 34 *Buffalo Law Review* 50, criticised Gilligan's ethic of care on the grounds that it represents the voice of a subordinated and victimised group.

47 R West *op cit* n 23.

48 N Chodorow, *The Reproduction of Mothering; Psychoanalysis and the Sociology of Gender* (1978) University of California Press.

The claim that mothers have a capacity to form empathy which should inform political life is summed up in the notion of 'maternal thinkers'. In Sara Ruddock's view maternal thought is not biologically based, but arises from experience. It is presented as not just a different set of values or commitments, but a different way of thinking altogether, giving 'priority to preserving vulnerable life' and honouring a moral 'style' that makes central the values of humility, good humour and attentiveness to others.[49] Jean Elshtain argues that maternal thinkers might transform public values, and create an ethical polity that will displace the individualism of political discourse.[50] There is reason for scepticism at this vision, especially when placed alongside prescriptive political statements about mothers, particularly single mothers. Furthermore certain aspects of feminist theory emphasise individual access to the 'glittering prizes' reserved for men in the past.[51]

I have already argued that past confinement of women to family life and exclusion from public life perpetuated an unjust sex/gender system, excluded women from citizenship, and educated children in injustice. It is true that a close relationship with children, the possibility of becoming a maternal thinker, was women's compensation for subordination. But surely if nurturing has something to offer citizenship, all citizens should be encouraged to undertake it. To argue otherwise is to return to a biologistic position. As Jean Grimshaw says, what is likely is, 'that the principles on which they [women] act are not recognised (especially by men) as valid or important ones'.[52]

From this it does not necessarily follow that women's moral reasoning is sharply opposed to that of men. Rather, one's experiences, and the way one lives, create different priorities.

If experiences gained from nurturing are to alter political life it is likely to be on the basis of conceptions of equality and liberty which recognise that the content of liberty and equality is not given, but open to debate, and that women's experiential understandings of vulnerabilities gives them valid priorities and concerns.

Cultural feminist arguments based on women's family roles are not without their critics. Mary Dietz argues that mothering is the wrong model for citizenship as it is based on an inequality of power between the helpless infant and the nurturer. If equality is a central conception then citizenship is an activity where:

> ... human beings can collectively and inclusively relate to one another not as strong over weak, fast over slow, master over apprentice, or mother over child,

---

49 S Ruddick, 'Maternal Thinking', in J Treblicot (ed), *Mothering: Essays in Feminist Theory* (1984) Rowman & Allanheld.

50 J B Elshtain, *Public Man, Private Woman: Women in Social and Political Thought* (1981) Robertson.

51 N Wolf, *Fire with Fire* (1993) Virago.

52 J Grimshaw, *Philosophy and Feminist Thinking* (1986) Wheatsheaf at p 210.

but as equals who render judgments on matters of shared importance, deliberate over issues of common concern, and act in concert with one another.[53]

The issue of a reordering of priorities still remains, despite Dietz's well-taken point about equality. A focus on nurturing does create an alternative vision. It is also not clear how we are to be transformed into equals. Must maternal thinkers learn to think in another way? How will this help the attainment of equality? If we go along with Dietz in rejecting mothering as a model for citizenship, gender inequalities remain. Unless mothers' voices can be heard in debate their values and their value will remain unrecognised.

It is evident from what is written above that gender is continues to be relevant to the citizenship debate. Yet some theorists think that the way out is to give minimal effect to gender, according it no more significance than eye colour. Susan Moller Okin advocates a minimally gendered society in which sex/gender roles are not prescribed. Intimate relationships to which partners wish to give legal effect will be recognised on an agreed and voluntary basis. Shared parental responsibility for children will be assumed and facilitated; employment practices and laws will share this assumption. Schools will not only co-operate with shared parenting, but will educate children to value a variety of roles and to participate as citizens.[54] Power will be shared by partners with a consequent elimination of physical and sexual abuse of family members. Values derived from parenting will be recognised. By contrast, Luce Irigaray argues for a recognition of women's values and priorities through 'special rights'.[55] This is an argument for recognition of difference, but Nicola Lacey argues that it unintentionally reintroduces gender essentialism.[56] In other words, these utopian visions of some women are not shared by all.

Cultural feminists valorise the experiences that women have of domestic life and child rearing. At issue here are different conceptions of the self which challenge much of Western political writing, particularly that based on a binary system of oppositions between body and mind, emotion and reason, private and political, object and subject. The association of women with the first part of these dualities and the negative valuing of body, emotion and nature lead to calls for an integrated self. While many conceptions of selves emerge, there is also emphasis on the shared experiences and understandings that women share as a group. Giving up a shared culture to become a neutral *citoyenne* in a genderless society is not necessarily seen as desirable by cultural feminists. But does the debate have to be structured in this way? Citizens do not necessarily have to

---

53 M Dietz, 'Citizenship with a Feminist Face: the Problem with Maternal Thinking' (1985) 13 *Political Theory*.

54 S M Okin *op cit* n 42, ch 7.

55 L Irigaray, *Thinking the Difference* (trans K Montin, 1994) Athlone; L Irigaray, *Je, Tu, Nous: Towards a Culture of Difference* (trans A Martin, 1993) Routledge.

56 N Lacey, 'Feminist Legal Theory Beyond Neutrality' (1995) 48 *Current Legal Problems* 1.

pursue the same general concerns. For some citizenship is about the coalition of groups working together while retaining their perspectives and identities.[57]

Iris Young points out universal citizenship must not repeat past history of 'incorporating' the silenced in the body politic:

> In a society where some groups are privileged while others are oppressed, insisting that as citizens persons should leave behind their particular affiliations and experiences to adopt a general point of view serves only to reinforce that privilege; for the perspectives and interests of the privileged will tend to dominate this unified public, marginalising or silencing those other groups.[58]

For Iris Young the answer is the 'rainbow coalition' in which groups can work together while retaining their identities, unabsorbed into the 'establishment view'. She does not insist on universalisability, but anticipates claims made on the basis of difference, on special needs. What citizens will share is a common membership of a community, and mutual respect. Particular responses to claims will be agreed upon as a form of compromise, but not necessarily on the basis of universal application. This marks a break with formal notions of equality under the law, a tradition which has not always been observed in practice. A unitary model of citizenship and of the legal subject is abandoned in this version of citizenship.

The rainbow coalition ideal is contrastable with ideas of abstraction currently used by other theorists to escape the dilemmas of difference and fragmentation. Abandoning the Kantian imperative of universal principles to guide conduct worries feminist writers, such as Okin and Lacey, as explained above. Although they acknowledge that movement away from individual concerns to abstraction has been the traditional tactic for avoiding particular concerns of excluded identities, nevertheless there is an attempt to reclaim universality.[59] The trick is to do so inclusively. Some theorists have argued that women's shared concerns can be identified in a practical programme; others suggest a set of procedures to allow particular interests or fears to be voiced. As Anne Bottomley points out there are different ways of telling a story, not so much as a difference in imaginative potential, as in the ways in which the narrator hopes to be heard, and by whom. Thus strategy enters into the way in which the debate is shaped.[60]

---

57 I M Young, *Justice and the Politics of Difference* (1990) Princeton University Press.

58 I M Young, 'Polity and Group Difference: a Critique of the Ideal of Universal Citizenship' (1989) 99 *Ethics* 250.

59 N Lacey *op cit* n 56; S Okin *op cit* n 42.

60 A Bottomley, editorial comments on this paper, August 1995, writes: 'I think it all goes back to "different ways to tell stories", but the issue here is not so much the imaginative potential in the telling, as in the possibilities of the stories being listened to (heard) ... by women, who can then operate within a consensus of claim and action, and by men (as the establishment) ... because the stories (form and content) key into codes and forms of rhetoric which they (men) not only understand but are under a kind of imperative to respond to. A kind of radical liberalism. This approach also counters any claim of a system being finally closed or of radical intervention being finally and fatally incorporated'.

In a programme of citizenship for the new republic of Australia, four feminist legal theorists have identified five equalities for women.[61] Equality of access to, and equal freedom to move with, public spaces is the first. This encompasses physical security, freedom from violence, access for those unable to walk. Physical security is identified as the greatest of freedoms, which is not accessible to women, particularly after nightfall. Equality of access to economic life is the second. This encompasses recognition of the value of unpaid work, such as nurturing, economic independence, freedom from gender discrimination. Equality of access to and participation in social life is the third. According to the authors, 'to the extent that women (and other groups) are excluded from full participation as members [of clubs], they are denied access to the professional and occupational opportunities which are as much a part of the role of those clubs as are the social opportunities'.[62] Equal access to and participation in political life is the fourth equality. This refers to under-representation in political life. Equality before the law is the fifth equality and refers to interests and harms specific to women denied legal protection, and access to knowledge and help in the legal system.

The equalities identified above are accompanied by a practical programme of law reform and measures of implementation. Although these proposals give priority to women's concern, they are not gender specific. All citizens, for example, will benefit from greater access to legal services. In this sense the programme is universal. Yet in another sense any notion of membership depends on non-membership. Citizenship is, in this sense, an exclusionary concept. Chantal Mouffe distinguishes between social relations which are gendered, and the domain of politics, where citizenship makes sexual difference irrelevant.[63] Although this represents an effort at inclusivity, and non-discrimination, issues of practicality, priorities and exclusions remain. Davina Cooper criticises Mouffe's model of citizenship as containing a narrow view of the political realm, which denies the relevance of the private. Notwithstanding her belief that citizenship does not have an essential meaning, but depends on the historical circumstances under which it is advocated, Cooper argues that legal citizenship may be significant in the 'empowering citizens project'.[64]

A procedural step to maintain universalisability, yet take account of women's concern, is offered by other theorists. Iris Young[65] and Anne Phillips[66] argue

---

61   S Berns, P Baron, M Neave, B Gaze, *Citizenship Theme* (1995).

62   *Ibid.*

63   C Mouffe, 'Feminism, Citizenship and Radical Democratic Politics' in J Butler and J Scott (eds), *Feminists Theorise the Political* (1992) Routledge.

64   D Cooper, 'The Citizen's Charter and Radical Democracy: Empowerment and Exclusion with Citizenship Discourse' (1993) 2 *Social and Legal Studies* 149 at p 168.

65   I M Young, 'Impartiality and Civic Public' in S Benhabib and D Cornell (eds), *Feminism as Critique* (1987) Polity.

66   A Phillips *op cit* n 24.

that there should be certain aspects of our lives that we are entitled to treat as private, such as our sexual lives, but that 'we should also be entitled to demonstrate publicly on all sexual issues, and none should be excluded from public discussion as inappropriate or trivial or better suited to the private domain'.[67] This is to advocate a collective sphere of justification in which all actions can be challenged where an infringement of liberty of equality is in question. Thus the idea of a personal zone of life is maintained, except where the freedoms of others are threatened. This goes some way to deal with the difficult issue of personal morality and beliefs, but it does not provide a complete solution to issues, for example, of patriarchal preferences for the behaviour of daughters.[68]

The debate about citizenship and the British constitution has not made much impact outside the academy. Yet we have come some way from dominance and separatism, particularly in the recognition that what goes on in private is relevant to theories of justice. The issue of universal against group rights remains unresolved not only in feminist theory, but also in debates on constitutional reform. Those concerned about democracy should not be disappointed in this. It is not for theorists to resolve such matters. Their role is to clarify issues, and to provide analytical frameworks. They may also make suggestions and express preferences; but it is for that 'vain abstraction', otherwise called 'the people', to decide.[69]

---

67 A Phillips *ibid* at p 85

68 This point can be explained on a variety of levels. On one level children are raised according to the preferences of their parents. This may result in prescriptions about gender roles, invasions of personal liberty, but because of notions of privacy and 'family autonomy', very little help is given to such children. On another level this could mean the rejection of culture, concepts, categories, as 'patriarchal' or as 'masculinist'. See S Wright, 'Patriarchal Feminism and the Law of the Father' (1993) 2 *Feminist Legal Studies* 115.

69 This is intended as a reference back to Lord Hailsham's view that experience and culture make the British constitution, *op cit* n 10. As before the questions are: 'Whose experiences? Of what? Is this a reference to the culture of the governing class, and of traditional deference thereto by the subject class?'

CHAPTER THIRTEEN

EQUALITY OF TREATMENT IN EUROPEAN COMMUNITY LAW: THE LIMITS OF MARKET EQUALITY

GILLIAN MORE*

INTRODUCTION

It is generally accepted that European Community (EC) Law has had a significant influence upon the development of sex discrimination law in the legal systems of the Member States. In the United Kingdom, in particular, sex discrimination lawyers have seized eagerly upon provisions of EC Law as a means of challenging the inadequacy of rights enshrined in national legislation.[1] Yet, although provisions of EC Law have undoubtedly advanced the cause of women's rights in certain spheres, the argument I make in this essay is that the vision of equality offered by EC Law is ultimately limited. In particular, I will advance the argument that as long as EC equality law continues to separate falsely the sphere of work from the sphere of the home (and family), the equality it guarantees is incomplete.[2] This rigid adherence to separate sphere ideology is, I argue, further evidence of the fact that EC equality law is constructed according to a male norm.[3]

THE LIBERAL IDEOLOGY OF SEPARATE SPHERES OF WORK AND FAMILY

Liberal thought is premised on a dichotomy between state and civil society: it assumes that there are naturally separate and identifiable spheres of life which of themselves define the appropriate parameters of state intervention in society. Interlinking with this is the dichotomy of the market and the family; the idea

---

*   Special thanks to Gráinne de Búrca for her comments on an earlier version of this paper.

1   See, for example, *R v Secretary of State for Employment, ex p Equal Opportunities Commission* [1994] 2 WLR 409, HL; *Webb v EMO Cargo* [1995] RLR 645, HL. See also C Barnard, 'A European Litigation Strategy: The Case of the Equal Opportunities Commission' in G More and J Shaw (eds), *The New Legal Dynamics of European Union* (1995) Oxford University Press.

2   See also K Scheiwe, 'EC Law's Unequal Treatment of the Family: The Case Law of the European Court of Justice on Rules Prohibiting Discrimination on Grounds of Sex and Nationality' (1994) 3 *Social & Legal Studies* 243-265; J Sohrab, 'Women and Social Security: the Limits of EEC Equality Law' (1994) *Jo SWFL* 5-17.

3   In another critique of EC equality law, I demonstrate how EC equality law is conceived of according to a model of 'sameness and difference', using man as the measure of comparison. See G More, 'Equal Treatment of the Sexes in European Community Law: What does 'equal' mean?' (1993) 1 *Feminist Legal Studies* 45-74.

that our 'productive lives' in the workplace are quite separate from our 'affective lives' in the family and home.[4] The family (itself given a 'natural' form) is constructed as the 'non-economic' sphere of our lives:[5] it is the realm of care and human relationships, of privacy, altruism, emotions and irrationality. Crucially, it is woman's sphere. This is contrasted with the 'economic' sphere of the market: this is man's sphere, the public world of work, objectivity, selfishness, challenge, and competition. The primary purpose of the dichotomy is, like that of state and civil society, to define the limits of government intervention: government may intervene in the market and in the workplace; yet the family is a 'private sphere', beyond state regulation. As Rose notes:

> Designating [activities as] personal, private and subjective makes them appear to be outside the scope of the law as a fact of nature, whereas in fact non-intervention is a socially constructed, historically variable and inevitably political decision. The state defines as private those areas of life into which it will not intervene, and then, paradoxically, uses this privacy as the justification for its non-intervention.[6]

Thus, non-regulation of particular issues should be regarded as being as equally significant as regulation itself: the failure to intervene both obscures the importance of the 'private' and, moreover, tends to legitimate the *status quo*.

Feminist thought has consistently underlined how the construction of the separate spheres of family and market constitutes a fundamental barrier to the full realisation of women's equality.[7] Whilst women have won many rights for example: recognition as legal 'persons';[8] the right to hold property;[9] to vote;[10] to an education;[11] and to be free from discrimination, these rights are market rights, accorded in the public sphere. Indeed, historically, many of these rights were conferred without displacing the prevailing view that woman's natural place was the home. The work of the liberal reformer, Mill, for example, has been criticised for exhibiting,

> ... an inherent tension ... between advocacy of sexual equality in the realm of civic rights for women and a simultaneously held implicit acceptance of

---

4   F Olsen, 'The Family and the Market: A Study of Ideology and Legal Reform' (1983) 96 *Harvard Law Rev* 1497-1578 at p 1498.

5   A Jagger, *Feminist Politics and Human Nature* (1983) Harvester Press at p 144.

6   N Rose, 'Beyond the Public/Private Division: Law, Power and the Family' (1987) 14 *Journal of Law and Society* 61-76 at p 64.

7   See for example, Z Eisenstein, *The Radical Future of Liberal Feminism* (1981) Longman at pp 89-132.

8   See A Sachs and J H Wilson, *Sexism and the Law* (1978) Martin Robertson at pp 4-66; also Mary Jane Mossman, 'Feminism and Legal Method: The Difference it Makes' (1987) 3 *Wisconsin Women's Law Journal* 149.

9   For example, the English Married Women's Property Acts of 1870 and 1882. See K O'Donovan, *Sexual Divisions in Law* (1985) Weidenfeld & Nicholson at pp 112-18.

10   See Martin Pugh, *Women's Suffrage in Britain 1867-1928* (1980) Hart-Walden for the Historical Association.

11   See Sachs and Wilson, *supra* n 9 at p 173.

traditional sex roles, together with an expectation that most women will in fact choose marriage as their career and should restrict themselves to home duties during their child-rearing years.[12]

This tension in liberal thought has led to the result that the equality accorded women in the public sphere is largely formal. Significantly, the sphere of life that is identified as woman's domain is excluded from the remit of equality: assumptions about women's role, about their natural abilities and about their position in the household remain untouched. Moreover, the connection between women's role in the private sphere and their capacity to enter and 'compete' within the public sphere is obscured.

In the late 20th century, it is possible to argue that the boundaries of the public and private sphere have shifted. The imperatives of the capitalist economy have broken down certain assumptions about woman's rightful role in the home: women now form a core element of the workforce, although their work is still to a significant degree both horizontally and vertically segregated from men's work.[13] Moreover, certain aspects of what were previously considered 'private' are now subject to state regulation:[14] the government intervenes in the family in areas such as divorce, child custody, child abuse and in welfare provision.[15] Nonetheless, the contention of this essay is that the family/market divide remains a potent force in limiting women's equality. In particular, in the field of sex discrimination law, the ideology of the public and the private allows both legislator and judge to disregard crucial factors in women's lives which influence their ability to claim equal treatment in the workplace.

For example, European Community law has recently witnessed a spate of litigation (initiated by men) concerning equality of treatment in relation to pensionable age for retirement pension schemes.[16] Yet the legal debates over the differential in pensionable age between women and men were conducted on a level completely isolated from the realities of pension provision for women. Whilst the mantra of these cases was equal treatment of men and women, and whilst an assumption was made that women have equal access to retirement pensions, the reality is that women's actual ability to achieve the same pension

---

12 Gail Tulloch, *Mill and Sexual Equality* (1989) Harvester Wheatsheaf at p 13.

13 And, moreover, women's employment is still to a large extent considered to be 'secondary': secondary to their private domestic role and secondary to the employment of their male partner, J Millar and C Glendinning, 'Gender and Poverty' (1989) 18 *Jnl Social Policy* 363-81 at pp 372-73.

14 Olsen characterises this as the 'regulated family', a form of regulation analogous to the idea of market management. *Supra* n 5 at pp 1517-18

15 Certain writers underline how state intervention in the private sphere in fact strengthens state control over women, through, for example, its construction of 'a proper mother'. See, for example, J Brophy, 'Child Care and the growth of power: the status of mothers in child custody disputes' in J Brophy and C Smart (eds), *Women in Law* (1985) Routledge & Kegan Paul; K O'Donovan, *Family Law Matters* (1993) Pluto at pp 30-42 and pp 75-79.

16 Case C-262/88 *Barber v Guardian Royal Exchange* [1990] ECR I-1889; Case C-110/91 *Moroni v Firma Collo GmbH* [1994] IRLR 130; Case C-200/91 *Coloroll v Russell and others* [1994] ECR I-4389; Case C-9/91 *R v Secretary of State for Social Security, ex p EOC* [1992] 3 CMLR 233.

provision as men is severely limited. Women's low earnings are often insufficient to reach the minimum threshold at which contributions towards a basic state pension commence.[17] Figures for the United Kingdom show that whilst 94% of men retire with a full state pension, only 15% of women do so.[18] Moreover, as retirement pension provision shifts inexorably towards the private sector, further problems arise.[19] Even if women do contribute to a pension scheme, their ability to contribute is often prejudiced by interruptions in their career patterns to bear children, or to care for elderly relatives. The level of pension contributions made by women is also prejudiced by the fact that many women are segregated into low-paid and precarious employment, often working part-time in order to accommodate competing family responsibilities.[20] The structure of pension provision has therefore led one writer to describe it as a system 'designed by men to benefit men', and based upon 'the traditional belief that the world is composed of only two categories of people: full-time participants in the labour market (husbands and fathers), and the people they support (women and children)'.[21] The system is based on a dichotomised view of the family and market, and it is this very vision which severely restricts women's access to adequate pension provision. The legal system's formal focus upon the issue of equalising pensionable ages simply serves to divert attention from the substantive inequalities faced by women in relation to pensions.

Separate sphere ideology operates in another way to disadvantage women in the context of sex discrimination law: it permits certain inequalities to be dismissed as 'natural', rather than constructed. For example, in the context of equal pay for work of equal value, the evaluation of the characteristics of a job is generally presented as a neutral process.[22] Yet perceptions of skill are undoubtedly gender-biased: work which produces goods is valued more highly than human service work.[23] In this respect, the market/family divide continues to exercise an influence on an assessment of what is considered economically

---

17 Or, alternatively, women's low earnings during a certain period of their working life will prejudice the final calculation of their pension entitlement, such as in the case of the UK State Earnings Related Pensions Scheme (SERPS) where entitlement is calculated in relation to average earnings over 44 years.

18 Fawcett Society, *Equal Treatment in State Pensions – Improving the system for Women. Introductory Briefing* (1995) Fawcett Society.

19 See Maureen Donnelly, 'The Disparate Impact of Pension Reform on Women' (1993) 6 *Canadian Jo of Women and the Law* 419-454.

20 Only 20% of women aged over 65 have an occupational pension of their own, compared with 66% of older men. Of women currently employed, 36% belong to occupational schemes, compared to 64% of men. Fawcett Society *ibid*.

21 L Dulude, 'Getting Old: Men in Couples and Women Alone' in G Hofmann Nemiroff (ed), *Women and Men: Interdisciplinary Readings on Gender* (1987) Fitzhenry and Whiteside 323 at p 330, quoted in Donnelly *supra* n 20.

22 A good example of assuming neutrality can be found in the judgment in Case 237/85 *Gisela Rummler v Dato-Druck* [1986] ECR 2101.

23 P Armstrong and H Armstrong,, *Theorizing Women's Work* (1990) Garamond Press at p 112.

valuable or wealth-producing. In other words, it works subtly to ensure that women's work is undervalued precisely because it is women's work.

In summary, therefore, the argument in this essay is twofold: first, women's claim to equality is severely restricted by the State's refusal to recognise that woman's (traditional) role in the home and the family has an enduring impact on her rights in the workplace. Liberal separate sphere ideology facilitates blinkered vision on the part of legislators and judges, meaning that effective solutions to women's problems in the workplace are rarely found. Secondly, continuing assumptions about women's natural place in the home remain largely undisturbed. Yet these assumptions 'infiltrate' the public sphere and serve to reify the perception that women's characteristics are different (and hence inferior) to those of men. Thus, the false separation of market and family not only allows the State to fail to confront inequalities faced by women; it also perpetuates women's unequal status. As Thornton observes:

> The public/private dichotomy ... constitutes a malleable political mechanism which can be effectively utilized to safeguard dominant interests under the guise of seeming neutrality and naturalness.[24]

ECONOMIC/NON-ECONOMIC AND THE EUROPEAN UNION

The dichotomy of the market and the family is, I have argued, strongly linked to notions of 'economic' and 'non-economic'. In the case of the European Union, a similar division between 'economic' and 'non-economic' can be identified. This division has its roots in the history of the common market: the Member States originally transferred competence to the Community to legislate only in those areas which directly affected the creation of the customs union and the free movement of the factors of production. Whenever the Community sought to expand its competence, such as, for example, in the case of environmental legislation, it could only do so by demonstrating the economic need for action; that is, by showing that such matters directly affected the competitive conditions within the common market. Thus, to a large extent, the Community has competence only to regulate the 'economic' sphere: matters considered 'non-economic' are left to the national legislator (or to the domain of non-regulation). Although the process of integration has given new 'non-economic' powers to the European Union (such as powers to legislate in relation to education, culture and public health),[25] these powers are weak and heavily circumscribed. It is therefore predominantly still the case that the Union must demonstrate (single) market-oriented motives for introducing new legislation.

---

24 M Thornton, 'The Public/Private Dichotomy: Gendered and Discriminatory' (1991) 18 *Journal of Law and Society* 448.

25 Articles 126-129 EC.

EC SEX DISCRIMINATION LAW

In the field of EC sex discrimination law, the market orientation of the legislation is immediately apparent. The central pillar of EC sex discrimination law, Article 119 EC, which guarantees to men and women the principle of equal pay for equal work – was included in the Treaty, not because of feminist demands, but due to the economic necessity of maintaining uniform conditions of competition.[26] It originated in the fact that, at the time the Treaty was drafted, French employers were already required to pay equal wages to men and women. France was therefore concerned that her producers would suffer a competitive disadvantage, should other Member States not require their employers to respect the principle of equal pay.

However, in its famous ruling in 1976 in *Defrenne (No 2)*, the European Court of Justice held that Article 119 EC in fact pursued a double aim, both economic and social. The court underlined, moreover, that:

... the principle of equal pay forms part of the foundations of the Community.[27]

The court's influential decision in *Defrenne (No 2)* coincided with the early 1970s initiative of the Community to develop its social dimension.[28] Together they gave the necessary impetus for the adoption of a series of directives by the Council, which expanded the remit of Community sex equality legislation beyond the basic principle of equal pay. As will be argued below, however, the focus of these directives is again largely limited to a narrow conception of 'harmonising' women's integration into the workplace in the various Member States. The directives' focus on 'market' activity means that the family/market divide is particularly pronounced in both their conceptualisation and application.

The first directive, Directive 75/117 on equal pay, was issued in 1975, its purpose being to implement the wider principle of equal pay for work of equal value.[29] It was followed in 1976 by Directive 76/207 on equal treatment for men and women, as regards access to employment, vocational training and promotion, and working conditions.[30] This directive introduced a much broader prohibition of gender discrimination in the workplace into the Community legal order: it is discussed in detail below. Social security was excluded from the

---

26 Nielsen describes the equality provisions of EC Law as a form of 'state feminism', Ruth Nielsen, *Equality Legislation in a Comparative Perspective – Towards State Feminism?* (1983) Kvindevidenskabeligt Forlag.

27 Case 43/75 *Defrenne v Sabena (No 2)* [1976] ECR 455.

28 The Community's 1974 Social Action Programme, *EC Bull Supp* 2/74.

29 Council Directive of 10 February 1975 on the approximation of the laws of the Member States relating to the application of the principle of equal pay for men and women, OJ 1975 L45/19.

30 Council Directive 76/207 EEC of 9 February 1976 on the implementation of the principle of equal treatment for men and women as regards access to employment, vocational training and promotion and working conditions, OJ 1975 L 39/40.

1976 directive; hence in 1978, Directive 79/7 on equal treatment in social security was adopted, albeit with a number of significant exceptions.[31] One such explicit exception was the subject of occupational pension schemes; and to cover these, Directive 86/378 was issued in 1986.[32] A guarantee of equal treatment was extended also to self-employed women in the form of Directive 86/613, a primary aim of this directive being to reach women employed in agriculture.[33] Finally, in 1992, Directive 92/85 concerning the protection of pregnant women at work was adopted.[34] The aim of this directive, as its title suggests, is to protect the health and safety of pregnant workers. The directive guarantees – of particular significance for women in the United Kingdom – the right to a minimum period of maternity leave and the right of protection from dismissal on grounds of pregnancy, regardless of the length or hours of service of the employee.

Beyond these directives, the Community has also developed a body of 'soft law', of non-binding measures, which seek to persuade the Member States to adopt certain principles within their legal systems.[35] Significant examples are the recommendation and the code of conduct in relation to the protection of the dignity of women at work and the recommendation on child care (the latter is discussed further below).[36]

---

31 Council Directive of 19 December 1978 on the progressive implementation of the principle of equal treatment for man and women in matters of social security, OJ 1979 L6/24. The directive however excluded the equalisation of retirement ages, survivors' pensions and family allowances. In October 1987, the Commission proposed a further directive in the area of equal treatment in social security, intended to complete the programme of equal treatment. This proposal has not, however, been adopted. See Draft Directive supplementing the Implementation of the Principle of Equal Treatment, COM (87) 494 final.

32 Council Directive of 24 July 1986 on the implementation of the principle of equal treatment for men and women in occupational social security schemes, OJ 1986 L225/40. However, the validity of certain provisions of this directive is now in question due to a series of judgments from the Court of Justice, which have drawn the issue of occupational pensions into the ambit of Article 119 EC, Case C-262/88 *Barber supra* n 17; Case C-109/91 *Ten Oever v Stichting Bedrijfspensioenfonds* [1993] ECR I-4879; Case C-152/91 *Neath v Steeper* [1993] ECR I-6935; Case C-200/91 *Coloroll supra*; Case C-408/92 *Smith v Avdel Systems* [1994] ECR I-4435. See also Whiteford, 'Lost in the Mists of Time: The ECJ and Occupational Pensions' (1995) 32 *CML Rev* 801-840.

33 Council Directive of 11 December 1986 on the application of the principle of equal treatment between men and women engaged in an activity, including agriculture, in a self-employed capacity, and on the protection of self-employed women during pregnancy and motherhood, OJ 1986 L359/56.

34 Council Directive 92/85/EEC on the introduction of measures to encourage improvements in the safety and health at work of pregnant workers and workers who have recently given birth or are breastfeeding, OJ 1992 L348/1.

35 For an overview of such measures, see R Nielsen and E Szyzsczak, *The Social Dimension of the European Community* (1993, 2nd edn) Handelshojskolens Forlag at pp 163-67.

36 Commission Recommendation on the protection of dignity of men and women at work (including a Code of Practice to combat sexual harassment) OJ 1992 C27/4; Council Recommendation 92/241/EEC on child care OJ 1992 L 123/16.

THE PERPETUATION OF SEPARATE SPHERES
IN EC EQUALITY LAW

The roots of EC equality law in the economics of the common market are the first strong indicator that the effect of the law is likely to be limited to the 'market' only. In fact, there is a wealth of examples which demonstrates how EC equality law applies to women only in their capacity as 'market' actors. This perpetuation of separate spheres can be observed both in the construction of the legislation itself and in the jurisprudence of the Court of Justice.

Legislation

The adoption of Directive 76/207 on equal treatment as regards access to employment, vocational training and promotion, and working conditions (henceforth, the 'Equal Treatment Directive') was a significant step beyond the purely economic rationale of Article 119 EC. Indeed, the Community's 1974 Social Action Programme, which gave birth to the directive, went some way towards considering the relationship between woman's role in the family and her role in the workplace, requiring the Community to give priority 'to enable women to reconcile family responsibilities with job aspirations'.[37] In this same vein, the ad hoc group involved in the drafting of the directive proposed that women's special needs and women's family responsibilities be emphasised.[38] However, despite such views, the Equal Treatment Directive was drawn up in much narrower terms, focusing solely on equality for women working outside the home.[39] The decision to exclude any reference to the family appears to have been heavily influenced by legal opinion that the Community had competence to legislate only in relation to employment matters. To legislate in relation to the family would, it was argued, have surpassed the limits of legality. Such reasoning demonstrates once more how the family and work are constructed as mutually exclusive spheres. Hoskyns, in her excellent account of the drafting of the directive, describes how men took charge of the finalisation of the wording of the directive. She suggests that:

> The gradual down-playing of the importance of the issue of family responsibilities in the whole question of the position of women in the labour market was partly due to a genuine doubt about Community competence, but was also due to the gradual imposition of the patriarchal view.[40]

---

37 EC Bull Supp 2/74 at 23. C Hoskyns rightly criticises the draft for assuming that only women can have family responsibilities, 'Women's Equality and the European Community' (1985) 20 *Feminist Review* 71 at p 79.

38 *Ibid* at pp 79–83.

39 See COM(75) 36 final.

40 *Supra* n 38 at p 84.

Hoskyns also views as significant the fact that the reference to 'the adoption of appropriate measures to provide women with equal opportunity' was deleted from the key definition of equal treatment in the directive.[41] Instead, a clause permitting measures to 'remove existing inequalities which affect women's opportunities' was inserted as a derogation from the principle of equal treatment.[42] This formulation of positive action as an exception to the norm is, it is argued, stuck within a particularly formal view of equal treatment as identical treatment.[43] It militates against positive action being viewed as an integral component of achieving equality and, moreover, it entrenches the division between the family and the market yet further.[44] As the subsequent discussion of cases before the Court of Justice dealing with the question of positive action will show, the formulation of the Equal Treatment Directive has severely impaired the perception of positive action in Community law.

Whilst the Equal Treatment Directive excluded any mention of the family, the memorandum accompanying the draft directive indicated that the Community would in the future consider legislation concerning parental leave and child care facilities at work.[45] A directive in relation to parental leave was proposed by the Commission in 1982, but failed to achieve agreement in the Council of Ministers.[46] The question remained dormant until the 1989 Community Charter of Fundamental Social Rights of Workers once again raised the issue of the need to 'develop measures to enable women and men to reconcile their occupational and family obligations'.[47] On the basis of the Charter, the Commission proposed the adoption of a recommendation on child care, that is a non-binding measure to encourage the Member States to introduce child care facilities for working parents. The Commission's choice of a recommendation rather then a (binding) directive was criticised at the time, particularly by the Women's Rights Committee of the European Parliament.[48] However, as had been the case with the Equal Treatment Directive, the prevailing opinion in the Commission's Legal Service was that the Community did not have legal competence to intervene in child care provision, this being a matter that went beyond mere regulation of the workplace. For this reason, therefore, the first Community measure that goes some way towards recognising

---

41   *Ibid* at pp 82–83.

42   Article 2(4).

43   See More *supra* n 4 at pp 61–63.

44   If, for example, positive action is taken in relation to women's family responsibilities, the fact that this happens as an 'exception' to the norm serves to separate it from the usual identical treatment principle of the workplace. See Case *Commission v France infra* n 78.

45   *Supra* n 40 at pp 24–27, 36.

46   COM (84) 631 final.

47   *Social Europe* 1/92, point 16. Note that the 1989 wording differed from the 1974 SAP in that the need to reconcile work and family obligations was extended to cover both men and women.

48   EP Committee on Women's Rights, Hearing on Child care, 25–26 June 1990.

the falsity of the family/market divide was adopted as a non-binding, advisory measure only.[49]

The Recommendation on Child Care, adopted in 1992, invites the Member States to encourage initiatives in a number of areas: in the 'provision of children care services while parents are working ... training ... or are seeking a job'; providing 'special leave for employed parents with responsibility for the care and upbringing of children'; proposing changes to 'the environment, structure and organisation of work, to make them responsive to the needs of workers with children'; and ensuring 'the sharing of occupational, family and upbringing responsibilities arising from the care of children between women and men'.[50] Whilst the recommendation can in no way be enforced to impose obligations upon the Member States, it can be used indirectly; that is, as a tool of construction by national courts when interpreting national legislation.[51] Moreover, it is possible to argue that it is incumbent upon the Court of Justice to take the principles of the recommendation into account when interpreting provisions of Community law. Creative litigators should consider the possibilities for employing such techniques!

Also originating in the statements of the 1989 Community Charter of Fundamental Rights of Workers is the 1992 Protection of Pregnant Workers Directive.[52] This directive has obliged the Member States to introduce legislation providing for a 12 week maternity leave for all pregnant employees, regardless of their length of service. It must, to a certain extent, be regarded as breaking through the family/market divide in EC law, since it legally validates 'a child care related employment interruption'.[53] Such interruptions, as Scheiwe has noted, have traditionally always been regarded as private risks, the cost to be borne by the mother and not by the state or employer.[54] However, given the entrenched, formalistic view of equal treatment in EC law as being identical treatment,[55] the weakness in the Pregnant Worker's Directive is that it seems to conceptualise pregnant women's rights as special, exceptional rights, rather than represent them as an integral part of women's equality.[56] Whilst on a practical

---

49 *Supra* n 37.

50 Article 1.

51 Case C-322/88 *Grimaldi v Fonds des Maladies Professionelles* [1989] ECR 4407 at para 18. This principle of interpretation has recently been used to interpret the UK Sex Discrimination Act 1975 with reference to the Commission's Code of Practice on measures to combat sexual harassment, see *Insitu Cleaning v Heads* EOC Review 59, 44; *Stewart v Cleveland Guest (Engineering) Ltd* [1994] IRLR 440 (latter case decided against plaintiff).

52 *Supra* n 35.

53 Scheiwe *supra* n 3 at pp 258–59.

54 *Ibid.*

55 See Fredman, 'European Community Discrimination Law: A Critique' (1992) 21 ILJ 119; More, *supra* n 4.

56 See J Jacqmain, 'Pregnancy as Grounds for Dismissal' (1994) 23 ILJ 355; G More, 'Reflections on Pregnancy Discrimination under EC Law' (1992) *Jo SWFL* 48; W Williams, 'Pregnancy and the Equal Treatment/Special Treatment Debate' (1984) 13 *New York University Review of Law and Social Change* 325.

level the rights are undoubtedly a step forward for women in many Member States, they could, as employers' associations have argued, militate against women being recruited. The recent relaunch of the Commission proposal for parental leave (to be adopted under the Social Protocol procedure, thus excluding the United Kingdom) may, however, go some way towards solving this problem.[57]

The jurisprudence of the Court of Justice

The demarcation of work and family

The Court of Justice has generally exhibited a firm adherence to the intention of the Community legislator that the equality provisions of EC law should apply only in the case of 'workers'. This it has done sometimes to the point of absurdity and often, therefore, avoided the real issues in the cases before it. Its 'bottom line' was stated in the case of *Achterberg*, in which it held that Article 119 EC and the Equality Directives were not intended to,

> ... implement equal treatment between men and women generally but only in their capacity as workers.[58]

Consequently, the court defined a woman who had never been employed outside of her home as a person 'who had not had an occupation'.[59]

In the case of *Hofmann v Barmer Ersatzkasse*, a German father challenged the '*Mutterschutzgesetz*' a law which guaranteed a six-month paid maternity leave to mothers but not to fathers – as contrary to the Equal Treatment Directive.[60] Hofmann argued that the aim of the German law was the reduction of 'the multiplicity of burdens' imposed on a woman by her work and her child, and that this aim could be equally met if the father were allowed to bring up the child. In opposition to his claim, the German government relied on the formal structure of the Equal Treatment Directive, submitting that maternity leave should be considered as a derogation from the principle of equal treatment; that is, it was a 'provision concerning the protection of women, particularly as regards pregnancy and maternity'.[61] The Court of Justice agreed with this view and held that granting maternity leave to mothers only was covered by the derogation in the directive. In response to Hofmann's argument, the court replied:

---

57 SEC(95) 276.

58 Joined cases 48, 106 and 107/88 *JEG Achterberg-te Riele & Others v Sociale Verzekeringsbank, Amsterdam* [1989] ECR 1963 at para 12.

59 *Ibid* at para 13.

60 Case 184/83 [1984] ECR 3047.

61 Article 2(3) of the Directive.

[T]he Directive is not designed to settle questions concerned with the organisation of the family, or to alter the division of responsibility between parents.[62]

In this statement, the court sought to follow the intentions of the drafters of the directive. Yet, the court's conservative stance served to reify the distinction in EC law between the market and the family and, importantly, blinkered the court's vision of equality for the future. Moreover, the delegation of the right to maternity leave to the realm of special treatment for women, that is, exceptional to the norm of equal treatment, served to alienate further the notion that accommodating child-bearing and child rearing is an integral element of equality in the workplace.

The refusal to link family responsibilities to workplace equality

The impact of women's family responsibilities on equality in the workplace has been raised directly before the Court of Justice on a number of occasions. Yet the court has always found a way to evade addressing such questions. A clear example is the case of *Bilka Kaufhaus v Weber*, where a woman employee challenged the policy of a German department store that required employees to have worked for at least 20 years (15 years of which full-time) in order to qualify for the store's (non-contributory) pension scheme.[63] Frau Weber argued that the pension scheme policy discriminated indirectly against women in its requirement that an employee should have worked 15 years full-time: women, she argued, were more likely to take part-time work in order to look after their family and children and were less likely to fulfil this requirement. Indeed, figures confirmed that for every one man who worked part-time for the department store, 10 women worked part-time. The questions referred by the Bundesarbeitsgericht to the Court of Justice focused on the circumstances in which an employer could justify an indirectly discriminatory pay practice: Was the store's claim that it wished to encourage full-time working sufficient justification? In addition, the German court submitted the question whether the undertaking was under an obligation to structure its pension scheme 'in such a way that appropriate account is taken of the special difficulties experienced by women employees in fulfilling the requirements for an occupational pension'.

The first part of the judgment is well-known: the Court of Justice held that national courts should apply a strict proportionality test to determine whether an employer could objectively justify an indirectly discriminatory pay policy.[64] However, on the question of whether the prevention of discrimination stretched as far as requiring the employer to organise its pension scheme in a particular way, the court responded negatively. Again, it reasoned that an obligation to

---

62 *Supra* n 61 at p 3075.

63 Case 170/84 [1986] ECR 1607.

64 At para 36 of judgment.

accommodate family responsibilities fell outwith the scope of Community competence:

> The imposition of an obligation such as that envisaged by the national court in its question goes beyond the scope of Article 119 and has no other basis in Community law as it now stands.[65]

Arguably, the court missed an ideal opportunity (in what is generally considered a progressive judgment) to introduce an even more stringent principle into the justification of indirect discrimination. A duty to accommodate the needs of particular employees is, for example, a known principle in North American anti-discrimination law.[66]

A more recent example of the court's failure to appreciate the impact of women's family responsibilities on their market equality in relation to pensions can be found in the case of *Rita Grau-Hupka v Stadtgemeinde Bremen*.[67] The case arose from the fact that the German Collective Wage Agreement for Federal Employees excluded workers pursuing a secondary activity (that is, if their employment as a federal employee was not their main occupation). Workers not covered by the collective agreement could be paid a lower wage. Moreover, for the purposes of the agreement, the receipt of an old-age pension was considered equivalent to having a main occupation. The plaintiff, Frau Hupka, upon retirement continued to work part-time as a music teacher in a state school. Since she was in receipt of a both a state and an occupational retirement pension, she was excluded from the more favourable pay rates of the collective agreement for her part-time employment. Frau Hupka challenged the provision of the collective agreement which excluded workers pursuing a secondary activity as contrary to the German *Beschäftigungsförderungsgesetz*, a law which prohibits employers from exercising any form of unequal treatment as between full-time and part-time workers, unless it can be justified by objective reasons. The German Labour Court held, however, that the fact that Frau Hupka was in receipt of a retirement pension constituted an objective reason for treating her differently from full-time workers.

The complicating factor in Frau Hupka's case was, however, that her pension had been reduced by the fact that during her pensionable working life she had worked five years part-time in order to bring up her children. The question was raised as to whether receipt of a pension could constitute an objective reason justifying discrimination, when the pension had been reduced due to the fact that a woman had been absent from the workforce in order to bring up children. The reduction in the pension amounted in itself to indirect discrimination

---

65   At para 42 of judgment.

66   B Vizketely, *Proving Discrimination in Canada* (Toronto: Carswell, 1987) at 96-104; M David Lepofsky, 'The Duty to Accommodate: a purposive approach' (1992) 1 *Canadian Labour Law Jo* 1-22.

67   Case C-297/93 [1994] ECR I-5535.

against women: could this then form part of the objective reason justifying the differential treatment of part-time and full-time workers?

The facts of the case raised two fundamental issues relating to women's equality: first, the disadvantages faced by women in relation to pension provision; secondly, the possibility that a reason used to justify indirect discrimination within the legal process may itself incorporate gender bias.[68] Yet these vital issues were avoided by the Court of Justice in its response to the questions referred. In a terse judgment, it held that Community law,

> ... in no way obliges the Member States to grant advantages in respect of old-age pension schemes to persons who have brought up children or to provide benefit entitlements where employment has been interrupted in order to bring up children.[69]

Thus, yet again, the court was able to avoid the issue of family responsibilities by denying that there was any Community competence in this sphere. Whilst, arguably, the court wished to steer clear of establishing new principles in relation to the organisation of state social security schemes,[70] it could still, in my opinion, have explored further the important issue of what types of objective justifications for indirect discrimination are acceptable. Considering its view that, ' ... the principle of equal pay forms part of the foundations of the Community',[71] the question of justifying pay discrimination is undoubtedly within its competence.

What the discussion of these few cases shows, therefore, is how the Court of Justice, whenever it is confronted with a radical question,[72] will take refuge in the argument that the competence of the Community is limited only to the question of 'work', understood in an extremely narrow sense. On the one hand, it could be argued that what this demonstrates is the inherent limitation of the role of a supranational court, which has to be careful not to impinge on the legislative prerogatives of the Member States. Were it a supreme court, working with a constitutional guarantee of equality, it would have more scope in which to give judgment. Yet, to take a contrary view, the European Court of Justice has quite obviously forced the hand of national and Community legislators on a number of occasions and has not seen itself bound by the wording of secondary legislation.[73] The question of the limit of Community competence is often treated in practice as being as flexible as the court allows it to be. The court's

---

68 On this point see the critique by Fredman ('Equal Pay and Justification' (1994) 23 ILJ 37–41) of the ECJ's admission of a market forces defence in Case C-127/92 *Enderby v Frenchay Health Authority* [1993] IRLR 91.

69 At para 27 of judgment.

70 The court also criticises the referring court for not submitting clear questions: it was not clear whether the reference referred to Hupka's state or occupational pension. See para 26 of judgment.

71 Case 43/75 *Defrenne v Sabena (No 2) supra* n 28.

72 By 'radical question', I mean a question that invites it to recognise that the workplace is not isolated from the family, see Eisenstein *supra* n 8.

73 An obvious example is Case C-262/88 Barber *supra* n 17.

reasoning that Community equality extends only to the workplace is, I would argue, merely a convenient guise for the conservatism of the court. Despite the court's reputation as being in the vanguard of women's rights, it is blinkered by the liberal ideology of the separation of the family and the market and has limited vision of the obstacles faced by women in attaining equality in the workplace.[74] This must, in my opinion, be explained to a certain extent by the fact that, despite its quarter century of existence, there have been no women judges in the Court of Justice.[75]

THE QUESTION OF POSITIVE ACTION

My thesis that it is not only the limited competence of the Community, but also the limited vision of the court that has reinforced the family/market divide in Community equality law, is borne out by an examination of the court's case law in relation to positive action. Whilst positive action in favour of women is explicitly permitted by a derogation in the Equal Treatment Directive and, moreover, is encouraged by the Commission's 1984 Recommendation on Positive Action, the Court of Justice has interpreted such provisions narrowly.[76]

The court's limited approach to positive action was illustrated first in the case of *Commission v France*,[77] where a provision in French labour law, which permitted collective agreements and individual employment contracts to continue providing for 'special advantages granted to women by reason of their family responsibilities', was challenged by the Commission. The French government defended these rights – rights such as leave when a child is ill, extra pension points in respect of second and subsequent children, and the payment of child care allowances – on the ground that in order for women even to begin to realise equality in the workplace, specific action was necessary to remedy the *de facto* inequalities they faced in relation to their family responsibilities.[78] The French government argued that the provision of such rights was permitted by Article 2(4) of the Equal Treatment Directive, which allowed measures 'to promote equal opportunities for women, in particular by removing existing inequalities which affect women's opportunities ...'.

---

74 See also the decision of the ECJ in Cases C-63 and 64/91 *Jackson and Cresswell v Chief Adjudication Officer* [1992] ECR I-4737, and commentary in Sohrab *supra* n 3; P Durston, '*Jackson and Cresswell v The Chief Adjudication Officer*. No Help for Women in the Poverty Trap' (1994) MLR 641-48. This decision has been superseded (albeit in relation to a different benefit) in Case C-116/94 *Meyers v Adjudication Officer* nyr of 13 July 1995.

75 There has been one woman Advocate General (for a short period of time). However, with the entry of Sweden and Finland into the EU, two women judges were appointed to the Court of First Instance in 1995.

76 Article 2(4) Equal Treatment Directive; Council Recommendation 84/635 EEC on the promotion of positive action for women, OJ 1984 L331/34.

77 Case 312/86 [1988] ECR 6315.

78 Report for the hearing *ibid* at pp 6322-23.

The Court of Justice found, however, that the French provision violated the Equal Treatment Directive. The positive action exception in the Equal Treatment Directive did permit measures which, 'although discriminatory in appearance, are in fact intended to eliminate or reduce actual instances of inequality which may exist in the reality of social life'.[79] However, the French government had failed to demonstrate that 'the generalized preservation of special rights for women' would, in fact, reduce such inequalities. The court's approach to such a vital decision was, to say the least, rigid and briefly-reasoned.[80] It appeared to favour the view of the Commission that women's interests would be served best by extending the provision of such rights also to men. This, it is submitted, misses the core of the French government's argument, namely, that it is women who are in fact disadvantaged in the workplace by their family responsibilities.

The court demonstrated once more its preference for a blanket norm of gender neutrality in the case of *Integrity v Rouvroy*, a case concerning the application of Directive 79/7 on equal treatment in social security.[81] This directive, unlike the Equal Treatment Directive, contains no specific provision for positive action. The court held that certain provisions of Belgian social security law, which compensated 'married women, widows and students' for the low level of social security contributions they had accrued (since their main activity did not constitute 'work' for the purposes of labour law), were in breach of the rule of equal treatment contained in the directive. The court merely applied its rigid rule of identical treatment, failing even to address the fact that the purpose of the impugned legislation was actually to combat discrimination against women in the labour market.[82]

The final indicator of the court's approach to positive action will be given in its judgment in *Kalanke v Freie Hansestadt Bremen*, which, at the time of writing, is still awaited.[83] The judgment has been preceded by the publication of the Opinion of Advocate General Tesauro.[84] Assuming that the court follows his approach, the judgment will demonstrate, once again, extreme conservatism in relation to the question of positive action. The facts of *Kalanke* concern a law relating to the equality of men and women in the public service in the German state of Bremen. Section 4 of the law, which relates to the recruitment, reassignment and promotion of employees, requires that priority be given to women in cases where women possess equivalent qualifications to those of men, and where women are under-represented in the class into which

---

79 *Ibid* at para 15 of judgment.

80 Indeed, Advocate General Tesauro takes the view that the decision was too harsh ('*avec une sévérité excessive à notre avis*') in his Opinion in Case C-450/93 *Kalanke infra* n 85 at point 18.

81 Case 373/89 [1990] ECR 4243.

82 For further discussion, see Fredman *supra* n 56 at pp 128-30.

83 Judgment given confirming Advocate General's Opinion on 17 October 1995, Case C-450/93 [1995] IRLR 660.

84 Opinion in Case C-450/93 of 6 April 1995.

recruitment/promotion is being effected. At the suit of a man who was not promoted to a senior position, the Court of Justice was asked by the German Federal Labour Court to consider the compatibility of the German provision with the Equal Treatment Directive.

Advocate General Tesauro, in his advisory opinion to the court, distinguishes between two forms of positive action: the first he describes as action which creates equality of opportunity by eliminating the barriers which prevent women from achieving the same results as men. This type of action, he reasons, creates an equal starting point for men and women. The second type of positive action he describes as aimed at equalising the finishing point: through the use of quotas and goals, an attempt is made to achieve an equality of results.[85] Tesauro criticises, however, this second type of scheme for failing to address the underlying barriers which cause the imbalance of representation in the first place. For this reason, he advises the court that the exception in the Equal Treatment Directive can only encompass the first type of positive action. The German provision in question did not fall within this exception, since it was aimed at achieving a numerical balance of women and men, but without addressing the underlying causes. Moreover, he reasoned, the German provision was disproportionate to the aim it pursued.

The Advocate General's Opinion, although in general well-reasoned, is unconvincing. Advocate General Tesauro fails to explain why a policy of achieving a numerical balance of women and men in occupational categories (and, in particular, in senior categories, such as the one in question) should not also be combined with other policies aimed at eliminating barriers. Furthermore, he fails to consider the question of invisible barriers, or the so-called 'glass ceilings', which prevent women from being promoted into senior positions, not because of tangible obstacles, but because it is thought that women cannot do the job (precisely because they have rarely been allowed to). Such barriers cannot be 'eliminated' *per se*. A policy of promoting women to such positions may, on the other hand, be such a way to break through the glass ceiling. It would tend to promote a critical mass of women within a certain job and, in this way, break down the perception that it was not a woman's job. The Advocate General's interpretation of the derogation in the Equal Treatment Directive is, therefore, in my opinion, unduly restrictive. When looked at in conjunction with the earlier judgments of the court on this topic, the provision in the directive is more or less deprived of its practical effect. Above all, the Opinion demonstrates a very limited comprehension of the barriers which prevent women attaining equality.

Should the Court of Justice follow the Opinion of its Advocate General in Kalanke, there will be severe repercussions for the use of positive action as a result of the judgment. This will particularly be the case in Germany, where the use of positive action programmes is fairly widespread.

---

85   At point 14 of Opinion (author's translation).

CONCLUSION

The aim of this essay has been to debunk the widely-held perception that EC sex discrimination law, as interpreted by the European Court of Justice, is an unreserved force for good in the advancement of women's rights. I have argued that Community equality law merely replicates the family/market divide of liberal ideology and that the decisions of the Court of Justice reinforce this distinction. This means that wherever women seek to advance an argument showing how family responsibilities impact upon their workplace equality, the court fails to recognise the foundations of their claims. This, I have argued, is not merely due to the fact that Community competence is limited to the workplace, but also to restricted vision on the part of the Court of Justice.

As with any pattern, there are always exceptions which will diverge from the rule.[86] Thus, the court's recent decisions in *Vroege* and *Fisscher*,[87] in which it recognised that failure to allow part-time workers access to occupational pension schemes may be indirect discrimination against women, can be presented as an example of the court indeed recognising how women's family-related employment patterns impact negatively on their rights in the workplace. Yet, whilst it is clear that the use of the concept of indirect discrimination has, to a certain extent, enabled the court to acknowledge 'the effects of women's family situations upon their labour-market status',[88] the rights bestowed upon women in indirect discrimination claims are in no way absolute. In the case of access to occupational pension schemes, it is open to employers to justify part-timers' exclusion on a number of grounds; for example, on grounds of administrative convenience. Ultimately, therefore, the outcome of women's claims depends on the stringency of the approach of the national courts to the issue of justification. Moreover, the Court of Justice endorsed the possibility that Member States could limit the possibility for successful claimants to backdate their pension claims.[89]

My conclusion remains, therefore, that women can make only limited gains using EC law. As long as the EC legal system is permeated with the notion of the 'economic', and as long as family activities continue to be portrayed as other than 'economic', then the actual impact of EC sex discrimination law will be far from radical.

---

86 Alternatively, there are examples which show how the rule is not applied uniformly across the whole field of Community law. For example, Scheiwe shows how the ECJ has been willing to recognise the relationship between the family and work in the context of the free movement of workers. Scheiwe *supra* n 3.

87 Case C-57/93 *Vroege v VCIV Instituut voor Volkshuisvesting* [1994] ECR I-4541; Case 128/93 *Fisscher v Voorhuis Hengelo BV* [1994] ECR I-4583.

88 Scheiwe *supra* n 3 at pp 254–255.

89 Case 128/93 Fisscher *supra* n 88. For criticism of this aspect of the judgment, see Whiteford *supra* n 33.

CHAPTER FOURTEEN

THE INTERNAL MARKET AND THE EUROPEAN UNION: SOME FEMINIST NOTES

*LEO FLYNN**

INTRODUCTION

When the European Economic Community (EEC) was established by the Treaty of Rome[1] it was clearly intended by its founders to form part of a move towards greater integration amongst the states of western Europe. The preamble to the original Treaty famously refers to the signatories' desire to foster 'an ever closer union amongst the peoples of Europe'. The mode chosen to advance this process focused on the mechanisms of trade and production, grounding the whole enterprise in so-called 'low politics'.[2] The decision to pursue a common market was, to some extent, a second-best option; it had been forced on the original Member States because of their lack of success in two attempts to launch integration in the spheres of high politics, namely, a failure to ratify the Treaty establishing a European Defence Community and the still-born Statute for a European Political Community. Forty years of experience with the process of economic integration demonstrated that integration of the Member States' economies could not be confined to that domain alone; as a result, the activities of the EEC tended increasingly to spill over into other fields such as social policy, environmental policy and education and training. These changes came about through a variety of routes, including policy initiatives on the part of the Commission, *ad hoc* projects developed by subsystems of Member States and the judicial activism of the Court of Justice.[3] They were formalised in amendments to the founding Treaties and provided the platform for a relaunch of the unsuccessful drives for political union and a common security policy attempted in the 1950s. However, because of this history, as we shall see, the process of the economic integration still retains centre stage. In terms of the legal dynamics of European integration, the internal market (as the common market is now known) provides the conceptual foundations in the development of the laws of the European Union.

---

* I wish to acknowledge the helpful comments and suggestions made on earlier drafts of this paper by Maleiha Malik, Aileen McColgan and Gillian More. However, all responsibility for its final form and contents rest with myself.

1 Treaty of Rome 1956. The European Economic Community became the European Community in 1993 as a result of amendments to the original Treaty contained in the TEU.

2 See Arthur P J Mol and J Duncan Liefferinkm, 'European Environmental Policy and Global Interdependence: a Review of the Theoretical Approaches' in J D Liefferink, P D Lowe and A P J Mol (eds), *European Integration and Environmental Policy* (1993) Belhaven Press at p 18.

3 See, generally, William Wallace (ed), *The Dynamics of European Integration* (1990) Pinter.

The pivotal role of the internal market in EC law has important implications for any feminist perspective on the area. Feminist perspectives on law have offered a set of powerful critiques of many aspects of law, and these insights have been applied in relation to key features of the legal system in many jurisdictions. However, in relation to EC law, the contribution made by feminist lawyers and scholars has been relatively limited. In particular, it has tended to be confined to a more restricted range of issues then one encounters in other fields of law. Thus, there has been sustained feminist commentary on EC social policy (in particular relating to equality between women and men at work and in relation to social security); however, relatively little work has been written about other areas of EC law which employs feminist scholarship or which seeks to examine the origin and/or impact of EC law from a feminist stance.[4] This leaves large areas of EC law almost untouched, including the agricultural and fisheries policies, regional policy, competition law, external affairs, substantial parts of Union constitutional law, and many aspects of the EC internal market.[5] This essay seeks to make an initial contribution towards going beyond the existing limits of feminist EC law writing. The aim here is to examine some of the central characteristics of the European internal market law from a feminist perspective. The analysis will then shift to the new player in the integration game, the European Union. The claims made above that this legal entity is heavily dependent on the existing law of the internal market will be substantiated, and the feminist critique offered of the legal regime in the internal market will be carried over to the European Union.

PRELIMINARY THOUGHTS ON FEMINIST LEGAL SCHOLARSHIP

Feminist legal scholarship has developed a diverse and powerful set of critiques and analyses of the legal system and legal reasoning. The most important achievement of feminist jurisprudence has been to develop a distinct method, refuting the theory/practice distinction employed in much of liberal thought,[6] and establishing alternative approaches based on women's experiences.[7]

---

4   Thus, in a recent bibliography of books dealing with Europe, all the books under the heading 'Women' deal with aspects of employment. See Eva Evans, *A Selective Bibliography of Books on European Integration 1990–1994* (1995) UACES at pp 34-35. However, there is some literature which has taken up this challenge in respect of free movement of persons. See, eg, Kirsten Schiewe, 'EC Law's Unequal Treatment of the Family: The Case Law of the European Court of Justice on Rules Prohibiting Discrimination on Grounds of Sex and Nationality' (1994) 3/2 *Social and Legal Studies* 241.

5   Where the internal market has been examined it has been principally in connection with free movement of persons. See, eg Kirsten Schiewe *ibid;* Tamara Hervey, 'Migrant Workers and Their Families in the European Union: the Pervasive Market Ideology of Community Law' in Gillian More and Josephine Shaw (eds), *New Legal Dynamics of European Union* (1995) Oxford University Press.

6   See, eg, Catherine A MacKinnon, 'From Theory to Practice, or What is a White Woman Anyway?' (1991) 4 *Yale Journal of Law and Feminism* 13.

7   *Ibid.*

Accordingly, this essay will seek to refer to women's experiences as they are influenced by the operation of EC law. However, an additional note must be made at this point. There is a familiar danger within this experiential approach, namely, the charge of essentialism. This paper does not seek to make claims about all of law, or about all women, or about all men; nor does it claim to have a single lens through which all of EC law is to be seen. The arguments here are intended to be local in nature, so as to provide a more effective critique of EC law.[8]

When we look more closely at the forms in which feminist analyses have been developed, a variety of strategies can be isolated, not all of which are necessarily compatible with others. For example, Carol Smart has outlined three principal variants of feminist analysis of law, from arguing that the law is sexist, to claiming that the law is male, and finally asserting that the law is gendered.[9] The 'law is sexist' set of claims focuses on the manner in which law allocates resources, opportunities and power and demonstrates that it perpetuates the disadvantage of women as a group in society in its operations. Work of this kind formed the basis for much of the critique offered on the legal system by 'first-wave' feminism, with attention given to the inability of women to vote and to participate fully in education and the market because of various discriminatory prohibitions.[10] Arguments that the 'law is male' proceed on the basis that law incorporates values, attitudes and norms which are perceived as masculine in our culture. This strategy explains why the application of seemingly gender-neutral rules, drafted in an objective fashion, often works to the systematic detriment of women. What counts as 'objective' or 'neutral' in our society reflects a set of deeply embedded assumptions which are valued above competing considerations and are considered by many feminists to be 'masculine'.[11] To treat the law as gendered is to analyse law as 'a process of producing fixed gender identities rather than simply as the application of law to previously gendered subjects'.[12] The 'law is gendered' stream of analysis has produced accounts of how legal discourse helps to shape many of the social structures which we encounter, including that of gender.[13]

---

8   Emily Jackson, 'Contradictions and Coherence in Feminist Responses to Law' (1993) 20 *Journal of Law and Society* 398.

9   Carol Smart, 'The Woman of Legal Discourse' (1992) 1 *Social and Legal Studies* 29 at pp 30-34.

10   Thus Kate Millet wrote that, 'Our society, like all other historical civilizations, is a patriarchy ... [E]very avenue of power within the society, including the coercive force of the police, is entirely within male hands', *Sexual Politics* (1971) Abacus at p 25.

11   See, eg, the argument made by Genevieve Lloyd that the ungendered 'rational individual' of liberal thought is male: 'The Man of Reason: "Male" and "Female"' in *Western Philosophy* (1984) Meuthen.

12   Carol Smart, 'The Woman of Legal Discourse' (1992) 1 *Social and Legal Studies* 29 at p 34.

13   For example, Sally Sheldon, in her work on English abortion law, explores how the female legal subject placed under legislative scrutiny in the passage of the Abortion Act of 1967 relies on 'certain assumptions about (a) women's maternal role and (b) the essential irresponsibility and (c) sexual immorality of the sort of Woman who would seek to terminate a pregnancy'. See 'Who is the Mother to Make the Judgment?:The Construction of Woman in English Abortion Law' (1993) 1 *Feminist Legal Studies* 3 at p 15.

It might be argued that EC law is sexist, given the overwhelming preponderance of men in positions of power within its institutions. For example, in a study of the Court of Justice, the authors observe before giving an outline of the judges' biographical details that these will deal exclusively with men because, 'a woman has still to be appointed to this office, although ... the French, with true republican *egalité*', chose a woman for appointment as advocate general in 1981'.[14] However, changing the number of women within the top ranks of the Community's legal and political order would not necessarily change the nature of the system in the absence of a major culture shift. Therefore, this essay will use the two other strategies which are identified by Smart, the claim that law is male and that it operates as a gendering mechanism. These elements will be developed once the role of the internal market in EC law has been considered.

THE INTERNAL MARKET

The primacy of the market in EC law

Writing about feminist perspectives on Anglo-American legal systems, Sharon Roach Anleu notes that:

> Jurisprudence and legal doctrine based on liberal notions of individual rights, freedom, and reasonableness, while purporting to be value-neutral and objective, favour men's interests and actually reinforce male domination. The whole structure and organization of law and legal knowledge require transformation, achievable not just through the opening up of law schools and the legal labour market to women but also by incorporating women's perspectives, experiences, and approaches which value social relations and empathy.[15]

These concerns are also applicable to the realm of EC law but they have largely been manifested in the area of EC social policy. There is no doubt that this an important area of research from a feminist perspective for at least two reasons. EC law is superior to all forms of domestic law[16] and is capable, in certain circumstances, of creating rights to be enforced by national courts without the need for domestic implementing legislation.[17] As a result, it can provide leverage for change to be exercised against Member State governments whose policies do not adequately address the systematic disadvantage experienced by women as a group. Secondly, feminist legal scholarship can offer powerful insights and

---

14 L Neville Brown and Tom Kennedy, *The Court of Justice of the European Communities* (1994, 4th edn) Sweet & Maxwell at p 55.

15 Sharyn L Roach Anleu 'Critiquing the Law: Themes and Dilemmas in Anglo-American Feminist Legal Theory' (1992) 19 *Journal of Law and Society* 423.

16 Case 106/77 *Amministrazione delle Finanze dello State v Simmenthal SpA (No 2)* [1978] ECR 629.

17 Case 26/62 *Van Gend en Loos v Nederlandse Administratie der Belastingen* [1963] ECR 31.

prescriptions for EC social law in its own right. However, the role of social policy within the wider framework of EC law is relatively unimportant. Social policy has always been the poor relation amongst the internal market policies, both in terms of legal content and political commitment.[18] This has been true since the original Treaties were drafted; these contained no coherent social policy framework[19] and, indeed, it was not until the 1972 Paris Summit that serious attention was given to this issue. The underdeveloped nature of social policy was not very different from other areas of EC law, from the early 1970s onwards, when moves towards greater integration stalled in the face of economic difficulties. The gap between social policy and other elements of EC law reopened when the attempt to relaunch the internal market set out in the 1985 White Paper on the Single Market[20] (the 1992 initiative) proved highly successful; however, the Commission deliberately decided not to link social policy to this drive for increased integration when it was first launched.[21] Attempts were made at the Athens and Madrid Summits of the European Council in 1988 to connect the internal market programme to social policy, but while 11 of the Member States were willing to do this, the United Kingdom refused, leaving a neutered Social Charter in its wake. These trends culminated in the failure to include the Social Chapter in the Treaty on European Union, a decision which is, potentially, a debacle for those who are seriously committed to social justice as a key objective in the integration process.[22]

The Treaty of Rome established the European *Economic* Community and although the name was changed to the European Community in 1993, the creation and maintenance of a common or internal market remains close to the heart of the Community's activities. The goal of the Community has always been one of integration but the 'four freedoms' of the internal market have been given a singular prominence in integration processes. In fact, the culture of the market and principles of market efficiency and competition are central to the creation of the internal market, and to the legitimacy of the legal order founded on it.[23] Article 7(a) EC defines the internal market as 'an area without internal

---

18   Erika Szyszczak speaks of social policy having started as 'the Cinderella of the common market', only to become 'an ugly sister of the internal market'. See 'Social Policy: A Happy Ending or a Reworking of the Fairy Tale?', in David O'Keeffe and Patrick Twomey (eds), *Legal Issues of the Maastricht Treaty* (1994) Chancery at p 313.

19   Although Articles 117 *et seq* EEC did refer to social policy this title was under-utilised during the first 15 years of the Community's existence and has never been the focus of concerted attention. In Case 126/86 *Zaera v Insituto Nacional de la Seguridad Social* [1987] ECR 3697 the Court of Justice held that Article 117 EEC was programmatic only and did not provide a legal basis for binding social policy measures to be adopted.

20   Commission of the European Communities, White Paper on Completing the Internal Market COM (85) 310 final (June 1995).

21   Lord Cockfield, *The European Union: Creating the Single Market* (1994) Chancery at pp 44–46.

22   See Elaine Whiteford, 'Social Policy After Maastricht' (1993) 18 *European Law Review* 202.

23   Joseph Weiler, 'Problems of Legitimacy in Post-1992 Europe' (1991) 46 *Aussenwirtschaft* 411 at p 428.

frontiers in which the free movement of goods, persons, services and capital is ensured in accordance with the provisions of this Treaty'. Because the concept of the internal market provides a key foundational concept for the Community, it also underpins the dynamics of legal doctrinal change in many fields of EC law. For example, if the prohibition of discrimination on grounds of nationality within the scope of the Treaty set out in Article 6 EC were given a minimalist reading, it might be seen as merely prohibiting direct and indirect discrimination. However, the Court of Justice has accepted a broader interpretation to the effect that the provisions of the Treaty are designed to create a single market in, for example, the provision of goods and services, and not merely to prohibit discrimination between traders and the providers of services.[24] This means that a national measure which restricts the free movement of goods or the provision of services is *prima facie* prohibited under the Treaty even if it is not specifically directed at goods or services originating in other Member States and even if it imposes an equal burden on national and imported goods and services. Thus, the desire to create and maintain the internal market has, in effect, trumped a powerful conception of discrimination in respect of economic transactions.

Developing a feminist critique of the market

As Francis Snyder pointed out, when developing a critical perspective on EC law, any 'reconsideration of the concepts of European Community economic law must not only include their economic implications: it must also treat these legal ideas as concepts of social law – that is, of law in society'.[25] Kirsten Scheiwe builds on this, noting: 'a definition of the market concept cannot be derived from a mere description of market policies', and suggests that, '[i]t is not simply a "market logic" that affects and fuels the dynamics of these developments, but a selective logic (with a gender dimension) which excludes or includes certain policy areas according to criteria of relevance other than ill-defined "market-connectedness"'.[26] Unfortunately, she does not develop this idea in any detail. However, it is an important one; and it will be argued here that the dominant conception of the internal market reflects a set of male norms and assumptions. In this sense, it is claimed that EC law is male because its assumptions, values and modes of reasoning are associated with masculine traits in our culture. This argument picks up strands from the work of Carol Gilligan who asserts that our culture suppresses a 'different voice' in matters of moral reasoning and problem

---

24 See, eg, Case 52/79, *Procureur de Roi v Marc JVC Debauve* [1980] ECR 833.

25 Francis Snyder, *New Directions in European Community Law* (1990) Wiedenfield and Nicolson at p 89.

26 Kirsten Schiewe, 'EC Law's Unequal Treatment of the Family: The Case Law of the European Court of Justice on Rules Prohibiting Discrimination on Grounds of Sex and Nationality' (1994) 3 *Social and Legal Studies* 241 at p 247.

solving,[27] and that this style of reasoning is associated with women.[28] Gilligan posits a style of reasoning that rests on the value of interconnection with other individuals and the world, and which operates from within a holistic world view rather than employing a conflict-laden perspective to wholly discrete entities. This stands opposed to the (masculine) market logic which sees relationships with other humans and the natural world as a series of *ad hoc* calculations to be made about the balance of pre-allocated rights in situations of conflict. While Gilligan does not use her work for a direct critique of market primacy,[29] it is contended that it has scope for such a reading.[30]

Feminist legal scholars have done work on the values which are enshrined in the market, and the writing of Patricia Williams on commercial and constitutional law is particularly interesting.[31] She recognises that while those first encountering legal concepts of property and the rules governing its exploitation and transmission (ie the rules of the market) may find these confusing, in her experience, they are 'paralyzed by the idea that property might have a gender'.[32] There has been recognition elsewhere that women have often been (and often still are) considered as property objects[33] but Williams goes on to explore the implications of the dominant conceptions of property and the market on self-identity and the manner in which relations between people and transactions are perceived in law.[34] She notes that, '[m]arket theory always takes attention away from the full range of human potential in its pursuit of a divinely willed, rationally inspired, invisibly handed economic actor'.[35] This market actor is not, however, without a body or a context, and when its traits are examined in more detail it appears that this figure is gendered as masculine.

---

27 Carol Gilligan, *In a Different Voice: Psychological Theory and Women's Development* (1982) Harvard University Press.

28 I do not intend to claim that any such different voice is essentially feminine, or that it is necessarily superior to other 'voices'. See, generally, Mary Jeanne Larrabee (ed), *An Ethic of Care: Feminist and Interdisciplinary Perspectives* (1993) Routledge.

29 Although it could be argued that the dilemma about the scarce life-saving drug facing Jake and Amy in Gilligan's study implicitly criticises the adequacy of market-based solutions alone to address this problem.

30 While it may be objected that this work champions 'domestic and traditionally feminine' reasoning without challenging the order of the public/private and market/domestic dichotomies, I will go on to argue that both forms of reasoning have a valid role to play in the market (when that has been defined), rather than privileging one over the other.

31 Although as Williams herself notes, her work is very (and, I would add, wonderfully) difficult to place within any particular category. See Patricia J Williams, 'The Brass Ring and the Deep Blue Sea' in *The Alchemy of Race and Rights* (1991) Harvard University Press at p 6.

32 *Ibid.*

33 See Mary Murray, *The Law of the Father?: Patriarchy in the Transition from Feudalism to Capitalism* (1995) Routledge.

34 Patricia J Williams, 'On Being the Object of Property' in *The Alchemy of Race and Rights* (1991) Harvard University Press.

35 *Ibid* at p 220.

This can also be seen in the work of Robin West, a cultural feminist, who has directly taken issue with the assertion that the market represents an adequate account of the conditions for human flourishing and offers a sound basis for the construction of social institutions including law.[36] Her work in this field is concerned with the 'Chicago School' of Law and Economics in the United States but her critique of that movement is also applicable to the market primacy of EC law. She argues that over-dependence on an uncritical conception of the market in establishing institutional structures and legal norms is inherently bound up with a failure to discern or to acknowledge the motivational complexity of individuals. As an alternative, she suggests that 'we need to develop rich and true descriptions of the subjective experiences of our institutions [including legal norms]'.[37] She rejects descriptions of our behaviour and interactions which purport to be neutral by virtue of their foundation in market norms but which actually privilege only a narrow range of interests and attitudes. Her project requires, in turn, that we abandon these attempts to subordinate all experience to a framework which is constructed around the market. West also identifies the key market mechanism of commodification, allocating rights in subjects, and over objects who are constructed as existentially separated, as a way of seeing the world which is built on male experience.[38] West's critique of market centred perspectives as reductive and hierarchically ordered, can be applied to the EC legal order and it is also intimately linked to other feminist perspectives. These processes of reduction and hierarchy have been identified by many feminist writers as patriarchal values;[39] the deeply embedded place of these values within EC law grounds the claim made here that EC law can be described as male.[40]

Applying a feminist critique to the internal market

This claim will be examined in relation to several aspects of the law of the internal market. It is first necessary to delineate the scope of the market. If the market is not a pre-ordained entity, its conceptual boundaries should be established and the origins of those contingent limits should be identified with

---

36 Robin West, 'Authority, Autonomy, and Choice: The Role of Consent in the Moral and Political Visions of Franz Kafka and Richard Posner' (1985) 99 *Harvard Law Review* 384.

37 *Ibid* at p 427.

38 Robin West, 'Jurisprudence and Gender' (1988) 55 *University of Chicago Law Review* 1.

39 See Diane Polan, 'Toward a Theory of Law and Patriarchy' in David Kairys (ed), *The Politics of Law* (1982, 1st edn) Pantheon Books at p 294; Janet Rifkin, 'Toward a Theory of Law and Patriarchy' (1980) 3 *Harvard Women's Law Journal* 83.

40 See also Margaret Jane Radin, 'Market-Inalienability' (1987) 100 *Harvard Law Review* 1849. Radin carefully analyses calls for universal commodification found in many strands of liberal legal thought. As demonstrated above, a similar dynamic of commodification can be discerned within EC law. Radin also argues that this market-centred vision distorts any attempt to account for our attachments and desires, and notes that particular damage which this perspective can inflict on women. See pp 1921-36 on prostitution, baby-selling and surrogacy.

particular attention to its gender determinants. The institutions of the EC have, for the most part, taken the view that any activity and any object can be assimilated to the market. The key issues here are what constitutes the object(s) of market activities, and who are the subjects who execute these activities. In identifying the objects and subjects of the EC internal market's legal order, a very broad approach can be discerned. For example, in 1984, the Commission stated that, 'Contrary to what is widely imagined, the EEC Treaty applies not only to economic activities but, as a rule to all activities carried out for remuneration, regardless of whether they take place in the economic, social, cultural (including in particular information, creative or artistic endeavours and entertainment), sporting or any other sphere'.[41] This approach provided it with the basis for regulating certain aspects of television and other audio–visual services but clearly claims many items and activities for the market. The Commission also has followed this approach in its decisions on the scope of competition law. In *RAI/Unitel*[42] an opera singer was treated by the Commission as an 'undertaking', a phrase which therefore covers any collection of resources carrying out an economic activity. This approach also embraces many individuals and institutions which would not necessarily be seen by those who are unfamiliar with EC law as participants in the market.

The Court of Justice has also taken a broad view of the scope of the market, as is clear from its jurisprudence on what constitutes 'goods' for the purpose of the free movement rules contained in the Treaty. The court's approach does not flow automatically from any internal rationale of EC law, found within the norms and the jurisprudence of the rules of EC law; rather it is a question of bringing transactions, administrative actions and individuals within their jurisdiction. What emerges from a critical consideration of its case law is that the court defines the market, it does not discover it. In *Commission v Italy*[43] the court considered the impact of Articles 9 (establishing a customs union) and 12 (prohibiting the imposition of charges having equivalent effect to a customs duty) of the Treaty on Italian rules imposing a tax on the export of art treasures. The Italian government argued that the tax was not levied on goods within the meaning of the Treaty, claiming that these items were of cultural and artistic and not commercial significance. The Court of Justice rejected this argument, holding:

> By goods ... there must be understood products which can be valued in money and which are capable, as such, of forming the subject of commercial transactions. The articles covered by the Italian law, whatever may be the characteristics which distinguish them for other types of merchandise,

---

41 Commission of the European Communities, *Television Without Frontiers* Green Paper on the Establishment of the Common Market for Broadcasting especially by Satellite and Cable, COM (84) 300 final (Luxembourg: OOPEC, 1984) at p 6.

42 [1978] 3 CMLR 306.

43 Case 7/68 [1968] ECR 423.

nevertheless resemble the latter, inasmuch as they can be valued in money and so be the subject of commercial transactions.[44]

As the court went on to observe, it is clear that the Italian government's arguments in this case were somewhat disingenuous as it was prepared to make an economic assessment of the art treasures in order to calculate the export tax to be levied on them.

Such double standards were not evident in the Belgian government's arguments in *Commission v Belgium*[45] where the Commission claimed that an import ban imposed by the Walloon Regional Authority on waste products was incompatible with Article 30 EC. The ban affected two types of waste product, recyclable and non-recyclable waste, and was intended to stop Wallonia from being the final halting site in 'waste tourism', the movement of by-products of industrial processes from wealthier regions to poorer regions for disposal or treatment. Waste is unlike other products in that it ceases at a certain stage to have any commercial value. Amongst the arguments raised by Belgium was that when waste can no longer be recycled or reused, and so has no commercial value, it cannot come within the scope of the rules on free movement of goods. This case caused some difficulty for the Court of Justice which had two oral hearings into the case and received two Opinions from Advocate General Jacobs on the matter. In his first Opinion the Advocate General took the view that non-recyclable waste was 'goods' within the Treaty rules because, although it had no intrinsic value, it could form the subject of commercial transactions in that waste disposal companies are paid to dispose of it.[46] He confirmed this interpretation in his second Opinion, relying on *Commission v Italy*.[47] The Court of Justice took a similarly robust view, holding that objects transported over a national border to effect a commercial transaction must be subject to Article 30 EC, irrespective of the nature of the transactions.[48] In doing so, it rejected the views of, amongst others, the German government which took the position that none of the fundamental market freedoms should apply to waste disposal because it does not belong to the 'economic activities' envisaged by Article 2 EC.[49] Clearly, the court's approach gives pre-eminence to a market paradigm, ignoring critics who assert that, 'The central problem is that the EEC fails to differentiate between different kinds of goods. One *should* look to the nature of the goods because all goods are not the same. After all, some commercial transactions have a negative environmental impact'.[50] This critique of the court's

---

44 *Ibid* at 428–29.

45 Case C–2/90 [1993] 1 CMLR 365.

46 Paragraph 16.

47 Case 7/68 [1968] ECR 423.

48 Paragraph 26.

49 See Peter von Wilmowsky, 'Waste Disposal in the Internal Market: The State of Play After the ECJ's Ruling on the Walloon Import Ban' (1993) 30 *Common Market Law Review* 541 at p 544.

50 David A Demiray, 'The Movement of Goods in a Green Market' 1994/1 *Legal Issues of European Integration* 73 at p 109. Emphasis added.

inability to see a difference in products related to their effects on the environment treats this perspective as a local anomaly. However, when the masculine nature of EC law is identified, a systematic failure can be recognised. A basic feature of EC law is its powerful impulse towards market deference,[51] and that failure cannot be addressed until EC law adopts other values, of connection and solidarity, and a different epistemology, contemplating 'masculine' assumptions of atomistic, de-contextualised objects and individuals as well as a 'feminine', holistic vision.

Different voices in EC law?

However, while a market paradigm is dominant within EC law, other perspectives can be detected. For example, recent debates on the draft Bio-Technology Patent Directive involved a clash of approaches to the limits of commodification. The Commission originally proposed a directive in October 1988[52] which sought to protect inventions developed through biotechnology and genetic engineering and took the view that such inventions should not be refused protection simply on the ground that they involved living matter. The proposal then went to the European Parliament which proposed far-reaching amendments to the draft directive.[53] The Parliament took the view that the original focus on economic and technical matters alone was too narrow and in its proposals observed:

> Whereas it is desirable to include in the body of the Directive such a reference to public policy and morality in order to highlight the fact that some applications of biotechnological inventions, by dint of their consequences or effects, are capable of offending against them ... .

> Whereas, in the light of the general principle that the ownership of human beings is prohibited, the human body or parts of the human body *per se* must be excluded from patentability ...[54]

These specific amendments were accepted by the Council when it adopted a common position on the amended proposal, but it rejected certain other proposed amendments which were also concerned to limit the untrammelled

---

51 See also Rossa Phelan, 'Right to Life of the Unborn v Promotion of Trade in Services: The European Court of Justice and the Normative Shaping of the European Union' (1992) 55 *Modern Law Review* 670; Ian Ward, 'In Search of a European Identity' (1994) 57 *Modern Law Review* 315 at p 327. It is also worth noting that the primacy of market access as a value in EC law often subordinates other core, legal values such as consistency. See, for example, Case 27/76 *United Brands Company and United Brands Continentaal BV v Commission* [1978] ECR 207 and Case 185/84 *Commission v Italian Republic* [1987] ECR 2013, the 'market for bananas' cases.

52 Proposal for a Council Directive on the legal protection of biotechnological inventions, OJ 1989 C13/3.

53 Amended proposal for a Council Directive on the legal protection of biotechnological inventions, OJ 1993 C44/36.

54 *Ibid* at 37.

operation of the market.[55] The dispute over the amendments went to a Conciliation Committee and eventually back to the European Parliament which then vetoed the legislation.

The basic objection to patenting human genes and living animals raised by the European Parliament is well expressed by Ruth Chadwick writing on the related topic of organ sale as: 'one undesirable consequence of the selling of our own bodies is that it contributes towards a society in which the bodies of persons are regarded as resources. The action of selling one's own body contributes to the prevailing ethos of everything being for sale, everything having a price. It reinforces the ethic of the market'.[56] However, although the market failed to trump all other values on this occasion, it should be noted that it is not necessarily desirable to be placed *outside* the market. Patricia Williams points out that the market is a plastic construct whose precise boundaries vary over time. She goes on to observe that it is, nonetheless, constant in one feature:

> Whether something is inside or outside the marketplace ... has always been a way of valuing it. Where a valued object is located outside the market, it is generally understood to be too 'priceless' to be accommodated by ordinary exchange relationships; if the prize is located within the marketplace, then all objects placed outside become 'valueless'. Traditionally, the Mona Lisa and human life have been the sort of objects removed from the fungibility of commodification, as priceless. Thus when black people were bought and sold as slaves, they were placed beyond the bounds of humanity.[57]

This insight, that to be excluded from the market is not to share even the limited benefits which it offers, reminds us that it is not the market itself which is the only source of concern for those casting a critical eye over EC law from a feminist perspective. Instead, our attention should also be on the way in which the market could become the only source of valuing others and the world around us. This issue might be addressed in several ways. If the exclusion of the feminist perspectives on sources of value canvassed above is an integral part of the formation of the market concept, a real challenge to EC law's dependence on the market may require a fundamental transformation of the presumptions used to construct that concept. It may be, however, that feminist perspectives militate towards abandoning the market because the concept cannot endure the pressures created by such transformational pressures and/or because the market cannot deliver what feminists require of it.

---

55 Common position (EC) No 4/94, OJ 1994 C101/65.

56 R F Chadwick, 'The Market for Bodily Parts' (1989) 6 *Journal of Applied Philosophy* 129 at p 137.

57 Patricia J Williams, 'On Being the Object of Property' in *The Alchemy of Race and Rights* (1991) Harvard University Press at p 227. As shown above, EC law is not so deferential toward art treasures as Williams might expect.

THE EUROPEAN UNION

The legal regime created by the internal market's operation had the effect of giving 'citizen-like rights'[58] to transnational corporations but at the same time it did not view natural persons as citizens. However, the adoption of the Treaty on European Union creates a new legal subject, the Union citizen; all persons who possess the nationality of the Member States shall be citizens of the Union (Article 8 EC).[59] These citizenship provisions provide a core element in this novel dynamic entity, the EU; and as such they have attracted study and comment from many writers.[60] What will be argued here is that the figure of the Union citizen carries within itself the legacy of the internal market and, more specifically, that this entails in turn that both the citizen and the Union are shaped by concepts and values which are usually valorised as masculine. As a result these new legal concepts are vulnerable to critique from a feminist perspective which can in turn provide an important corrective to those unbalanced constructs.

The addition of Union citizenship to the founding Treaties formally marks a major paradigm shift, from a market-centred integration project towards the formation of a European political space.[61] Article A of the TEU expresses this as 'a new stage in the process of creating an ever closer union among the peoples of Europe, in which decisions are taken as closely as possible to the citizen'. The introduction of rhetoric and norms which refer to citizenship must be viewed cautiously by feminists. A well-developed body of feminist political theory argues that the conceptions of citizenship which are dominant in liberal legal discourse carry a history of misogyny which is not merely incidental but is integral to their meanings.[62] The exclusion of women from participation in the public sphere of political activity and from those arenas where the virtue of justice[63] was applicable leaves its legacy in contemporary views on citizenship.

---

58 Gordon Laxer, 'Opposition to Continental Integration: Sweden and Canada' (1995) 2 *Review of Constitutional Studies/Revue d'Etudes Constitutionnelles* 342 at p 347. See also Malcolm Chapman, 'The Commercial Realization of the Community Boundary' in Victoria A Goddard, Josep R Llobera and Cris Shore (eds), *The Anthropology of Europe: Identities and Boundaries in Conflict* (1994) Berg p 227 at pp 238–42.

59 On the concepts' origins and the intergovernmental negotiations on the issue, see Malcolm Andersen, Monica den Boer and Gary Miller, 'European Citizenship and Co-operation in Justice and Home Affairs' in Andrew Duff, John Pinder and Roy Pryce (eds), *Maastricht and Beyond* (1994) Routledge.

60 For an introduction, see David O'Keeffe, 'Union Citizenship' in David O'Keeffe and Patrick M Twomey (eds), *Legal Issues of the Maastricht Treaty* (1994) Chancery.

61 Dawn Oliver and Derek Heater, *The Foundations of Citizenship* (1994) Harvester Wheatsheaf at pp 133–46.

62 J Elshtain, *Public Man, Private Women: Women in Social and Political Thought* (1981) Princeton University Press at p 176; Susan Okin, 'Women and the Making of the Sentimental Family' (1981) 11 *Philosophy and Public Affairs*, 65 at p 85.

63 Carol Jones, 'Since She's My Queen Well I Must Be King' (1995) 1 *Res Publica* 41; C Pateman, 'Feminist Critiques of the Public/Private Dichotomy' in A Phillips (ed), *Feminism and Equality* (1987) Blackwell at p 107; Iris Young, 'Polity and Group Difference: A Critique of the Ideal of Universal Citizenship' (1989) 99 *Ethics* 250 at pp 253–54.

This is not to say that citizenship is an irredeemably 'male' construct;[64] feminism has done much to rebalance the concept. For example, there is no doubt that one of the main achievements of 'first wave feminism' was the partial extension of those components of citizenship, based on civil and political rights, to women. Similarly, 'second wave feminism' brought with it a renewed drive to complete that process and to add women to those who participated in the full social rights of citizenship.[65] This process is not complete; it has been argued that 'the new issues of citizenship appear to centre around gender politics and around the Green movement'.[66] As such, feminism has a great deal, in general terms, to offer in relation to contemporary citizenship debates. However, following on from the feminist critique of the internal market set out earlier, feminist perspectives on the figure of the Union citizen also have an added, local dimension.

It was probably inevitable that the creation of the European Union would have to build on the previous achievements of the EC, but it appears that the outline and contents of this new figure, the Union citizen, is almost entirely determined by existing, market-centred norms and practices.[67] At a superficial level, the creation of the citizen appears a marketing exercise in its own right, the latest product in a line which has brought us Euro-passports, a Euro-flag and anthem, and sundry European years dedicated to worthy causes.[68] In this guise it can be seen an additional attempt to legitimise or 'sell' the idea of Europe to the very people, mainly ignorant or apathetic or sceptical about the Union, who have recently become its citizens.[69] However, the Union citizen is reliant on the previous market-based legal dispensation at a deeper level. It appears that the key rights conferred by the citizenship provisions, to move and reside freely throughout the Union, remain linked to economic status.[70] Thus, as O'Keeffe notes: '[t]he free movement of persons is the cornerstone of the Union citizenship provisions, as it has been throughout the evolution of the concept of European citizenship.' He adds: 'the emphasis on free movement as a source of citizenship rights is in fact odd ... [because] the right is economic rather than

64 Barry Hindess, 'Citizenship in the Modern West' in Bryan S Turner (ed), *Citizenship and Social Theory* (1993) Sage at p 33.

65 See *supra* nn 11 and 12.

66 Bryan S Turner, 'Contemporary Problems in the Theory of the Citizenship' in Bryan S Turner (ed), *Citizenship and Social Theory* (1993) Sage at p 13.

67 While the relevant provisions of the Treaty do give the Union citizen certain political rights of participation and representation, for the most part, they are neither novel nor confined to Union nationals, and it is difficult to see what gives them any distinctive character. See Hans Ulrich Jessurun d'Oliveira, 'Union Citizenship: Pie in the Sky?' in Allan Rosas and Esko Antola (eds), *A Citizens' Europe: In Search of a New Order* (1995) Sage.

68 Cris Shore and Annabel Black, 'Citizens' Europe and the Construction of European Identity' in Victoria A Goddard, Josep R Llobera and Cris Shore (eds), *The Anthropology of Europe: Identities and Boundaries in Conflict* (1994) Berg at pp 286–87.

69 Gerard Delanty, *Inventing Europe: Idea, Identity, Reality* (1995) Macmillan at p 128.

70 Siofra O'Leary, 'The Social Dimension of Community Citizenship' in Allan Rosas and Esko Antola (eds), *A Citizens' Europe: In Search of a New Order* (1995) Sage at p 173.

overtly political'.[71] This oddness should not, however, be treated as an anomaly. In fact, the Court of Justice has taken the view that 'free access to employment is a fundamental right which the treaty confers individually on each worker of the Community',[72] elevating these market freedoms to a status of legal principles, on a par with human rights.[73]

It has been claimed that the introduction of Article 8(a-e) EC means that 'the mobility of economically active persons has now been elevated to the core of European citizenship and expanded into mobility for persons generally. In other words: economically irrelevant people have been promoted to the status of persons'.[74] This is not a wholly accurate assessment because these mobility rights are expressed as subject to the limitations already set out in the Treaty. The central figure, therefore, in the Union citizen's origin is the EC worker who enjoys rights under EC law when working, seeking work, or having worked, in another Member State by virtue of Article 48 EC and associated legislation. For the most part these rights are taken up by those in work; a factor which already disadvantages women as a group. In 1991 the average female unemployment rate in the EC was 50% higher than the average male rate.[75] Another important consideration is that the ability and willingness of individuals to migrate is dependent on several factors, including real income differentials, attitudes to risk, and age,[76] as well as a variety of 'push' and 'pull' factors.[77] Given the uneven distribution of caring responsibilities between the sexes and, consequently, the greater exposure to risk from uncertainty for women, their opportunities for free movement are even further reduced.[78] It is, therefore, legitimate to express concerns about the way in which 'the burdens of citizenship will fall on young women given the stereotypical assumptions about women's role as carers'.[79] As such, we can argue that the configuration of rights set out in Article 8(a-e) EC renders the concept of Union citizen a sexist one, unevenly distributing resources and opportunities on the basis of sex.

---

71 David O'Keeffe, 'Union Citizenship' in David O'Keeffe and Patrick M Twomey (eds), *Legal Issues of the Maastricht Treaty* (1994) Chancery p 93 at p 94.

72 Case 222/86 *UNECTEF v Heylens* [1987] ECR 4089, 4117.

73 Jason Coppel and Aidan O'Neill, 'The European Court of Justice: Taking Rights Seriously?' (1992) 12 *Legal Studies* 227.

74 Hans Ulrich Jessurun d'Oliveira, 'European Citizenship: Its Potential, Its Meaning' in Renaud Dehousse (ed), *Europe After Maastricht: An Ever Closer Union?* (1994) Law Books in Europe at p 132.

75 Mike Artis and Nick Weaver, 'The European economy' in M J Artis and N Lee (eds), *The Economics of the European Union* (1994) Oxford University Press at pp 47–48.

76 D G Mayes, 'Factor mobility' in Ali M El-Agraa (ed), *The Economics of the European Community* (1994, 4th edn) Harvester Wheatsheaf at p 441.

77 See Loukas Tsoukalis, *The New European Economy: The Politics and Economics of Integration* (1993, 2nd rev edn) Oxford University Press at pp 153–54.

78 See Tamara Hervey, 'Migrant Workers and Their Families in the European Union: The Pervasive Market Ideology of Community Law' in Gillian More and Josephine Shaw (eds), *New Legal Dynamics of European Union* (1995) Oxford University Press.

79 Neville Harris, 'Social Citizenship and Young People in Europe' in B S Jackson and D McGoldrick (eds), *Legal Visions of the New Europe* (1993) Graham & Trotman/Martinus Nijhoff at p 200.

However, the Union citizen can be subjected to a feminist critique on a deeper level. A key point of concern must be the manner in which the Court of Justice has defined *who* is to be seen as economically active and so entitled to mobility rights. The court stated in *Walrave and Koch* that an economic activity, 'has the character of gainful employment or remunerated service',[80] which covers workers and persons who provide and receive services. It has been observed that the core of Union citizenship rests on the EC worker, a concept developed by the Court of Justice over the past three decades.[81] 'Worker' is defined broadly; it is not necessary for a worker to earn income equal to a national minimum,[82] nor even to reach the minimum means of subsistence.[83] Trainees,[84] those engaged in 'social employment' schemes,[85] and contract workers without any guaranteed hours[86] have all been held to be workers. The extensive definition of worker produced by the Court of Justice is based on a requirement that the individual is involved in genuine and effective work as opposed to marginal and ancillary activities under the direction of an employer for remuneration. In *Steymann*[87] the court held that this test did not cover the situation of a German member of a Bhagwan community in the Netherlands who carried out plumbing jobs and general chores for this religious community in exchange for his lodgings and food. The court was not willing to extend a right to reside to him and did not accept the Commission's argument in the case that there was a moral and legal obligation for work to be done and for payment in kind to be made. The court observed that work was an important and normal part of Steymann's communal life and that he received various services as an indirect *quid pro quo* for his work. However, it did not resolve the question of his status as a worker and it held that he did not enjoy rights as a service provider. The court was ultimately sceptical of extending rights to a working relationship which was premised on a religious or philosophical basis. Given this approach it is unsurprising that the category of 'worker' does not embrace women who are economically active within the home and do not engage in paid employment. There are two obstacles to conferring this status on such women: the perception of the value of such work and the motives ascribed to such women in 'choosing' to work in this way. The possibility of treating these women as workers might exist if traditional assumptions about the worth of work within the home

---

80 Case 36/74 *Walrave and Koch v Assocation Union Cycliste Internationle and others* [1974] ECR 1405, 1417.

81 Commencing with Case 75/63 *Hoekstra (née Unger) v Bestuur der Bedrijfsvereniging voor Detailhandel en Ambachten* [1964] ECR 177.

82 Case 53/81 *Levin v Staatssecrataris van Justitie* [1982] ECR 1035.

83 Case 139/85 *Kempf v Staatssecrataris van Justitie* [1986] ECR 1741.

84 Case 66/85 *Lawrie-Blum v Land Baden-Württemberg* [1986] ECR 2121.

85 Case 344/87 *Bettray v Staatssecrataris van Justitie* [1989] ECR 1621; Case C-30/90 *Bernini* [1992] ECR I-1071.

86 Case C-357/89 *Raulin* [1992] ECR I-1027.

87 Case 196/87 [1988] ECR 6159.

(usually none)[88] were set aside, in light of the minimal value of the labour which a 'worker' in EC law must produce. However, given the common assumption about the altruistic nature of this 'private' labour, it is unlikely to be treated as an economic activity and so will fall outside the scope of the Treaty and of relevant secondary legislation. Thus, in *Achterberg*[89] the Court of Justice held that a woman who had not been in employment outside her home could not claim rights under EC law which was directed at workers as she 'had not had an occupation'.

As a result, notwithstanding the evolution of an increasingly liberal response to the question of who is a worker in EC law, the jurisprudence of the court still overlooks the value of a significant segment of the economically active female population.[90] The category of 'worker' provides a foundation for citizenship rights, but the use of a narrow, male style of reasoning to identify workers serves to exclude many women. This partial, gendered approach is compounded in the area of freedom to provide and receive services. The Court of Justice has held that only services provided for remuneration come within the scope of the Treaty's rules;[91] this overlooks the manner in which many women participate in informal economies, exchanging goods and services without the use of cash.[92] As it stands, these individuals are also beyond the scope of the mobility rights. Thus the core right of the citizen, that of mobility, remains anchored in the categories of economically active persons already established in EC law and is available to women in a more restrictive fashion than to men because of the court's failure to include in its decisions modes of economic existence which are informal, unstructured and largely experienced by women.[93]

The definition of spouse is the final issue to be examined from the court's case law on the rights of workers, in order to support the claim made here that the implicit incorporation of this jurisprudence into the figure of the citizen

---

88   See Leo Flynn and Anna Lawson, 'Gender, Sexuality and the Doctrine of Detrimental Reliance' (1995) 3 *Feminist Legal Studies* 105.

89   Joined Cases 48, 106 and 107/88 *JEG Achterbeg-te Riele and Others v Sociale Verzekeringsbank, Amsterdam* [1989] ECR 1963.

90   Tamara Hervey also notes that by extending mobility rights only to those workers who are nationals of the Member States EC law appears to confer universal market rights to workers while denying rights to groups who can provide a captive source of labour for low-paid or peripheral work, 'Migrant Workers and Their Families in the European Union: The Pervasive Market Ideology of Community Law' in Gillian More and Josephine Shaw (eds), *New Legal Dynamics of European Union* (1995) Oxford University Press. See also Avtar Bhah, 'Black Women and 1992' in Anna Ward, Jeanne Gregory and Nira Yuval-Davis (eds), *Women and Citizenship in Europe: Borders, Rights and Duties* (1992) Trentham Books.

91   Case 20/88 *Belgium v Humbel and Edel* [1989] ECR 393; Case C-159/90 *SPUC v Grogan* [1991] ECR I-4685.

92   See Madelaine Leonard, 'Women's Paid and Unpaid Handiwork in a Belfast Estate' (1994) 3 *Journal of Gender Studies* 187.

93   This critique of the restrictively gendered nature of EU citizenship can be adapted in tracing a racial critique of the concept as it applies to ethnic minority communities within the EU. See Tamara Hervey, 'Migrant Workers and Their Families in the European Union: the Pervasive Market Ideology of Community Law' in Gillian More and Josephine Shaw *supra* n 91.

ignores the interests of women. The rights of workers in EC law are extensive, encompassing rights to be accompanied by spouses, children and certain other relatives. However, these statuses have had to be defined by the court and in doing so it has limited those rights. The manner in which the limits are applied reinforces heterosexual marriage and fails to adopt a more egalitarian model of interpersonal relations. The leading case on this issue is *Reed v The Netherlands*[94] which arose from the claim of Reed, a British woman whose male partner was a British national working in the Netherlands, that she had a right to reside there by virtue of his rights as a worker in EC law. The Court of Justice held that the long-term companion of a worker, who is a national of a Member State and is employed in another Member State, cannot be treated as his 'spouse' for the purposes of EC law. However, the court took the view that the possibility of such a worker obtaining permission for his unmarried companion to reside with him can assist his integration in the host State and support the freedom of movement of workers. Thus, where Dutch nationals could obtain permission for their unmarried non-Dutch companions to reside with them, other EC workers could not be subject to discrimination because of their nationality (Article 6 EC) and could also obtain such permission. This judgment converts the relationship between an unmarried heterosexual couple into one where the presence of the partner who is not an EC worker is a 'social advantage', a material benefit for the other. *Reed* indicates that the attempt by women to define themselves as economic subjects rather than as objects to be traded[95] is one on which EC law's stance is ambiguous.

The judgment in *Reed* also discriminates directly against lesbians and gay men, who are unable in most of the Member States,[96] to enter into legally recognised spousal-like relations with members of their own sex. The result is that lesbians and gay men are unable to claim derived rights to mobility on behalf of their partners and will only, exceptionally, be able to claim that the presence of their partner constitutes a social advantage.[97] This legal situation also adversely affects those opposite-sex couples who do not wish to marry, but the effect is greater on same-sex couples who have no such option. It is not being claimed here that support for the institution of marriage is necessarily anti-feminist; however, as Katherine O'Donovan notes, it is an institution which carries a deep history of oppression for women.[98] EC law has deliberately chosen to subscribe to that history. In addition, the view which the Court of

---

94 Case 59/85 [1986] ECR 1283.

95 See Susanne Kappeler, 'The International Slave Trade in Women; or Procurers, Pimps and Punters' (1990) 1 *Law and Critique* 219 at p 235.

96 At present only two Member States, Denmark and Sweden, provide for legal partnerships between couples of the same sex.

97 See Hans Ulrich Jessurun d'Oliveira, 'Lesbians and Gays and Freedom of Movement of Persons' in Kees Waaldijk and Andrew Clapham (eds), *Homosexuality: A European Community Issue* (1993) Martinus Nijhoff.

98 Katherine O'Donovan, 'Marriage: A Sacred or Profane Love Machine?' (1993) 1 *Feminist Legal Studies* 75.

Justice takes of marriage is a wholly formal one; it is not necessary that the spouses co-habit at any point or that there should be or ever have been any emotional or sexual relationship between them. Thus in *Diatta v Land Berlin*[99] the court found that where a marriage had not been dissolved, it was to be treated as still existing even if the spouses were separated and had no intention of ever living together again.

When we look to see how this affects women, the creation of a new market can be seen. In London and other large cities located in Member States with strict immigration laws, a market in EC (as opposed to host State nationals) workers who are unmarried lesbians has emerged in recent years. Such women cannot enter into a legally recognised spousal-like relationship with other women and they are likely to be less well-off than men. If they are EC workers they have a right to the residence of a spouse of theirs in the same Member State, and this economically valuable right is, increasingly, being traded. The trade is, undoubtedly, one which occurs on a grey market but it is a real phenomenon. We are reminded of Chadwick's comments on the sale of bodies: 'One undesirable consequence of the selling of our own bodies is that it contributes towards a society in which the bodies of persons are regarded as resources [which] contributes to the prevailing ethos of everything being for sale, everything having a price. It reinforces the ethic of the market'.[100] The creation of the European Union and the construction of a new model of citizenship on the basis of the existing market order should be judged in light of this trade in women, a new variation on an old tale of female oppression which was authored by the European Community and is now continued by the European Union.

99   Case 267/83 [1985] ECR 574.
100 R F Chadwick, 'The Market for Bodily Parts' (1989) 6 *Journal of Applied Philosophy* 129 at p 137.

INDEX